AF816808

Tortured Souls

Based On a True Story

By

Tom Finley

Contents

CHAPTER 1

On July 4th weekend 2005, my wife Martha and I had a weekend alone. Our daughter Jennifer was away with close friends. She was our only child. Martha was 38 years old Italian and German, 5 foot 8 inches tall, slender built with brown hair about shoulder length and big brown eyes. To me, Martha was the prettiest woman in the world. She had a college degree and was soft-spoken. Jennifer was 13 years old, about five feet 5 inches tall, brown shoulder-length hair, and medium built with brown eyes with a light complexion. She was a happy child as well as a humble one. My name is Tom Frawley; I am 5 foot, 9 inches tall with Reddish blond hair, green eyes, and 210 lbs with a medium build. I am Irish. I was married to Martha for 18 years, with my 19th just 5 months away. During this day, we were working on some new landscaping. In the evening, we would sit on our 40 foot long deck having a few drinks. Night time was beautifully surrounded by multi-colored lights illuminating across the railings, overlooking the glowing 30 foot oval above ground pool.

We had a nice size 3 bedroom, 2 bath, ranch-style house on a half-acre lot in a middle-class suburb just west of Chicago. We bought this second home in 1996 for $175,000. It was somewhat old-fashioned but structurally sound. In the nine years we lived there, we completely remodeled the house inside and out. I was the jack of all trades and enjoyed carpentry. It was not all fun as I had several injuries. In 1989 while working on my first house, I severed the tip of my left ring finger and lost my pinky completely on a table saw. It was December 22, I was planning a surprise birthday party for Martha, and I was finishing trim around the bathroom door, something that I needed to complete for company to use the bathroom. I cut my thumb with a circular saw, stepped on many nails, one going completely through my shoe sticking out of the laces. I was electrocuted several times, one as recently as December 23, 2004, where I spent Christmas Eve in the hospital. Some people say I wasn't careful, but I always used this analogy: A man that crosses a highway every day is more likely to get hit a few times as opposed to a man that crosses once a year.

It was a normal weekend at home for Martha and I. We watched movies, worked around the house and were intimate several times.

Then on July 7th, Martha went out to eat with our daughter. When she returned, I saw a look on her face that I had never seen before. She looked ill and worried. Martha was walking out of the bathroom; I walked up to her and said, "Martha, could you come into the bedroom where we can talk?" She kept her head down as she walked ahead of me into our bedroom. Once inside, I shut the door. Martha sat down on the bed. I sat down next to her as she silently stared at me with a scared look on her face. Looking her in the eyes, I asked, "What's wrong Martha, is everything ok? You don't look well..."

"I want a divorce Tom," Martha replied in a soft voice as she put her head down. I was blown away. My heart was in my throat; this was surreal.

"Why, Martha, what did I do?" I asked.

"We are not getting along anymore," Martha uttered.

I looked at her in disbelief and said, "This is bullshit. We were intimate a few days ago and a few days before that." She sat there for a second before replying.

"I met a man."

I stood there in shock for several seconds. The next thing I knew, the questions came pouring out.

"Is he married?"

"Yes, he is."

"Are you crazy Martha, does he have children?"

"Yes, Tom, he has two, a seventeen-year-old daughter and an eleven-year-old son."

"How long have you known this man?"

Martha replied, "Five months."

Confused and distraught, tears started rolling down my face. With blood-shot eyes and a shaking voice, I looked at Martha and begged, "Please do not do this, Martha."

"I am not changing my mind, Tom; it's over." I took Jennifer to dinner to prepare her for the divorce." Martha immediately took off her wedding ring, got up, walked into Jennifer's room, and gave the ring to Jennifer.

I was in total shock; I fell backwards onto the bed. I did not understand, nor did I see this coming. Moments later, Jennifer came into my room crying.

"What did you do so wrong Daddy, can't you stop this?" she inquired. "Is there anything you can do to stop this, Dad?" Some People may think I was wrong for doing this, but I said,

"Jennifer, Mommy did not tell you?"

Jennifer replied, "Mommy said you and her don't get along."

"Mommy has a boyfriend, Jennifer." I was not going to lie to my thirteen-year-old daughter. I did not want her to believe that her Dad failed in his marriage. Martha just ripped my heart out of my chest and then wanted me to just go along with her affair and lie to her child, so she did not look bad.

Jennifer went back into her room to confront her mother. Within seconds, Martha came running into our bedroom crying and screaming, "Why did you tell her? Why would you tell her? You bastard!"

Hurt, angry and confused, I shouted, "You are with a married man and what you are doing is wrong, not only for our family but his as well. You are a cheater, a liar, and I will not join in on this lie, especially to my daughter. Have you lost your mind?"

"You are an asshole!" she said as she turned around and went back into Jennifer's room. I stayed in our bedroom alone.

An hour later, Jennifer came into my room, climbed into the bed and said, "Dad, I am going to sleep with you."

"Ok, Jennifer, maybe I could talk to Mom tomorrow and try to stop her." Jennifer stayed close to me and fell asleep; however, I could not fall asleep. This was a sudden shock. I had no clue whatsoever. I would just lay there and think. Hoping that if I could just fall asleep, I would eventually wake up from this nightmare. I would not sleep at all.

The next morning I went to work at 8:30AM. I was walking around like a zombie; I was installing electrical switches and outlets in a second-story addition working for my construction job. I could not remember what I did ten minutes ago. I was dazed and confused.

At 11:30 AM, I walked into another room where my boss Bob was talking to a coworker. I approached him. "Hey Bob, could I speak to you in private?"

"Sure, Tom, let's go outside."

Once outside, I looked at him with glassy eyes and said, "Hey Bob, I really need to go home." He looked very concerned as he asked me if everything was ok.

"Martha asked for a divorce; she is with a married man." Bob and his wife were long-time friends of Martha and me.

"Get the hell out of here, Tom!" Bob said, looking confused. "That is unbelievable! I did not think Martha would ever do that; let's go have a quick beer."

Bob jumped into his truck, and I followed him to a nearby bar. Inside, I sat at a table as he went up to the bar and bought us two bottles of beer. Besides the female bartender, we were the only people there. It seemed Bob was as in much shock as I was. He just kept saying, "Unbelievable." I could not hold a conversation. I was not functioning. My body felt light, as if I was on a cloud. We had one beer before I told Bob I needed to go. Bob stood up, gave me a hug," I am so sorry, Tom, use whatever time you need off. "

In a soft voice, I replied, “Thank you," and I left. I drove home with the blazing sun beating down through my windshield. I was starving and weak, still not having slept yet.

When I arrived home, I went straight to my bedroom and lay in bed with all my clothes on, including my shoes. I finally fell asleep.

On Friday, July 8, Jennifer went away for the weekend with a friend so her mother and I could discuss this further. I waited for my wife to come home from work. I was sitting on the couch in silence, no TV, no radio, just sitting there thinking and nervously awaiting her arrival. She arrived around 4:15PM. Martha walked in, dropped her bag, and left the front door open behind her.

Martha said, "I have to go to Diana’s house.”Diana was her best friend.

I looked at her with disappointment. "We need to talk, Martha."

"I have to do this," Martha uttered.

"Are you coming back?" I asked.

"Yes, Tom"

From what I heard, she went to tell Diana the good news, but Diana thought otherwise. Diana said, what you are doing is wrong as she cried. I called Martha’s cell phone several times, inquiring when she was coming home. I was not going to give up. I loved her more than anything in the world; I was not going out without a fight.

After a couple of hours, Martha arrived home. She walked in, sat on the couch across from me. We were both silent for a moment when Martha started in.

"Tom, I am so sorry, this just happened. You are my first love, and if you ever need anything, I will be there for you."

I replied, "This man brainwashed you. Do not do this; think about our daughter. This person is married. What is wrong with you? I love you."

She just kept saying, “I am sorry!"

We talked through the night, falling asleep on and off. I noticed she would not put her cell phone down, even sleeping with it. We slept in the same bed, but she wore shorts, a tee-shirt, as well as her bra. It was as if she belonged to someone else now, as she was very distant from me.

On Saturday, July 9th, we were sitting on our enclosed back porch. I was still trying to save my marriage. I was begging Martha to not throw 19 years of marriage away without thinking about it. I continued to tell her that I loved her as I cried. Martha was sitting on a couch opposite me and had a blanket over her with her cell phone in her hand underneath. As we were talking, her cell phone rang. She pulled it out and looked at the number, looked at me, and said, "I have to take this."

"Is it him, Martha? “I was getting pissed now when I suddenly blurted out “This man is going to call you at my house?"

Martha said, “If you do not let me take it, I will leave to call him because he cares about me." I turned in disgust and walked into the house. I would constantly look out the kitchen window as Martha was sitting in the middle of the yard talking on the phone to that man. Martha sat in the middle of the yard privately, talking for about 30 minutes. I could not believe what was happening before my eyes. I went into the yard, walked up behind Martha, and angrily said, “Hang up that phone!"

Martha looked up at me, then she put her head down and softly whispered into the phone, "I have to go; I will call you back." Then, she hung up the phone, got up off the grass, and walked toward the house.

While walking right behind her, I said, "Do you have any idea what you're putting me through?"

“I am sorry, you are right." As she walked into the house, I was right behind her.

We sat up most of the night talking. We were sitting on the couches for long periods, sometimes saying nothing. Every now and then, I would utter a question like, "Martha, why are you doing this?"

Her reply, "I don't know Tom, it just happened; I am so sorry. Then, unexpectedly, Martha stated, "You know Tom, I told this guy I was not sure if I was doing the right thing, I told him that I have been with you my whole life."

"What did he say when you told him that, Martha?"

"He started crying, Tom."

As thoughts rolled through my head, I thought that this man only knew her for five months and my tears were of over twenty years with her. During some of these remarks, Martha would switch gears.

"Tom, if we use the same attorney, we could save a lot of money. If we fight, it will cost us. What do you want from the house?"

I could not answer those questions; my mind was on her. Martha was lying on the love seat with a blanket and her cell phone underneath. I could hear it vibrating from time to time. She was going to the bathroom often. Martha would get up off the love seat several times, saying," I am so sorry, Tom. "

I sat there most of the night in a trance. Martha and I did not eat anything all weekend.

Jennifer arrived home Sunday at noon from her trip. When she came into the house, I could see the look on her face. I could tell she was hoping for good news but expected the worst. Martha looked at Jennifer as she closed the door behind her and said, "Jennifer sit on the couch so your father and I could talk to you." Jennifer sat down next to Martha, keeping a few feet of distance between them. I could tell by the worried look on Jennifer's face that she was nervous about what she was about to hear. Martha started doing all the talking. I could not say anything. I was numb. I lost my composure within the first few words and went out to the back porch.

Jennifer was home for *only* an hour when Martha decided to take her to our friend's house for a few days. Martha let me know she was taking her and left the house with our daughter.

Martha returned a few hours later. We again stayed up most of the night talking. I was trying everything to save my marriage. Martha kept saying, "You were my first love, and if you ever need anything, I will be there for you."

I would constantly beg Martha not to leave, to consider what this will do to Jennifer. At one point, I said to Martha, "Give me some closure; why did you make love to me a few days ago? Why did we buy a new pool two months ago and put in a new deck? Why did we go out to buy a new front room set? Why would you do all that if you were going to leave me?"

Martha replied in a cold voice, "I don't know."

Baffled by Martha's answers and demeanor, I sat forward on the couch and told Martha, "Look me in the eyes and tell me you do not love me."

Martha did not look at me or say a word. I did not understand. She just sat there staring into space as if she were in a coma. We fell asleep on and off the rest of the night.

Monday morning, Martha was getting ready for work. As I walked past her, I asked Martha, "Will you do me a favor?"

She replied, "What?"

"Please do not date this man until we are divorced. Can you give me that much respect?"

"Yes, Tom, I would never do that to you."

I walked into the kitchen and opened the fridge looking for something to eat. Although I was browsing through the food, I had no appetite. I shut the door and walked into the front room. I saw Martha packing a suitcase. "What's that for Martha?"

"Oh. Martha replied, ``I have a conference downtown Chicago, and I have to stay at a hotel." She traveled with her job, but I found that a little strange, being that we live in a Chicago suburb. Martha was behaving strangely while packing her suitcase, lost in her own world like I was not there. She was packing things like perfume, lotions, and even douche. I said nothing as I watched Martha zip up the suitcase, roll it across the hardwood floor out the door without looking back or saying a word.

I knew she was meeting this man. In a way, I could say I have always thought it would happen like this. In the traveling business world, men and women meet states away from home in exhibit halls and hotels for trade shows or other businesses as their families are behind at home. They work by day and meet by night for dinner and drinks, carrying on how bad their life is back at home and then returning to their rented bedroom as affairs bloom.

I did not go to work that day because I knew I was worthless and could not function. I walked around the house in circles. Walking into different rooms and not knowing why I was there. I was devastated; it was as if I was having an out-of-body experience. I started losing my mind, and by Monday afternoon, I called Martha's sister Carrie. Carrie was one year younger than Martha and had similar looks. She had short brown hair, big brown eyes, about five foot 7 inches tall with a slim to medium build. Carrie and I always got along; she was like a loving little sister.

Carrie answered my call, "Hi Tom."

I responded, "Did Martha tell you what is going on with us?"

"Yes, she did, Tom."

"What do you think, Carrie?"

"I don't know what to say except how could you stay with her and ever trust her again?"

I told Carrie, "I could not go on, and I hung up."

I went into the basement and walked to the back computer room where I had a gun safe. I opened the safe and took out a 22 caliber gun and a box of shells. I shut the safe and went back upstairs to the living room. I sat on the couch, took out one bullet, and put it into the chamber. I took the safety off and put the gun against my head with my finger on the trigger. I thought to myself, I have to do this fast without any thought in order to succeed. It felt like forever as my arm was getting tired of holding the gun up. Just when a tear rolled down my cheek, my arm dropped. The next thought going through my head was I could not do it there, not at home, what that would do to Jennifer. My mind was fighting two demons. When I thought of Martha, my finger wanted to squeeze, but when I thought of Jennifer, my finger let go.

I dropped the gun on the couch and went into the kitchen to get my cell phone. I called Martha's cell phone and got her voice mail. I left this message.

I have a gun. I am going to kill myself. I hung up.

Within minutes Martha called back, I answered.

Martha was crying hysterically! “Tom, please don’t do this; I will stay with you. Please, Tom, don’t do this." In all the years I have known Martha, I have never heard her scream that way.

I yelled back, “You’re full of shit, I had no warning and I know you’re meeting that man. When Jennifer looks into your eyes, she will be looking at the person who killed her father! If you call the police, I am not at home." I hung up, grabbed the gun, box of shells, and ran out to my truck. I jumped in the truck and drove to the city. I knew Martha would call the police. My phone was constantly ringing throughout the 14-mile ride, but I did not answer.

I called my older brother Paul who happened to be in from his home in Italy. He answered, "Hey Tom, how is it going?"

I briefly explained my situation to him and told him I had a gun. He convinced me to meet with him; that he understood, because he, too, was going through a divorce. We walked around Bridgeport for a few hours stopping for a slice of pizza. It was very difficult to eat. I have not eaten anything in 4 days. Paul was talking about my assets and Jennifer. I knew he was trying to take my mind off Martha. After walking a while more, we went by Paul's apartment. He had me stay the night. My cell phone was ringing throughout the night, but I did not answer.

It was family, friends, and Martha. I did not want her to know that I was still alive. I guess I wanted her to suffer. Martha was calling my family members throughout the night. My younger sister Anne drove out to my house, trying to get in to see if I was alive or dead inside the house. I had two vehicles, a Tahoe and a Van; the van was in the driveway.

Anne called Martha. Martha answered. "What's up, Anne?"

Anne replied, "I'm at your house. Can you please come home and open the door so I can get in to see if my brother is there and if he is alive?"

To Anne's surprise, Martha said," I can't because Tom might hurt me."

Anne said, concerned with an angry voice, "What's the matter with you?" Anne hung up in disgust. The police arrived and informed Anne they could not break in unless they knew for sure there was a body inside. Martha never came to let Anne or the police in the house.

I woke up about 8:30am Tuesday at my Brother Paul's apartment. He was sitting at his computer when I approached him and said, "I'm going to leave now, Paul."

Paul replied, "Are you going to be ok?"

"Yes, I'll be ok" As I turned and headed toward the door, Paul blurted out, "Hey Tom, can you leave the gun here?"

I looked at Paul; I pulled the gun out of my pants, walked over to him, and handed him the gun. Then, I turned around and left.

I got home about 9:30 Tuesday morning. I called friends and family to let them know I was all right. I decided to call my wife. When she answered, she was more angry than relieved.

"I don't want to talk to you, Tom," with a hateful, angry tone. Before she could hang up, I said with a stern voice,

"You are going to bury me this week, and I hung up. "I spent most of the day on the computer going through Martha's work directory, trying to find out who this person was. Then it hit me; I went online and checked her cell phone records. I found the number that she was constantly calling. It was a cell phone number, and while going through her directory, that number was next to a work number as well. I now knew who this person was. His name was Todd. He did not actually work in the same company as Martha but was a vendor for her company and worked at Geneva Molding in Elgin, Illinois. I was not one hundred percent sure, but I believe I may have met this man at Martha's company's Christmas party. I called Martha several times throughout the day, but she would not answer me.

That evening I decided to go by our best friend's house where Jennifer was to spend the night. Roy was my best friend. Dianna was Martha's best friend. I needed to see how she was doing. While I was sitting on a basement couch with my friend Roy, I overheard Jennifer in the stairway on the phone with her mom. Jennifer was shouting, "No, Mom, I don't want to meet this man." The last thing I heard was Jennifer say, "You know what, Mom, you're a liar," and then she hung up. Jennifer came downstairs, and I asked her to take a walk around the block so we could talk. Once we were several feet from the house, I asked Jennifer how she was doing with all of this?"

"Dad, I want to ask you something. Please tell me the truth. Were you going to kill yourself?"

"Yes, Jennifer, I thought about it."

"What stopped you, Dad?"

"You did. All I kept thinking about was you. I'm sorry, Jennifer, sometimes adults get weak and selfish. I don't know how to explain what I'm going through."

"I'm glad you are here with me Dad."

"I am too, Jennifer."

We talked a little more, mostly Jennifer telling me about fun things she did. When we got back to the house, we went inside. I stayed the night to be with her. Jennifer and I stayed in Roy and Dianna's basement. Jennifer and I were lying on couches opposite of each other, awake, talking.

"Jennifer, are you ok?" I asked.

"You know what, Dad, when I came home Sunday and Mom sat me on the couch, and you went into the back room, Mom said," Jennifer, you have to meet this new man. That he is nice, he is going to buy us a new house with a big yard and a pool. She said, “She told me he lives in Wisconsin and that we will go on vacations together. She even asked me if I wanted to see a picture of him. His name is Todd Scum."

“I told her I never want to meet him. I already have all those things, a house, pool and a big yard. Do you believe that, Dad?"

"Really, I don’t know Jennifer; she’s lost her mind. Let’s get some sleep, Jennifer." It took a while for Jennifer to fall asleep. As for me, I was awake most of the night.

I went back home the next morning, leaving Jennifer behind. I decided to investigate more on the computer. While looking at Martha’s phone records, I noticed that the calls were minimal to her boyfriend in the past two days. I decided to call his phone. He did not answer, so I left a message, "Was my wife good in bed last night?" I hung up. My next call was to Martha, got her voice-mail, and said, “Was your boyfriend good last night?" My phone suddenly rang, the caller ID showed that it was Martha. By the time I answered, she had already hung up. I did not hear from Martha the rest of the day. I knew she had to be freaking out.

That evening my phone rang at about 4:00pm, it was Diana.

"Hi Diana"

"Hey Tom, do you want me to bring Jennifer home so she can spend some time with you?"

"Sure, Diana, I really need that."

Diana brought Jennifer to my house and stopped in with her two young boys. She stood by the door and commented, "I figured you would want to be with Jennifer."

"Yes Diana, thanks."

After Diana left, Jennifer and I spent the remainder of the evening together, mostly talking about looking at condominiums for me. Martha called Jennifer around 4:30pm and told her she would be home at about 6PM that evening. Six o’clock came and no Martha. She never came home or called back.

On Thursday morning, July 14, 2005, Jennifer and I went looking at condominiums in Countryside. At about 11:30 AM, Martha called Jennifer's phone. Jennifer answered, "Hello!"

"Hi Jennifer, its Mom. Could you have your Dad drop you off at my work for lunch?"

"You know, Mom, I have not seen you for days, and you told me you were coming home yesterday, now you want to go to lunch? I don't know, Mom," Jennifer hung up.

I said. "Are you sure you don't want to have lunch with your Mom?" She did not answer. I felt that although Jennifer was upset with her mother's recent behavior, she actually wanted to see her Mom. "It is ok if you want to go see your Mom; I don't have a problem with that. I think you should go see your mother and she should see you."

"Ok Dad."

After looking at condominiums, it was about noon when I headed to Martha's work. It was less than a mile away. As I was pulling into the parking lot, I suddenly felt strange. I told Jennifer, "Something is not right; I don't feel good about this. I don't know. Something just doesn't seem right." I pulled up about 50 feet from the front door. I turned toward Jennifer, "You go inside; if something happens, honey, I love you!"

"I love you too Dad, I will call you later! "It felt as if we were saying goodbye.

I headed back home and was there for about two hours when the doorbell rang. I opened the door. There was a man in plain clothes showing me a badge.

Step outside the house, sir. Are you Thomas Frawley?"

"Yes, I am," I replied.

"I am a Cook County Sheriff, you have five minutes to get any belongings from your home, and then you have to leave." He started reading from papers he had in his hand. "Stay 100 feet from Martha, 100 feet from Jennifer, 100 feet from your home, and 100 feet from Jennifer's school. You are to have no contact whatsoever with Martha, and Jennifer Frawley, not even through a third party. If you violate these orders, you will be arrested and spend time in jail." I just looked at him as he read on. I said nothing. When he finished reading, he looked at me and said, "I am not saying your right or wrong; I am just doing my job." I believed he made his last statement, as I was sure I was considered dangerous. However, from his point of view, I must have looked more confused, like a harmless deer in the headlights. That I was.

He gave me the papers, and I went into the house to get what I could. I grabbed some clothes and a cup with some of my jewelry. With my eyes full of tears, I wrote this note and put it on Jennifer's pillow. "Goodbye Jennifer, I will miss you, love Dad" I left $400.00 in cash for Jennifer and all my credit cards on the table, and then I left. I got in my truck, drove a few blocks, and pulled over to read the papers.

The Papers:

PETITION FOR DISSOLUTION OF MARRIAGE

- MARTHA is 38 years of age, currently residing in Countryside, Illinois, having been a resident of the state of Illinois for ninety days preceding the filing of this Petition for Dissolution of Marriage. MARTHA is presently employed.
- THOMAS is 44 years of age, currently residing in Countryside, Illinois, having been a resident of the state of Illinois for ninety days preceding the filing of this Petition for Dissolution of Marriage. THOMAS is presently employed.
- The parties were lawfully married on November 22, 1986, in Chicago, Illinois. Said marriage was registered in Cook County, Illinois.
- There is no other dissolution of marriage proceedings in any other State or County.
- THOMAS is guilty of extreme and repeated acts of mental cruelty, without cause or provocation on the part of Martha, all in accordance with the provisions 5/401, Chapter 750, and Illinois Compiled Statutes.
- Alternative grounds for the dissolution of the parties' marriage exist in that irreconcilable differences have arisen between the parties that have caused the irretrievable breakdown of the marriage. Past attempts at reconciliation would be impractical and not in the best interest of the family. As a result, the parties have lived separately and apart for the required statutory period to the date of a Judgment of Dissolution of Marriage in this case.
- One child was born as a result of this marriage, namely JENNIFER FRAWLEY, born October 31, 1991. No other children were born or adopted by the parties hereto as a result of this marriage, and Martha is not presently pregnant.
- It is in the best interest that MARTHA be awarded the sole care, custody, control and education of the parties' minor child.
- The parties acquired, during the course of the marriage, certain items of marital property.
- MARTHA lacks sufficient income to provide for the needs of the minor child. THOMAS is employed earning sufficient income to provide for the minor child's expenses as established by the family's standard of living prior to this dissolution of marriage proceedings commencing.

WHEREFORE, Petitioner, MARTHA FRAWLEY, prays as follows:

- The parties be awarded dissolution of marriage, dissolving the bonds of matrimony heretofore existing between them.

- Petitioner be awarded the sole care, custody, control and education of the minor child of the parties.
- Petitioner be awarded child support commensurate with the parties' standard of living during the marriage.
- The marital property of the parties be divided in just proportions.
- Each party be barred from receiving maintenance from the other, whether it be past, present, future, or statutory maintenance.
- Each party be required to pay his or her own attorneys' fees and costs.
- For such other and further relief as in equity this Court deems just.

___________Martha Frawley

Subscribed and sworn to before me

This 13th day of July 2005

Jennet K Wilford

NOTARY

AFFIDAVIT IN SUPPORT OF

PETITION FOR ORDER OF PROTECTION

MARTHA FRAWLEY, under penalties of perjury, the deposes and states as follows:

- I am the petition in the above-entitled cause.
- If called upon, I could testify competently as the matters contained herein.
- I give this affidavit based upon my own personal knowledge.

THOMAS Frawley and I were married on November 22, 1986. We have one child, Jennifer Frawley, born October 31, 1991, currently aged thirteen, who will be attending lindens township high school this fall as a freshman.

- We reside at **** S. Catherine in countryside Illinois in a single-family residence jointly owned by the two of us.
- Our marriage has been in serious trouble for a number of years. Thomas was a product of a broken home and was severely abused by his stepfather, and I have not had a cooperative relationship for a long time. On this, THOMAS becomes abusive verbally and emotionally

while at the same time he tries to exert control over me by telling me that I am the only good thing in his life and that I can't leave him because he cannot live without me.

- On Thursday, July 6, 2005, I told THOMAS in one of our many ongoing discussions over the last several years that the marriage was over and done with and that I was going to file for a divorce. THOMAS became upset and abusive and accused me of being unfaithful to him. I told them that we argue every day, we don't get along, that habitual spending habits have kept us from accumulating anything, that we are just barely keeping our heads above water and that the marriage was over and done with. THOMAS kept on arguing and arguing, and finally, in frustration, I admitted to him that I was involved with someone else, at which point he became distraught and started saying things like, "if I can't have you,\, nobody else can. If I find out who it is, I'm going to kill him. "
- I was so afraid and upset that I slept in my daughter's bedroom.
- THOMAS stayed awake the entire night, would not let me sleep and repeatedly kept me awake, coming into the room and saying things like I can't believe this is happening. "I can't believe you would do this; how could you leave me for another man."
- I had a scheduled business trip Monday, July 10, 2005, through Tuesday, July 11, 2005. I made arrangements to have our daughter Jennifer stay with my best friend. On Monday afternoon at approximately 3:45 PM, my sister Carrie Mullen received a phone call from THOMAS, during which THOMAS said he intended to kill himself. Carrie tried to get a hold of me but couldn't because I was in a meeting. Carrie left a message repeating what THOMAS said. I have saved that message on my voicemail.
- A few minutes later, I received messages from Thomas insisting that I call him immediately. I called THOMAS, and in that conversation, Thomas was crying throughout and said, "I can't go on. I can't do it." THOMAS stated that he was going to kill himself and every time that Jennifer looked in your eyes she would look into the eyes of the person who had killed her father", and that he " had a gun to his head right now" and " I am not at home if you send the police."
- THOMAS is the owner of two firearms, a double-barreled shotgun and a handgun. There is ammunition for both weapons in the residence.
- I believe that THOMAS had a firearms owner's identification card, and I believe that it was not renewed at the appropriate time, so these guns may not be lawfully possessed by him.
- By the time I called my sister on July 10, 2005, she had already called the Countryside Police who went to our residence, but THOMAS was not there.

- Monday night all evening, I tried to locate THOMAS by calling various family members. THOMAS has a sister Ann Blake, And a brother, Paul Giano, both of whom live in Chicago in separate residences in the Bridgeport neighborhood with whom he can live in an emergency. None of the family members I called were aware of THOMAS's whereabouts.
- I later found out that Thomas spent a good portion of Monday evening in a bar in Bridgeport.
- Monday morning, I received a phone call from THOMAS where he said that even though he had not killed himself on Monday, he still could not go on, and he was going to kill himself. THOMAS stated, "Better get a grave for me because you're going to bury me this week."
- It is unclear to me whether THOMAS, as he claimed in one of his phone messages left on Monday that he has turned over his weapons to the Countryside Police Department. I do not believe him.
- I live in constant fear that THOMAS will hurt me and/or my daughter because he has made statements that every time Jennifer looks into my eyes, she will see the person who has killed her father. I believe that what he really means is that he can't stand the thought of me not living with him, and I believe that he would harm not only myself but my daughter and himself.
- My daughter was mostly unaware of the problems going on until THOMAS deliberately told her last Friday that I was involved with another man. Jennifer was upset and cried for hours after THOMAS cruelly divulged my relationship to Jennifer.

FURTHER AFFIANT SAYETH NAUGHT.

Martha Frawley

Subscribed and sworn to before me

This 13th day of July, 2005

Jonathan J. Baxton

Notary

I was in total disbelief. I was not aware that my marriage was over for years. We were intimate several times just days before as well as anytime I wanted it. Just six months earlier, I got a tattoo with Martha and Jennifer's name on my arm. Five months earlier, for Valentine's Day Martha asked for a red heart-shaped ring , which I bought for her. Back in December, while shopping at a mall, Martha asked me to pick something out for her at Victoria's Secret. These were not signs of a Marriage being over; it just did not make any sense. As far as my habitual spending habits, Martha and I months earlier bought a new swimming pool in which she insisted on the larger, more expensive one. We just bought a new leather front room set, and while doing so, she bought a bedroom set for Jennifer. Oddly, Martha was spending money. My problem was I put my money into my house. I was a jack-of-all-trades. I remodeled my entire home over nine years, labor-free. Our house was now worth over two hundred thousand dollars in equity. I worked very hard in construction, making good money. I built a dream home with my own hands. I did not hang in bars, nor did I do drugs. Keep our heads above water? We had more than most people I knew, mostly all paid for. We never struggled with a single bill. For most of my life with Martha, I worked two jobs, taking on side jobs over the years for extra cash. In 2001, I was laid off from a company that I worked for 12 years. Martha insisted that I stay home to care for Jennifer because she traveled and made enough money. I agreed but continued working side jobs for extra money. In 2004, I decided to go to work full time for one of my friends in construction.

Martha stated she had a business trip from Monday, July 10, 2005, through Tuesday, July 11, 2005. According to my calendar, Monday was July 11, and Tuesday the 12th. As far as my guns, they were legal, and my gun card was up to date. I later willingly turned them into the police, except the one my brother Paul took from me. I did not spend any time in a bar; that was a total fabrication. On Martha's claim, she lacked sufficient income to provide for her child, on a salary of 60,000 annually. Martha stated that on Thursday, I said I was going to kill the man she was with, that she was so afraid, yet she returned home from work Friday and spent the weekend alone with me in our home, even slept in the same bed. Martha was so afraid that I was going to kill her that she filed a restraining order 7 days later. Did the court actually read these papers? Amazing how the paper states "under penalties of perjury." I never said those words. Everything was a lie. I figured that Martha painted an evil picture of me to get me removed from my home. I was very confused. Where was all this coming from? If my marriage was over, Martha definitely kept it to herself. It was like a punch in the stomach that I didn't see coming.

I continued driving around and not knowing where to go. I ended up at our best friend's house, and they said I could stay as long as I needed. They set me up in their basement. Having slept there many times before, I was very comfortable there.

That evening Diana was at school, and when she returned home, she came down in the basement and asked, "how are you, Tom?"

"Surviving," I replied. She noticed the restraining order and dissolution papers on the table. I said, "Go ahead, and told her she could read them." After reading the papers, she did not say much, but I understood that Martha was her best friend.

After a few days of listening to both sides of the story, it appeared our problems were disrupting the lives of Roy and Diana. I felt this was unfair, so the next morning, while they were at work, I left them a thank you note and left before they returned home.

My younger sister Anne previously offered me to stay with her in the city, so I took her up on that. Her oldest daughter moved out, and I would stay in her room. Anne was married with two daughters. And I got along with my brother-in-law Louie very well. Anne was 5ft 7in tall with dark brown hair, blue eyes, with a medium build. She was always straight to the point, but she had a heart of gold.

CHAPTER 2

I was still working in construction, so I had plenty of money. I was sending Martha 150.00 a week for child support; however, I missed my daughter. What was she thinking? Does she miss me? Is she hurting? It was the first time in my life I would not hear my daughter's voice for days. I was devastated by the silence. My baby was taken from me.

For Martha, I was told that being with someone for all those years and losing him or her was like the same as if someone you loved died. It sure felt that way. You no longer like yourself. When looking in the mirror, you see an ugly person. Then you no longer look in the mirror. Food suddenly tastes bad, so you do not eat, you barely sleep, and all you do is think every waking moment. You seclude yourself in a single room. When watching TV, you just see people talking; you do not hear what they are saying because your mind is always elsewhere. You do not smile; you do not laugh. Your mind plays what happened over and over again, trying to justify what went wrong. If my mind was not on Martha, it was on my daughter. All you want to do is talk to people about what happened, simply. I needed to vent. Some get tired of it, some do not say anything, and others always want to know what you are thinking. You feel that you serve no purpose in life. I looked like the walking dead as I lost a lot of weight. Days and nights were long. You think to yourself, if I were dead, the pain would end.

After a few weeks passed, Martha called me unexpectedly.

"Hey Tom, I am having a garage sale today. I already sold some furniture, the Yamaha scooters, your van, and other various items. How much money do you want for the bear table and canoe you built?"

"I don't want to sell those things, Martha, what gives you the right to sell our belongings without me?" I was so angry and helpless. With a restraining order in place, I could not go near my home.

"Well, we need to clear the house out, Tom, so I need to get rid of things."

"How much money did you sell the scooters for Martha?"

"I sold them for 1500.00."

I said, "1500, that is the price for one. Those are brand new! How much did you sell my van for?"

"I sold it for 3000.00"

"That's crazy; the van is worth twice that amount."

Martha had always been greedy, so I knew she was lying about the amount of money she was receiving, knowing I had no way to prove it. She also knew there was nothing I could do and that she could do whatever she wanted.

"Well, I have to go, Tom, here is my attorney's number. We can do this fast and easy with one attorney; if we fight, we could go through all our money."

"Well, it seems that you are already going through all our money." Martha read me the number and hung up.

I figured let me call this attorney and see what he has to say. I dialed the number, and the phone rang.

"Hello, this is Donald Burnburg!"

"Yes, Mr. Burnburg, this is Tom Frawley."

At this point, his demeanor changed to arrogance and authority. "Oh yes, Mr. Frawley, you know I represent your wife."

"Really," I uttered.

"Are you working, Tom?"

"I'm on vacation, I replied."

"This is the deal I have for you, Tom. If you go to the first court date and sign the papers, you will be allowed to see your daughter."

"Are you kidding me?" I thought to myself, just like that. If I sign divorce papers, I would no longer be considered a dangerous threat to my daughter despite a restraining order that claims I verbally said I was going to kill people. A simple thing as a pen and paper is proof to the Cook County Court System that I am sane enough to see my child, and if I do not, I am a dangerous man.

"Here is the date and time, as well as the location of the courthouse. Are you showing up with an attorney? If I were you, I would, Tom."

I replied, "I will let you know," and hung up.

Wow, what happened to a quick and easy divorce? "It will be cheaper to use one attorney; we will go through all our money." Boy, did this person have Martha in his grips? Martha put herself through college part-time, graduating with all A's, but one thing was for sure, she was lacking, when it came to common sense.

Mr. Burnburg was a downtown loop attorney. He was considered to be one of the best divorce lawyers that Martha acquired through her sister Carrie. He charged a $5000.00 retainer fee and $375.00 an hour. Did she actually think he would get her a quick divorce? Who knew, but I was sure of one thing. I certainly was not going to tell Martha that the attorney she chose to settle this matter quickly suggested I get an attorney and fight. I figured if she was going to continue liquidating my assets for some fast cash, I might as well make her give it all to this person. I did not have anything to lose. I was homeless!

CHAPTER 3

My brother Paul decided to pay a visit to Martha at our home in Countryside, hoping to talk some sense into her. After about an hour, he realized that was impossible. Although unsuccessful, he used the opportunity to talk to Jennifer. While Martha was busy doing her own thing, he was alone with Jennifer.

Paul said, "Hey Jennifer, I know you're not supposed to have no contact with your father, but what are they going to do if you contact him? I could see the headlines now, a 13-year-old goes to jail for contacting her father because she misses him." Jennifer laughed! Paul said, "I'm serious; they can't put a kid in jail for loving their father."

"You’re right, Uncle Paul. I didn’t think of it that way!"

Jennifer took Paul's advice and started contacting me through her friends. I would get text messages from numbers I did not recognize. They would say things like, "Hi Mr. Frawley, I'm Jenn's friend. She says hi, and she misses you."

How awesome is that? The things kids do for each other to help. Jennifer would also start to call me from her friend's cell and house phones.

On some days, Jennifer contacted me. I noticed her Mom was dropping her off by friends and family members as much as possible. When I asked Jennifer where she was, she said, “I am not supposed to tell you, Daddy. “I could easily tell by the voices in the background and dogs barking where she was. I understood and did not pressure her. It was simply nice to hear her voice.

CHAPTER 4

My older brother Paul was also negotiating with Martha. Martha was claiming she would be fair in the divorce. Although Paul thought, based on experience, that I should come to an agreement with Martha and end the divorce fast, I called a lawyer friend of mine, and he said I have to be crazy to go to court without representation.

July 25, 2005, first court date, I did not go, and that meant not seeing my daughter for another month. I did not have an attorney, nor did I trust Mr. Burnburg. I knew my daughter was wondering why I did not go, especially that it meant seeing her. That was the toughest decision I ever had to make in my life. Because I did not show in court, Martha would do everything in her power to keep Jennifer from contacting and visiting me. I still could not contact Jennifer due to the restraining order, and I feared Martha would use phone records if I made any attempts. Jennifer did, from time to time, use her own phone.

I knew I had to do something. A friend of mine referred me to Attorney Daniel Simmons, whom I decided to hire. Daniel was in his late 40's about five foot seven with a stocky build. I could not use Tim because he was not a divorce lawyer and was friends with Martha as well. Mr. Simmons and I arranged to meet at his office, where he broke everything down for me.

"Mr. Frawley, I charge a $2500 retainer fee and $250 an hour. It is a good decision not to go to court alone." I will need a list of all of your assets including bank accounts, summer homes, retirement plans, and anything else you can think of. I will get you a copy of the Marital Settlement Agreement and send it via email. Let me know when you get it."

"Thanks, Daniel, I will."

I received a copy of the MSA a few days later. It was insane. It stated I made more money than Martha; therefore, she would need child support and that I waive the right to seek maintenance. I made about half of what she made. I also stated that Martha shall have sole custody of Jennifer and that I should give Martha all bank accounts, including Jennifer's college account. That I shall remain in counseling for 2 years, and that I am not to consume alcohol in the presents of Jennifer. That I promise not to touch Martha's 401K and a two-year restraining order for Martha but would be permitted to see Jennifer. Basically, give Martha everything and walk away.

With the next court date a month away, I was depressed and missed Jennifer even more. After a few weeks of silence, my phone rang. I did not recognize the number. I answered, "Hello."

"Hi, Daddy!"

“Hi Jennifer"

"Where are you calling me from? Does your Mom know you are calling me?"

"I’m not supposed to tell you where I am, but I’m at a friend’s house. Mom is not here, and she doesn't know I am calling you. (Starting to cry) I miss you Dad, why won't they let me see you? Why didn’t you go to court so you can see me?"

"I couldn’t go to court because I did not have an attorney to represent me. I am very sorry and cannot wait for the day that I will see you again."

"Well, please do something, Dad, so I can see you."

"I’m working on it, Jennifer."

"Well, I have to go now, Dad, before someone finds out I’m talking to you. I just wanted to tell you that I love you and miss you."

"I love you too and miss you very much Jennifer, thank you for calling me."

"Bye Dad!"

"Bye!"

Jennifer stayed in touch with me by secret phone calls but only when she was not with her mother. She told me that Martha started checking her phone for my number.

Meanwhile, I went to work one morning and my boss Bob approached me. “I am worried about your wife going after us because we pay you cash. I heard that Martha told a friend she was going to tell the courts."

"Bob, I would not let that happen to you, especially since you have been a longtime friend." I resigned and said, "I need to find a job with insurance now anyway, that soon I will be off my wife’s insurance. “Martha claimed she would not go after my job, but it was starting to show that she had become a good liar.

Despite the restraining orders, Martha called me and agreed to let me come by the house one day to get a suit for court. She was a very different person at times, making her hard to figure out. I pulled up in front of my house, but I stayed on the street instead of pulling in the driveway. I waited in my truck for a few minutes when I saw Jennifer coming out of the house with my suit. She came up to my window, stuck her head in, and kissed me.

"Hi, Dad!"

"Hi Jennifer, how are you?"

"Good Dad, I miss you."

"I miss you too, Jennifer."

"Well I have to go now, Dad. Mom said only for a minute because you are not supposed to be here."

"Jennifer, Can you do me a favor? Give this envelope to your Mom. Here is my wedding ring, this is for you. I know you have Mom's and thought you might want mine too."

"Yeah Dad, I was going to ask you if I could have it, thanks. Here, Dad, this is from Mom, it's $2500.00."

"Tell her thank you."

"I love you Dad."

"I love you too Jennifer, Bye!

I pulled away as the tears rolled down my face. In the envelope was a letter telling my wife how much I loved her. I did not want to give up. I used the money to pay my attorney. After that day, Martha suddenly became cold again. She would not answer my calls, and when she did, she would say, "talk to your attorney," and hang up. She was mean, a voice of hatred. Jennifer and I continued to stay in touch as much as we could, usually on weekends. We always had a special bond. From the time she learned to walk, we made dozens of funny home videos together, including just months before my demise. We would dress up in crazy outfits with wild wigs as if we were rock stars. We were like best friends. Sure, we had our fights, but I was like another kid to Jennifer, yet still a father.

Jennifer was a violinist and a pianist. I played the guitar and a little piano. We had our own little music room at home. We even had microphones and amps. We enjoyed playing instruments and making up our own music together. She was very talented but humble. We had a beautiful home in Countryside, IL. It was completely remodeled, with a huge fireplace in the front room. We had a half-acre lot with a huge pool right off the deck. Our basement was finished with knotty pine walls with a fireplace and dry bar. We had full-size arcade games, a pool table, Ping-Pong, and a dartboard. Jennifer and I shared an office in the basement where we had our computers.

I was missing everything. Up until now, I have never missed a school concert, where I video recorded every one. Because I was not allowed to go within 100 feet of Jennifer's school, I would miss many. What did she feel when she was up on stage, and her father was no longer watching her play. She knew how much I loved to watch her play. Jennifer also loved playing softball in the summer. I even helped coach her team one year in which we won the championship. Jennifer was very proud as some friends repeatedly told her I wish I had a father like yours.

With me out of the picture, Martha started contacting some of my family members, trying to find out where I was living. Her attorney was leaving messages on my phone asking the same question. During one of my conversations with Jennifer, she would tell me that Martha told her she knew my every move. She even mentioned a few things that were true, like whose house I was by and when. There was definitely someone in my family that could not be trusted. I would constantly tell my family members that I would appreciate it if they would not talk to Martha, yet I learned quickly that friends and family choose sides during a divorce.

July 27, 2005, while staying with my sister Anne, I was using her computer daily to search for employment. I was eating a few bites at dinner, coffee in the morning, and nothing for lunch. Despite Anne trying to get me to eat, I had no appetite. One morning I was on the computer, I went to get another cup of coffee and the next thing I knew, I woke up on the floor. This was the second time this had happened. A little dizzy and nervous, I decided to go to the doctor. I did not call; I just got in my truck and drove there. It was in Countryside about 14 miles away. I walked into the waiting room, and it was a little busy, so I sat down. I was feeling dizzy and light-headed. The next thing I knew I was on the floor with paramedics standing over me, saying I passed out. I also heard a woman's voice.

"He has lost a lot of weight. He is getting divorced. "She was a friend of Martha's that worked there as a nurse. They put me on a stretcher and wheeled me out to an ambulance. As the paramedics were putting me in the ambulance, the police arrived.

One officer jumped into the ambulance, stood over me, and said with a loud voice, "Where is the gun, is it in your truck?"

"I don't have a gun," I said in a weak voice.

Just then, one of the paramedics jumped into the back of the ambulance and started in with questions. "Are you on drugs? Have you been drinking?"

"No! No!" I stated. I could hear another officer telling one of the paramedics that this guy is crazy, and he threatened to kill his wife."

Oh my god, I thought. The restraining order plainly stated that Martha said I feel he may harm me, my daughter, and then himself. Police officers are now starting a rumor that I actually verbally threatened I was going to kill her. What bestowed them that right? The side door of the ambulance was open, and I could see the police searching my vehicle. I realized I was labeled in my own town.

I was taken to the emergency room. They expressed that I was totally dehydrated and something about my sugar level. They put an intravenous in me. While lying there, the phone by my bed was ringing. I could not reach it. After several rings, a nurse walked in. She answered the phone.

"Hello! Yes, he is" and handed me the phone, "It's for you."

I said, "Hello, hello," but no one answered. I knew it had to be Martha because nobody in my family knew where I was, and I knew her friend that worked at the doctor's office would call her. I did not know why she would call. Once I was in a regular room, I called my sister Anne to inform her that I was in the hospital. My sister Anne called Martha's sister Carrie.

"Hi Carrie, this is Tom's sister Anne. Do you know where Jennifer is?"

"She is here with me," Carrie answered.

Anne responded, "Can you have Jennifer call her father? He is in the hospital."

Carrie rudely replied, "That is up to her Mom," and then hung up.

I was lying in a hospital bed staring at the walls when a woman walked into my room. "Hi Mr. Frawley, my name is Bell, and I am a hospital counselor." She stated with an accent. What is going on with you today, Mr. Frawley?"

"Well, I have not eaten for days, I am in the middle of a divorce, and my wife has restraining orders against me. She lied about me going to harm her, my daughter, and her boyfriend."

"Why don't we call your wife and have a family session here at the hospital."

I firmly replied, "You cannot do that; my wife will have me committed. There is a restraining order!"

"Mr. Frawley, you know it is up to me when you will be released from here. You are angry, and I think that maybe you contributed to the divorce."

I replied in frustration, "You don't even know me or my situation. Can you please leave me alone right now? I'm not feeling well."

"Ok, Mr. Frawley, but I'll be back tomorrow."

In a panic, I called my sister Anne who worked at a hospital and asked her to get me out of there. Knowing the rules and regulations at hospitals, she had me out the next morning just before the return of this crazy hospital counselor.

Anne drove me to the doctor's office where my truck was. The doors were unlocked. I was still driving around with pillows, blankets, clothes, practically everything that Martha gave me. My truck was a mess. The police threw things everywhere.

July 30, 2005, at 7:00 a.m., I decided to take a ride by my house. I also had a child support check in the form of a money order that I was going to put in my mailbox. As I pulled up to the house, a strange car was parked in the driveway, to my surprise. Also in the driveway was my big screen TV and boxes by the garage door. The TV was a little older but in working condition. It was originally in the garage with many other things we were storing for a future garage sale. I went to the police station and asked a woman in her fifties at the front desk if she could send an officer to my home. I needed to get inside and because of a restraining order, I would like an escort. The woman said she would have a car meet me by the house. As soon as I returned to my home, there was a police car in the street. Female and male officers were standing in my driveway. I pulled up, jumped out of my car and as I walked up, one of the male officers immediately asked what was going on.

I explained, "I am in the middle of a divorce, and I drove past my home to put a child support check in the mailbox, and I noticed some of my things outside." I explained.

"Yes, I have noticed the big TV in the driveway," the officer said.

I replied, "I would just like to know why my things are outside where they could get damaged or stolen."

The female officer said, "Yes, someone could have taken these things. What is your wife's name?"

"Her name is Martha."

"The woman officer looked at me and said, "Well, let's knock on the door and find out."

As the officers walked toward the front door, I walked around my property to look at the other items that were outside. Christmas decorations were piled on the curb by our mailbox, waiting to be picked up by the garbage men. The TV, which was on wheels, was at the top of our 20-foot driveway and could have easily been rolled away. There were several boxes by the garage door containing new picture frames, tools, and other various items. I took pictures of everything, including the strange car and the plates.

The officers were having no success with anyone answering the door. I could hear the female officer knocking and saying, "Open the door, Martha, it's the police." After several attempts, the female officer turned to me and said, "I am sorry, sir, that is very rude for your wife to put your things outside where anyone can take them. I suggest you try to get a truck and get someone to help you come back and get these things."

I uttered," I really do not have anywhere to store them, but I will try to think of something."

The officers informed me they would try again later.

I did not make it back until the next day, but there was nothing outside. I did not know if everything was put back into the garage or taken. Martha refused to answer my calls. I later found out the car in the driveway was her mother's new car, and Martha was out of town. Her mother was watching the house and did not answer the door, which I did not blame her for. I wondered what she thought of her daughter's behavior, watching the house with my belongings outside while her daughter was away with a married man.

When I got home, I called my lawyer to inform him of what transpired and later brought him the pictures as proof. He told me that he would look into it and bring it up in court, but that never happened.

Things have suddenly changed for me in Countryside. When walking down the street, people I knew looked at me strangely, even some of the kids I knew avoided me. I would see some of my daughter's friends in local stores and when I would wave, they would either turn around and walk away or wave slowly from their waist as if they wanted to say hi but shouldn't. My looks alone probably scared people. I looked like a skeleton. In my small town, things got around. Martha painted a picture of me that scared people. The local police watched me every time I returned. This was not something I knew how to respond to. People that I knew stared at me as if I were a known criminal. This would extend to my old neighborhood.

While walking down the block in my old neighborhood Bridgeport, I saw Martha's cousin outside with her children. She looked right at me as I began walking toward her across the street. She grabbed her children, pulled them into the house, and shut the door. I was sure Martha hit them with her side of the story. I never hurt any of these people. However, my relief was my old neighborhood. Friends and family were always around. Nobody judges you. Down there, everyone has been through something.

CHAPTER 5

August 3, 2005, Court date, 9:30 am. I met with Mr. Simmons in the hallway around 9:15 am, where he briefed me on what to expect. He told me that we would sit in the back inside the courtroom until my name was called, at which point we would go to the front of the courtroom and stand at the left side and Martha at the right. He also informed me that we were there to agree on an order for visitation with me and Jennifer.

I went inside and there were a few dozen people sitting in seats, to the left and to the right. I went and sat in an open spot to my right. There was a case currently in session. A few moments later, Martha walked in through the doors with her attorney. They walked in and sat several rows in front of me. I was sitting there for about 30 minutes before I heard "Frawley."

I got up and stood where my attorney had previously instructed me, to the left, and Daniel Simmons stood to the left of me. Martha and Mr. Burnburg were to my right. The judge was a white woman in her fifties with grey hair. I was unsure if this was good or bad for me. The Judge looked over at Mr. Burnburg, "Good morning Donald." Then over to Mr. Simmons and asked, "Who are you?"

"Hi, Your Honor, my name is Daniel Simmons; I represent Mr. Frawley."

"I am Judge Mary Nobal, and I will be handling The Frawley case. What do we have today?"

Mr. Burnburg stated, "Martha Frawley is seeking a divorce. She currently has a restraining order against Mr. Frawley. He has threatened her and attempted to commit suicide."

Mr. Simmons, "Mr. Frawley never threatened her."

Mr. Burnburg, "Your honor, we have an order here for restricted visitation for Mr. Frawley for his daughter.

The judge looked over at Mr. Simmons and said, ``Is this order agreed?"

"Yes, Your Honor," Mr. Burnburg replied.

I was curious as to how this case was going to go as Judge Mary Nobal and Mr. Burnburg were on a first-name basis.

IN THE CIRCUIT COURT OF COOK COUNTY, ILLINOIS

Martha Frawley__________

Petitioner

V.

Thomas Frawley__________

Respondent

ORDER

AGREED ORDER

THIS CAUSE coming to be heard by agreement of the parties, the Court having jurisdiction over the parties and the subject matter, and the Court been fully advised in the premises;

WHEREFORE, IT IS HEREBY ORDERED THAT:

- By separate Order to Order of Protection in the matter herein shall be modified so as to allow THOMAS FRAWLEY ("THOMAS") visitation with JENNIFER FRAWLEY ("JENNIFER"), the minor child on Mondays and Wednesdays each week from 6:00 P.M. until 8:00pm and on alternate weeks commencing Friday, August 12, 2005, from 6:00 P.M. until Sunday evening at 7:30 PM.
- THOMAS may have telephonic visitation on days when he does not see JENNIFER limited to one time per day call limited to ten minutes.
- All pickups and drop-offs shall be from the curbside. THOMAS shall not for any reason enter the premises, including but not limited to drive his car onto the driveway or exit his car and come onto the parkway or otherwise approached the residence at **** South Catherine, Countryside, Illinois.
- Thomas shall prior to the commencement of any overnight weekend visitation, supply MARTHA FRAWLEY in writing the address and the landline telephone where JENNIFER will be staying overnight.
- Thomas shall prior to the commencement of any overnight weekend visitation, start individual psychotherapy with the licensed clinical psychologist. Such therapy shall be on a weekly basis and shall continue until further order of the court and his continued pay is a precondition to continuing overnight visitation. This paragraph shall be revisited at the next status date, and it is entered without prejudice to be either party. Responded to have the evaluation performed within the next fourteen days as a provision to starting any program of psychotherapy.
- Thomas shall be permitted to remove his personal clothing on 7th August 2005 at 12:00 p.m.
- Status is set for September 9, 2005, at 9:30 PM without further notice.

AGREED:

Donald Burnburg

Daniel Simmons

The personal items in the driveway were not brought up in court, but I did not stress that subject due to the fact I was allowed to see Jennifer

I was able to see Jennifer that evening. When I saw her, my eyes filled up with tears. She jumped into my truck and, as she greeted me, said, "Hi Dad!" "Hi Jenn!" I saw her eyes turn glassy as she looked over at me because my body looked frail as I lost so much weight since the last time she had seen me. Nevertheless, she maintained her composure to show me she was strong. She looked very pretty. We went to the park and walked around as she was excited to fill me in on her life and everything I have missed. Martha always told me that Jennifer never tells me anything. Little did she know, Jennifer told me everything. I had her for two hours; I just let her talk away. When our time was up, I took her home, kissed her goodbye, and headed back to Bridgeport. As the week went on, I directed my attention to Martha. I heard she was having a garage sale. She was denying the sale, but I did not believe her. I bought the Wednesday edition of our neighborhood newspaper, and there was not an ad for the sale. Thursday, after thinking all night, I went to the building department in Countryside to see if a permit was pulled for a garage sale at my address. I went into the building, went up a staircase to the permit department. There was an elderly man at the counter. I walked up to the man and said, "Excuse me, sir, is there a permit pulled **** S ****** for a garage sale?

"Let me check," the man said. He opened up a binder and searched. He then looked up at me and said, "Yes, sir, there is."

"Can I have a copy for my attorney? That is my home, I'm in the middle of a divorce, and my wife should not be selling our things."

He replied, "I can't do that sir, you will have to get your attorney with a court order to come in and get it."

I left in frustration. When I got into my truck, I called Martha. She Answered.

"Hey Martha, you have a permit for a garage sale, and I want to be there."

Martha replied, "No," and hung up.

I then called Mr. Simmons.

"Hello Daniel, Martha is having a garage sale; I want it stopped."

"Let me call her attorney Tom, I'll call you right back.

"Ok Daniel," I hung up.

Shortly after, Daniel called back.

"Hey Tom, I talked to Mr. Burnburg, and he said if you allow the sale, you can attend."

I agreed.

Friday before the sale, my heart was pumping because the thought of being in the driveway with Martha selling my life piece by piece for two days was going to be unbearable. I wanted to be there so bad, and now I did not know if I could handle it.

August 12, 2005, I was sitting on the couch at my sister Anne's house when she came home from work. She walked in the door, and I said, "Hey Anne,"

Anne seemed upset about something. She kept walking toward her bedroom and said, "I'll talk to you later."

I felt she needed to be alone with her family and I left the house and drove out to Countryside. I did not know what was wrong with Anne, but I had my own problems to face. I went to the Holiday Inn and got a room for the night. I then went to the liquor store and bought a 12 pack of light beer. I returned to the hotel and started to consume my beer, just sitting there in silence, thinking about the next morning. I decided I want to die. I could not function in my new strange world. It was a lonely existence. I just wanted the pain to end.

I called Martha. She answered the phone. "What do you want, Tom?"

"Martha, pour my ashes in Michigan."

Michigan was our friend's lake house where we vacationed for years.

Martha said, "Here we go again!"

I hung up.

I called a couple of my friends to say goodbye and hung up on them. They were calling me back, but I did not answer. I do not remember the exact time, but it was dark outside. I went down to my truck that was parked in the back of the hotel. I looked around to see if anyone was around. It was very dark in the back parking lot. I had duct tape and an aluminum dryer hose that I purchased some time earlier. I taped one end to the exhaust pipe, and the other I put through the rear window and rolled it up as far as it could go. I got into the truck and called Jennifer. We talked for a little bit, she told me she was on her way home after being out with friends. I did not tell her my intentions, for I did not want to hurt her. We finished our conversation, and I said goodbye. I do not know how long I was sitting there with the keys in the ignition and my hand on the keys. Then suddenly, out of the corner of my eye, I see police cars coming from my left and then my right. They pulled up, jumped out, and pulled me from my vehicle and stood me by the back doors of my truck. One of the officers said, "What are you doing?"

I did not say anything. There were officers everywhere. Unexpectedly an officer blurted out, "She's not worth it." Who was this person? I did not know him. They put me in an ambulance and took me to the hospital. Upon arrival to the emergency room, the doctors were questioning me. A woman doctor in her forties asked, "Were you drinking, are you on drugs, if so, how much?

I replied, “I was only drinking beer."

"Did you start the car?"

I said, “No, I did not get that far." A woman police officer was standing in the room. She said, "It was running."

I said, “Whatever."

My car was not running, no exhaust in the car. Why would they lie?

They put me on oxygen and took blood samples. Shortly after, they took me to a room. It was a regular hospital room where I was alone. I was nervous and scared. A nurse came into the room and gave me something to put me to sleep. Before I fell asleep, I was lying there thinking what is wrong with me, what has happened to my life, what Jennifer would think of me. Finally, I fell asleep, and the next morning a hospital Psychiatrist came into my room to talk to me. He asked me, “What is on your mind? “I did not answer, fearing being locked up. "Well, anyway, Mr. Frawley, I am going to send you to another hospital where they specialize in the treatment you need." I did not have a clue what he was talking about. He suddenly left my room. That afternoon two paramedics came into my room with their traveling bed. They put me in that bed, and they strapped my legs and arms. I asked, "Why do I have to be strapped like this?

One of the men replied, "For your safety. “I thought this was standard procedure for an ambulance ride. They strapped me in the first ambulance. I arrived at the hospital by the emergency entrance. I knew this hospital. My mother was a heart patient there. They took me down a hall toward a room with double-thick doors and two small windows. They had to ring a bell to be let in. I was wheeled inside toward a desk with a couple of nurses. They un-strapped me and took me into one of their many rooms. A woman in her late fifties came in and sat down at a table across from me.

"Hi Mr. Frawley, I am Nurse Pat, and you are in the psychiatric ward. I need you to give me all your personal belongings and your shoes. You can keep your pants, shirt, and socks. You can make it easy by signing yourself in; if you do not, the hospital will file a court order to keep you longer. You will be here for at least seven days, depending on your progress."

"I am not signing any papers," I said.

"Ok, suit yourself, Pat replied. You are assigned to room three with another male patient, we have two showers, but one is broken. You can shower once a day in the morning or at night before you go to bed. We will supply you with soap, shampoo, towels, toothbrush, toothpaste, shaving cream, and razor. However, if you need to shave, you are not allowed to shave alone. One of the nurses will accompany you and bring you the razor. When you are finished, you are to return the razor to the nurse. Three times a day, you will get a breakfast, lunch and dinner menu. You will have different choices to choose from for each meal. Down the hall is a TV room with chairs and tables. We use this room for meals as well as a visitor room. During the day there will be activities, I suggest you participate. The activities for the week are posted in the TV room. There is also a payphone at the end of the hallway. You can use this anytime except during meals and after 9:00PM. Your doctor will be in once a day to check on your progress. The TV room is shut down every night at 10:30. Visiting hours are from 6:00 to 8:00 PM Monday – Friday, Saturday, Sunday & Holidays 1:00 to 2:00 PM., and 6:00 to 8:00 PM. Do you have any questions?"

"No," I replied!

Oh my god, I thought, just two months ago, I was a normal, hard-working guy with the American dream, a family, dog, house, cars, and now I'm in the nuthouse. I accepted the fact that I and I alone were the reason why I was here. I was the only one to blame for my own actions. There was nothing I could really do now but deal with what was ahead of me.

I got to know one of the young nurses. She was about 30 years old, dark brown hair, and brown eyes, with a slender build. She convinced me to sign the admittance papers; she said being in the position I was in, I could not win against the hospital. She had a sweet personality, and I think she believed I was not crazy and that I was a regular person who got knocked down. She was on the night shift, and I spoke to her regularly.

There were about six rooms with two people in each room. Men paired with men and women paired together. This place had many characters. A woman in her 40's was in for alcohol problems, another woman signed herself in for fighting with her teenage daughter. Most of the other people I was not sure about. I heard one man claiming to hear voices in his head and later heard him say he was faking crazy to get a state check. The man I was paired up with never spoke to anyone. He just sat around and stared into space. This person looked crazy. Other patients feared him. He never said one word to me while I was there. I did not fear him, I tried talking to him, but he just stared into space. He mumbled once.

I learned the system after a day. They had three activities a day, and they monitored who attended. I noticed a man with a clipboard. He was always sitting in the activities room. He was marking down whether you stayed in your room or were active throughout the day.

Once a day, a doctor would come in and talk with us individually to monitor our progress. The days were long. At about nine o'clock every night, it was medicine time. I only asked for sleeping pills. I did not want any medication written in my file to show depression. I knew Martha was going to hang me in court now.

I would lay in bed at night wondering what happened in my life, hoping to fall asleep and wake up in my own bed. In the morning, I would wake to this harsh reality. Day to day, I was observing the routines of the hospital staff. They would mark down how often people visit you. If you had no outside support, they considered this a risk to let you back into society. My brother Brendan and sister Anne came to see me just once. I understood they had their own families. A childhood friend and his wife, Kal and Sally, came to see me as well. That was a nice surprise, for I have not seen them in years; Sally gave me a phone card to make outside calls. They stayed the duration of the visitation hour. They wanted to reassure me that there were people who cared that I was alive. One day I decided to call Martha. She answered in a cold voice. Her comment to me was, "What is wrong with you? I do not want to see my daughter grow up without a father."

I do not know why I called her. I guess in my mind I thought deep down she still cared. I was very wrong. I called Jennifer. This was the call I feared. She said, "Dad, are you ok? Please do not ever leave me, Dad. I need you, Dad."

"I know Jennifer, I am so sorry. I love you, Jennifer. I have to go now but take this number down if you want to call me." She called me every day.

It was the 7th day, and I was waiting for the doctor to release me. When he finally arrived, he called me into a private room where we sat at a table. I was excited to finally get out of this Looney bin. "Hi Mr. Frawley, how are you doing today?

"I feel great," I replied.

"Well, Mr. Frawley, your sister Anne called and said she thinks that you should be kept here a few more days."

My heart dropped, my blood went cold, sitting two feet across from him suddenly felt like a mile. The lump in my throat almost rendered me speechless when I regurgitated the words, "I am fine, please, and I just want to go home."

"I am sorry Mr. Frawley, I am keeping you here for a few more days. " They did just that.

I was so angry, I called my sister Anne and told her "How dare you keep me here longer. Who do you think you are? When I get out of here I am not coming back to live with you, put my stuff in my truck." and I hung up. What a mean thing to say to someone who wants you to live.

I had a few more days to reflect. That I did. People consider a person that commits suicide a coward, a selfish person. Are they correct, or are they judging from a life of no problems, extreme happiness, financial stability, a family, supportive friends, and surrounded by unconditional love.

I believe it is more of a lack of understanding. It is easy to judge when you are up, as I wonder what these judges would do if they lost it all in a blink of an eye and fell down. Only then can they see through the eyes of a suffering soul and feel the pain of a broken heart.

I was one of those judges, but for the first time in my life, I was on the bottom looking up. Unanswered questions were pondering in my mind. How can a single person have so much power over you that you are willing to take your own life? That question cannot be answered. You have no control of your emotions. Do we control when we laugh, when we cry, or when we are happy or sad? I think not, but these are things that can be controlled by others.

On the third day, I was up at 7:00AM. The doctors usually started seeing their patients at 9:00 AM. It was a long morning. I waited nervously. Finally, at about 10:00 am, my doctor arrived. Once again, we sat at the infamous table. It was an eternity as Dr. Peck slowly went through papers on a clipboard. He looked up at me and said, "Well, Mr. Frawley, I am going to release you, do not come back here."

"Trust me, I said, you will not see me again!"

I called my sister Liz. My heart skipped a beat at every ring. Then like music to my ears, "Hello!"

"Liz, this is Tom. I need you to come and get me from the hospital. Can you do that?"

"Yes, Tom, I'll leave now."

"Thank you so much Liz! Please get to the hospital by 11:00 AM. If you are not here, they will not release me!"

"I'm on my way, Liz replied!"

I constantly paced up and down the hallway impatiently.

It was five minutes to eleven when Liz arrived. I was very glad to see her. I could see her through the small thick windows on the doors. They gave me my release papers, and they buzzed the double doors to let me out. I was free. I thanked Liz and said, "Let's get out of here fast."

Liz took me to Anne's house to pick up my truck. I was sure Anne did not want to see me after the way I treated her. I did not blame her. If I were her, I would slap my face. At least twice!

I was homeless once again. Liz was living with her boyfriend's parents and was getting an apartment in a few weeks. Liz said she would have an extra room for me. Sometimes I would stay at motels. During the day, I would walk around the Bridgeport neighborhood visiting family members to kill time and conserve gas. At night, I would frequent a neighborhood bar called Home Base, just to have somewhere to be. A friend of mine owned the bar.

Even though I had many family members here, their homes were full, and they had their own problems. I would go to my younger brother Dan's house daily. He is an amazing person. Dan was about 5-foot 7 inches tall, with brown hair, blue eyes, and a slender build. He practically raised five children on his own and always had company and a full house. I would sometimes sleep on his floor. Other times, I would sleep in my truck. Dan was very concerned about me, often waking me up from his floor, offering me soup or food, trying to get me to eat. Everyone was aware that I was slowly starving myself. It was not something I was trying to do; I just did not have an appetite.

I had about five hundred dollars left, and it was running out quickly. So I decided to go to my bank in Countryside for some money. I went up to the teller and said," excuse me, but I do not have my bankbook, but I have a checking and savings account". It was a woman in her 30's, she asked, "Can I have your driver's license so I can look up your account?" I gave her my license. She was entering my information in the computer in front of her when she said, “there is nothing in the savings and 20 dollars in the checking."

I frantically said, “There were 14,000 dollars in the savings, are you sure?"

"Yes, Mr. Frawley that is all that is there."

I stared at her for a second in disbelief and walked out of the bank. Wow, Martha took all the money. I went out into the parking lot and called Mr. Simmons.

"Mr. Simmons, This is Tom, I just went to my bank, and Martha emptied the bank accounts."

"I will look into it, Tom."

That evening while at my brother Dan’s house, I decided to call Martha’s Aunt and uncle. Uncle Fred and Aunt Barb were always good to me. Uncle Fred answered the phone. I said, “Hi Uncle Fred, did you hear anything about Martha and me?"

"He said no Tom, where are you?"

"I am in the neighborhood, Uncle Fred."

“I am at home; come and see me," He replied,

I went to visit, and they welcomed me as they always did. I told them my story, and they were sad for me, considering I was with their niece for over 20 years. They said we are here if you need anything. They were not picking sides, but they would treat me like family. That meant a lot to me. I would visit them from time to time. Martha’s parents and her uncle and aunt were not on speaking terms for over ten years because of a dispute over money when the grandmother died.

September 1, 2005, Liz would finally get her apartment, and I would move in with her. Liz had two daughters, twelve and nine. I had a small room with a bed and a computer table. I would stay in my room almost 24 hours a day, only coming out to eat a few bites of dinner. This was when I started writing my story. I was not trying to write a book; I would buy spiral notebooks and write my unconceivable events daily as they happened. This was my personal therapy, a way to vent silently without boring other people who did not want to hear my drama. Besides, most people did not believe me.

After moving into Liz's house, I was seeing a counselor ordered by the court. It was a woman in her fifties, Jaime Frazer, and I would get to like her very quickly. She was straightforward. She told me to get my shit together because there is a little girl who needs me. I did not have to worry about paying her because Martha’s insurance was covering the visits. I was scheduled to see her once a month. It got to the point where I was glad to see her. She listened to all my problems, assuring me that I was a normal person who was knocked down in life.

I dreaded this day.

September 9, 2005 Court date:

My attorney advised me that we agree to the order and leave to buy some time.

IN THE CIRCUIT COURT OF COOK COUNTY, ILLINOIS

COUNTY DEPARTMENT-DOMESTIC RELATIONS DIVISION

Martha Frawley_________________

Petitioner

v.

Thomas Frawley_________________

Respondent

ORDER

AGREED ORDER

THIS CAUSE coming to be heard on MARTHA FRAWLEY's Petition for Additional Relief, notice having been given, counsel for both parties present, and the Court being fully advised in the premises;

WHEREFORE IT IS HEREBY ORDERED THAT:

- All visitation between THOMAS FRAWLEY and JENNIFER
- FRAWLEY he and is hereby suspended for fourteen days pending till further order
- THOMAS FRAWLEY may speak to JENNIFER FRAWLEY
- Telephonically one time each day limited to fifteen minutes.
- THOMAS FRAWLEY is ordered to enter an intensive Psychotherapy program and report to the Court periodically on the progress of same.
- Any further visitation ordered by this Court and between
- THOMAS FRAWLEY and JENNIFER FRAWLEY shall be subjected to terms expressed by this Court.

The Plenary Order of Protection heretofore entered August 03, 2005 shall be modified in conformance with this Order and a separate Disposition Order shall be entered.

Status set for

9-23-05 AT 9:30 ENTER Mary noble

JUDGE

This time I knew there was no one to blame but myself for losing Jennifer once again. I just did not understand why my punishment would include not seeing my child. What did she have to do with it? If a child attempted to hurt themself, would the court keep them from seeing their parent as a consequence?

After this incident, Jennifer started giving me a hard time saying things like, "Dad, get a job, Mommy said you are trying to take my college fund, they are never going to let you see me without a job." Jennifer's voice was cold and hateful. This was way out of character for her.

On this particular call, I said, "Jennifer, do you know how hard it is to get a job, and that is not true about me wanting your college fund. You should know me. I would never lie to you."

Instead of arguing with Jennifer daily, I did not answer her calls for several days. I knew Martha was the driving force behind her. Nevertheless, I knew how to control the evil Martha was trying to feed into my daughter. I decided to initiate a call with Jennifer. I called Jennifer's phone and when she answered, I yelled! "Jennifer, I am your father, and you do not tell me what to do. Do you understand me? That has nothing to do with me being your father. That has nothing to do with us! That is between your mother and me. Your mother should not be involving you. Do you understand, Jennifer?"

She said, "Yes, Dad." with a pouting voice.

I said, "I do not want to yell at you, but I am your father, and I cannot let you talk to me that way. One day you will see the truth, honey."

Jennifer never said anything like that again, and we went right back to our old selves.

September 13, 2005, another petition from Martha:

IN THE CIRCUIT COURT OF COOK COUNTY, ILLINOIS

COUNTY DEPARTMENT-DOMESTIC RELATIONS DIVISION

MARTHA FRAWLEY,

Petitioner,

And

THOMAS FRAWLEY, COURTROOM

Respondent, 1623

PETITION FOR ADDITIONAL RELIEF

NOW COMES Petitioner, MARTHA FRAWLEY ("MARTHA"), by and through her attorneys, BURNBURG & GORDON, P. C. , and pursuant to Section 501 of the Illinois Marriage and Dissolution of Marriage Act of 1986 (750 ILCS 60/101 et.Seq.) States as follows:

- The above-entitled cause of action was filed on July 13, 2005, and remains pending and undetermined.
- The parties have one minor child. JENNIFER FRAWLEY ("JENNIFER"), born October 31, 1991, and currently age 13.
- On August 3, 2005, a plenary Order of Protection was entered in the above-entitled cause, which provided in certain points that:
- MARTHA would have custody of JENNIFER.
- THOMAS FRAWLEY's ("THOMAS") access to Jennifer would be specified in a separate court order, which was also entered the same day.
- MARTHA and Jennifer remain protected parties.
- Subsequent to the entry of the Plenary Order of Protection, THOMAS attempted to commit suicide in Countryside, Illinois, by running tubing from the tailpipe of his vehicle into the cab and starting the engine. This took place in the parking lot of a hotel In Countryside, Illinois.
- THOMAS did not complete his suicide attempt but was interrupted by the police when they notice the tubing from the tail pipe into the cab. Police took THOMAS for evaluation and ultimately admittance to the McNally hospital psychiatric ward.
- A blood test and clinical evaluation of THOMAS revealed that THOMAS had a 0.13 alcohol level with the presence of carbon monoxide noted in his system. THOMAS was diagnosed with severe depression.
- THOMAS was released from McNally hospital and, upon information and belief, is no longer residing with his sister in Chicago, Illinois, which was his given place of residence at the time of the entry of the Plenary Order of Protection.

- MARTHA Is informed and believes that THOMAS is not seeking any intervention of any nature or sort to deal with his severe depression and whatever other psychological/psychiatric issues THOMAS may have.
- MARTHA Believes that THOMAS is a danger not only to himself but to JENNIFER and MARTHA if the present terms of the Order of Protection are not changed and order to adequately protect MARTHA and Jennifer.

WHEREFORE, MARTHA FRAWLEY prays as follows:

- That the visitation ordered in the Order of Protection be immediately suspended until further Court Order other that THOMAS FRAWLEY be allowed to have daily contact by telephone limited to fifteen minutes each day with JENNIFER FRAWLEY.
- That THOMAS FRAWLEY not be allowed any different or other contact with JENNIFER FRAWLEY unless and until he enrolls and continues to remain enrolled in an intensive program of psychotherapy.
- That until such time as this court is satisfied that THOMAS no longer presents a danger to himself and to others that any and all future visitation between THOMAS and a minor child, JENNIFER FRAWLEY, be supervised by a non-family professional.
- For such further, different and other relief has this Court deems meet and just.

CERTIFICATION

Under penalties of perjury has provided by law pursuant to section 5/109 of the Illinois Code of civil procedure, undersigned certifies that the statements set forth in this instrument are true and correct, except as to matters therein stated to be on information and belief has to such matters the undersigned certifies as aforesaid that I verily believe the same to be true.

Martha Frawley

Martha Frawley

BURNBURG & GORDON, P. C

Wow, I was blown away by "Petition for Additional relief" What did that actually mean. Because I tried to hurt myself, Martha gets to make demands. Paragraph number 3-C. "Martha and Jennifer remain protected parties." Whether I succeeded or not in my attempt, at what point was Martha and or Jennifer's life in danger or threatened. Wasn't my life in danger? The system was right in sending me to the mental hospital. Their job was to protect me from myself, not protect Martha from me. If I were dead, what harm could I possibly cause her?

Number 4 gave me the chills. How in the world could Martha get so much detailed information? Is it not against the law for police to give out such a detailed report to a party that was not involved, especially a civilian? Then my medical records without my consent. They had more information than I had. Considering the circumstances, I would agree that the courts would want to know about this but wouldn't the proper way be by a "Court Order"? The police knew I was in the middle of a divorce. I asked for a copy of a garage sale permit, but I was told, because of being in the middle of a divorce, to have an Attorney with a court order for such an important piece of paper. When you arrive at a hospital, they usually make you sign a piece of paper, "who has the right to your records, who can make medical decisions on your behalf. "I certainly do not remember putting Martha's name on anything. I am sure if I came in half dead and had some consciousness, I would have written Jennifer. I never received any court orders to release my private records.

Number 6, at the other Hospital, "THOMAS was diagnosed with severe depression." Who knows, maybe there was a court order requesting my diagnosis? The doctor did not mention it to me.

Number 7, how dare I move from a "given place of residence?" Is that against the law? I remember it being no big deal when my "given place of residence" had a license plate.

Number 8, another sentence with severe depression but now topped off with psychological/psychiatric issues. What did they expect of a man who has lost everything? It is against the law to be depressed, alone, broken at the hands of another human being. To upper society, you are not normal; there is something wrong with you. I have a real hard time with that. When you spank a child, and they cry, are they not normal? When you starve them, deprive them, put them out in the cold, are they the ones who are psycho because they become depressed, confused, disoriented?

Martha believes that I am a danger to her and my child. "Under penalties of perjury," Martha knew I was seeing a psychotherapist paid for by her insurance.

It was obvious that those words meant nothing. If Martha believes, the court will act upon it. The courts granted all of Martha's requests.

A week later, Martha emailed me,

"Tom, what can we do to get this divorce over with?"

RE:

"Give me half of everything, including my daughter, half of my money, half of the house, and half of the furniture. I just want my half, nothing more, nothing less."

Martha called me on the phone later that same day, and we went through the papers Item by Item. It took about half an hour to go through all the papers. Martha said she would give the revised copy to her attorney, and I should have them in a few days. During that conversation, Martha came from left field with a comment.

"I just want you to know Tom, I never slept with this Man until after we were divorced."

"I thought for a second and replied," Martha, we are still married. "There was a moment of silence on her end, and then she changed the subject. At this point, I was starting to wonder who the hell this person is that I was with my whole life. Was that comment for her own piece of mind? How did I miss the signs?

I never received the revised copies.

As time went on, I kept begging Martha to let me see my daughter. Little did I know Jennifer was giving her mother a hard time on the other end to see me as well.

September 19, 2005, my attorney filed this petition:

IN THE CIRCUIT COURT OF COOK COUNTY, ILLINOIS

COUNTY DEPARTMENT-DOMESTIC RELATIONS DIVISION

MARTHA FRAWLEY,)

Petitioner,)

And)

THOMAS FRAWLEY,) COURTROOM 1623

Respondent,)

PETITION FOR TEMPORARY MAINTENANCE AND OTHER RELIEF

NOW COMES, the RESPONDENT Thomas Frawley, by and through his attorney, Daniel Simmons, and as and for her instead petition, states as follows:

- That move the petitioner herein Martha Frawley, filed her Petition for Dissolution of Marriage on the 13 day of July 2005, which Petition remained pending and undetermined.

- Simultaneously with the filing of her petition for Dissolution petitioner has also filed a Petition for Order of Protection.
- Pursuant to Petitioner's Petition for Order of Protection and ex parte Order for Protection was issued barring respondent from contact with Petitioner, the minor daughter, and entry onto the form marital property.
- Since the entry of the Order for Protection, the respondent has been unable to find permanent living quarters and has stayed with various friends, family, slept in motels, and on a number of occasions slept in his work truck.
- Although regularly employed as a carpenter, the respondent has been unemployed since mid-August.
- During the course of their marriage, at the insistence of Petitioner, Respondent has frequently been the "stay at home" parent raising their minor daughter, Jennifer.
- In large part, Petitioner has typically had a higher annual income than Respondent.
- Since Respondent vacated the marital residents, Petitioner has had complete control over all marital assets and has sold via garage sale and private sale, many items from home.
- With the exception of proceeds derived from the sale of two motor scooters, Petitioner has not accounted for Respondent for the funds received.
- On information and belief, Petitioner is holding funds from the sale of a van.
- The Respondent has been looking for a replacement job and anticipates new employment with a "start-up" company in mid-September.
- Respondent is currently unable to support himself.
- Petitioner is employed full-time at Through-View and Countryside, Illinois and earns approximately $60,200.00 annually.
- The Respondent lacks sufficient property, income, or other means with which to provide for his reasonable needs and requirements.

WHEREFORE, the respondent Thomas Frawley prays as follows:

- That he may be awarded temporary maintenance in a fair reasonable sum from the Petitioner, Martha Frawley.
- The Petitioner be ordered to account for all sums acquired by her through the disposition of property of the marital estate.
- That Petitioner be restrained from the further disposition of property of the marital state without further order of the court.
- For such other and further relief in the premises this Court may deem reasonable.

Daniel Simmons

Nothing was done to stop Martha from liquidating my life's worth.

September 24, 2005, Martha sent me an email:

"Tom, I am going to bring Jennifer to the city to see you. I will bring Jennifer to Liz's house Monday at 7:00 P. M."

RE: "Ok, Thank you."

I was so excited; it had been days since I saw my little girl. I was still skinny, but I have been lifting weights to look strong again, and I was starting to eat again. It was a Monday evening; I was waiting anxiously, looking out the second-floor apartment window. I saw Martha's red truck pull up. I watched as the passenger door opened and Jennifer got out. She walked to the front of the building; I could hear her coming up the stairs. She knocked on the door. When I opened the door, I saw a little girl that was turning into a woman. She was beautiful. Her hair was longer, and she had colored braces. She even had makeup on. It looked like she had grown a foot. I grabbed her and gave her a bear hug. I had to fight back the tears. I could see her eyes were glassy, and by her facial expression, she was very happy to see me. Jennifer said, "Here Dad, this is for you."

She gave me an envelope along with two pictures of her.

"Thank you Jenn, I will open it later. Let's go for a walk. "We went down the stairs out the front door, and Martha's truck was still there. Jennifer said, "Oh, I have a bag of clothes for you Dad; they are in Mommy's car. "Jennifer went up to the truck, turned around toward me, and said, "Dad come here; they are in the back seat. "I opened the back door, reached in for my clothes, gripped the bag in my hand, and paused and said thanks, Martha.

"You are welcome, Tom; I will meet you in front of the house in two hours."

"I would have her back by then," I replied.

Jennifer and I walked all through the neighborhood. She talked a mile a minute. She was telling me about her first year of high school, and the boys are so cute. In the two hours, together Jennifer would make a few comments about Martha being mean. Saying things like, "Mom is always yelling at me; she is always talking about court stuff."

I did not comment; I just let her go on. I just let her talk, she wanted me to be proud of her, and I was. The only question I asked her was, "Jennifer, how did you get your mother to bring you to see me."

"I tell her all the time I want to see you; I guess I drove her crazy. "After our two hours were up, we met Martha back at the house. I kissed and hugged Jennifer goodbye. I went up into the house and went straight into my room. I lay on the bed, and I opened the envelope that Jennifer gave me and inside was a letter on three small pieces of paper with flowered borders. This was her exact letter.

"Dear Dad, I know that you love me, but I just wanted to make it extremely clear that I love you too. I think about you every minute of the day. I miss you so much. If someone were to ask me how much I love you. I wouldn't be able to tell them because words can't come close to showing my love for you. I see a picture of you in my mind, and I don't ever want it to go away!

I NEED you in my life because without you, I am not whole. If you weren't here, I would be like a flower without a stem that would die slowly. I keep a picture of us right on my dresser, along with the card you made me.

Therefore, I am giving you these two pictures, one for your wallet and the other for whatever else you want to do with it.

I love you with all my heart, and deep inside, this letter is really not enough? I love you Dad, nothing will ever change that, and NO ONE can ever take your place. I hope by this you can kind of realize how much I love you. I can't wait until I am able to see you again. I LOVE you with ALL myHEART!!

Always & forever, Jennifer (Funghi)

Funghi is Jennifer's nickname, an Italian word for mushroom.

After seeing my daughter that night, I felt much stronger. I was looking for a reason to stay alive. Looking at that precious little girl, I knew she needed me, and I needed her. I was praying for an angel to save my life. Little did I know that all along, Jennifer was that angel.

Although I appreciated Martha letting me see Jennifer, something was resonating in me. Martha was supposed to be afraid of me, afraid that I was capable of harming her and Jennifer. Despite having restraining orders protecting her from the crazy dangerous person I am seen by the courts, and by ink from Martha's pen as well as a sworn statement, Martha was within inches of me all alone, unprotected as she handed over her only child to me not knowing where I was taking her. I guess you can call it bittersweet, as there was nothing I could do about it. Martha knew I would bring Jennifer back. Martha also knew I was not capable of harming neither Jennifer nor her, but she also knew that if I said anything, she had the power to keep my daughter from me.

My main weakness was not being with Jennifer.

The long absence of Jennifer again would wear me down. Days later, I went out to a bar and got intoxicated. I drank for hours, beer after beer. It was about 2AM, I was driving past Paul's house, and I saw him getting out of his car. Paul was in town from his home in Italy. He was 47 years old, about 5ft 7in tall, athletic build and balding. He was a non-drinker, doing well with his own business in pharmaceuticals, but he had his own problems. Paul, like me, was in the middle of a divorce and had a son with a life threatening disease called Thalassemia he always found the time to help others. I got out of my truck, and I am sure he noticed I was drunk. Paul stood in the street as I walked toward him.

"Paul, I need the gun," I said.

"What do you need it for, Tom?"

"The courts and police are hounding me to turn it in."

Paul said, "Come back tomorrow. I got in my truck and left.

The next day Paul gave me the gun along with a warning. He said, "Do the right thing, do not hurt anyone else, or yourself, and think of your daughter. Show them the Tom I know."

I had no intentions of hurting anyone or myself at that point, but I did not turn the gun in to the police. The gun was unloaded, but I had three shells in my truck. However, I did go to the police station to see if they were looking for the gun. I was told that Martha has reported it, but they told her that I have not committed a crime; therefore, I didn't need to turn it in.

I got to know a young Policewoman in her 30's. She would be the person that I frequently talked to from time to time. Her name was Dianna. She had a medium build, blond hair, and light color eyes. I believe she saw through Martha's lies, especially that she already knew my situation when Martha called. Dianna's husband was a police officer as well, working at the same station. Dianna was very understanding. She told me to call her anytime for legal advice. I did it several times.

October 3, 2005, Saturday morning, I was awakened by loud noises in the house. I sat up on the bed, and I could hear Liz arguing with her boyfriend, Bob. I jumped out of bed and walked through the front room into the dining room. I could see Liz screaming and throwing whatever was in her reach. It was something that frequently happened during my stay. It always made me uncomfortable. I needed to get out of there. I turned around and went back into my bedroom. I grabbed my Cell Phone and called Jennifer.

"Hi, Jenn, what's up?"

"I'm sleeping at a friend's house, "she said with a soft sleepy voice.

"I'm calling you Jenn to let you know I cannot live here anymore."

"What, Dad, Why?

Just then, I heard Liz I coming toward my room.

"Jenn I Have to go!" Just as I hung up the phone, Liz was in my doorway. She was screaming, explaining what was going on.

I got up, put my shoes on, walked past her, and headed toward the door. I did not want to get into the middle, and I left.

I went to the gas station down the road and purchased a coffee. I jumped back into my truck and was driving around for about 30 minutes with nowhere to go. I was uncomfortable, and I needed to get out of there. I wanted to rest my head somewhere in peace. Without much thought, I decided to get on the highway and go to Michigan. My best friend's parents live out there, a place Martha, Jennifer, and I frequented several times a year. They were like parents to Jennifer and me. Jenn considered them Gram and Pa. They were retired and had a big beautiful house on the lake, but bigger than their house was their hearts. Anyone who knew them wished they had parents like them.

I arrived in Michigan about two hours later but decided to stay at a motel in Dowagiac, about eight miles away. I paid the 40 dollars and checked into my room. It was an inexpensive motel, a typical room with a queen bed, TV, and small fridge. I was sitting on the bed just watching country music videos. I was actually paying attention. A lot of country musicians sing of pain. It is amazing how a person can relate to the story they are telling. It was the first time I watched TV and was coherent since July.

After about an hour, I decided to walk around the small town. It was early afternoon, a sunny day. I walked through their downtown area, so to speak, looking through store windows as if I were browsing. It was different here, nobody knew me, and nobody judged me. I was not afraid. It was safe here. A feeling I had not had in a long time. It was almost as if I was the only person in the world. It was like a strange tranquility. I walked around for several hours. There were not that many people around, kind of like a holiday back home.

I found a grocery store where I bought a 12 pack of beer and some chips. I went back to the motel, sat on the bed, turned on the country music videos, and drank throughout the evening until I fell asleep.

The next morning I showed up at Pa and Grams house unannounced. I was unsure how they would take it, seeing they loved Martha like their own daughter as well. But, I think they were glad to see me. They acted as if nothing had changed. Just like good parents, they gave me good advice and never spoke poorly of Martha, just as I expected. They took me out to dinner that evening and had me stay the night.

The next morning I said goodbye and thanked them for letting me stay, then returned to Chicago. When I walked in the front door at Liz's house, she was freaking out.

"Oh my god Tom, where have you been? Everyone thought you were going to kill yourself! You need to call Martha."

"Call Martha, I am not calling Martha! What is going on?"

Liz screamed, "Paul wants you to call him!"

I thought to myself, oh boy, what am I in for now. I called Paul, he answered screaming, "Tommy, what is wrong with you? Your daughter called me screaming and crying, saying my Dad is going to kill himself. It is on my voicemail. Do you want to hear it?"

I said, No, I do not want to hear that. I have to let you go so I can call Jennifer.

I called Jennifer's phone, but there was no answer. I called Martha, and I got her voice mail. I left her a message.

"Is Jennifer in school today?

I wanted to assure Jennifer that she had it all wrong. I sent her this email.

"Jennifer, I am so sorry, but you have it all wrong. I said I could not live in my sister's house anymore, not this world. I will always be here for you. I will be around to see you graduate and walk you down the aisle when you get married. This is my promise, Jennifer that I will never leave you.

Martha saw this email and called the police, informing them that I might take Jennifer.

Jennifer called me after school; she was angry at first but soon calmed down.

"Dad, I was so scared. I thought you were saying goodbye and that you were going to kill yourself." In a whimpering voice.

"Jennifer, Daddy is never going to leave you. I understand the way I said things and just disappeared scared you, and I am very sorry! Trust me, I had no intentions whatsoever of ending my life. I want to be here with you. You are my reason for living. "

"You know Dad, Mom just uses these things against you. There is a picture of you at my school. If someone sees you enter the building, they should call the police."

I was unaware of the one at the school. I knew there was a picture of me at Martha's work.

“Jennifer, trust me, you could not get rid of me if you tried. I am here to stay. You got that, honey?”

"Yes Dad, " she laughed. I have to go now, Dad.

Ok Jenn, I am just a phone call away.

I realized how stupid I was. I had to be very careful of the way I said things to Jennifer. She was fragile enough with her parents getting a divorce, let alone a suicidal father. I just could not convince Jennifer enough not to worry about me. How do you tell a child not to worry about losing a parent she loves so much? The answer is you do not tell them; you show them. I guess I was a little too selfish with my mind constantly on Martha that I lost focus on the little girl who was suffering the most.

Jennifer needed one stable parent. Looking at it from her perspective, her mother broke up her happy home, demonstrating hate against her father that she loves so much, and when she depends on her father to help her through this, he is self-destructive, rendering her all alone in a fight she does not understand nor can she handle.

I had to change, and she needed my help.

Paul called me the next day.

"Tom, I want you to go with me to go meet some people. They have some work for you. They were friends of Paul's, Fred and Carl Carbuchi's. They were two brothers, both of whom were divorced. Paul figured why not put me with people who have something in common. He wanted to keep me from sitting in my room for 24 hours a day thinking. It did not pay much but put money in my pocket. Fred had three daughters of his own and just like me, they were his everything. Carl had two sons, and on his own time, would run a drug and alcohol program at his local church. He preached to me now and then, telling me that if I had faith, everything I lost, I would get back tenfold. He was even sure that Jennifer in time was going to come to me. From time to time, Fred and Carl would ask me for the gun because we worked in a bad neighborhood.

One day I gave them the gun even though I knew their true intentions were to assure themselves and Paul that I would not do something stupid. Now that I had money coming in, I was a little more powerful.

October 14, 2005 court date: As soon as they called our case, The Judge asked the attorneys to meet in her chambers. They were in the judge's chambers for several minutes. When they came out, Judge Nobal looked toward Martha and stated,

"The law is 50/50, you better fix the numbers in the divorce papers, and Mr. Frawley deserves half of your 401k."

I felt I had a good day in court. When the short court hearing was over, I asked Mr. Simmons, "When am I going to get in my house?

He said, "I am going to file that next court date."I just looked at him and rolled my eyes.

Mr. Simmons gave me a piece of paper stating I was allowed to see Jennifer Mondays and Wednesdays from 6:00 PM to 8:00 PM. However, the visits were to be supervised.

With my visitation back in place, Jennifer and I would frequent the same restaurant to have dinner.

October 17, 2005, while on my way to pick up Jennifer, I gave her a call, "Jennifer, can you ask your mother if I could have some of my clothes."

"Hold on, Dad!" I could hear Jennifer in the background talking to her mother." Mom, Dad wants to know if he could have some of his clothes."

"No Jennifer, he is not getting anything until he signs papers," Martha said with a cocky voice.

Jennifer said, "Whatever, Mom! Sorry Dad."

I said, "That is ok, it is not your fault. I will see you shortly."

Jennifer started sneaking things from the house. She would use her duffle bag when I picked her up on my visitation nights. She bowled on Saturdays and would put small things in her bowling bag like hats, gloves, CDs, whatever she could fit.

Martha would ask Jennifer who was supervising each visit. It was usually my brother John, his girlfriend, or my mother. Just to give us a hard time, Martha would tell Jennifer they are not on the list. I did not know anything about a list. I called Mr. Simmons and asked him if he knew of the list. He said, "Martha created the list in her mind."

Visitation with supervision also depended on the mood Martha was in. Sometimes she would say to Jennifer, "Your Dad does not have to bring anyone with him tonight. Other times if she was in a bad mood or things were not going her way, she would turn supervision back on.

It was not hard to figure out Martha's motives. I knew when her boyfriend was coming over, I did not need supervision because otherwise, she would be stuck with Jennifer, and she knew she could not see her boyfriend with Jennifer around. It was not because of me. Jennifer told me that her mother was constantly trying to get her to meet this man. Martha finally gave up when Jennifer said, "If you ever bring that man around me, I will kick him in the balls and stab him with a knife. I don't ever want to meet him!" Martha blamed me for that. She could not accept the fact that Jennifer was an individual. I also believed when Martha's boyfriend was away visiting his children, and it was on one of my visitation days, she would make it as difficult as possible for me.

There were many nights when I could not get anyone to go with me. They had families and jobs of their own, and it was a 28-mile round trip. So I would not see Jennifer.

I called Mr. Simmons once again. I was trying to stop Martha from dictating supervision. He said he would call Mr. Burnburg. Nothing was ever done about it. I was so upset.

One evening I was walking through a city alley and spotted an unclothed female mannequin. Suddenly an idea struck me. There was a thrift store several blocks away. The next day I went to the thrift store and did some shopping. I could only imagine what the cashier thought of me as I bought a wig, hat, coat, and a pair of glasses on the counter. She looked at me strangely as I paid the bill of fewer than five dollars. I went back home and dressed the mannequin, and put her in the back seat of my Tahoe.

On the next supervised visit that I had no one to accompany me, I decided to try it out. I usually had to call Jennifer and let her know that I had someone to supervise our visit. So I called Jennifer and said, "Jennifer, I will be picking you up at 6:00 PM tonight!"

Jennifer asked, “Who is coming with you? Mom said you have to have supervision tonight."

"I said, Nonie."

Although nervous, it was worth the risk. I wanted to see my daughter. I headed out to Countryside. I pulled out in front of the house. I hit the Dome button so that the dome light does not come on when the door is open. Jennifer came out of the house walking toward the truck. I could see Martha peeking through the blinds. My heart was pounding, and my hands were shaking. Jennifer opened a truck door, and with no light on inside and my windows tinted, Martha could not tell who was sitting in the back seat. Jennifer shut the door, and I pulled away. Jennifer looked in the back and said, "What the heck, where is Nonie?"

"I said, “She could not come, so I found someone else instead." Jennifer laughed and blew it off. She was happy to see me.

Wow, I could not believe it. I was laughing and thinking to myself, Martha always has the upper hand. In her mind, she was superior to me; she was smarter than I was, and yet she watched out the window as she approved my visit with my plastic supervisor.

While eating dinner at a restaurant during this visit, Jennifer said, “Dad, please do not make me choose between you and Mom."

I said to Jennifer, "You go with your Mom. I will not put you through that kind of pressure. We will still have our weekends together."

"Thanks Dad," she said. Even though I wished she would go with me, I felt I had to spare her from a tug of war. By Jennifer saying that, I felt that was where she wanted to be. I always enjoyed the 2-hour visit; it was what I lived for.

My youngest brother John came to stay at Liz’s house for a while. He was having domestic troubles himself. John had a restraining order against him from his girlfriend, the mother of his child. He understood what I was going through and was always willing to go with me when I needed to see Jennifer. We sat up many nights talking about each other’s problems. We formed a closeness that was not there before. There were many times when I started to lose control. John would always tell me that this is just what they want. Do not let them get the best of you. I took his advice. John spent most of his life in and out of prison. He was not a bad person or a dangerous criminal; he just made stupid decisions. There is one thing for certain, if you do not have an attorney and money to pay for a good one, they will make an example out of you. John once told me, when you walk into a courtroom, and you face a judge, they do not see you, that all they see is a piece of paper. To them, the paper is who you are. You are defined by a single piece of paper. It does not matter if you are a loving brother, father, son, or anything else that is good about you. They wear blinders like racehorses, so they are not distracted by any good; they only see that you are an evil soul.

October 24, 2005, during a phone conversation with Martha, she tells me,

"Tom, I cashed in our $25,000 CD."

"I said shockingly, “How did you do that? That is in my name too."

"I needed the money Tom."

I immediately hung up the phone and called Mr. Simmons to tell him the news.

"Mr. Simmons, Martha just informed me she cashed in a $25,000 CD we had together," I said in an angry voice.

He said, "She will have to give you half when she sells the house."

I replied, "Why is it that our money and assets cannot be frozen until the divorce is final?"

"I will take care of it, Tom."

I decided to go to the Bank in Countryside where we had our CD. I walked in and stood in a line for several minutes. I was upset and disgusted. How were these things happening to me? What did I do to deserve this? I was agitated, as I could not wait to get to the counter and get answers. I was staring at the floor when I heard, "Next."

I looked up, and I was next in line. I walked up to the counter to a woman in her late fifties; I pulled out my wallet and put it on the counter with my license visible.

"Excuse me, but I had a 25,000 dollar CD in this bank, and my soon-to-be ex-wife informed me that she cashed it in. So my question is, how is that possible when it is a joint CD?"

"Let me look up your account, sir."

Waiting impatiently, did you ever get the feeling all eyes are on you? I turned around and looked at the line of people behind me. Most of them were looking in my direction. As I turned back around, I looked over to my left and saw a female customer at another teller window. She was staring at me as if she overheard my conversation. When I stared back, she put her head down. What she was thinking, I thought. Did she feel bad for me, or was what happened to me helpful information? Who knew, but I was the focus of attention as it seemed they too, were waiting for my answer.

"Mr. Frawley,"

"Yes," I replied.

"Our system shows that you did have a 25,000 dollar CD and that Martha Frawley cashed it in."

"Ok," I said sarcastically, "How is it that she cashed it without my signature? Don't you need two signatures on a joint CD? Is that not the purpose?"

"No, Mr. Frawley, any one of you can cash it in."

"I exhaled and put my head down, embarrassed and disgusted. I grabbed my wallet off the counter, turned around, and walked past the line of people and out the door, never looking up.

October 31st is Jennifer's birthday. It was also one of my days to see her. I called Jennifer up to wish her a happy birthday.

She said, "Dad, "Would you mind if I go with my friends to go Trick or Treating? Mom said you could have me tomorrow."

I said, "Sure, no problem, you go and have fun and be a kid."

"Thanks Dad, I am sorry."

"We will have our day tomorrow, honey."

"Ok bye, Dad!"

The next day Jennifer called me up and said with a sad voice, "Dad, you cannot see me today."

"Are you kidding me Jenn, why not?"

"Mom said it is not your day."

"But I did not see you yesterday, Jennifer."

"Mom said no, it is not your day."

I was frustrated and angry. After hanging up with Jennifer, I called my attorney Mr. Simmons.

"Daniel, Martha is playing games again. I was supposed to see Jennifer yesterday, it was a scheduled visitation, but Jennifer wanted to go trick or treating with her friends, and Martha said if I was ok with it, I could have Jennifer today. Now she is telling Jennifer I cannot see her because it is not my scheduled day. Does Martha have this right?"

He said, "No, I will call her attorney and tell him what she is doing."

Martha continued with her torturous control.

On November 13, 2005, Jennifer called me. It was a Sunday, and I was supposed to see Jennifer on Monday.

"Hi Dad, I'm at Aunt Carrie's house, and I was wondering if I could stay one more day and you see me Tuesday?"

"No problem Jenn, as long as Mom will let you see me on Tuesday."

"I asked Mommy before I called you, she said sure, no problem."

"Ok Jenn, see you Tuesday!"

Tuesday, November 15, 2005, Jennifer called me up, this time crying.

"Mommy said you cannot see me."

"Why would she do this to us, Jennifer?

"I do not know; she just said no, Dad."

There was nothing I could do to stop her. My child and I were victims of power.

I often called my attorney, and numerous emails were exchanged between lawyers, but no action was taken to stop her.

November 17, 2005, my brother Paul called me up and said there was an apartment available in his building that I could have right away. I jumped right on it. I never told Liz I was leaving. I grabbed my mere bag of clothes and my computer and left when she went to the store. She was mad at me for a while, but I think she forgave me.

I was excited to have a place of my own where I could have quality time with Jennifer. When Jennifer came to spend the weekend with me. At first, I was a little embarrassed. When she came in, she saw I had nothing but a computer and a blanket; it did not seem to bother her. She had fun roughing it. We slept on the bedroom floor with just pillows and blankets. We went to the dollar store to buy bowls, silverware, cooking pots, and whatever else we needed. She enjoyed picking things out for me. It did not matter if I had nothing. All that mattered to her was being with me. Jennifer would slowly get me more things from home. She told her mother, "I am giving my Dad some things he needs, so do not stop me, Mom." She got away with it for a while.

One evening while at my apartment, Jennifer approached me and said," Dad, I am always arguing with Mom."

"Really," I said.

Jennifer said, "Dad can I see your Divorce papers?"

"No, why do you want to see them? I cannot do that, Jennifer."

Jennifer said, "Dad, they are saying bad things about you. Defend yourself, so I know who is lying. If you do not, I have no choice but to believe them. Someone is lying, Dad. Please show me!"

I let her see the divorce papers and restraining orders. I gave her the papers and she sat on the front room floor. She read every paper, every word. It took her about 30 minutes to go through everything. When she was done, she stood up, walked up to me, hugged me, and said, "Now I know you are telling the truth now, Dad." Little did I know she was already giving her mother a hard time defending me?

More and more often, Jennifer would tell me about problems she was having with her mother. She told me that Martha would often explain why she left her father, with the reasons changing with every explanation. Jennifer said she was not asking for reasons; Martha just gave them to her. "I did not get along with your father, he spent too much money, your Dad was mean to you, he abused me, and he worked on the house too much," a different reason every time.

Jennifer said her Mom would close her bedroom door at night, and she could hear Martha talking on the phone with her boyfriend, saying I love you. During the day, Martha would constantly be in another room on her phone. Jennifer was always alone in a different room. Jennifer was spending most of her weekends at Martha's family or friend's houses.

Jennifer had a Doberman pinscher. Her name was Daisy. She was black with brown cheeks and eyebrows. Daisy was 4 years old. She was a birthday gift for Jennifer's 10th birthday. Daisy went to an obedience school and won second place. She failed to sit all the way down because she was stung in the behind by a bee that evening. She was very tame. When Jennifer was not home, Daisy would cry and search for her throughout the house. Jennifer told me she feared her Mom giving her dog away. But when Jennifer asked Martha if she was going to give Daisy away. Martha said," I would never give her away, Jennifer. ``

Jennifer also told me that a man I worked with in construction was constantly making repairs on our home. Martha would pay him with the items that belonged to me, such as tools, electric heaters that I had in the garage, and other various items. Martha denied those allegations, but I later confirmed they were true from a friend of the man I worked with. I tried several times to get a hold of this person, but he did a good job of avoiding me. However, I was glad as I don't know what

I would have done to this man due to the fact he was trying to console me when I was confiding in him about my suffering at the loss of my wife, and he was gaining from my loss without my knowledge.

My bond with Jennifer would become even stronger. When I did not have her, all I thought about was our next weekend together. On some of Martha's weekends with Jennifer, Martha was out of town on business. I asked her several times if I could have Jennifer through emails and voice mail. She would not answer. Martha would send Jennifer to her parents', sister's, or friend's houses. Jennifer would often ask her mother, "Why couldn't I go with Dad when you travel?" Martha would say things like, "Don't you want to spend time with your granny? You need to be with your friends, and your Dad will have you next weekend."

I called my attorney asking to have my child when her mother is traveling. He said, "you should be able to have Jennifer."

He said he was going to file a motion in court to allow me to have Jennifer when Martha travels."

I started to learn the powerful system of attorneys and money. When filing such a motion, it takes a month to be heard. By the time that court date arrives, other situations arise, and that motion would not be heard, it would be discarded into a divorce file. More time, more money. Martha, knowing I was trying to file such a motion and nothing was ever done about it, started becoming increasingly abusive with her control and power. Jennifer felt the effect as well.

Jennifer's way of life was now rapidly changing. Martha shut off the home phone and the internet. Jennifer watched as her mother took family pictures down from the walls. She watched as other house items were slowly disappearing. Life as she knew it was disappearing piece by piece. When Jennifer returned home after weekends with me, something new was gone.

One day Jennifer went into the basement and noticed the Ping-Pong table was missing. With an upset voice, she asked, "Mom, where is the Ping-Pong table?"

Martha replied in a calm tone, "I sold it."

Jennifer started to cry, "That was mine and my Dad's! How much money did you get for it?"

Martha said, "Twenty dollars."

Jennifer just walked away in frustration and hurt. Jennifer would walk to the bus stop and wait for a bus in the cold, something she was not used to. Martha was either sleeping or just getting up for work. Jennifer said her mother was always tired because she could hear her talking on her phone for hours late at night. I used to take her to school many mornings, especially when it was freezing outside. In the evenings, Jennifer either went to a friend's house or went home to cook for herself. She would eat alone. She became self-reliant. I used to get home before Martha most of the time and cook or go out to eat with Jennifer. We would play Play Playstation, pool, and Ping-Pong, whatever we felt like doing.

Jennifer loved baseball. The Chicago white sox were in the World Series. Jennifer and I, worlds apart, often talked about the games. One night during a series, Jennifer was watching the game, and knowing how much that meant to her, Martha shut the game off and made her go to bed. Jennifer said, "It was punishment because of an earlier argument she had with her Mom."

Every night I would send Jennifer a text, "Good night my love." She would always reply. "Good night Daddy!" Jennifer called me every morning on the way to school, sometimes crying because of fights she had with Martha. I felt so helpless.

One morning at about 8:30 AM, Martha called my cell phone. I did not answer, and she left a voicemail. She was angry!

"Jennifer ran away, and if she is not in school, I am going to put out the red alert!" and hung up.

Not knowing what was going on, I tried to call Jennifer's phone, but there was no answer. Within minutes, Martha left me another voicemail. This time she was crying.

"Why won't you talk to me? I'm so sorry for everything!"

I called her back. She was screaming and crying!

"Jennifer was fine until she started seeing you!"

Confused, I said, "I do not know what you are talking about, what is going on in that house; I do not live there."

Martha then jumped right in, "You know I left you because we did not get along; you spent too much money,"

I could not understand some of what she was saying; she was speaking so fast. Like with Jennifer, her reasons would change with every explanation.

I said, "You keep believing yourself!" and hung up on her. Martha called back ten minutes later. I answered.

"What now?"

"Jennifer is in school, and you are lucky!"

I hung up.

After school, Jennifer called me while she was on the bus.

"What is going on Jennifer, your mother called me talking crazy this morning"

"I got into an argument with Mom this morning and walked out the door earlier than usual. It was no big deal to me, Dad but Mom made a huge ordeal. School security came into my class to see if I was in school. Mom accused me of stealing a necklace from her room that her boyfriend gave her. I said, where was it, Mom.

Mom said, "It was hidden."

I said, "Where was it hidden?"

Mom said, "I am not going to tell you, but you are the only one who could have taken it."

"I did not take the necklace."

Mom said, "If you did not take it, then one of your friends took it, and you cannot have any more friends over."

"I walked away upset Dad! Mom found her necklace sometime later. I asked her, ``Where was it?" She would not answer me and then did not apologize. "Do you believe that, Dad?"

"Yeah, I believe it, Jenn. I don't know what is wrong with her."

"Yeah, Dad, first of all, I would not want anything that man gave her, and it was a skimpy cheap necklace anyway. He probably only paid thirty dollars for it!"

I was laughing hard! "Ok Jenn, I will talk to you later!"

The following weekend, I had Jennifer. I decided to go to the Bowling alley in my town. It was a 24-lane alley. There was once a month league that I had started several years ago but no longer participated in because of my situation. The league went from September through May. It consisted of friends, family, and Martha's sister Carrie. When Jennifer and I arrived, we sat with my sister Anne, her husband, and a couple of friends. Jennifer noticed Martha's sister Carrie. She said Dad, can I go over and say hello to Aunt Carrie.

I said, “Sure honey.”Jennifer went over, hugged, and kissed her Aunt. A while later, Jennifer and I were walking toward the counter to get something to drink. As we were walking, Carrie was walking toward us with one of her friends. As soon as she saw me, she suddenly stopped and ducked behind her friend to avoid me. Carrie and I were like a loving brother and sister. That really hurt, especially in front of my daughter and in public. Jennifer said, “Dad, why would Aunt Carrie hide from you like that?

"I have no idea," I said. After that happened, I did not stay much longer. The public rejection was another punch in the stomach. I never did anything to hurt her.

November 20, 2005, Paul called to tell me that he is going back to Italy. Paul had an apartment that he rented year-round in Bridgeport, so when he was in town, he had a place to live.

"Hey Tom, I was thinking, I am going back to Italy, and I think you should stay at my place and we could share the rent, saving us both money. I paid November and December's rent. You would not have to pay until January. I agreed. The apartment was furnished and had internet. I lived on the net.

We would miss Paul. He had not seen Jennifer in a few years with him living so far away. Jennifer got to know her uncle Paul and really enjoyed being around him. He would always ask about her grades. She was usually on the honor roll, and Paul kindly rewarded her. His analogies on life were always straightforward and funny. Jennifer got a kick out of them. So did I.

Jennifer and I moved our things to Paul's Place. As we were getting situated, Jennifer started this conversation. Dad, "I dread the holidays with Mom."

"Why is that Jenn?"

"Well, in October, Mom put a single pumpkin light in our big front windows. That was it. She doesn't care about them like we used to."

Because Jennifer’s birthday was Halloween, we had just as many Halloween decorations as Christmas. Jennifer and I would spend a whole day just decorating the yard with creatures, ghosts, pumpkins, spider webs, coffins, colored lights, as well as lights in all the front windows. Jennifer and I would also decorate the basement as if it was haunted. We would do this every year. Jennifer said, "Mom took me out to eat and while eating she asked Jennifer what you want for your birthday, and do not say your father because that’s never going to happen. I told her I do not want anything. That day when we went home Dad, I was in the basement in our computer room on my computer, and Mom came down there and sat by yours. She turned it on. I looked over to see what she was doing, and she was deleting any pictures of you and her together. I did not say anything; I just turned back around." Do you believe she would do that in front of me? She doesn't care about my feelings Dad, she knew I saw her."

"Really, I don't know what to tell you, Jennifer other than she is just selfish."

What a cruel thing to do, I thought. Martha might as well have torn pictures of us in half in front of Jennifer and threw them in her face. Maybe she did not realize what she was putting her own daughter through, nor did she realize that she was tearing her relationship in half with Jennifer. Either way, it was obvious she was not considering the consequences.

Jennifer continued. "Dad, I went to Granny's house last week with Mom, and we took Daisy along."

This was not unusual. They took the dog many times before. "When we were leaving to go home, Mom said leave Daisy here." I said, "Mom, why are we leaving Daisy?"

"Jennifer, it is hard to show our house with the dog there. "I did not say anything to Mom the rest of the way home. I know Mom's boyfriend has been in our house when I am with you on the weekends.

I said, ``what makes you think that?"

"When I go back home, certain pictures of you are gone and then reappear a few days later. She thinks I am stupid Dad.

Her bed had new pillows and pillowcases of woods, bears, and snow. Mommy was never into that, and she said she was selling the bedroom set. Why would she buy new stuff for a king-size bed, Dad?"

I was suddenly learning that Jennifer was far more intelligent than I thought.

Jennifer said, "Mom leaves too many clues. You know what else, Dad? I saw Mom watching football. I said, why are you watching football now, Mom? You never watched football. Mom said, "I watched football with your Dad a few times." I told her, Mom, I never saw you watch football with Dad. She said, ``Well, I did, Jennifer."

In 22 years, Martha has never watched any sports.

The November court date arrived, but I did not have to attend because it was something they called a "status update" where the lawyers go to court just to tell the judge what the current status of our divorce was. They had them every couple of months. Basically, neither party needs to show up, but you still pay your attorneys to attend court.

On November 22, I had Jennifer. After dinner, Jennifer went into the bedroom, sat on the bed, and started crying. I went in after her and said, "What is the matter Jennifer, why are you crying?"

She said, "Do you know what today is, Dad?"

"No honey, I do not."

She said with a crackling voice, "Today is your and Mom's 19th wedding anniversary."

I said, "Oh yes it is., I was not thinking about that." "Well, I was, Dad. I sat down on the bed by Jennifer and held her until she regained her composure.

While living in the city, I was visiting my Step Father now and then. He was the man that had beaten me as a child. He was old and had not had a drink in a few years. He had been divorced for over 20 years and was living alone in an apartment. People often wondered why I went to see the man that abused me. I really did not know why. I think I was looking for something. I guess I did not want to carry hatred around the rest of my life. He was a different man who was dying alone. He was on oxygen 24 hours a day. He was told he did not have long to live. We would just sit around and talk, hanging out for a few hours. He was a good listener. I let him get the chance to get to know Jennifer. He was very kind to her. He was not the man I knew as a child. I think he was trying to make up for what he has done to me through my childhood. Martha was correct in her restraining order about me being beaten as a child. I did not understand what that had to do with us. In the 22 years I have known her, we had one bad fight. She was hitting me, and I hit her back in the arm. She had a bruise. I would never put my hands on her again.

November 24, 2005, Thanksgiving Day. This would be my first holiday without my family. Jennifer was with her mother. Although Martha's Aunt Barb invited me to her house, I did not attend. It would have been too hard. I was sure I would not have been good company with my body in one place and my mind somewhere else. I stayed home alone, watched TV for a while, and spent a few hours surfing the net. It was very strange knowing the rest of the world was sitting at a large table in front of a feast surrounded by family and enjoying life. I could have gone to my sister's house a few blocks away. She always hosted Thanksgiving for the family in Bridgeport, but I did not want to be somewhere and be the topic of the evening because I would have been antisocial as well as unhappy. It would not be fair to the happy people. I believe it was better for me to be absent and them thinking I was just somewhere else celebrating than for me to be there looking depressed and unhappy. Although you think that you can hide these types of emotions inside, you do not realize that the truth is written all over your face.

I may have been alone on this Thanksgiving, but as I lay in bed waiting to fall asleep, I was thankful. I was thankful to be alive. I was thankful I had a daughter somewhere else, wishing that she was here with me. I was thankful that we had the same wish, and I was thankful we had the same dreams. Then I fell asleep.

November 28, 2005, I was on my way to pick up Jennifer on a visitation night, and Jennifer called me. She said,

"Dad, you cannot see me today."

"I said why not?

"Because I am in New York with Mom."

I said, "How come nobody told me?"

Jennifer said, "Here is Mom," and put her on the phone.

Martha started to explain, "Tom I..."

I interrupted her,

"You have no right!" and hung up.

Martha told Jennifer not to say anything to me about the trip. I was not upset with Jennifer. I was unable to get a hold of my attorney until the next day. I called my attorney,

Daniel, "Yesterday was my visitation day, and I could not see my daughter because she is in New York with her mother. I was not notified until I was driving out to get Jennifer."

"Ok Tom, I will bring it up at the next court date."

It is now December and 5 months since Martha filed for divorce. Martha was seeking full custody of Jennifer. Something I would continue to fight. I was working on a letter from my counselor to say that I was fine. That I was.

When I would pick up Jennifer, Martha would give her my mail. Often there were a few opened letters—usually credit card bills. I called Martha and told her, opening other people's mail is a federal offense. She paid no attention to my warning.

December 15, 2005: My attorney files this motion:

IN THE CIRCUIT COURT OF COOK COUNTY, ILLINOIS

COUNTY DEPARTMENT-DOMESTIC RELATIONS DIVISION

MARTHA FRAWLEY,)

Petitioner,)

And

THOMAS FRAWLEY,) COURTROOM 1623

Respondent,)

MOTION TO DISSOLVE RESTRAINING ORDER

NOW COMES, the RESPONDENT Thomas Frawley, by and through his attorney, Daniel Simmons, and it has and for his instant petition, states as follows:

- Aid barred visitation on the part of the Respondent (Tom) and provided for no contact with the petitioner (Martha) or the formal marital residents. A copy of Petitioner's Petition for order of protection with the Affidavit in Support (Affidavit) is attached as exhibit A.
- The initial order for protection was extended, subject to relaxed and visitation prohibitions, to August 3, 2007.
- In lieu of specific allegations and paragraphs J of her Petition for Order of Protection, Martha submitted her Affidavit in Support as a reference to exhibit as above.
- Although her Affidavit speaks for itself, Tom submits that nowhere instead Affidavit is there any factual allegations that Tom has ever posed a threat to either Martha or their daughter, Jennifer.
- When read on its own, the Affidavit is substantially insufficient to support entry of an Order for Protection.

- Tom did make it a threat to kill himself over the breakdown of the marriage and, on two occasions, made feigned attempts to carry out his threat.
- Because of the threats of suicide, it was decided to extend the Order for Protection until such time as Tom's mental state could be more fully evaluated.
- Tom has sought and received counseling through a therapist, Jamie Frazier.

- Jamie Frazier has indicated that Tom is not and never was a Bonafide threat to Martha, Jennifer, or to himself.
- A written report has been requested from Ms. Frazier and will be submitted to the court for consideration upon request.
- Since the entry of the Order for Protection and subsequent modifications, Martha Has voluntarily allowed Tom visitation without supervision even though agreed modifications required supervised visitation.
- Recently, Martha has insisted on supervised visitation and
  Tom has complied on each occasion.
- At no time has Tom posed an actual or perceived threat to the health and safety of either his daughter or wife.

Wherefore, Movant Thomas Frawley respectfully requests that this court enter an order to solve the Order for Protection or alternatively grant Thomas Frawley a full hearing on the propriety of said Order for Protection.

Thomas Frawley

By: Daniel Simmons

Daniel Simmons, his attorney

IN THE CIRCUIT COURT OF COOK COUNTY, ILLINOIS

COUNTY DEPARTMENT-DOMESTIC RELATIONS DIVISION

MARTHA FRAWLEY,)

Petitioner,)

And

THOMAS FRAWLEY,) COURTROOM 1623

Respondent,)

ORDER

This matter coming to be heard on the Motions of Respondent, Thomas Frawley, to Dissolve Order for Protection and for Appointment of a Child's Representative, due and proper notice having been given.

IT IS HEREBY ORDERED THAT:

- Petitioner Martha Frawley is granted 7 days to respond to the petitions.
- This matter is set for status on January 6, 2006, at 9:30 AM room 1623.

ENTER

John Stahl

December 15, 2005

December 20, 2005: Martha's response to my motion

IN THE CIRCUIT COURT OF COOK COUNTY, ILLINOIS

COUNTY DEPARTMENT-DOMESTIC RELATIONS DIVISION

MARTHA FRAWLEY,)

Petitioner,)

And

Respondent,)

THOMAS FRAWLEY,) COURTROOM 1623

RESPONSE TO MOTION TO DISSOLVE RESTRAINING ORDER

NOW COMES, the PETITIONER, MARTHA FRAWLEY ("MARTHA"), by and through her attorneys, BURNBURG & GORDON, P. C., and as for her response to a THOMAS Frawley's ("THOMAS") Motion to Dissolve Restraining Order states as follows:

- MARTHA admits the allegations contained in paragraph 1 of

  THOMAS' Motion.

- MARTHA admits the allegations contained in paragraph 2 of

  THOMAS' Motion.

- MARTHA admits that on August 03, 2005, a Plenary Order of Protection was entered in the matter herein, a copy of which is attached hereto and incorporated hereby as Exhibit "A. " MARTHA further states that Thomas was represented by present counsel at the entry of the Plenary Order of Protection.

- MARTHA admits the allegations contained and paragraph 4 of THOMAS' Motion.
- MARTHA denies the allegations contained and paragraphs 5 of THOMAS Motion and further affirmatively states that the following allegations among many were made in the Affidavit in support of the Petition for Order of Protection:
- That THOMAS possesses firearms
- That THOMAS has made threats in the past to kill others as well as himself.
- THOMAS had deliberately told the minor child, Jennifer, about the marital problems of the parents.
- MARTHA denies the allegations contained in paragraph 6 of THOMAS motion and further states that whether or not the Petition was legally sufficient is a moot point. THOMAS has acquiesced to the entry of the Plenary Order of Protection.
- MARTHA admits that Thomas has made threats to kill himself and has, in fact, attempted to kill himself twice since the inception of these proceedings. That any attempt by Thomas to characterize these attempts as "feigned" is a serious understatement of the gravity of THOMAS' fragile mental state.
- MARTHA denies the allegations contained in paragraph 8 of THOMAS Motion and further states that until such time as THOMAS no longer presents a threat to himself and/or others, his access to the minor child should be and ought to be restricted.
- MARTHA admits that THOMAS has received some therapeutic service from Jamie Frazier. The nature and extent, and efficacy of said treatment are unknown to MARTHA.
- MARTHA has insufficient information with which to admit or deny the allegations contained in paragraph 10 of THOMAS Motion and further affirmatively states that under the Mental Health and Developmental Disabilities Confidentiality Act, MARTHA was prohibited from obtaining the information about the allegations and paragraph 10 of THOMAS' Motion. By separate Motion, MARTHA is requesting this court to allow the discovery deposition of Ms. Frazier and to obtain her records.
- MARTHA has insufficient information with which to admit or deny the allegations contained in paragraph eleven of THOMAS Motion and therefore denies the same.
- MARTHA admits that due to pressure from THOMAS and THOMAS' pressure exerted on the minor child, JENNIFER that on several occasions THOMAS was allowed unsupervised access to the minor child. Fortunately, on those occasions, nothing untoward happened except THOMAS to use the opportunity to grill JENNIFER about matters pertaining to this case.
- MARTHA admits the allegations contained in paragraph 13 of THOMAS Motion. \

- MARTHA Denies the allegations contained in paragraph 14 of THOMAS Motion.

THOMAS Motion.

WHEREFORE, MARTHA FRAWLEY prays that this court deny THOMAS FRAWLEY's Motion to Dissolve Restraining Order and all relief requested therein.

Respectfully submitted,

MARTHA FRAWLEY

BY Donald___________

BURNBURG & GORDON

Her Attorneys

The restraining order was not lifted.

Christmas was coming, and knowing I would not have much money for Christmas, I bought a used laptop from someone for only a hundred dollars. It was in great shape with a docking station. It needed to be fixed because of a virus. I was good at fixing these small problems. I would give it to Jennifer weeks before Christmas because she needed it for school. Martha would question Jennifer. Where did your Dad get the money? The only thing on her mind was child support, money. Even though I was not paying child support to Martha at that time, I gave Jennifer money weekly. At least $25.00. Martha was not giving Jennifer any money; in fact, Jennifer said when she wanted to spend money to go out with her friends or the show, Martha made her use her own money from her savings. Jennifer depleted her savings over several months. One thing that was true about Martha, she was very cheap. She complained about a Quarter. I remember a day Martha and I were grocery shopping. After paying at the register and receiving the receipt, Martha stopped and read the entire receipt. She turned around, went back to the cashier to complain. She was angrily complaining that she overpaid for 6 cans of green beans. Her complaint was that she paid 63 cents per can instead of the sale price of 60 cents per can. Embarrassed, I walked up to Martha, whispered in her ear, "Here is a quarter; let's get the hell out of here!" She continued to argue in the car; I just ignored her. This was coming from a woman making $90,000 a year at that time.

I could only imagine how much money she really took from me. For several years we made over $110,000 a year. For 20 years, Martha handled all the banking. I gave her my checks every week. If I needed money, I asked her. If I wanted to buy something, I had to go through her. It was never easy, "How much is it? It's too much money; I don't think we need it!" At the beginning of our marriage, we had a huge argument because I found out Martha had a secret bank account with several thousand dollars. She admitted that her father taught her to do this. I do not think it ended there. If you think about it, in the 20 years together, we made about 2 million dollars. Let us say 1 million were houses, cars, bills, insurance, and whatever else we bought through the years. That leaves 1 million dollars. Now let's say 500,000 were taxes, which is a crazy 50%, but I'll give her the benefit of the doubt. Now we are left with 500,000. Now let's go with money Martha says we wasted on whatever I don't know at 250,000. Therefore, that leaves us with 250,000, yet my bank account represents 39,000 dollars. Maybe my calculations are way off, but I think about this. The last year Martha and I were together, Martha made 60,000. Tax that and you have 43,200, and I made 36,400 in cash, equaling 79,600. Our mortgage was 1200 including taxes, a month, Car payment 300, groceries 400, gas for cars 100, utilities 400, clothes and necessities 300, eating out 200, car insurance 300. All of these things equal 32,000 dollars. So just for one year, 79,600 minus 32,000 equals 47,600, yet Martha claims we only have 39,000 for 20 years of savings. Just one year of savings, which is at least the last 10 years. How can someone get away with this? Is this not a crime because it is domestic? I wonder what they would do to me if I went to Martha's house, broke in, and stole all of my furniture. I wonder if I can use the domestic defense and avoid 2 years in Jail. Nevertheless, there is absolutely no doubt that Martha took thousands of dollars from me. She claimed we couldn't keep our heads above water. I begged to differ as I was skiing on top of the waves, and she cut the rope and watched me sink.

Jennifer complained about the way Martha showed interest in Christmas. Jennifer said Martha put up a 2 foot Christmas tree with a single strand of lights. The family Christmas decorating was gone for Jennifer. It would take all day for Jennifer and me to decorate inside and outside the house. Jennifer mentioned shopping at a Mall with Martha. Martha was searching for the new Xbox Game. Jennifer said she had a feeling that the game was for the boyfriend's son. It was something Jennifer had not asked for, and Martha would not spend that kind of money. Maybe Jennifer was mistaken, but the feeling of being second was there. There was nothing I could do but try to lift Jennifer's spirits when we were together.

During the Christmas holiday, Jennifer would be off school for two weeks. I would have Jennifer from Christmas day until New Year's Day. Christmas day was Martha's birthday. On Christmas Eve, Jennifer asked Martha, "Mom, can I go with Dad at 9:00 AM tomorrow?"

Martha said, "What about opening your presents?"

Jennifer said," I will get up earlier; I want to go with my Dad early. "Martha was scheduled to have Jennifer Christmas evening. Martha told Jennifer that she did not have to return home because Martha had other plans. I picked up Jennifer early and brought her back to my apartment. Jennifer looked at me and said, “Dad, do you believe Mommy does not want me on her birthday?"

I looked Jennifer in the eyes and said, “I want you!"

She gave me a kiss and said, “I would rather be with you anyway, Dad."

Even though I knew Jennifer wanted to be with me instead of her mother, it still hurt Jennifer that her mother wanted to be with someone else instead of her.

Jennifer surprised me with a special gift. She gave me a little jewelry box that had a picture slot on the top. In the slot was a picture of me holding Jennifer when she was 2 years old. I opened the box, and there was $300.00 in cash. I said, "What is this, Jennifer?"

"It is half of your rent Dad."

"Why would you do that," I said.

Jennifer replied, "I know you needed 300.00 for rent."

"Where did you get this?

She laughed, "Do not worry about it."

She was looking at my face to see what I thought about her. I hugged her and said, "Little girl, you are a special child and have a big heart!"

She had a cell phone before all the other kids and an iPod, a pink razor phone, whatever she wanted. I spoiled her, but she was not a brat; she was very humble. I think she wanted to be my hero for a moment. I let her have that moment.

New Year’s Eve would be the first time in 22 years without Martha. The good thing was having Jennifer with me. I had to be strong for her as well. Her holidays were now with one parent. It was no longer a family thing. We went to my brother Dan’s house. Most of my family members were there. I felt it was better to be around many people rather than Jennifer and I being alone. I was wondering If Jennifer was thinking like me. She seemed to be having a good time.

January 1, 2006 at the stroke of midnight, everyone was yelling and celebrating. For a few seconds, I thought about Martha. I then went up to Jennifer, wished her a happy new year, and gave her a kiss. She celebrated with everyone as if everything were just fine. I would take Jennifer back home the next morning. We had a great week together, and I knew I would miss her.

We had a great time playing cards, on the internet, going to restaurants, and visiting family members. This visit would be different from all the others. Jennifer was starting to look at me differently. She was glowing and stayed very close to me, no matter where we went. She was a little unusually happy. I asked her, "What is going on with you?"

"Nothing Daddy, why?"

"You seem different."

"I do not know," she said and changed the subject.

I started to notice when I was getting Jennifer for the weekends, she would ask Martha to come with me earlier and stay later. My weekends were from Friday 6:00PM until Sunday at 8:00PM. Jennifer would want me to pick her at 4:30 PM and take her home at 9:00 PM Sunday. Martha did not give us too much trouble. She would often offer us extra time. On the Sundays I had Jennifer, Martha would call Jennifer around 7:30 and ask, "What time are you coming home? Where are you?" Jennifer told me, "I know why Mom calls every Sunday before you take me home, so she could get rid of her boyfriend before I got home."

I laughed!

"Jennifer said, "What is so funny, Dad?"

I said, "You just crack me up!"

"Whatever, Dad!" Jennifer was definitely smarter than Martha gave her credit for.

Over the past month, Martha was leaving voicemail stressing that Jennifer needs to seek counseling because she is not normal. With the few conversations I had with Martha, I expressed my thoughts, reiterating that Jennifer is fine, and told Martha that you are not normal. As Martha told me Jennifer refused to seek counseling, I stated I would not force her to go.

January 03, 2006 court date: As usual, Martha's attorney Mr. Burnburg started the show. "Your Honor, Mr. Frawley's crazy; he has an illness and suicidal tendencies. "Even though it did not pertain to the filings of that day, it would frequently become his opening line. We were mostly arguing about the MSA.

Mr. Burnburg stressed, "The child is giving her mother a hard time because of Mr. Frawley. Martha would like the court to order counseling for the child."

Judge Nobal turned to Mr. Simmons and said, "How do you feel about this?"

Mr. Simmons turned to me and whispered, "I suggested you convince Jennifer to attend counseling to expose the truth about Martha." I agreed to the order.

Mr. Simmons spoke up, "Your Honor, my client requests that the court appoint an attorney for Jennifer."

I was pressing my attorney for months to make this happen. I figured it would be beneficial for Jennifer to have someone solely representing her.

Mr. Burnburg, "Your Honor, in addition, we would like to request the records be released to the courts from Mr. Frawley's therapist."

I agreed to that. I had nothing to hide. I was fine.

Mr. Burnburg stated, "We would also request that Martha get the Tahoe from Mr. Frawley because it was in her name."

The Judge turned to Martha, "Do you have your own vehicle?" Martha said," Yes."

The Judge said, ``No, you do not get both vehicles. "Martha had a list of what money we had and owed.

Judge Nobal was overlooking our MSA papers. She looked up at Martha and stated, "The law is 50/50, and that includes your 401k."

According to Martha's papers, she wanted everything.

The judge ordered both attorneys and clients to go in a room in the back of the courtroom to hash out the numbers. Once in the room, my attorney gave me a list from Martha. As I was looking at the list, I noticed several things that Martha was trying to get away with. For example, our cell phone bill was something like $350.00 for the month of September. Monitoring her calls on line for months, my memory was fresh.

I looked over at Martha and said, "You used 1400 minutes; I used 400 minutes and Jennifer 200 minutes. I will be damned if I pay for all the calls you made to your boyfriend. "The room was silent.

I also noticed that in the column of my bills, there was the amount of three hundred dollars titled Christmas gift. Hmm, I thought, that was the money Jennifer gave me. I never said a thing about that. Going down the list, I said, "Where is the $3,000 that you sold my van for?"

Mr. Burnburg looked over at Martha and said, “Do you want me to investigate to see if you paid some other bills with that money?"

I replied, "Yes, go right ahead, Martha, pay your attorney $375.00 an hour to investigate the 1,500 you owe me."

Martha said in a soft voice, "No, give him his share of $1,500."

All of a sudden, Martha looked at me and said, “You know Tom, our marriage has been over for years."

I looked at her and thought, where the hell did that come from? Baffled by the comment, I said, "You surely could have fooled me when we were having sex on the back porch two days before you made your announcement. “ The attorneys were silent, and the look on Martha’s face was priceless!

She did not say a word and put her red face down. It was weird, as if Martha was trying to convince me to believe her lies. You just do not live with someone for twenty years and not see through them. That conversation ended our meeting and court appearance.

For months, Martha was trying to get me to sign papers for the sale of our home. Today I will sign the papers. I needed the money. We would put the house up for $499,000.

We owed the bank $177,000.

The Court Orders:

IN THE CIRCUIT COURT OF COOK COUNTY, ILLINOIS

COUNTY DEPARTMENT-DOMESTIC RELATIONS DIVISION

Martha Frawley__________________

Petitioner

And

Thomas Frawley_________________

Respondent

ORDER

THIS CAUSE coming to be heard on Martha Frawley's Oral Motion for Leave two Obtained Documents and Take Discovery Deposition of Jamie Frazier, Psychotherapist for Thomas Frawley do notice having been giving and the court been fully advised of the premises:

WHEREFORE, it is hereby ordered that:

- Martha Frawley Is given leave to issue a subpoena for deposition (Records only) to Jamie Frazier for all records in her possession or control concerning the care and treatment of her patient, Thomas Frawley. Martha Frawley has given leave to issue a subpoena for the discovery deposition of Jamie Fraser.
- By agreement of the parties, Jennifer Frawley ("Jennifer") shall immediately commence individual psychotherapy with the licensed clinical psychologist. Both parties shall encourage Jennifer to attend all therapy sessions, and each parent shall stress the importance of Jennifer getting help and having someone other than their parents to whom she can express her views or problems over the dissolution of the marriage of her parents.

ENTER JUDGE Mary Noble

Donald J. Burnburg, Esq.

BURNBURG & GORDON, P. C.

Attorneys for MARTHA FRAWLEY

South ** Street, Suite ***

IN THE CIRCUIT COURT OF COOK COUNTY, ILLINOIS

COUNTY DEPARTMENT-DOMESTIC RELATIONS DIVISION

Martha Frawley_________________

Petitioner

And

Thomas Frawley_________________

Respondent

ORDER

This matter coming on to be heard for a pretrial conference and the court having met with the parties and council.

It is hereby ordered that:

- The order for protection entered on August 3, 2005, is vacated.
- Visitation schedule, as set out in the order of August 03, 2005, remains in full force and effect.
- Hearing date set for January 6, 2006, on Tom Frawley's motion to appoint GAL and to dissolve order for protection is stricken.
- This matter is set for status as to settlement on January 20, 2006, at 9:30 AM room 1623.

ENTER Mary noble

JUDGE

January 9, 2005, Jennifer called me. She was upset.

"Dad, I have to start counseling with a woman tonight. I don't want to go!"

"Jennifer, maybe this counselor could help you. Maybe your Mom will not be so mean if she knows you are telling a counselor what is going on at home."

"I know, but I really don't want to go. Mom told me that she is seeing a counselor too."

"Really," I said, "Now there is someone who needs counseling!"

After a few sessions, Jennifer was getting more comfortable with this woman as she felt this counselor believed her and understood her pain. However, Jennifer told me that Martha stopped seeing her counselor after a few sessions.

January 19, 2005, Jennifer called me up, once again upset.

"Dad, there is a dance that is coming up in March. It is the King of Hearts Dance where a girl asks a boy to the dance. Mom had just left town. I asked Mom for money for a dress and school lunch. Mom only left me 14 dollars. I am shopping with my friends and I'm at the mall. Dad, I found a dress that I really like, but I do not have any money."

I replied, "Can you put it on layaway and I will go buy it when I have you on the weekend?"

"I will ask them Dad, Thank you!"

Jennifer put the dress on layaway. When we went back to the mall, we gave the woman at the counter the ticket, and she went in the back to get the dress. A few minutes later, she brought the dress out and put it on the counter.

Jennifer looked at me and said, "Dad, it's expensive."

I picked up the dress and looked at the price tag, and it was eighty dollars. I laughed and bought the dress.

Jennifer said, "Thank you, Dad!"

"You are welcome, Jennifer." I did not want my child to do without. I got an extra 15% off for applying for the store credit card. I was surprised that I was approved.

For several months, I have been trying to reestablish my credit. I have been applying for some credit cards but have been turned down every time. I did not understand because I had excellent credit. Martha started giving me hospital bills that were overdue. I asked her to pay them and deduct it from the money she took from me. She agreed but never paid them.

January 23, 2006, Jennifer and I were at our favorite restaurant, she was rattling on, and she blurted out, "I can't wait until you get your own place, Dad."

"Why," I Asked.

"Because I want to come live with you."

My heart skipped a beat. Did I just hear that?

I said, "Jennifer, are you for real?"

"Dad, I cannot live with Mom. I want to be with you; she is crazy. I want to run away, Dad, but I am afraid Mom will have me locked up in a boarding school."

"Do not run away Jennifer, I am sure she will do something to punish you!" I think I asked her 20 times if she was sure. It was yes every time. I took Jennifer back to Martha and on my way back home. All I could do was smile. It was too good to be true.

I gave Jennifer time to make sure that was what she wanted. Her decision would never change. After several weeks, I asked Jennifer if she told Martha about her decision. She said, "No Dad, I do not want to tell her. Can we wait until the divorce is over and the house is sold?"

"No, Jennifer, your mother is fighting for sole custody of you. I think you should tell her what your intentions are."

"I am not ready to tell her, Dad."

"Jennifer, if you want to be with me, you have to tell her. With the court knowing your wishes, it will be easier for me to fight for you. "I thought maybe by Martha knowing Jennifer's intentions, she would back off her abusive behavior towards Jennifer. Jennifer was so afraid of telling Martha. Knowing that, I decided that I would spare Jennifer from that fear. My first approach, I called Martha. "Jennifer wants to tell you something; you should sit down and talk with her.

"What are you up to now?"Martha asked?

"Sit down and talk to your daughter, she wants to talk to you. Why won't you talk to her?

Martha uttered, "I was advised not to talk to Jennifer."

"What? Someone else advised you not to talk to your own daughter." I replied. Martha hung up.

After a few days passed, Jennifer told me Martha had not approached her about a talk. It was then I decided to tell Martha Jennifer's desire to live with me. I called Martha again.

"Martha, Jennifer wants to live with me"

"Oh really, Tom, you are brainwashing Jennifer into making that decision." Martha hung up again!

I knew then that it was a huge mistake because Martha did not want to accept that Jennifer did not want to go with her. Their feuds would escalate. Martha was very angry. She could not accept the fact that her daughter wanted no part of her new life. For her, Jennifer ruined her plan. As Jennifer once put it, "Mom is mad because her fairytale did not go according to her plans."Because her child refused to start a new family with a strange man, she was considered not normal and needed psychiatric help. Jennifer told me that Martha would come into her room at night thinking Jennifer was asleep checking her phone for text messages and or calls from me. Martha was reading our text messages. I showed Jennifer how to lock her phone in which Martha became very angry. Martha was so angry with Jennifer one evening that she told Jennifer, "You know what Jennifer, I have the power to make sure you never see your father again." What a hell of a thing to say to her daughter. Did Martha think she had the power to take her child by force? Would she and could she take her against her will? At this point, I was unsure what Martha was capable of. However, I was sure I was in for a long hard fight.

I continued to reassure Jennifer That I was doing everything I could to get full custody of her.

It was income tax time, and I called Martha to ask her how she was filing. I had a feeling she was going to claim me, knowing I had no income on paper.

"Martha, are you claiming me on your taxes?"

"Yes Tom, I'm filing jointly if you want."

I said yes, "I deserve half of the return."

"I will give you half when I get it Tom"

I knew that was a lie, so I called my attorney,

"Daniel, Martha is filing jointly, and I know she is not going to give me half of the return."

"You have a right to half."

"We will see, Daniel"

On February 1, 2006, I was on my way to see Jennifer. I was running late due to highway traffic. It was about 5:50 PM., and my cell phone was ringing. I answered. It was Jennifer crying hysterically.

"Dad, I am by Jenny's house. Mommy threw me out! Mommy threw me out!"

"Calm down, Jennifer, I will be right there!"

"Ok Dad, hurry!"

When I arrived, I pulled into Jenny's driveway. Jennifer came out and ran in my arms, crying even harder.

I held her and said, "You are safe now; daddy has you. Where is your jacket?"

"It is at home," she said. I put her in the warm truck and gave her one of my spare jackets, and we went to the restaurant. I got Jennifer to calm down. Even though I was happy to have her, I felt sorry for her because she was truly hurt that her own mother would throw her out. Jennifer started filling me in.

Martha took her cell phone and house keys and told her to get the F*** out! Jennifer's Grandmother was also present but did not intervene.

About 20 minutes later, my cell phone was ringing, and the call was coming from Jennifer's phone. I knew it was Martha and I answered the phone,

I said, "What?"

Martha said, "Do you have Jennifer?

"Yes, I have her!"

"Are you going to bring her home?"

I replied, "Just to get her clothes. You threw her out."

Martha said, "Well, I am going to call the police and say you kidnapped her."

I said, "Whatever, and hung up!"

I figured if Martha did call the police, it would not be kidnapping until I left Countryside with Jennifer, or I kept her after 8:00pm.

After dinner, we went to Best Buy to buy a cell phone for Jennifer. As soon as we were done, we were walking out and noticed a police car parked on the street in front of the store. Jennifer said, "Dad, do you see that police car?"

"Yes, I do Jennifer, don't worry, I have a plan."

We walked past the car, headed to the parking lot, and jumped into my truck. We pulled away heading to the exit of the mall. We caught the red light. I turned around to see if the police car was still sitting in front of Best Buy. I noticed the car coming in our direction. The light turned green, and I made a left turn on La Grange road. We drove 6 blocks to 55th street. I could see the police car in the rearview mirror trailing behind by a block. I turned right onto 55th street. This was the way back to the city. I drove another 2 blocks, constantly checking the mirror to see if I was being followed. The police car turned right onto 55th street again, not far behind us. I came upon East Ave; straight across the intersection was crossing the border of Countryside. It was a red light. I could see the police car closing in behind us about a half-block away. The light turned green. I looked over at Jennifer and smiled, then I made a right turn, headed a half block, and turned into the police station. "Jennifer said, what are we doing here, Dad?"

I said, "We are going to go inside and file a police report that your Mother threw you out."

"Oh," Jennifer said.

We went inside and asked the woman sitting behind the glass if we could file a report. She called a police officer from the back to take care of the report. The woman came through a door and said, follow me please. We followed her into a room where a large conference table was. She said, "Have a seat; what is going on?"

I replied, tell her what happened, Jennifer.

Jennifer explained to her what happened, and the officer started writing things down. When Jennifer was finished, I asked for an escort back to the house so we could get Jennifer some clothes. The woman said, "Yes, just follow me there."

We followed the police car to the house. The woman police officer got out of the car and waited for us to get out of ours. We walked up to the officer, and she said, "I will go in with Jennifer and try to make peace with her and her mother." They went up to the front door, and the police officer rang the doorbell. Martha answered! Jennifer and the officer went inside. While outside, I thought to myself, "Make peace with Jennifer and her mother," her Mother should be arrested for throwing a child into the street on a February night with no coat, hat or gloves. What was this officer thinking?

A few minutes passed, and another police car pulled up. It was a male officer. He got out of his car and approached me. I was standing outside of my vehicle. He asked me what was going on. I told him, and he said he was going inside. He came back out very quickly. He said I guess your wife thought I was you and was shouting, "What are you doing in here? You're not supposed to be in here. Get the hell out of here! "He said she looked up and was shocked to see it was a police officer. He just looked at her and stepped back outside. Shortly after, the woman police officer came back out with Jennifer. She said she could not resolve the matter with Martha. The officer looked at me and said, "Your daughter went into the house stomping her feet; she seems like an angry teenager."

I said, "She was just thrown out on the street; how do you expect her to act?"

"Well Mr. Frawley, you have to have Jennifer back home by Monday. It was Wednesday, so I would at least get to have Jennifer for 5 days.

When we arrived home, we stayed up for a while and talked. Jennifer said, "It is nice to be with you Dad.

I said, it is nice having you with me, Jennifer. Jennifer was a little emotional and tired and wanted to go to sleep. When she fell asleep, I just stared at her. I had my baby but I was worried about how Martha would react when Jennifer returned. Jennifer said when she went into the house, Martha was very angry! Martha said, "I figured this was going to happen." Jennifer ran down to the basement and grabbed her suitcase. She ran back upstairs, went into her room to pack the suitcase. Martha followed Jennifer into her room. She stared at Jennifer for a few seconds and went back into the front room by the police officer. Martha suddenly returned, hovering over Jennifer. Jennifer said, "What do you think I am going to steal something?"

Martha said sarcastically, "You never know."

Jennifer told me that she packed as fast as she could.

The next morning I immediately called my attorney.

"Daniel, Martha threw Jennifer out last night!

He replied, "Do you have a police report?"

"Yes, could you file some kind of emergency custody petition?"

"Yes Tom, I will take care of it."

Monday came, and I drove Jennifer to school in the morning, and she was going to a friend's house after school. Martha was going to pick Jennifer up there. While driving Jennifer to school, Jennifer said, "Dad I am afraid of what Mom is going to do. I know she is going to start another argument with me especially that we came back with the police."

"If anything happens, you call the police, and then you call me even if you have to run outside, Jennifer."

At about 4:30 that evening, Jennifer called me on my cell phone. She was excited and talking fast. "Dad, Mom just called me and said I can stay with you; I do not have to go back home."

"You're kidding me Jennifer!"

"No Dad, I am not. Mom said, ``Jennifer, you do not have to come back home, you can stay with your father."

"Oh my god Jennifer, This is great! Ok I will be right there to pick you up."

Jennifer called Martha back and said, "Can I come by after school tomorrow and get my clothes?"

"Martha replied, I am out of town, and I will not be home until Wednesday."

Jennifer hung up. Jennifer was so happy, and I was as well. Jennifer did not have to fear Martha anymore!

Tuesday morning, while driving Jennifer to school, we were traveling down 55th street. We were passing Catherine Ave when Jennifer said, “Look Dad, there is Mom in her truck turning on 55th street. I thought she said she was not coming home until tomorrow. That is what she told me Dad. "Jennifer immediately called Martha on her cell phone. Martha answered. "Mom, I thought you were not coming home until tomorrow."

Martha uttered, ”Oh well, I came home late last night."

"Whatever Mom, I need my mouth guard for my braces and my clothes."

"You can come by tonight, Jennifer.

"Put my stuff in a bag and put it on the front porch; I do not want to go in the house with you. “Jennifer hung up.

I started buying Jennifer clothes and women's things that she would need. It would be a rapid but rough transition. My boss Fred helped me make this all possible. I started work at 5am, and Fred would let me leave at 6:45 to go back home, pick Jennifer up, and take her to school. The school was about 14 miles away. I would drive Jennifer to school and turn around and go back to the city to work. Fred would also let me leave at 2 p.m. allowing me enough time to get Jennifer by 3 p.m. After picking Jennifer up, we would drive back to the city where we were staying. I drove 56 plus miles every day, just taking Jennifer back and forth to school and work. This did not include going shopping for clothes or food. Every Saturday, I took Jennifer to see her counselor. That was also over 15 miles one-way. Jennifer also bowled every Saturday. This cost ten dollars a week. With gas prices well over $2.50 a Gallon, it was costing me about $70 dollars every two to three days. Jennifer needed about 25 dollars per week for school lunches and to have some money in her pocket. Jennifer’s cell phone was about $30 a month.

Between school and after school sporting events, we were always on the road, so we were continuously eating out at restaurants. Things were slow at work because Fred was waiting on a business license. Fred was trying to keep me busy getting me side jobs as well. I started racking up charge card bills. I would do whatever it took to keep Jennifer. Martha was not contributing any money for Jennifer.

A few weeks have now gone by, and I called Mr. Simmons up.

"What happened to the emergency custody order, Daniel?"

He said, "The police report was not detailed enough."

"It says Mother threw a 14-year-old minor out of the house! What more do you need? I do not understand."

"It is not detailed enough."

I thought to myself, if that were me throwing out my daughter Mr. Burnburg would have a two-page Court Order requesting jail time.

Nothing was ever filed.

Jennifer and Martha would talk once a day, and usually every call was a fight. Jennifer did not want anything to do with Martha, especially because she was lying to everyone, saying she let Jennifer go with me and she did not throw her out. A few weeks went by, and Martha wanted Jennifer for a weekend. Jennifer did not want to go, so I did not force her. Martha called her attorney, Mr. Burnburg complaining, and shortly after, my attorney called me.

"Tom, I suggest that you make Jennifer see her Mother. If you do not, it would look bad on you in court."

Hmm I thought, it didn't look bad on Martha when I didn't see Jennifer.

Against my better judgment, I told Jennifer,

"If you do not see your Mother, they are going to blame me."

"Ok Dad, I will do it for you, but I'm not happy about this!"

Friday, February 17, 2006, I called Martha,

"I will drop Jennifer off by Gracie's house, and you could pick her up there at 6 P.M."

"Ok Tom."

I dropped Jennifer off at about 5 P.M. and drove back to the city. I was at my mother's house when my phone rang at about 6:10 pm. It was Martha yelling, "Jennifer would not come out of her friend's house to go with me!"

I said, "let me call her and see what happened."

I called Jennifer, "What is going on? Mom just called me."

"I do not want to go with her, Dad, please do not make me."

I said, "I am not going to force you, Jennifer."

She replied, "Thanks Dad," with a crackling voice.

I called Martha back and said, "Jennifer doesn't want to go with you. What do you want me to do? Drive all the way out there and grab her by her hair and put her into your car?"

Martha said, "No," and hung up.

I still forced Jennifer to talk to her mother at least once a day; she did not want to call her mother at all. One less thing that Mr. Burnburg has to attack me.

February 19, 2005, Martha called Jennifer and said, "You can stop by anytime to pick up your clothes or whatever else you need."

February 20, 2005, Jennifer and I decided to stop at the house to get some things. We pulled into the driveway just at the edge. Jennifer got out and went up to the door to ring the bell. There was no answer despite the fact that Martha's SUV was in the driveway. Jennifer tried to call several times on her cell phone. I rolled down my truck window and said, let's go Jennifer. Jennifer got back into my truck and was very angry. She was saying, "He is there! He's in there!"

I said, "Who?"

Jennifer said, "Her boyfriend, who do you think?"

"What makes you think that, Jennifer?

"I'm not stupid Dad; Mommy's truck is parked to one side of the driveway, allowing another vehicle to get past to get into the garage. There are also tire tracks in the snow going into the garage, and it just started snowing. Mommy always parks in the garage. That's why she threw me out Dad, to move her boyfriend in," she said with her eyes all teary.

I had no words for Jennifer because I was thinking the same thing. She even said, "You know he's in there too, Dad."

I remained silent; I had no words to comfort her.

The next day Jennifer called Martha.

Martha replied, "Oh hi Jennifer!" and was just rattling on and was not acknowledging that Jennifer came over last night or called her cell phone.

Jennifer said, "Mom, I came over last night to get some of my things, and you didn't answer the door."

Martha said, ``Oh, I must have been in the shower."

Jennifer said, "Then whose tire tracks were in the driveway?"

"The realtor was here."

"Did she park in the garage, Mom?"

Martha said, "Nobody was in the garage."

"Then why didn't you call me back, Mom?"

"I didn't know that you called honey."

"You're such a liar Mom, your phone beeps when you miss a call."

Jennifer, frustrated with her Mom's lies, hung up on Martha.

The city life would be a strange transition for Jennifer. The city was life in the fast lane as opposed to the suburbs. Jennifer adjusted to the city life very quickly. There was always someone to go by. I had two sisters, four brothers, my mother, and my stepfather, all living in Bridgeport. I also had about 13 nieces and nephews there. We would even visit some of Martha's relatives. Two of my brothers lived in a tougher part of the neighborhood. Jennifer learned quickly how to adapt to this part of the neighborhood. I taught her to look people in the eyes and show them you're not afraid. I told her people mess with those who are scared. In addition, Jennifer knew her last name protected her as well. My brothers are fighting Irish men who I think actually enjoyed it sometimes. They definitely had a reputation. I also was known for brawling in the neighborhood a few years back. I had many friends, and every time I ran into them, I would always introduce Jennifer. Jennifer would get to know many people there. I could tell Jennifer thought she was all that in Bridgeport, and she was.

This was a true test of survival. I was told by my attorney that Martha did not take Jennifer back because she thought I wasn't capable of taking care of her and that Jennifer would get tired of living a tough life and want to go back home, therefore saving her the cost of a custody battle in court.

We sometimes struggled money-wise, but there was always a family member who cooked large dinners. Family and friends were always close by.

Jennifer was surrounded by a great group of friends that she went to school with. There was a main group of kids—all girls except one boy. There were the Couch twins, Nancy and Candy, Emily, Jenny, Sandra, Gabby, Gracie, Karen, and Andrew. These 14 and 15-year-olds had Jennifer's back as well as mine. They would listen to all of Jennifer's problems and provide her with support and a place to stay if needed. These kids were some of the few people I trusted as well. They had my cell number, and I had theirs. If I couldn't get a hold of Jennifer, I would call them. If Jennifer was upset, I could call them, and they would take care of her. If I had to work late, there was always one of her friends who would let Jennifer stay at their home until I arrived. I don't think they knew how special they really were.

It is now March. Jennifer was refusing to call Martha because she would hear nothing but lies from her. Martha would call Jennifer only once a day, usually in the late evening, yet when we went to court, Martha would complain that she misses Jennifer so much and I am responsible for Jennifer not talking to her as if she made 10 calls a day. I had to force Jennifer to call her mother every day because they were beating me down in court. Jennifer was not happy at all. I told Jennifer, "Mom is saying you don't call her because I will not let you. They are saying that I am brainwashing you."

Jennifer said, "But you're not Dad. I don't want to talk to her."

"I know Jennifer, but we have to, or they will keep saying that I am a bad parent."

March 9, 2005, Martha calls Jennifer,

"Jennifer, you have an F in one of your grades. What is your father doing to help you?"

Jennifer argued with her Mom, "If you went online, then you have read it wrong. I had one F paper, not for the whole course, not for the grade." Jennifer hung up.

My attorney also called me about the accusation.

"Tom, Martha is saying that Jennifer is failing at school."

"Oh really, I have Jennifer's progress report, and it is A's, B's, and a C."

"Ok, we will need it for the next court date. That will shut Mr. Burnburg up."

Martha tried to be a mother for a whole 2 minutes during the calls. "Jennifer, did you make your counseling appointment? Jennifer, did you floss? Your grades need improvement. Jennifer, your Dad is going to get in trouble with the courts if you do not see me. "Then Jennifer would start with the questions. Martha insulted Jennifer's intelligence with lies. Just about every call, Jennifer hung up crying. Once Jennifer made her daily call to Martha, that would be the last she would talk to her mother in twenty-four hours.

March 13, 2005, Jennifer, during a call, asked Martha for some of her things.

"Mom, could you put them out in front of the house, and we will pick them up.

Martha said, "The only way you are getting any of your things, Jennifer, is if you come and see me."

Jennifer said, "Then I do not want them, Mom. I do not want to see you."

After several of these phone calls, I decided to call Martha. I rarely spoke to her, but I decided to try to reason with her. Normally when I talked to her, I yelled—this time, I did not.

"I calmly asked, " What is wrong with you Martha? Why don't you give Jennifer some of her things the way she asked and show her that you can be nice? That is how you win her over, not hold her stuff for ransom."

Martha stubbornly said, "She is not getting her things until she comes to see me."

I said, "Whatever!" and hung up.

Jennifer and I would go past our house after I had picked her up from school. We knew Martha was still at work. We would pull up by the mailbox, which was on Jennifer's side. She would roll down the window, open the mailbox, grab any mail that was for her or me. All mail addressed to Martha Jennifer would put back into the mailbox and shut the door. I had one of my credit card accounts issue a card for Jennifer so she would be able to purchase clothes and things when she was out shopping with friends. The credit card company said it would take from seven to ten days. 14 days passed, and still no card was received. I called the credit company up and asked where the card was. They stated that I should have had the card days ago. I also discovered that I did not receive my monthly bill statements.

I called up Martha and said, "Do you have my bills and a letter for Jennifer?"

She said, "No."

I said, "That's funny, they were sent to our house."

Martha stated, "I don't know what you are talking about."

I hung up!

A few days later, while Jennifer and I were getting our mail from the house, we noticed Jennifer's letter and my bills. Jennifer looked through the mail and uttered, "Dad, Mom opened all the mail except the junk mail."

When we arrived home, I went through the mail. My bills were late, and I would have to pay late fees. I once again called my attorney and said, "Martha is opening my mail."

Mr. Simmons said, "Get a P.O.BOX."

I took that advice.

With work still slow, I decided to buy a smaller car because the gas was eating my money rapidly driving a big SUV. I also wanted to hide my truck in a parking garage owned by Fred. I had a feeling that Martha wanted that truck because it was in her name too. The Judge told Martha not to touch the truck, but Martha had no rules. I did not trust her. I didn't want to buy a beater and break it down all the time. I knew I needed something dependable and affordable. I bought a little Ford Taurus for about five thousand dollars. I used a credit card for the down payment of $1,000.00. The payment was $120.00 a month. It was a small six-cylinder and would start saving me money immediately.

March 20, 2005, I called Mr. Simmons.

"What are you doing about the custody? I need child support from Martha as well."

He said, "You have to establish a residence and get a tax-paying job first."

My reply to him was, "I have a half-million-dollar residence with my wife and her boyfriend living in it, and I have to go get another place to prove I can take care of my daughter."

He said, "That is what you have to do."

I said, "Why can't my daughter and I move back in the house, and Martha moves out."

He said, "That will never happen."

"You mean to tell me, my wife throws Jennifer and me out of the house and for me to keep my child, and I must prove that I am a stable parent, especially that Martha has all my money, furniture and clothes. This is unbelievable! I want you to look into getting a court-appointed attorney for Jennifer. I want someone to protect her. When are you going to get me in my house? It has been nine months and I haven't been in my house since. Martha could have sold everything.

He said, "I'll take care of it."

I was getting more and more frustrated every day.

On March 28, 2006, my attorney filed this motion:

IN THE CIRCUIT COURT OF COOK COUNTY, ILLINOIS

COUNTY DEPARTMENT-DOMESTIC RELATIONS DIVISION

MARTHA FRAWLEY,)

Petitioner,)

And

THOMAS FRAWLEY,) COURTROOM 1623

Respondent,)

MOTION FOR APPOINTMENT

OF CHILD'S REPRESENTATIVE

NOW COMES, the RESPONDENT Thomas Frawley, by and through his attorney, DANIEL SIMMONS, and as and for his instant petition, states as follows:

1. That the Petitioner herein Martha Frawley, filed her Petition for Dissolution of Marriage on the 13th day of July 2005, which Petition remains pending and undetermined.

2. The parties have one child, Jennifer Frawley born October 31, 1991.

3. Jennifer currently has been staying with the father because the mother "threw" her out of the formal marital residence some months ago. During the course of her residence with Tom, Martha has repeatedly refused to allow Jennifer access to clothes and necessary school items.

4. Tom, through discussion with Martha and as well as Jennifer, has learned of numerous conflicts arising between Jennifer and her mother.

5. Jennifer has repeatedly threatened to run away from the mother and has expressed a desire to live with Tom.

6. Jennifer has further been exposed to the relationship, which developed during the marriage, between Martha and another man.

7. Martha has blamed Tom for the strife, which has arisen between herself and Martha and has accused Tom of "brainwashing" Jennifer and most recently has blamed Tom for a perceived drop in school performance on the part of Jennifer.

8. Jennifer is presently caught in the middle between her mother and Tom.

9. Versions of events related by Tom are diametrically opposed to versions of events as related by counsel for Martha.

10. It would appear that the only way to reconcile the constant "he said, she said" situation is to appoint an independent third party to evaluate the situation and report to this Court.

11. Tom verily believes that it is in the best interest of Jennifer that the Guardian ad Litem be appointed to interview her and report to this court.

Wherefore, Thomas Frawley respectfully requests this court appoints a Guardian ad Litem them to look out for the interest of Jennifer Frawley.

Thomas Frawley

Daniel Simmons

By: Daniel Simmons, his attorney

IN THE CIRCUIT COURT OF COOK COUNTY, ILLINOIS

COUNTY DEPARTMENT-DOMESTIC RELATIONS DIVISION

MARTHA FRAWLEY,)

Petitioner,)

And

THOMAS FRAWLEY,) COURTROOM 1623

Respondent,)

RESPONSE TO MOTION FOR APPOINTMENT OF CHILD'S REPRESENTATIVE

NOW COMES the PETITIONER, MARTHA FRAWLEY ("MARTHA") by and through her attorney's BURNBURG & GORDON, P. C. And as and for her response to THOMAS FRAWLEY's ("Thomas") Motion for Appointment of a Child's Representative ("Motion") states as follows:

1. Martha admitted the allegations contained in paragraph 1, paragraph 2, and paragraph 3 of Thomas' motion.
2. Martha has insufficient information for which to respond to the vague allegation of "numerous conflicts" as alleged in paragraph 4 of Thomas' Motion and therefore denies the same.
3. Martha denies the allegations contained in paragraph 5 of Thomas' Motion.
4. Martha denies the allegations contained in paragraph 6 of Thomas' Motion.
5. Martha denies the allegations contained in paragraph 7 of Thomas Motion.
6. Martha admits that Thomas visitation is supervised and denies that "numerous occasions have occurred where Thomas visitation was permitted on an unsupervised basis.
7. Martha denies the allegations contained in paragraph 9 of Thomas' Motion and affirmatively states that Thomas' visitation has always been supervised except on one or perhaps two occasions where Thomas insisted and put such pressure on the minor child that in order to reduce the immediate strife Martha acquiesced to Thomas pressure.
8. Martha denies the allegations contained in paragraph 10 of Thomas' Motion.
9. Martha admits that on at least one occasion, the parties have discussed counseling for Jennifer.
10. Martha denies the allegations contained in paragraph 12 of Thomas's Motion.
11. There are no allegations of fact alleged in paragraph 13 of Thomas's motion, and Thomas's belief is irrelevant in the matter herein.
12. Parties have yet to be ordered to attend Marriage and Family Counseling Services to resolve Thomas' quixotic quest for joint custody and unsupervised visitation on the matter herein. Thomas is barely employed (he works part-time on call at McCormick place directing traffic in the parking lots) and has no money to contribute to the payment of the child's representative. In fact, Thomas does not pay child support with any regularity. Accordingly, it is premature and financially unsound for Thomas to request the appointment of a child's representative in the matter herein.

WHEREFORE, MARTHA FRAWLEY prays this court denies Thomas Frawley's Motion for appointment of child's representative.

Respectfully submitted,

MARTHA FRAWLEY

By Donald_Burnburg________

BURNBURG & GORDON P. C.

Her Attorneys

Every day I would send out at least ten résumés online. I received a call now and then, but nothing usually came out of it. I was desperately searching for a job with insurance and a decent wage. Fred was still keeping me busy, but I knew he was doing more out of his heart, going into his own pocket to keep me busy. My longtime friend Ray was a Fireman, and on the side, he would get electrical jobs. Ray and I had been doing side jobs for years. He would call me if he had work. This would help me out greatly. I was doing whatever I could to stay afloat and prove to everyone I could take care of my daughter. Jennifer and I did not have the things we were used to, but we made the best of it. We did not have our half-acre yard, pool table, arcade games, Ping-Pong, music room, etc., but we played cards, listened to music, watched DVD's and we also started walking a few miles at night. It did not matter to Jennifer as long as she was with me. I tried to keep Jennifer's life as normal as possible. I would take her to our neighborhood in Countryside as much as possible to see her friends. She would spend some weekends at a friend's house. I wanted her to do the normal things that she was used to and continue to be a kid.

My Mother lived in Bridgeport, and Jennifer would get to know her a little better. My mother was 65 years old and was on disability most of her life. She had a severe stroke at the age of 33. Her right arm was paralyzed, and she had a limp in her right leg. She had several heart surgeries over the years, replacing the main valve in her heart.

Jennifer did not see my mother as much over the years as she did Martha's Mother. Some days while I was at work, she would hang out with her Nonie. My mother lived alone and enjoyed the company. They would play cards and other games and go shopping together. Jennifer would become a big help to my mother. Even though she was capable of taking care of herself, she loved having Jennifer around. My brother Paul would come in from Italy from time to time, and Jennifer and I would stay with my mother.

I was getting desperate for money. I decided to go down to public assistance for food money. This would be the first time in my life that I had to get help. I went down to apply, and they gave me a link card for food, but no other assistance was awarded to me. They said I would receive about one hundred and seventy-nine dollars in food money every two weeks. They said they would also go after Martha for child support if I wanted them to. I didn't want Martha knowing that I was getting assistance. She would have used that against me in court. The food money would make my life with Jennifer much easier.

Martha was telling people that I was a loser justifying her reason for leaving me. My best friend Roy was always telling me to make a liar out of her. I was doing everything in my power to hang on to Jennifer.

March 30, 2006, the court date arrived, and to my surprise, Martha agreed to allow the court to appoint Jennifer her own attorney. I was told that Martha did this because she knew I did not have the money. The judge appointed a woman attorney. As we were on our way out, we were introduced to her. Her name was Mrs. Rachel Davis.

"Hi Mr. and Mrs. Frawley, I will be representing your daughter Jennifer. My retainer fee is $2,500. Both of you will have to pay half. If I piss off one of the parents, then I am doing my job."

She set up an appointment with Martha and me separately.

I did not have the money. I would have to ask Paul. I did not want to ask him for the money, but I had no other choice. Paul, without hesitation, gave the money to Jennifer's attorney.

I went to my appointment to pay Mrs. Davis. While I was there, she invited me into her office to tell her my side of the story. I briefly described everything that happened between Martha and Jennifer up until this point. She took notes, and then we set up an appointment for Jennifer. Jennifer would spend an hour with Mrs. Davis. I felt this was the answer to my prayers. Jennifer would now have a voice in court and expose the truth about what Martha has done to her. Mrs. Davis told Jennifer," I suggest you and Martha attend counseling together."

Jennifer said, "I'm already in counseling, and I don't want to go with my Mom because she will lie and nothing will get accomplished."

Mrs. Davis told Jennifer, ``Why don't you try a session and if you don't like it, then let me know and I'll see what I can do."

Jennifer said, "That is fine."

Mrs. Davis also suggested, ``Jennifer, I think you should talk to your mother."

Jennifer replied, "All we do is fight."

Mrs. Davis said, "We will see what happens in counseling."

When we left, I told Jennifer, This attorney is supposed to work just for you; hopefully, she will tell the courts how crazy your mom is.

Jennifer had school concerts for the violin. Martha would not attend some of the concerts. When she did show up, she would sit on the other side of the concert hall. She usually came a few minutes late so she could see where I was sitting. She came with her parents a few times, and after the concert, they would run out the doors immediately after the concert to avoid me. Martha's parents, after being with their daughter twenty-two years, no longer spoke to me. I had no idea what I had done so wrong to them that they would act as if I never existed. I was very close with them, especially her father. Over the years, I went on many fishing and hunting trips with him, more than his own son. He would often stop by my house, and the two of us would go to lunch and just spend the day together. Even though I didn't call her mother Mom, I felt she was a mother to me. This would be a pain I would carry with me. Martha's father told a neighbor that Martha was divorcing me because I didn't know how to save money, yet when Martha first announced the divorce, her father told me, "She must be crazy." Her mother called me and said, "I don't understand Tom, why my daughter is doing this. Martha is going to fall flat on her face." I understood that it was their daughter no matter what. To act as if they never knew me was a horse of a different color.

Jennifer would now try out for the school badminton team. She was very nervous because there were a lot of girls trying out. It would be a three-day elimination tryout. Jennifer was excited that she made it through the first round. I was praying that she made the team, which would take her mind off things. The second day I waited outside the school for the news. Jennifer came out and was walking toward me, and the look on her face looked a little sad. Right as she approached me, she started jumping up and down, screaming, "I'm on the team Dad, I'm on the team!" I was so happy for her; I was excited as she was. I had to buy her the required uniform, but it was not too expensive. Jennifer would become very good at this sport. She would become the number two player. This would be a grueling schedule because she traveled to other schools, and games would end late in the evening. I went to all of her home games and a few road games. Even though Jennifer did not want Martha at any of her games, Martha never attended one game. It did not bother Jennifer at all, but it did bother me. Martha's new life was continuously pulling away from her child.

I was getting calls about jobs I applied for on the internet, but they were only temporary agencies looking to fill temporary positions. They mislead people into thinking there is a position available, then they have you drive miles away to their office to apply. When I arrived, I filled out paperwork and had to take a test. When finished, I found out that there is no position like the one I applied for online; they put you in their computer system and will call you if a position becomes available. After going through this twice, I asked if it was a temp agency before going any further.

April 25, 2006, I took Jennifer to school in the morning, and I had to go to the bathroom. I went into the Dominick's store that was by the school, and on the way out, I picked up the job finder. I drove back to the city to work. At lunch, I was reading the Job Finder, and I came across a job in Countryside, my hometown. The position was for a Machine assembler. After work, I was headed to pick Jennifer up from school and decided to stop and fill out an application for the job that was in the job finder. The person who was interviewing was not in at that time but I was still able to fill out the application. A few days later, I got a call for an interview. I went in for the interview and took an aptitude test. He told me that he would let me know by the end of the week and that there were a few more people to interview. I was nervous for a few days. At the end of the week, I got the call. He said that I was hired, but I had to take a physical and a drug test. Knowing I was in good health and clean of drugs, I was overwhelmed with excitement and relief. When I hung up, I jumped up and screamed, "Thank you, God! “This was the answer to my prayers. I was due to start on May 1st. The starting pay was $12.00 an hour with plenty of overtime.

April 27, 2005, I found a new job in Countryside. My new job required me to have my own tools and toolbox. I owned a few thousand dollars in tools that were at my home in my garage. I called my attorney,

"Daniel, I am starting a new job, I need to get into my garage to get my tools."

"I will inform Mr. Burnburg."

I called him a few days before the weekend in the hope to get the tools by Saturday or Sunday. By Sunday, April 30, I did not get my tools. I had to go and buy new tools costing over four hundred dollars, and this was just to get started. On Monday, my attorney left me a voicemail: "You probably got your tools by now."

I called him during my lunch break and said, ”I did not get my tools from Martha; I had to buy new tools."

His reply, ”Save the receipt."

May 1, 2006, A few days later, Mr. Simmons called me, " You can go get your tools tonight at 6:00pm; I suggest that you bring a witness to assure there are not any problems between Martha and you."

My witness would be Jennifer. Jennifer and I drove to our home to get the tools. We pulled into the driveway, and I got out and rang the doorbell. Martha opened the door and when she saw it was me, opened the garage. I got back into my truck to turn around and back up to the garage when I noticed Martha's Mother come out of the house and watch me as I backed up to the garage. I walked into the garage and was looking around. All the shelves were emptied into boxes mixed with other things like clothes, holiday decorations.

I had over twenty years of accumulation of tools. I could not remember every tool, but I knew there were some big tools missing. As I was standing there, looking around, Martha's Mother came into the garage within a few feet of me and stared at me. I looked over at her only once. She never said a word, nor did I. Jennifer got out of my truck and walked into the garage. Martha's mother saw Jennifer and said hi, and went over to her to give her a hug. Jennifer did not say hi or hug her grandmother back.

A few minutes later, Martha came into the garage explaining something about my tools in a voice of anger and hatred. She said, "Tom, I put some of your tools in bins. There is so much stuff I do not know where to put it all. "I did not say a word. She was vapor to me. In a split second, she looked toward Jennifer, said, "Oh hi Jennifer," and walked toward her with her arms starting to open to give her a hug. Martha did not get two steps before Jennifer firmly stated, "don't even." Martha stopped in her tracks and turned around, and told her mother to go into the house with her. Jennifer and I gathered whatever tools we could find and packed them into the truck, and pulled away. Most of my tools were gone.

That same evening Jennifer and I went to the Laundromat to do our laundry. Jennifer went outside for a moment. I was checking on the clothes, and I decided to go outside to see what Jennifer was doing. She was on her phone. I heard her talking to Martha.

Jennifer said, "Mom, how dare you treat my father like garbage in front of me, and what did my Dad ever do to Granny that she didn't talk to him. I hate the way you are now, Mom!" and hung up.

By now, it had been three months since I put my house up for sale, and the realtors in charge of the sale of my home had not contacted me. I didn't even know who they were. I went to the Countryside realtor's office. I walked in, and there was a woman at a desk on my left. I walked over to her, and I asked,

"Who is in charge here?"

She replied, "The boss is not in right now. Can I help you?"

I said, "Who are the realtors that are selling the house on Catherine Ave?" She went through some papers and said, "There are two agents, why, what is wrong?"

I said, ”I own the house on Catherine, and it has been for sale for three months. Nobody has called me since it has been for sale. This real-estate company is going to make about $20,000 off the sale of my house and my signature will be on that check. Someone had better start calling me on the status of my home. I want to be treated as if my name is on that house! People that were sitting at their desks heard me and were looking at me. I was loud and angry. The woman apologized and assured me that someone would call me.

I said, “I am sorry that I was loud with you. I know it is not your fault, but put yourself in my shoes." I walked out.

On the way back home, one of the realtors called me. He said, ”I'm sorry Mr. Frawley..." Before he could say anything else, I boldly stated, "That is my house as well as Martha's, I signed that contract, and I want to be updated as often as possible on the progress of selling my home."

He said, ”I understand Mr. Frawley. Many people have been looking at your home, but no offers yet."

I replied, ”Are you going to stay in touch with me?"

"Yes Mr. Frawley!" I never heard from that man again. He was the assistant of the primary seller.

May 2, 2006 court date arrived; it was Jennifer's attorney Rachel Davis's first appearance.

Mr. Burnburg started off, ”Mr. Frawley is a sick person with an illness, and he is brainwashing the child, keeping her from talking to her Mother."

I responded, ”That is not true, your honor."

Mr. Simmons jumped in, "The child does not talk to the mother because of conflicts between the mother and child." Judge Nobal looked over at Mrs. Davis, "What are your thoughts on the whole situation?"

Mrs. Davis stated, "I feel the mother and daughter should go to counseling together."

I interrupted, “Jennifer is already in counseling."

Martha said sarcastically, "Jennifer misses appointments and does not like the counselor."

Arguing back, I said, that is not true; we rescheduled, not canceled appointments because of Jennifer's sports and school events. Jennifer is comfortable with her counselor."

Martha replied, "You are brainwashing Jennifer to keep her away from me."

The judge then asked Mrs. Davis, "What is your thought on this?

Mrs. Davis said calmly, "Well, I think the teenager just doesn't like counselors."

I angrily interrupted, "Call Jennifer's counselor up, and get the records!"

It fell on deaf ears.

Judge Nobal, "I hereby order Martha and Jennifer to attend joint counseling. The counselor will be chosen by Martha through her insurance."

I said, "What about the counseling Jennifer attends now?"

Martha said, "Jennifer does not have to see this person anymore."

Wow, I thought silently; thanks for the ruling on that issue, Martha!

The court was over; I stopped Mrs. Davis in the hallway. I asked, "Are you aware that it was me who wanted an attorney for Jennifer? Why would you say she does not like counselors?

Mrs. Davis replied, "Just because I do not agree with you does not mean I am not doing my job.

I stared at her for a second in disbelief, turned and walked away.

When I picked Jennifer up from school that day, I gave her the news. She started crying, saying "I do not want to change counselors, Dad. Why can't Mom go to my counselor? All she is going to do is lie in there, Dad."

I do not know what to tell you Jennifer, your attorney ordered this.

The Court Order:

IN THE CIRCUITCOURT OF COOK COUNTY, ILLINOIS

COUNTY DEPARTMENT-DOMESTIC RELATIONS DIVISION

Martha Frawley_________________

Petitioner

And

Thomas Frawley________________

Respondent

ORDER

This cause coming to be heard for status and the court been fully advised on the premises:

It is hereby ordered:

- Martha Frawley and Jennifer Frawley shall attend counseling With John Dawson. The frequency of the sessions shall be determined by John Dawson.
- The parties shall cooperate on ensuring Jennifer attends the sessions.
- This matter is set for status on 6-21-06 at 9:30 AM.

Mary noble

JUDGE

I find it ironic that "Martha will be choosing the Counselor through her insurance." Then 20 minutes later, I am handed a court order with a chosen counselor. With Martha to my right and Rachel to my left, the judge in front of me and no one behind me, I felt like a human pinball with a paddle hitting me to the left and then smacking me back to the right, bouncing off of bumpers surrounding me as I hear the ringing of Martha's high score. With Martha dropping all the quarters, I could only wonder, did she also choose Rachel Davis in her arcade game of lies?

To take Jennifer's mind off things, it was a Sunday afternoon, and Jennifer and I decided to go to a White Sox game. It was within walking distance from my mother's house. Jennifer had her own Sox jersey. She was putting it on and said, "Dad put yours on."

I uttered, "I don't have one. "She reached down, opened her suitcase, and pulled out a very nice official White Sox jersey. Jennifer said, "I gave this to you last father's day. When I went back to the house with the police in February, I took your jersey."

I said, "Wow! Thank you, Jennifer." I had very little money on me, so Jennifer and I decided to go to the gas station across the street to get cash from the ATM using my credit card. I was able to obtain two new credit cards in my name. We walked in and went to the back of the store where the cash station was. I swiped my card and hit the button to withdraw $100.00. I went through all the transactions, and the screen said denied. I tried it again, but it was denied again. I had a different charge card and swiped it. Once again, I went through all the transactions, and this card declined. I said I do not understand, Jennifer; I am nowhere near my limits. We went outside of the gas station and started walking back to my mother's house. On the way, I called the 1-800 number on the back of the cards to see what the problem was. A representative answered the phone. I told this person that I was denied cash. He said, "Let me look up your account. "He then put me on hold. A few moments later, he was back on the line and he said, "There is a problem with your address. Do you live at ****Catherine in Countryside IL?"

"I said I have a home there."

"He said we received a call saying you do not live at this address, and that is the address that is on your account. You will have to contact customer service on Monday to resolve this issue. "I called the number on the second card. A woman answered. I told her my problem, and she said the same thing. Jennifer and I went back to my mother. I said, "I am so sorry Jennifer, I know how excited you were to go see the game. I am sorry I do not have the money to take you."

She said, "No problem Dad, it is not your fault. You know Mommy did this. Remember she was opening your credit card bills."

I said, "Jennifer, you are too smart. "Feeling bad, I wanted to do something. I called my brother Jim to see what he was doing for the game. He stated he was watching the game in his backyard and was going to barbecue some food. I told him what just happened to us. He firmly said, "Why don't you and Jennifer come by and join me." We went to Jimmy's house. It was just down the block from my mother. We had a good time. If there was anyone Jennifer enjoyed watching the game with, it was Uncle Jimmy. Jimmy was a sports nut.

May 8, 2006, we met the new counselor. When Jennifer and I arrived, we were a little curious because it was a house instead of an office. I thought that was odd. We walked up to the house, and there was a sign on the door that said walk in. Martha arrived just a second later. There was a living room with magazines spread over the table. There was a couch on one side and two chairs on the opposite side of the room. Jennifer and I sat in the chairs, and Martha sat on the couch. Jennifer and I ignored Martha. The counselor came from a different room. He gave papers to Martha and Jennifer to fill out. He introduced himself as John Dawson. He was a slim tall older man in his early 60's. He asked, "Do you mind if I eat a fast dinner while you guys fill out paperwork. It should take about thirty minutes to fill out. We said, "Not a problem."

Martha was getting very angry because Jennifer was whispering to me, asking questions about the paperwork. She was giving us dirty looks. I wanted to make sure that Jennifer was not signing anything she did not understand. I noticed that there were to be 26 sessions. There was one piece of paper I did not like. It was something about Martha getting access to Jennifer's records of the sessions. Mr. Dawson came back into the front room and sat on the couch next to Martha. He looked over the paperwork and noticed the sheet that Jennifer did not sign. He asked, ``Why is this not signed?"

I told him, "I do not agree with that paper."

He said, "If she does not sign the paper, I cannot start the counseling; this is nothing that you have to worry about. " I had Jennifer sign the papers. Once Jennifer signed the papers, Mr. Dawson suddenly became direct and influential. He looked at me and stated, "It is a good thing that you had Jennifer sign the papers because if you did not, you would have a problem in court." Mr. Dawson also stated, "You know I believed that all children should be with the mother because that's what I did in my divorce. Mothers are nurturing. Right after he said that, Jennifer and I looked at each other in disbelief. This is the person who will have a huge effect on the custody decision, and before the first session even began, his personal opinion was that my daughter should be with her mother. Neither Jennifer nor I said a word. The sessions began just minutes later with Martha and Jennifer. Mr. Dawson had a very arrogant demeanor.

I left Mr. Dawson's house and took a ride to get some water and a newspaper. I returned an hour later. When Jennifer came out of the house, her eyes were glassy. I asked her, "What is wrong?"

She said, "It's fixed Dad."

"What is fixed Jennifer, what do you mean?"

Jennifer said, "Mr. Dawson was taking us down a hallway and he said the room is on your left; your Mom knows where it is. She has been here before Dad, and he defends whatever Mom says. He justified all of the mean things Mom did to me. Not once did he say anything sticking up for me Dad."

Immediately I phoned my attorney, leaving him a message.

"Daniel, Martha knows Mr. Dawson that is a conflict of interest with this counselor.

I also had Jennifer phone her attorney Mrs. Davis. There was no answer. Jennifer left a voicemail for Rachel to call her back.

The next evening during a conversation between Jennifer and Martha, Jennifer asked Martha,

"Mom, have you seen that counselor before?"

"No Jennifer, I did not."

"Then how did you know where that room was in that big house?"

Martha replied, "Because I was there before to sign papers."

Jennifer said, "You signed the papers the same time we did."

Martha then admitted, "I have seen Mr. Dawson in the past. I had a few sessions with him."

Jennifer hung up.

I called my attorney Mr. Simmons and left a voicemail again. I said, "Martha admitted that she has seen that counselor before to Jennifer. Call me when you have time."

Mr. Simmons left me a voicemail saying, "Tom, you were right, that counselor is tainted. I will work on a file to have him removed."

Jennifer also called Mrs. Davis, leaving her a voicemail stating that her mother admitted seeing that counselor before.

May 9, 2006, I sent Mr. Simmons an email:

Daniel, Jennifer is scheduled for Tuesday with Dawson. So you know, we will not be attending. I do not trust this person whatsoever. This person who is deciding my life with Jennifer and told me in front of Jennifer that he thinks children are better off with the mother just because he gave his own children up! I am not saying we do not want Jennifer and Martha to go to counseling; we just want someone neutral. Jennifer also left a voicemail with Rachel. I do not want to go through Martha's insurance; I will pay out of my pocket as long as it is fair!

May 22 2006, Email from Daniel Simmons:

Tom

As I told you it would happen, the failure to keep the Dawson appointment has been spun back to you. Attached is a petition for contempt of court, which essentially alleges that YOU have refused to take Jennifer. I will respond as to the inaccuracies, such as the fact they left out the fact Martha tossed Jennifer out as opposed to Jennifer just refusing to live with her.

IT IS STILL MY OPINION THAT SHE SHOULD GO TO THE SESSION. It is to tell what Martha is really like. Right now, it just looks like we are not cooperating.

Daniel

My reply:

Amazing how things progress! Martha admitted to Jennifer in a phone conversation that she knew Mr. Dawson prior to their meeting! Just as Jennifer suspected and felt she could not trust someone who could hurt her. Your opinion was to continue to see this person. I really don't know how to take that! I wonder why Martha did not choose Jennifer's first counselor.

Daniel, I called you the same evening of the very first session to inform you of a critical comment made by Mr. Dawson, a comment that was clearly in Martha's favor. Also, the fact that he had past sessions with Martha. I had expected you to go to court and file some kind of conflict of interest. How is it possible for Mr. Dawson to remain neutral when he already knows Martha, the very reason she did not choose Jennifer's counselor! Because nothing was done on my behalf, I am now being attacked again. Why are we reactive instead of proactive? Martha set a nice trap, and all you can do is tell me to walk right into it. Martha made a lot of mistakes along the way, and I feel we did not take advantage of them. I now feel it is time to seek other help!

Sincerely,

Tom

Mrs. Davis has not returned any of Jennifer's calls.

PETITION FOR ADJUDICATION OF INDIRECT CIVIL CONTEMPT OF COURT

NOW COMES the petitioner, MARTHA FRAWLEY ("MARTHA") by, through her attorney, Burnburg & Gordon, P. C. , and as and for her Petition for Adjudication of Indirect Civil Contempt of Court states as follows:

- On May 2, 2006, an order of the court was entered, a copy of which is attached hereto and incorporated hereby as Exhibit "A," which stated in pertinent part:
- MARTHA FRAWLEY and JENNIFER FRAWLEY shall attend counseling with John Dawson; the frequency of the sessions shall be determined by John Dawson.
- The parties shall cooperate in ensuring JENNIFER attends the sessions. Notwithstanding the clear, unequivocal language of the order of court of May 2006, THOMAS FRAWLEY ("THOMAS") has willfully and contumaciously violated the order in the following fashion:
- A session was scheduled for Tuesday, May 16, 2006. Mr. Dawson called THOMAS to confirm that JENNIFER will be attending.
- On Tuesday, May 16, 2006, THOMAS failed to bring JENNIFER to the session schedule for that evening.

JENNIFER resides with THOMAS. The therapy is necessitated by

JENNIFERS's refusal to reside with her mother or, for that matter, even visit with her mother. Notwithstanding the clear dictates of the order, THOMAS has failed to bring JENNIFER to the court order therapy two out of the first three sessions.

- MARTHA has incurred attorney's fees in the preparation and Presentation of this Petition for Adjudication of Indirect Civil Contempt of Court.

THOMAS is an able-bodied man, allegedly gainfully employed and well able to pay MARTHA's attorneys fees necessarily incurred herein, which in any event, are mandatory pursuant to Section508(b) of the Illinois Marriage and Dissolution of Marriage Act.

- Upon a finding of contempt, this should and ought to fashion a sanction that includes incarceration for THOMAS so that he will suffer the penalty of confinement if he fails to ensure that JENNIFER attends the mandatory counseling ordered by the court on May 2, 2006.

WHEREFORE, the Petitioner, MARTHA FRAWLEY, prays as follows:

- That this Court enter a rule to show cause if any he has why THOMAS FRAWLEY should not be held in contempt of court for failing to bring JENNIFER FRAWLEY to the counseling sessions with John Dawson.
- Upon a finding of contempt, enter appropriate sanctions, including periodic incarceration for any subsequent failure to bring JENNIFER FRAWLEY to counseling.
- For her attorney's fees.
- For such further and different relief as this Court deems just and equitable.

Martha Frawley

MARTHA FRAWLEY

May 23, 2006, Email from Daniel:

I thought it was a good way for Jennifer to make a record as to what Martha has done to her. Notwithstanding the fact that you believe Martha had seen this person, I told you she should go anyway. I also told you that if the appointment would be canceled it should be Jennifer who makes the call, not you.

Your message also implies that I've been fired. You certainly have that right. Have your new lawyer contact me, and I will sign a substitution.

Daniel Simmons

May 23, Second email from Daniel

By the way, I also talked to Burnburg shortly after I called you yesterday. Among other things he told me, they are prepared to concede custody to you with a joint parenting agreement. This, you may recall, is from the person who said at the outset that even JOINT CUSTODY would NEVER be an option, considering your history.

I tried looking ahead to the ultimate result, not just her day-to-day Mickey-Mouse antics.

Have your new lawyer call me.

My Reply:

Sure, they are willing to concede now, especially that Jennifer tells her mother almost every conversation that she will never go with her. With that in mind, Martha has no choice but to settle for joint parenting, knowing her own daughter doesn't even want that! I will NEVER agree to any of Martha's wishes. Martha threw her own daughter out on the street in Feb. with no coat. She told Jennifer she has the power to make sure she never sees her father again. She yelled at her for having a family photo in her room. I can go on, CRUEL and EMOTIONAL ABUSE! As far as my history, I still continue counseling. I have a full-time job, and I have been raising an honor roll student for the past five months with no assistance from her mother. Jennifer, after one session, decided she was not returning. I agreed. Mr. Dawson shot down EVERYTHING Jennifer said as if Martha were the poor victim. How would this help us in court? My goal is to get full custody of my daughter, who wants the same! My question to you is this Daniel, Can you, and are you willing to make this happen? Jennifer and I have spoken to Rachel today on separate occasions. She is going to see what she can do to appoint a counselor that is truly neutral, someone who doesn't know Martha or Jennifer, therefore, making it difficult to be biased.

Tom

May 31, 2006 Email from Mr. Simmons:

It is my position that until the counselor is changed, Jennifer should go. I think it is a great chance for Jennifer to vent about all the crap Martha has put her through. If she is as mature as you believe, she will be able to "swing "Dawson into thinking that Martha is the unfit parent here. I happen to see it as a device to make sole custody actually happen. Dawson may very well report back to the Court as to just how screwed up Martha is and what she has done to this girl. I am trying to look at it objectively and from a global perspective as to the final outcome.

I am trying to coordinate an effort with Davis to have Dawson disqualified. I will be asking Davis to give me a written statement (from Jennifer) to the effect that Martha admitted to seeing Dawson in the past. The second party hearsay (Jennifer to you: you to me) is not really strong enough to use in court.

A Joint parenting Order is NOT joint custody. It simply means that the parents will cooperate in the attempt to raise a child. I. e., throw the petty BS behind and focus on the kid.

DS

My reply:

Daniel, I would agree, except for the fact that Dawson, in one session, defended Martha for all the bad things she has done to Jennifer. Wow, as my attorney, you would suggest walking into a setup. I am in shock! Dawson is clearly on Martha's side! Whose side are you on? HE JUSTIFIED Martha's throwing Jennifer out! How do you justify endangering a child? She could have been kidnapped and possibly killed! She didn't even go after her! I don't know what to think anymore.

Tom

Daniel Re:

Think what you want.

Tom Re:

No problem Daniel, You leave me a voicemail saying Mr. Davis is tainted!

Yet you suggest I have this tainted man evaluate my child. I'm sorry, Daniel but my better judgment caused me to wonder why. You even said that's probably why Burnburg didn't want him as a witness. But anyway, I got your other email!

Tom

Daniel Re:

Get someone else

Tom Re:

Like someone who will work for their clients. . . . .

There was never any effort to appoint a new counselor.

June 8, 2006 court date: I woke up that morning, jumped into the shower, and dressed for court. Before I left, I woke Jennifer. I said, "Jennifer, you know that I might not come back right."

She softly said, "Yeah."

"If I do not come back, you are going to have to go with your mother."

Jennifer said nothing as she stared at me with glassy eyes.

"You have to go with her. Promise me you will not run away. If you do, they will put you away. When Daddy comes back, I will fight to get you back. You have to stay strong for me. "She nodded her head as tears ran down her face. I hugged and kissed her and said, "I love you Jennifer. They cannot take that from us. I will see you later" and left for court.

I walked into the courtroom and sat down. They called my name shortly after. Mr. Burnburg started with the contempt of the court charge. He said, "Your honor, we are filing a Petition for Adjudication of Indirect Civil Contempt of Court."

Mr. Simmons jumped in, "Your honor, I am filing a Motion to Withdraw as Counsel for Mr. Frawley."

The judge looked at Mr. Simmons and rolled her eyes. Then Mrs. Davis stepped forward and uttered, "Your Honor, I think that the child just doesn't like counselors."

I was trying to fight back, "That is not true, she liked her first counselor. Why don't we get records from the first counselor?" My statement was ignored. The judge asked all of the attorneys, do you want to see a hearing judge for the contempt? They all agreed. The judge ordered us to another courtroom for the hearing to take place within the next half hour. I walked into the new courtroom first. Martha and the attorneys arrived shortly afterward. I sat down on the nearest seat. Martha sat a few seats away. The attorneys went into the judge's chambers. Martha and I were left in the room alone together. It was a very small courtroom. I did not say a word to her, nor did I look at her.

Moments later, everyone returned to the courtroom. We all sat at the table. Mr. Simmons and I sat on the left side of the table. Martha, Mr. Burnburg, and Mrs. Davis sat on the right. Seconds later, the Judge came out. It was a woman in her 50's. The judge started right in. She looked over at me and said, "I always promised myself that as a judge, I would never put up with contempt of court. You are going to spend thirty days in Cook County Jail. Do you have any questions?"

I said, "Yes, Your Honor, Can I explain what is going on?"

"No!" She stated.

Mr. Burnburg said, “Your Honor Mr. Frawley deliberately refused to obey a court order."

Neither Mrs. Davis, nor Mr. Simmons said a word. I sat there scared on the outside and crying on the inside as I looked in Martha’s direction. I saw a smile on Martha's face. As usual, Martha has rendered me powerless. The judge spoke with the attorneys a bit more, then looked at me and said, "Thank your attorney because I am not going to send you to jail just yet. This is what you are going to do. You are going to take the child to see the counselor tonight, and you will return to my courtroom tomorrow at 11am; and if you do not take that child, I will take her away from you and put you in jail. Do you understand me?"

"Yes, Your Honor," I said. I exhaled and thought to myself, thank my attorney, he is the reason I am here.

I hurried out of the courtroom toward the elevators. As soon as I came down to the lobby, I ran through the hallway to get outside. Jennifer was waiting alone at Paul’s apartment. I called her, and I said, ”I’m coming to get you Jennifer."

She said, ”You’re not going to jail Dad?"

"No honey, I am not. I’ll be right there." When I got to Paul’s apartment, I opened the door and hugged Jennifer. She was very happy to see me. I told Jennifer, "You have to continue to see Mr. Dawson."

With glassy eyes, Jennifer said, “Why is this happening to us, Dad? Why does Mom always get her way?"

"I said, I just don’t know honey."

That evening I took Jennifer to the session with Mr. Dawson. I waited outside in my car. After this session, Jennifer came out and I asked her how it went. She said it did not go too bad; he mostly asked me about my background. Do not be too sure of yourself Jennifer, this is only the second session out of twenty-six.

June 9, 2006, I returned to court. While waiting for the judge, I noticed Martha’s attorney passing some papers out to Mrs. Davis and Mr. Simmons. No one said anything to me. So I went up to Mr. Simmons and asked, "What are those papers they are passing around?"

He said, ”Oh, Your wife wants to send you to jail for 12 days and have you pay her attorney fees for today and yesterday for the sum of nine hundred dollars."

My heart was in my throat once again, sitting there, waiting, my body numb, and my hands sweating reading the papers. The judge finally came out. Martha’s attorney showed the judge the papers of what he wanted to happen. She looked over at me and said, “I see you did what I told you to do."

I replied, ”Yes."

She then looked over at Martha's side and said, ``I am not going to send him to jail, and he does not have to pay your attorney fees; he did what he was told."

I was so relieved! I did not look over at Martha. The Judge said to Martha and me, "You need to get along for the child’s sake."

Martha smiled; I said nothing.

Right before we were about to leave the courtroom, Mrs. Davis approached me and said, "I haven’t returned your daughter's phone calls for the last few weeks because my afternoons were busy."

I looked at her for about 3 seconds, turned around, and walked away without saying a word. I walked up to Mr. Simmons and said, ”Listen, if you can get me what I want, then I would like you to continue to work for me."

"He replied fine, but I think it is a good idea if you get together with Martha and try to work something out; you are going to have to deal with her for the next four years."

In 6 weeks, Rachel Davis has only seen Jennifer for one hour and has spoken to her only twice by phone.

Jennifer went to her third session. I briefed her on what to expect. "Be very careful with this counselor because we both know what his intentions are."

Jennifer said, "Ok," and went inside. I would wait outside in my car for Jennifer. When Jennifer came out of this session, I asked her, "How did it go?"

"Not too bad, Dad."

I said, "Do not get too comfortable with this counselor. I know you are very smart Jennifer, but this person does this for a living."

Jennifer was getting a little angry saying, "He only asked one question about you, Dad, and I didn't tell him anything."

I replied, "I know you wouldn't Jennifer, I just don't want him tricking you. You heard what that man said. He thinks you should be with your mother. Honey, for some reason, all the people that are supposed to be on our side seemed to give Mom whatever she wants. This counselor is definitely on her side."

My job was going well at this point; they were very understanding and said nothing about the constant court dates. There was plenty of overtime, and I would work as much as I could. If I lost time because of court, I would work on a Saturday at straight time just to show my loyalty. I needed my job and would do anything it took to keep it. I was getting deeper into debt with the credit cards. Jennifer needed clothes as well as me.

Paul was in town again and Jennifer and I moved in with my mother. She had a two-bedroom apartment. Jennifer and I had the second bedroom. We didn't have a bed, but we went out to buy a queen-size blow-up mattress. We lived out of laundry bags because we didn't have a dresser, and we were going from place to place. My mother was on a fixed income but knew we were trying to save for a security deposit. Sometimes my Mom would need twenty dollars to borrow. I gave her the money and said keep it. I also bought groceries for all of us. Jennifer and I were gone most of the day. We left at 5:30 am and got home at around 6pm. When Jennifer had counseling, or after school activities, we got back to the city between 9:30 and 10:00pm. We continued to eat out a lot because we were always on the go. I worked 10 hours a day Monday through Friday and 8 hours on Saturday.

During one of the few conversations Jennifer had with Martha. Martha told Jennifer, ``If you are not living in the school district by August 28, I will notify the school, and you will not be able to attend your school."

Jennifer said, "Mom, you would get me kicked out of my school?"

Martha replied, "Well, you're supposed to be living here Jennifer."

Jennifer started crying and hung up on Martha.

I could not recall one phone call that was ever pleasant between Jennifer and Martha.

I was checking the local newspapers constantly for an apartment I could afford. Most of the two-bedroom apartments were anywhere between eight hundred and fifty dollars and nine hundred and fifty dollars. I could not afford that much money. I was trying to raise Jennifer alone. Martha would contribute nothing. One-bedroom apartments were from six hundred fifty dollars to seven hundred and fifty dollars. I had to save between fourteen hundred dollars and sixteen hundred. Time was not on my side.

Jennifer was standing up for her girlfriend Gracie's Quinceanera, a Spanish celebration for a girl turning fifteen. This celebration was on Father's Day. Jennifer said, "Dad, I am so sorry I did not know it was going to be on Father's Day."

I said, "No problem Jennifer, this is a big thing to you and we will go out to dinner together tomorrow." Jennifer was very excited because she loved to dance, and one of the dances was from Grease. The girls involved have been practicing for weeks.

The ceremony started off in church. Jennifer was sitting in the pews with some of her friends, and they started passing a message from one girl to the next to tell Jennifer that her mother was there sitting in the back of the church. Jennifer told me after the ceremony that all the girls went to the front of the church to take pictures. Then all of a sudden, Martha came from the back of the church, walked up to the front and took pictures. Jennifer said she was embarrassed because her mother was dressed in shorts and a T-shirt. Martha was attacking me for not being with my daughter on Father's Day as if I were not a good parent.

The next day Jennifer and I went out to dinner. She gave me a homemade Father's Day card.

This was her card.

From Your Daughter

You've been a Superhero who chased away my fears.

A silly funny JOKER who clowned away my tears.

You've been a FUZZY teddy bear who gave me great BIG HUGS.

You're a big STRONG hunter who killed the icky bugs.

You've been a special STORYTELLER when it was time 4 bed.

And a super tucker inner when I was a sleepy head.

You've been my private tutor when my homework got real hard.

An extra fun to be with a friend to play with in the yard.

And though I may be older now DAD

You'll always be every bit as WONDERFUL

As you were back then to me.

HAPPY FATHERS DAY! Love always Jennifer

P. S. Sorry I couldn't spend father's day with you!

June 21, 2006 Court date and order:

MARTHA FRAWLEY,)

Petitioner,)

And)

THOMAS FRAWLEY,) COURTROOM 1623

Respondent

ORDER

This matter coming on to be heard upon the motion of Daniel Simmons to withdraw as counsel for responding Tom Frawley, Mr. Frawley being present in court.

IT IS HEREBY ORDERED THAT:

- Daniel Simmons Is granted leave to withdraw as counsel for Thomas Frawley.
- Thomas Frawley is granted 21 days to file his own appearance or appear through substitute council.
- This matter is set for status on July 25, 2006 9:30 AM.

ENTER Mary noble

JUDGE

It was July, and Jennifer started her summer softball league, something she did for the past six years. This was the last year she was able to play because of the age limit. The registration fee was fifty-five dollars. Even though I could have used the money for something else, I knew how much softball meant to Jennifer. It was her passion next to the violin. In the first game, Jennifer and I were worried about Martha showing up. After a few innings, we thought she would not come, and all of a sudden, I noticed Martha walking toward the field. She was dressed as if she was going out somewhere. I was standing in the dugout on Jennifer's team's side, talking to some of the players. As Martha walked past, she suddenly stopped in front of me, gave me a dirty look, and flipped her head back. I never looked up at Martha's face, and then she walked over to the bleachers and sat with two of her friends. Mostly all the people that were there had known Martha and me over the years. Many people knew our situation and saw what Martha had done. The young players, who were all girls, were friends with Jennifer outside of baseball and attended the same school. They also knew about Jennifer's situation with Martha and witnessed Martha's scene as well. Martha believed in her mind that people felt sorry for her, but most of these people looked at a person who cheated in her marriage and threw her only child out in the street to move her boyfriend to her daughter's home. The two people Martha was sitting with were one of Jennifer's friend's parents. These were Martha's new best friends. They were the only people out of Jennifer's friend's parents that thought what Martha was doing was ok. Their daughter was Jennifer's best friend until her best friend and her parents were getting involved with our personal life.

I changed Jennifer's phone number so Martha could not upset Jennifer anymore or leave a voicemail. I told Martha that Jennifer's phone broke and I didn't have insurance or money to get a new one. If she wanted to contact Jennifer, she was to call my phone, and I would have Jennifer return the call.

Jennifer's best friend told her mother that Jennifer had a pink phone and was talking on it. Her mother would convey that to Martha. Jennifer would no longer talk to this girl or her parents, nor would I.

Counseling Session 4,

Jennifer came out of this session crying hysterically, saying, "You were right Dad, Mr. Dawson said that I was depressed and needed to learn to respect my mother. Mr. Dawson said that I have goals to meet by a certain date and that if I did not meet them, I could get in trouble with the courts and you too, Dad. Jennifer said the way he said that was threatening to her. Mr. Dawson said, your mother tells me she could never get a hold of you. Jennifer said, that's a lie, my Dad makes me call my Mom when she calls, and my Mom calls only once a day, usually at night and sometimes not at all, especially on the weekends. Mr. Dawson then says, Jennifer, when you go to court in order to win, you need phone records. Jennifer replied, my Dad has phone records. Mr. Dawson looked at Jennifer with his mouth wide open and then looked over at Martha. Mr. Dawson says Jennifer, your counseling sessions are scheduled on Monday's and now I think we will add Thursdays.

Jennifer asked Mr. Dawson if we could change Thursdays to a different day because she had double-header days for softball on Thursdays. This was the last year she could play, and she loved playing. Mr. Dawson replied, no, I cannot reschedule, I'm busy, and as a matter of fact, we will make Thursday a double session from 7:00 to 8:00 and from 8:00 to 9:00. Jennifer sat there with tears rolling down her face as Martha, knowing softball is Jennifer's passion, said nothing. Martha was present for this session. Jennifer was crying so hard as if someone had beaten her.

Jennifer, while crying, said, "Dad, I don't understand, Mr. Dawson told me that I should be a kid and not think about the divorce, yet he won't let me play softball. Why are they doing this to me, Dad?" I had no words that would make Jennifer feel any better. I told Jennifer to call her attorney and tell her everything that she told me. Jennifer called her attorney immediately and left a crying voicemail. The next day was Friday, and no returned phone call from Mrs. Davis.

I called Martha,"So you know, I am taking Jennifer to Michigan from 6/30 to 7/4. I started shouting; Jennifer told me Mr. Dawson changed counseling on the nights she plays softball! What is wrong with you? Why do you continue to hurt her? You are a bitch!" I hung up.

Mr. Dawson gave this paper to Jennifer.

DAWSON COUNSELING SERVICES

TREATMENT PLAN AND AFTER CARE PLAN

Name: Jennifer C. Frawley

Counselor: John Dawson MHS, LCPC, CADC Diagnosis: 311: V61. 20

PROBLEMS * ** GOALS METHOD/FREQUENCY TARGET DATE COMPLETION DATE STAFF RESPONSIBILITY

1. Intoxication/Withdraw N/A

2. Biomedical Conditions N/A 2-3

3. Emotional/Behavioral/ Cognitive Major Depression NOS 3-4
Reduce/eliminate depression a) Develop health cognitive patterns and beliefs about self and the world that lead to alleviation of depression symptoms

4. Readiness to change Client appears unmotivated to treatment
Completion of all treatment plan goal and objectives

5. Relapse/Continued Use or Continued Problem Potential N/A.

6. Recovery Environment N/A

Other Family Conflicts 4-5 Reduce parental conflicts through conflict resolution a)Identify conflict situations and own role in conflicts b)Can have own feelings and thoughts apart from those in family c) Demonstrates and uses assertive communication skills

Other Continual arguing and/or not communicating with mother. 4-5
Increase awareness of the client's role in the relationship conflict. a) identify ways to initiate change b)increase frequency of communication c) Verbalize the needs of both parties in the relationship. D) Conduct conjoint sessions with mother

Severity Scale 0 = very mild 2 = mild 3= moderate 4 = severe 5 = very severe

** Goal Attainment 1=significant change 2= moderate 3=no change 4= worse

Email from Martha:

Tom,

Thank you for letting me know you are taking Jennifer to Michigan from 6/30 to 7/4.

Remember to call the counselor to reschedule her 7/3 appointment, or I can let him know when Jennifer and I see him tomorrow.

I don't appreciate the way you were yelling at me at the top of your lungs. I don't talk to you that way, and you don't have to scream at me. For Jennifer's sake, let's be civilized when communicating.

Martha

My Reply:

Oh, no problem, For Jennifer's sake, I was a little upset that you allowed Mr. Dawson to schedule sessions on the evenings of her softball games with you sitting right there. Knowing this is the last year she will get to play. She fell to the ground crying as if someone beat her. "They took my softball, Dad! Please don't let them take that away from me. I love softball. They said I should be a kid and do the normal things I've always done. Yet they won't let me. Why am I being punished, Daddy!" She cried in my arms all night.

Please do not send any more emails. I cannot communicate with someone who makes my child cry all the time.

I myself will save this email for my files as well.

Have a nice day!

Tom

On Saturday, my brother Jim called me and offered two White Sox tickets for Jennifer and me. He was going as well. He had four tickets but his girlfriend Caroline was not going. I told Jimmy what great timing. I told him what had happened to Jennifer Thursday, and this would be a great way to take things off her mind. Especially that the Sox were playing the Houston Astros, whom they played in the World Series. Jennifer was extremely excited! She put on her Sox Jersey and grabbed her baseball glove. We had great seats about twenty rows behind the Sox dugout. Jennifer was just like her uncle Jimmy; they both were baseball nuts. Jennifer had nothing else on her mind when all of a sudden, guess who walked right by us and sat 10 rows in front of us, Jennifer's attorney Mrs. Davis. Jennifer sitting right next to me noticed her at the same time and said, "Dad, that's my attorney."

"Yes, it is," I replied. We did not say anything else about her. After every inning, when the Sox were coming into bat, some of the players would throw baseballs into the crowd. Jennifer and I would run down toward the field to try to get a ball. On our way back to our seats, Mrs. Davis noticed us and would hide her face behind the man that she was with. I had no intentions of approaching her; we were there for the game. How sad is it that you see the little girl you were hired to protect, and when you see her in public, you hide from her.

It's now Monday, and I felt totally helpless. I had no idea who to call for help. Who in this world oversees that attorneys and counselors do not abuse their power? Not knowing where to turn, Jennifer and I decided to take matters into our own hands. Jennifer said, "Dad, I have a digital voice recorder. Why don't I record what happens in the counseling sessions, then they will believe us." I did not know if I could use this in court, but at least I would have proof Martha and Mr. Dawson were mentally, emotionally abusing, and trying to brainwash a 14-year-old little girl. Knowing there was nothing that I could do to help Jennifer legally, I told Jennifer that she could read any court documents that she needed to defend herself against these lying adults. I felt at least she did not have to sit there and take the punishment. I gave her the tools to fight back.

Counseling session five,

It was Monday night, and Jennifer had a 7pm session.

On Mondays, Martha did not attend the sessions. Martha only attended Thursday's second session from 8 to 9pm. The court order was for both mother and daughter to attend counseling together. Also, after every session with Martha and Jennifer, Mr. Dawson would ask Martha to stay after the session to talk to her alone. It was about 6:55pm, and we were a block away from the counselor's house. Jennifer and I got the recorder ready. We were a little nervous but somewhat at ease because the recorder has a hold button to assure that if any buttons such as the stop or play buttons are hit accidentally, nothing will stop the recording. I turned on the recorder and hit the hold button, and gave the recorder to Jennifer. The recorder was very small, making it easy to hide. Jennifer put the recorder under a cameo shirt, whatever that was. We pulled up to Mr. Dawson's house, and Jennifer went inside. Jennifer came out an hour later, and we pulled away before taking the recorder out. We got a few blocks away, and Jennifer pulled the recorder out and stopped the recording. We had about a fifteen-mile ride home, and I used this time to playback the recording. Jennifer said he didn't say anything that we could use against him, Dad. I said, no problem Jenn; I'm going to listen anyway.

Mr. Dawson: So you were into Taekwondo Jennifer.

Jennifer: yes.

Mr. Dawson: I was into Tai Chi. He rattled on for a while with his stories, and they started to talk about loyalty.

Mr. Dawson: Jennifer, you have a problem with loyalty. You don't know which parent to be loyal to, but you're loyal to your father because he feeds you.

Jennifer: That's not why I am loyal to my father. I am loyal to him because he is loyal to me.

Mr. Dawson: Tell me about the calls you have with your mother.

Jennifer: Well, my Mom always asks about court-related things, and that leads to arguments. I don't feel she should be asking me those things.

Mr. Dawson: Why don't you just answer the questions?

Jennifer: I do answer those questions, but they lead into other things, like my Mom would ask me if I was going to the other counselor before you, and I would tell her, yes, but then she would tell her attorney that I don't go.

Mr. Dawson: Why didn't you ask the counselor for the attendance records to bring to court?

Jennifer: I don't know.

(Jennifer informed me that Mr. Dawson was writing down) everything that she says.

Mr. Dawson: What do you like to do for fun?

Jennifer: Well, my friends and I like to play softball and go walking downtown. Me and my father joke around a lot, play on the computer and sometimes play cards and...

Mr. Dawson: Let's stop for a minute. I know this is going to be hard, but I don't want you to mention your father.

(Jennifer told me at the point when she mentioned me, the counselor stopped writing).

I lost the rest of this session.

It was now Wednesday, and Mrs. Davis finally returned Jennifer's call 6 days after her crying voicemail. Jennifer told Mrs. Davis that she felt this counselor is on her Mom's side and about not being able to play softball and that they always talk about court-related stuff. Mrs. Davis told Jennifer that she would call the counselor about rescheduling so that Jennifer could play baseball. Jennifer asked Rachel, "Could I go to court and say who I want to live with?"

Rachel said, "No."

It was Wednesday evening, and I was not sure if Mrs. Davis got a hold of Mr. Dawson to allow Jennifer to play her games the following Thursday. I also left a voicemail for Mr. Dawson informing him that Jennifer and I would be out of town from Friday to Tuesday for the fourth of July weekend. We were going to Michigan by friends, something we have done for over 10 years.

It was Thursday evening, and Jennifer started her game, but we had to leave after half an hour because we had not heard back from Mrs. Davis on the baseball issue.

It was a double two-hour session that night, and Mr. Dawson never returned my phone message about our vacation. As we were about to leave the game, Martha showed up. Jennifer and I turned our backs to her and walked toward our vehicle. As we were walking toward my truck,

Martha started walking toward us, calling Jennifer saying, "Mr. Dawson is running a little late tonight." We never looked back and kept walking.

Mr. Dawson did not call me to inform me he was running late.

Counseling session six/seven, Once again, we were a block away, and we got the recorder ready, hoping to reveal Mr. Dawson's intentions. As Jennifer got ready to go in, I told her, "You'll be ok." She smiled with confidence and went inside. I started using this time sitting in my vehicle and writing my story. After fifty-five minutes had passed, I could see Martha coming down the street in my rearview mirror. She pulled into Mr. Dawson's driveway. I noticed she had parked there the last session. Just then, to my surprise, Jennifer came out and jumped into my truck. I asked, "What is going on?"

She said, "I get a five-minute break." Jennifer looks at me and says very little because the tape was running. Jennifer and I checked the recorder to ensure there was enough time left to record.

Jennifer went back inside to start the session with her mother. It was 9:07 pm, and Jennifer was not out yet. I was getting very nervous. I decided to go into the counselor's house. He had a sign on the front door that said walk in. I walked in. There was a front room to the left that was like a waiting area with music playing in the background. I sat on the couch, waiting nervously. I knew they were in a room somewhere in the back of the house. I could hear some arguing, but I did not know what room it was coming from. It was now 9:17pm. I was even more nervous because I did not know how much time was left on the recorder or if it would beep when out of time. I decided to go back outside to ring the doorbell as if I just arrived. I paused for a moment, starting to panic. At that moment, Jennifer came out of the house. She was crying and angry. Jennifer was stomping her feet toward the truck at the same time ripping the recorder from her shirt. I said, "What are you doing? Are you crazy?"

Jennifer said, "They are in the back room," and threw the recorder in my chest and said, "Listen for yourself!" We got in the car and drove away. Jennifer was still crying, saying, "They're nuts! Mommy is such a liar." Jennifer calmed down somewhat, and I told her, "A few of your friends called; call them back." Jennifer would leave her phone in my truck during counseling. She took her phone and called Julie. I started playing the recorder back.

Session Six:

Mr. Dawson: Did you read a page from a book that I gave you from your mother?

Jennifer: No!

Mr. Dawson: Why?

Jennifer: Before I start doing anything, my mother would have to admit all the bad things she has done to me before counseling can even work for us.

Mr. Dawson: Jennifer, you know if I have to go to court and they ask me if she is cooperating, I'm going to have to say no. I wouldn't do that if I were you, I am the court-appointed counselor, and they are relying on my testimony. You don't want to hurt yourself. I diagnosed you with problems, and you shouldn't resist treatment.

Jennifer: You said I was depressed, and I'm not. I was seeing another counselor for months, and that counselor said there was nothing wrong with me.

Mr. Dawson: I don't care what that counselor said; I rely on myself and my expertise. That counselor could have been a yahoo. Why are you jumping around if you're so happy?

Jennifer: I'm excited because I'm going to Michigan on vacation.

Mr. Dawson: I don't get it. I would be relaxed if I was going on vacation.

Jennifer was telling Mr. Dawson about the time when Martha threw her out. Mr. Dawson seemed to be concerned at this point, saying that Martha's actions were neglectful and abusive.

Mr. Dawson: Does your attorney know about this?

Jennifer: Yes.

Mr. Dawson: Is your Dad paying for your attorney?

Jennifer: I think my Mom and Dad are paying.

Mr. Dawson: I don't think you should skip Monday's session for vacation. I think you should be in therapy.

Mr. Dawson: Jennifer, since this is a two-hour session, you could have a five-minute break with your father. What is your father going to do, sit out there for two hours and smoke? Why don't he go to the park or go get something to eat? What's with that?

Jennifer said nothing and walked out to my car.

Jennifer went back in for the second session with her mother.

Session Seven:

Mr. Dawson: Confront your mother about throwing you out of the house.

Jennifer, while crying: You told me to get out and give you the house keys and cell phone. You even swore, you said, get the Fuck out! You went through my backpack, took my keys and cell phone, and told me to get out. I left right away because I was scared of you. It was February 1st, and it was cold and dark outside. You did not follow me to see if I was ok. I was crying and scared that something could have happened to me. I walked three blocks to my friend's house. Her brother answered the door, and he could see I was crying, and he called his sister right away. I was let inside, and I called my Dad to tell him what happened and to pick me up at my friend's house.

Martha: Are you finished?

Jennifer: Yes!

Martha: I would never kick you out of the house, Jennifer. I love you more than anything. (Martha looking at Mr. Dawson) I was not actually throwing her out. I was calling her bluff because one time, she attempted to leave and just stood in the driveway. She wouldn't talk to me or eat dinner with me. You kept telling me that you wanted to go live with your father. I didn't know what else to do, so I said pack your bags and said go live with your father.

Jennifer: (Crying) No, Mom, you're lying. You told me to get the Fuck out, you went through my backpack saying where your cell phone and house keys is, and you told me to get out. It was dark outside, and I had no coat. As far as eating with you, I made my own dinner every night because you were always working late. You never went after me to see if I was ok and I walked 3 blocks in the dark, freezing.

Martha: I knew your father was coming to pick you up because it was a visitation night.

Jennifer: Mom, it was only 5:30, and Dad wasn't coming until 6:00. I had to call him from my friend's house to tell him what happened.

Mr. Dawson: That is child neglect, and I believe her, I don't know if the father knew right away that you threw her out, but she is only 14. You know I was in a store and this woman with two kids, small kids, toddlers, well, she was walking around shopping, not paying attention to these little kids. And wouldn't you know it, the kids ran off. Good thing I was watching this take place because something could have happened to those kids. I took the children to the woman and said, do you know what you have just done. That is child abuse and neglect. Someone could have easily taken these children. The woman just stared at me. She didn't care. What else do you want to tell your mother, Jennifer?

Jennifer: Mom, remember when we were by your sister's house on a night, Dad had visitation. I called Dad to see if we could stay longer and he could have his visitation the next day instead. Dad said no problem, and when the next day came, you said Dad can't see me because it's not his day. You agreed, Mom! I was so upset, and when I came home from school, I would not speak to you all night. When it was time for bed, you came into my room and started asking me questions. I told you why I was mad, Mom, and then we started arguing. I told you, Mom, I need to get some sleep, but you would not leave me alone. I had a feeling that night you were going to take my phone, so I took my phone and went into the front room to lay on the couch. Then you followed me saying, give me your phone. I started running from you, trying to get out the front door, but I couldn't get out fast enough. Then I crouched down on the floor because I was terrified of you! I ran to my room to get changed to get out of the house because I was so scared because of the way you were screaming at me. Give me your phone! I knew you wanted my phone, so I could not call my Dad. I went toward the front door, and you said, go ahead, and I'll call the police, and you will be put in the Audi home. I went back into my room because I was scared you would call the police. I finally went to bed very late. When I woke up the next morning, I asked you for my phone, and you said no because you're going to call your Dad. When I went to school, my friends noticed my eyes were red and puffy because I was crying and didn't get enough sleep. I was scared to go home from school because I thought you were going to start again. I have never seen you so angry like that in my life.

Martha: I don't remember that argument, I wanted your phone because you sometimes don't call me after school, and I was just trying to stop you from getting out the door.

Mr. Dawson: Martha, I'm assuming you missed your feeling to see that the child was terrified. Your interpersonal feelings did not let you see what you were doing. A lot of things were going on inside you, blinded you to see how your child was feeling. Martha, how do you feel about the evening you were trying to get her phone?

Martha: I was trying to get her phone because I thought she was going to call her Dad and he was going to take her away.

Mr. Dawson: I'm not sticking up for your Mom, but she was just going off her emotions because she was scared herself.

Mr. Dawson: Martha, how did your husband get thrown out of the house?

Martha: He had attempted suicide, and he said he was going to kill me, himself, my daughter, and my boyfriend.

Jennifer interrupts: That's not true, Mom! I read the papers, and that is not what you wrote down and signed, Mom.

Mr. Dawson: Martha, what action was taken by the Police and what was said in the divorce papers? I would like to see them. Why he was not arrested and put into a state mental institution?

Martha: He had many suicide attempts.

Jennifer: (Crying very hard): That's not true!

Martha: Five, six, seven, there were so many Jennifer that you don't know about.

Jennifer: You're a liar, Mom.

Mr. Dawson: I don't understand why the judge and police didn't do their job.

Martha: I'm still afraid of him to this day.

Jennifer: (Still crying) Mom, if you were so scared of Dad, then why would you drive all the way to Bridgeport under a restraining order and let me walk around with Dad? He even went in the back seat of your car to get his clothes. Why would you do that if you were so scared, Mom? Dad had plenty of opportunities to hurt you, and he never once tried anything! It doesn't make sense Mom, the facts don't fit.

Martha; I felt sorry for him.

Mr. Dawson: I think I know why your mother did that, because she makes poor choices. I think she makes them out of her feelings. She makes emotional choices trying to be a people pleaser to everyone. I think the courts should have checked your husband's counselors' credentials because I don't think your father is ok. Your Dad shouldn't have ended up with you, Jennifer. What do you think your father is going to do if he loses you to your mother?

Jennifer: I don't know.

Mr. Dawson; The court system didn't do their job, that is enough for tonight, but I have some fears that your father is not stable enough to take care of you, Jennifer.

Jennifer (cries harder!)I have been with my father for five months, and he's ok. This is not supposed to be about my Dad. Why won't everyone leave us alone? I want to be with my Dad!

Martha: I want what's best for you, Jennifer.

Jennifer: What's best for me is not throwing me out of the house.

Mr. Dawson: I just want to let everyone know I am neutral. You can go now, Jennifer.

What the hell was happening in there? What were they doing to my innocent daughter? What an insensitive bastard, attacking this child's father, a person he does not know. Praying on her emotions, he was like a Prairie dog attacking a young live wounded gazelle. Wild animals, I call them, as Martha was like a mother lioness eating her cub and spitting up lies. Five, six, seven, so many suicide attempts that Jennifer did know about. Wow, I was unaware of so many myself as Martha was writing her own fictional book in her twisted mind. However, she was missing one thing, her outline or confusing synopsis taken from several chapters she has not yet written.

Jennifer and I went on our vacation to Michigan with our close friends. This was the best thing for Jennifer as well as me. It was our first family vacation since this all started. Jennifer went tubing, swimming, rode on the wave runners, and took pontoon boat rides with her Pa and Gram, her cousins, and our close friends. The only thing on her mind was fun except for the fact that Martha said she was going to call Jennifer every day. Jennifer said, "Why Mom, you want to look like a good mother in front of our friends and family." Martha would not call every day. I actually made Jennifer call her because we were out of state, and I didn't want Martha claiming she could not get a hold of Jennifer. As for me, I enjoyed fishing, did some writing, and hung out with everyone. It was very relaxing for a change. It went by too fast.

Other games fell on nights of counseling, and Jennifer and I were forced to leave only a half-hour into the game. Martha showed up about ten minutes before we left. Jennifer and I started leaving the games the second Martha arrived. One of these games, as Jennifer and I were leaving, her coaches asked,

"Jennifer, why do you have to leave so early on certain games?"

Jennifer shouted loudly for everyone to hear, and pointed at Martha, and said, "Because of her!" Martha looked on and showed no emotion whatsoever. She would even smile when people looked at her.

On one evening, Jennifer and I were leaving a night game. We were walking along a dark path poorly lighted because of many towering trees blocking the light. We were carrying bats and gloves, and I had my arm around Jennifer's shoulder. We were walking slowly down the path, talking and joking. There was a man walking in our direction. I thought nothing of it as there was still a game going on in the field this man was headed for. As the man was passing by us, he walked toward my side of the sidewalk. Then all of a sudden, he bumped into me with his shoulder, leaned toward my ear, and said, "Back off of the custody!" He moved away quickly as I turned around and yelled," What the hell did you say? Come back here and say it to my face! Who the hell are you? I'll kick your ass!" He kept walking away at a fast pace and disappeared into the dark trees of the park. I turned and looked at Jennifer. Her mouth was wide open as she was shocked at what just happened. "Where did that guy come from Dad? Who is he?

"I have no Idea Jenn, but we know who sent him."

"Yeah, he is probably one of Mom's cop friends."

"I wouldn't doubt it, Jenn, but he doesn't scare me!"

Although Jennifer was scared for a moment, she knew I would always protect her and that I was not afraid to fight anyone. Martha could have her thug friends threaten me all she wanted, but they were tough because of a badge; I was tough because of my fists. I was not afraid of them arresting me for something they might create in their mind; they were Chicago police who had no jurisdiction here. However, I was afraid of what they might do if they caught me in Chicago. At this point, there was no telling how far Martha might go.

It was Thursday and session eight. We pulled up to the house, set the recorder, and it said "full, cannot record." I could not erase what was on it because I didn't transfer it to something else or write down what was said. I was upset, and we were out of time. I would not be able to record that session. I walked into Mr. Dawson's house with Jennifer. I saw Mr. Dawson, and I said, "Can I ask you a question?"

He said, "Sure."

I asked, "Is there any way my daughter can play softball and have counseling another day instead of Thursday?"

Mr. Dawson said, "I talked to Jennifer's attorney and told her I'm all booked up. That's just the way it is."

I turned my head and walked out of the house. I took a ride to buy another recorder because I did not want to miss the next session with Martha there. I pull up just in time for Jennifer to get her 5-minute break. She jumps into the car, we hit record, and Jennifer put it under her shirt. We talked a bit, and Martha pulled into Mr. Dawson's driveway. Jennifer waited until Martha was inside before going in herself.

The session.

Mr. Dawson: Does your Dad have the air conditioning on in his car?

Jennifer: I don't know.

Mr. Dawson: Martha, what's on your mind?

Martha: Jennifer, why did you leave your baseball game early?

Jennifer: Because, we had to come here and you showed up.

Martha: Well, you could have played 15 more minutes.

Jennifer: Dad had to get gas.

Mr. Dawson: Why don't you want your Mom at any of your games?

Jennifer: I don't feel comfortable when she's around, and the last game she came to, she walked right past my Dad and gave him a dirty look in front of everyone and then went and sat by her friends, and my Dad didn't do anything.

Mr. Dawson: It almost seems that you want to protect your Dad for whatever your Mom does to him. What's that about?

Jennifer: My Mom's behavior in public is childish and embarrassing.

Mr. Dawson: Protecting your Dad! Jennifer, express your feelings toward your mother.

Jennifer: Well, I would like my Mom to own up to everything, especially kicking me out of the house.

Martha: Jennifer, if I could take that day back I would. I didn't kick you out of the house, I said go with your father. Jennifer I don't get to see you; I have to go to your school activities, music, sports just to see you.

Jennifer: Mom, you did not go to one badminton game.

Martha: Well, they start at 4:30, and I get out of work at 5.

Jennifer: They don't last a half-hour, Mom.

Martha: You didn't tell me about your games, Jennifer.

Jennifer: Oh well, Mom, if you were letting me go with Dad, then why are you fighting for custody.

Martha: I'm looking out for your best interest Jennifer.

Jennifer: Throwing your child out isn't in my best interest, Mom.

(The room is quiet for a few seconds.)

Mr. Dawson: Martha, you told me on the phone you could see why Jennifer thinks she was kicked out.

Martha: Because of the way I said it. Jennifer, for that you don't see me for 5 months.

Jennifer: It's not just that Mom, it's the way you treated me the entire time I was with you, like the time when you came into my room, and you asked me, why do you have a picture of your Dad and me, and I said it's my family.

Martha: I didn't want to give you false hopes.

Jennifer: You took the picture frame and were selling it in a garage sale, and I took it from the sale, and it was in my room for a month, Mom.

Mr. Dawson: She was just trying to tell you the marriage was over. You need to understand that the marriage is over, and you need to accept that. You can go now, Jennifer.

Session 9, Everything went as usual, we set the recorder a block away, pulled up in front of Mr. Dawson's house, and Jennifer went in.

Mr. Dawson: Come on in, Jennifer. I just want to let you know your Mom tells me everything. Jennifer, pretend I'm a judge, and your Mom is in the courtroom. Is that person your Mom over there?

Jennifer: what?

Mr. Dawson: Pretend that's your Mom sitting there. Is that your Mom?

Jennifer: Yes.

Mr. Dawson: Did your Mom kick you out?

Jennifer: Yes.

Mr. Dawson: Should I send her to jail?

Jennifer: Yes.

Mr. Dawson: Why?

Jennifer: Well it's a crime to throw your underage kid into the street.

Mr. Dawson how many years should I put her in jail for?

Jennifer: They probably wouldn't ask me that.

Mr. Dawson: I can. I'm the judge.

Jennifer: I don't know.

Mr. Dawson: Did she kick you out with her foot or push you out the door?

Jennifer: No, she told me to get out.

Mr. Dawson: She didn't kick you out; you walked out with your own two feet. You have to prove she kicked you out. Jennifer, you were mad at your Mom, and you knew your Dad was coming, and you argued with your Mom because you knew you wanted to leave and your Mom was upset because of that, so she just said go, go with your father. She didn't throw you out.

Jennifer: Yes, she did!

Mr. Dawson: No, she didn't!

Jennifer: Yes, she did!

Mr. Dawson: No, she didn't. How many years would you give your Mom?

Jennifer: About two.

Mr. Dawson: You would put your Mom in jail? You know you will have to live with yourself.

Jennifer: Yeah.

Mr. Dawson: You're the one who is going to suffer later on.

Mr. Dawson: Should your Mom be put in jail for making mistakes? It would solve all your problems, and then your Dad would have you for sure because your Mom would be out of the way, right!

Jennifer: I guess I don't know.

Mr. Dawson: What is your attorney supposed to be doing for you?

Jennifer: I guess help me.

Mr. Dawson: When is the next court date?

Jennifer: I don't know.

Mr. Dawson: Jennifer, your Mom was insane; that's why she did what she has done. Insane people don't know what they are doing. She was sick, that's why she came to me for help. Repeat what this session is about, Jennifer.

Jennifer: That my Mom was insane, and she is sick.

Mr. Dawson: Ok, you can go now.

At this point, it was clear as day the intentions of this abusive counselor. I was so angry that this was actually happening to my innocent daughter. Jennifer's attorney was doing nothing to protect the child for which the court system appointed her to protect. I had contacted an attorney that my cousin referred me to. It was a woman. I told her about the taped counseling sessions, and she said I would not be able to use the tapes in court and that they are illegal. I said, "Child abuse is illegal, that this grown man is interrogating my daughter and mentally and emotionally abusing my daughter, her mother joining in at times. She cries every session; what are my daughter's rights?"

She said, "There is really nothing I could do to prove it. You and Jennifer should be living in the house. Martha should be paying child support as well as maintenance."

"Well, thanks for the advice but, I do not have the money to hire you."

"Tom, Martha will get to see her daughter."

I did not want to use any attorney that felt Jennifer should see her abuser.

At this point, I decided to take Jennifer to the police and report Mr. Dawson. We went to the Countryside Police Station and asked if we could speak to an officer in private. Jennifer and I went into a room with a female officer. I told her about Mr. Dawson and about my whole situation. The officer said there was nothing she could do and that we had to prove abuse, and even if we did, it was in the court's hands. She looked over at Jennifer and asked if this was true. Jennifer said yes. She advised Jennifer to keep a journal on what was happening at the counseling sessions to use them in court. Jennifer and I walked out of the police station and went home. Jennifer started writing her journal using the tapes at times to recall some things that happened.

Now that work was very busy, and Martha warned Jennifer about residing in the school district, we were continuously searching for apartments. I needed to be in the district by August 27, so Jennifer could attend her high school. Martha was hoping that I would fail to do so.

On July 25, I found an apartment that was in a small town next to our neighborhood. It was Hodgkin's Illinois. Jennifer and I knew many people in that town. It was like a sister neighborhood to Countryside. With heat and electricity included, it was five hundred and fifty dollars a month. It was a white house that stood on a hill with a small bar and grill to one side and several empty lots on the other side. To enter the apartment, you had to go through the backyard and up a steel spiral staircase onto a flat roof to the door. It was an attic apartment without any bedrooms but contained a large front room. It had a small kitchenette, a walk-in closet, and a very nice bathroom. It was a great hideout for Jennifer and me. This was all I could afford because of a variety of bills and no help from Martha. By staying with my mother, I was able to save up enough money for the security deposit. My mother was sad to see us go because she had developed a special bond with Jennifer. She understood that it was imperative that we moved back to our old neighborhood. The building manager gave us the keys right away to allow us to start moving our belongings in. We were set to be fully moved in by August 1. Jennifer and I were excited to move back to the suburbs. Jennifer's friends were right down the road, and the bus stop for school was within two blocks. As for me, my job was less than a mile away. The apartment was not much, but it was a start in the right direction. I informed Martha that I would have Jennifer in the school district, but I would not give her our address.

July 25, 2006 court date, I brought Jennifer's journal, the definition of conflict of interest, and phone records of Martha's calls to Jennifer for the past 5 months. This was the first court date that I was representing myself.

I walked into the courtroom, went up to the clerk to check in, and went to the back to sit down. Rachel Davis entered the courtroom. She walked past me and sat by Martha's attorney and Martha. She was talking to Martha, often whispering and smiling. I was sitting alone, and she never approached me unless I called her over. Nor did she ever look in my direction.

When they called our last name to approach the judge, I was ready with evidence. I started for once. I said, "Your Honor, I would like counseling for Jennifer stopped; I have the definition for a conflict of interest. This counselor is abusing my child. All they talk about in counseling is court-related things. It is supposed to be about the mother and daughter getting along. Martha knows this man, and he is abusing my daughter to gain custody for Martha."

Judge Nobal said, you mean to tell me that you think a counselor paid by insurance is trying to help your wife because of money."

I said, "Yes, he stated the first time I've met him that he believes the child should be with the mother. That is a conflict of interest."

The judge said, "I do not believe that."

I said, "They will not let my daughter play softball."

The judge said, "She should be in counseling and not playing softball."

I boldly stated, "I have a journal that my daughter has kept on what was going on at those sessions. The counselor told my daughter if she did not cooperate with his treatment, then her Dad will go to jail."

"Mr. Frawley, you mean to tell me your daughter was taking notes while the counselor is taking notes. Why would she do that?"

I replied, "A police officer told her to do that."

The judge said, "You went to the police, why would you do that?"

I said, "Because my daughter is being abused by this counselor."

"Do you have proof?" She asked.

I paused for a moment; I wanted to say it, I wanted to say it so bad that I have recordings of what this bastard did to my daughter, but deep down, I knew I would be punished.

"My daughter's journal is my proof. Don't you want to see it?"

"No," the Judge replied, "She is just a teenager. We know how they can be," as she looked toward Martha. She looked back at me and said with an angry voice, "Let me tell you something. In the end, who do you think will have the final say, me or the police officer?"

I said, "You, your honor!"

She turned to the court reporter and said, "Swear Martha in."

She then turned to Martha and said, "Raise your right hand, do you swear to tell the truth and nothing but the truth so help you, god?'

Martha said, "Yes."

The judge asked, "Did you know this counselor prior to the sessions with your child?"

Martha, "Well I. . ." Martha was stuttering.

The Judge asked again, "Did you know this counselor prior to the sessions with the child?"

Martha said, "No."

The judge turned to Jennifer's attorney Mrs. Davis and asked, "What do you think about all this?"

Mrs. Davis replied, "I've talked to the counselor, and he said that's not true."

Mr. Burnburg stepped in, "Your Honor, We request the court issue a restraining order against Mr. Frawley, keeping him from entering the counselor's home."

I jumped in and said, "I never enter Mr. Dawson's house. I always wait outside in my car."

The judge said, "Mr. Frawley, I am granting the restraining order against you."

The request was granted. Court was over.

On the way out of the courtroom, I stopped Mrs. Davis. I said, "Do you want to at least read Jennifer's journal?" as I was handing them to her.

She glanced down at the papers, looked back at me, and said, "Mail them to my office."

I replied, "Do you have an email address?"

"Mail them to my office," she replied as she turned and walked away.

I never sent the papers. At this point, I did not trust Rachel. I was glad she did not take the journal. I did not want her to know how much I knew of what was going on in the counseling sessions.

The Court Order.

IN THE CIRCUIT COURT OF COOK COUNTY, ILLINOIS

Martha Frawley__________________

Petitioner

V.

Thomas Frawley_________________

Respondent

ORDER

This cause coming to be heard for status Thomas Frawley appearing pro se, Martha Frawley present with counsel and the child's representative present and the court going fully advised in the promises wherefore it is hereby ordered that,

1 By appeasement Thomas Frawley shall not enter the location where John Dawson conducts therapy with the minor child, Jennifer Frawley.

2. Neither parent shall discuss in any fashion, including but not limited to advising notes, letters or memorandum, any of the issues discussed by Jennifer Frawley in therapy with John Dawson.

3. This matter is continued for status to August 28, 2006, at 9:30 AM without further notice.

Entered:

Dated: ____7/25/06___________

Judge Mary Nobal

Judge JUL 25 2006________

Circuit Court -****

Session 10, Mr. Dawson, arrogant, intimidating, authoritative

Mr. Dawson: (Coughing and clearing his throat) Gosh, sometimes it's like ha, ha, ha come on, are you ever going to go away. Ha, ha you know!

I'm glad we are here tonight together because I want to clear the air on a couple of things that are troubling to me. It's troubling to me. In addition, it's the court, the court communicates to me, Jennifer. I'm aware of what goes on in court. So when we talk about the judge, the attorneys, you know, Uh your Dad, and whoever else is there, I know what's going on! And it's because I'm the court-appointed counselor and it's good for me to know what's going on. I know who the players are; you know what I mean. Why don't you feed that back to me?

Jennifer: Uh, the court tells you what's going on.

Mr. Dawson: Right! And I know who the players are. What does that mean to you? Jennifer: Uh!

Mr. Dawson: Who is involved, like the players on your team, you know, the players on your team? Ok, I want you to help me with this now because I need clarity, because I thought you and I had an understanding. Uh, and I can tell you where the feeling level is coming from, you know, I was telling you that I was upset. I am upset! I'm upset for another reason. When I have somebody in here. I know trust is something you build upon. It comes after a while, but people, when they walk through that door and sit down. They sit down on the couch. I'm assuming they trust me a little bit. Otherwise, they wouldn't come into my house and come into a room with me by myself, you know. You know what I mean! There has to be a level of trust! Something! They trust me. Hmmm. But when that trust is broken. Trust is very important to me, and I think that, that, that trust, um when my trust has been broken, I realize that maybe something was said or done that I wasn't aware of. Something that was done, I was not even aware of it. That hurts!

It really hurts! I want to ask you something. When I, when I talked about how if the, how do you understand my relationship with your attorney and how I report to her about how you are doing in treatment. How do you understand that?

Jennifer: What do you mean?

Mr. Dawson: Well, what am I supposed to do if your lawyer, the one that's representing you, calls up, and she goes, hey, how's Jennifer doing? What am I supposed to do?

Jennifer: Tell her!

Mr. Dawson: And tell her what?

Jennifer: How am I doing?

Mr. Dawson: And what would that mean?

Jennifer: I don't know.

Mr. Dawson: Well, like when I ask you to, have you read that book yet?

Jennifer: No.

Mr. Dawson: Is that part of your treatment?

Jennifer: Uh Yeah, I guess!

Mr. Dawson: It is! This is yours, your file. That's right, oh! And by the way, billing! Excuse me for a second (looking at Martha) the way I am billing. I can't bill for the same person twice on the same day!

Martha: Ok!

Mr. Dawson: So had to go on to yours; that's why I pulled this chart here. So I'm going to pull your chart, Jennifer.

So if I'm supposed to, if your attorney calls anytime, what's her name?

Jennifer: Rachel.

Mr. Dawson: Rachel! If Rachel ever calls me, I have to report on how things are going in terms of family conflicts and um, are you motivated and uh, are you continuing to argue and or communicate with your mother, you know! Are you doing that um, are you following my recommendations? What do you think I have to say?

Jennifer: No.

Mr. Dawson: No, ok! Is that threatening to you?

Jennifer: Um no!

Mr. Dawson: Have you ever felt that at any one time in here like I threatened you with, I'm going to tell your attorney and your Dad's going to get in trouble?

Jennifer: Yeah

Mr. Dawson: You felt that was.

Jennifer: Yeah

Mr. Dawson: Ok let's clear the air on that; how did that happen? Tell me how you understood it!

Jennifer: Um,

Mr. Dawson: I keep asking you to feed it back to me because I don't know what your thinking is.

Jennifer: You said that if I, well I understand, but you said if I wasn't cooperating or something, you would tell the judge, and that could lead to my Dad getting in trouble.

Mr. Dawson: Ok, I'll tell you, I'm going to go back to what I said, and I'm going to say it in front of your Mom. We had a discussion about your failure to come to treatment for thirty days. Remember that? And I asked you who made the decision and you said well I did. You said you did. Then I said, If you're making decisions not to come to treatment, you're putting your Dad at risk because they'd had him in court, and he would be held in contempt. Contempt means to make them angry. And you would have to suffer the consequences. That's what I said to her. I never once said that if you didn't cooperate, he'd go to jail.

Jennifer: Well, no, you didn't say that.

Mr. Dawson: Huh

Jennifer: You didn't say that he'd go to jail, but you said my Dad could get in trouble.

(Jennifer told me that Mr. Dawson was reading from a notebook that she recognized to be Martha's)

Mr. Dawson: I'm going to read to you what was said in court. This was said by your Dad. The counselor is threatening you to listen, or she'll be in trouble, and I will go to jail. Your father said that!

Jennifer: Okay, well, you did say that I could get in trouble and he could get in trouble and last time, the contempt of court happened he could have gone to jail, so that's where that would play in.

Mr. Dawson: Well, not because you weren't cooperating with me because he wasn't cooperating with the judge.

Jennifer: Before, you said that if I don't cooperate with what I'm supposed to do or work with the treatment that I can get in trouble for it too.

Mr. Dawson: And what does that mean, get in trouble?

Jennifer: I don't know. Well, like, I don't know what happened, but.

Mr. Dawson: By those consequences, I don't know what those consequences might be, but would there be consequences?

Jennifer: Maybe

Mr. Dawson: So you think you should be aware of that. I mean, you could be doing something for yourself. And could it have been said out of kindness and not to be scary or threaten you or control you.

Jennifer: I guess.

Mr. Dawson: What do you think, Mom?

Martha: Um and Jennifer, you know when your Dad wasn't coming, bringing you to counseling, that was your choice for not wanting to come, and your Dad was letting you choose not to come and not bring you, and that's when you could get him in trouble.

Mr. Dawson: With who?

Martha: With the courts.

Mr. Dawson: Do I have any, any control if your husband goes to jail?

Martha: No

Mr. Dawson: Who makes that decision?

Martha: The courts and the attorneys.

Mr. Dawson: And how do they make that decision, based on what criteria?

Martha: If he is bringing Jennifer to counseling or not because it was a court order.

Mr. Dawson: So that's the truth, and I want you to hear the truth. That's it. And if your attorney calls me and says if you're not coop.... you know if she asks me well how she is doing, I'm going to be kind, I'm gonna say well we're trying to address this, this, this, and this. Here's the treatment plan and if she gets a release of information, I would give the treatment over to her. She's gonna see it's factual. Ok, feed it back to me.

Jennifer: Feed what back?

Mr. Dawson: What we said. Your Mom said, and I said. (Cough)

Jennifer: Well, that it was that my Dad could have gotten in trouble for what I decided to do.

Mr. Dawson: What you decided to do, not what I decided to do because I wasn't bringing you here. Do you see what I mean?

Jennifer: Yeah, kind of.

Mr. Dawson: Well what don't you get? I want you to get it because I don't want to go through this again. I don't want to go down this road again. I want you to get it. What kind of power do I have with your father?

Jennifer: I don't know.

Mr. Dawson: Do I have any?

Jennifer: No.

Mr. Dawson: I mean, I don't; I'm a counselor. Ok

Martha: Let me add a little bit more to that. Can I?

Mr. Dawson: Sure.

Martha: Your Dad wanted a counselor for you so you would have a voice. So getting, I'm sorry not a counselor, an attorney for you, so he got an attorney for you so that you follow her advice. And you're not following her advice through the courts. She's the one that recommended the counseling. And you refused to go to counseling, and that's why the attempt came into place, Jennifer. Because you refused to go to counseling. So we're paying an attorney to help advice you, and she's there for you to talk to you anytime. And she might not be available all day, every day, Jennifer, because she's in court and she has other clients. You can call her anytime you want.

Jennifer: I do call her anytime, and she doesn't return my phone calls.

Martha: Well, do you want me to give her a call and let her know to call you?

Jennifer: No

Martha: Why?

Jennifer: Cause I'm handling it.

Martha: But you just said she's not returning your calls.

Jennifer: She didn't; all of a sudden, she does, but.

Martha: Ok. If there is something I can do for you, Jennifer, I'm here for you.

(Pause)

Martha: The only thing she asks you to do is call me every day and tell me what's going on.

Jennifer: She never said that. She didn't tell me that.

Martha: You told me the reason you were calling me before was that she told you to call me every day.

Jennifer: Yeah, she told me that I should call you, and that, or we should be talking or whatever. And then you would call me too. Funny, you want to talk to me so much and care about me so much; you haven't called in what, about almost three weeks now? Yet you say you can't get a hold of me, and you don't even try.

Martha: I would get a hold of you every day if you would give me your phone number to get a hold of you.

Jennifer: You have it.

Martha: Calling your Dad's number

Jennifer: You, you have it,

Martha: Having your Dads. . .

Jennifer: But wait wait wait! When you were calling me three weeks ago, and you were calling me on that phone number. Was I talking to you?

Martha: I'd leave a message for you. . .

Jennifer: No, No, No! Wait No, No, No! Was I talking to you? Did I answer the phone?

Martha: Ah

Jennifer: Did I, wait, will you just answer the question? Did I answer the phone? Yes, I did!

Martha: Sometimes you called me, and sometimes you didn't.

Jennifer: Ok, but most of the time I answered the phone, did I not.

Martha: No!

Jennifer: Yes!

Martha: You let it go into voicemail:

Jennifer: No, Yes I did! And then you say in court because you were like Jennifer, I can't get a hold of you, Dad's not letting me talk to you.

Martha: I don't have a direct line to you, Jennifer.

Jennifer: I answered your phone calls. Yeah, my phone too. I answered your phone calls. But like I said, you were saying you can't get a hold of me, (Sarcastic) Oh, I need to talk to my child. I care about her, then why is it that you haven't even called in three weeks?

Martha: John, do you want me to address that one?

Mr. Dawson: Yeah, go ahead.

Martha: I talked to him about how our conversations were, that you weren't talking to me about anything, and I always have to leave messages on your Dad's phone for you to get back to me.

Jennifer: No, you don't always have to leave messages; that's why I answer your phone calls. Once in a while, yes, you have to leave a message because Dad will have his phone that day.

Martha: John and I talked about it, we decided I wouldn't call you. I would wait for you to call me.

Jennifer: Well, I'm not going to call you, so keep waiting.

Martha: So tonight, we decided I'll start calling you again.

Jennifer: Well, have fun. It doesn't mean I'm gonna talk! Yea now, I'm not going to answer the phone. I did it before, exactly like you said my attorney advised me to. I'm in counseling now, something that you wanted whatever, and I'm not, I don't want to talk to you now so I'm not going to.

Martha: What do you think the whole plan of this is Jennifer?

Jennifer: I didn't want it! Doesn't mean it's going to happen or it's gonna help!

Martha: Why not?

Jennifer: Because I don't want to talk to you!

Martha: What, you have to get your anger out, and the only thing is to talk about it, Jennifer.

Jennifer: Yeah, but you just keep lying, so I'm just wasting my breath.

Mr. Dawson: Ok the second thing I want to ask and we'll get back to this, the second thing is uh, tell me about the trip to the police department.

Jennifer: When?

Mr. Dawson: Did you go to the police department with your Dad?

Jennifer: Recently?

Mr. Dawson: Last month, last thirty days

Jennifer: Yeah

Mr. Dawson: Tell me about it!

Jennifer: To see what I should do. Like um, Yeah, to see what I should do. Like she advised me, and my Dad told her what was going on, and I was put into counseling and stuff and that I didn't agree with it, and that I felt you were backing my Mom and stuff, and she told me to write down a journal and that's what I did.

Mr. Dawson: Is that all you have to say about the trip to the police officer, the police department.

Martha: What would make you go to the police?

Mr. Dawson: Yeaah!

Jennifer: Um well, like, I said she wasn't answering my phone calls, she wasn't answering my phone calls, and then so that's why we went there! Who else am I supposed to talk to! They know the law and everything, so that's why I asked them. I got advice from a police officer. Because my attorney wouldn't answer my phone calls. Simple as that!

Mr. Dawson......Ok....... . That's not what was said in court.

Jennifer: What was said in court?

Mr. Dawson: See, we're talking about everybody being dishonest with each other, ok! Both sides alright. Pointing the fingers at, this one's lying, this one's lying, this one's lying! And everybody needs to get honest. I took, this is your Dad! I took her to the police because the counselor threatened her, and the police advised her to write down what was talked about in the sessions.

Jennifer: Saying Yeah Saying that

Mr. Dawson: You told the police officer that I threatened you.

Jennifer: I said that you were backing up my Mom and changing my story around and telling me that I would get in trouble if I didn't cooperate and that the court or that I'd have to deal with the courts and look bad on my Dad and me. Yea that's what, (loudly) I'm telling you what happened!

Mr. Dawson: You felt threatened.

Martha: Threatened, Jennifer!

Jennifer: (loudly) Yeah Threatening saying that I could get in trouble, that's a threat! .... If I say, Mom, you better do this, or you're gonna get in trouble by someone, that's a threat!

Mr. Dawson: That's a consequence, threatening is like, I hold all this power over your head, and you better do it.

Jennifer: Yeah, you do! You basically hold what goes on in my hands because whatever you say to the judge, is what the judge is gonna reflect back on us.

Martha: On us?

Jennifer: Yeah, me, you, Dad!

Martha: Jennifer, this counseling is all about me and you getting back to how...

Jennifer (shouts) Yeah and it's not going to happen! It's not going to happen Mom! Ok, I don't understand why you don't understand that, but no matter what anyone says to me, I don't mean to be mean or like offend you in any way, like I'm just, but whatever somebody says, what the judge does, if she gives custody to you or whatever. It doesn't mean that, that's what I'm going to do! It doesn't, you know, she doesn't control what I do. She can't make me talk to you......she can't make me love you! And that's too bad!

Mr. Dawson: On a personal level here, I care about you, and I have been working very hard to help you. Not to win, not to lose, not to get custody. And when you use those words, without even passing it by me. I care about you, and when you use those words, you hurt me.

Jennifer: What words?

Mr. Dawson: Threatened! And when you went to somebody. You went to the police, you or somebody went to the police. You hurt me. I'm trying to help you! Now how can I trust you?

Jennifer: (Loudly) by backing my Mom, and telling me what happened. And that doesn't hurt me!

Mr. Dawson: If we have a relationship, you need to be open with me so I can just clear it up....... Not try to hurt me; you hurt me! You know, unnecessarily.........It's not about winning in court. They're not going to look to me to say whether you go with your Mom or your Dad. They're not going to ask me that. You came here for counseling. Your attorney is probably going to call me up and say, write something up and tell me how she is doing. What she does with it, I don't know.... I don't know! ...Not at all...

So if you hurt me, or if you did hurt me, what am I supposed to feel now? Am I supposed to trust you? Huh?

Jennifer: It's up to you.

Mr. Dawson: You don't trust your Mom.

Jennifer: Ok.

Mr. Dawson: Right! Should I have that same kind of approach that you have?

Jennifer: If you want.

Mr. Dawson: Is it healthy? Is it?

Jennifer: No, but I guess not but

Mr. Dawson: If it isn't healthy for me, then it's not healthy for you to do that. I'm not gonna do that; I'm not going to mistrust you. You're 14, and you're in the middle of a battle between your Mom and your Dad, and somebody is trying to win, and I think I know who it is. And you're 14. And the things that were said here were confidential. Not to be shared with anybody outside this room unless the court asked for it. That's personal. And if you think. If you have any kind of feelings about what I am doing specifically and did you read the client rights, the confidentiality? Did you read that? It says you have a right to ask me! You have a right to ask me about anything. You have a right to express your feelings. I had you sign off on a document that says you can tell me that I'm uncomfortable with that question. You have a right to that.................This has nothing to do with you or anybody. . . The hurt is there, the hurt is there! And I'm going to forgive, I'm going to try to let go of it, but if this happens again, if someone makes liable comments about me, I will take action! Because it could have hurt me in the community, it could have hurt me. And there was no justification, there was no reason for it.... . Feedback to me what I said.

Jennifer: I don't know.

Mr. Dawson: Huh! What did I say?. . . . .

Martha: Jennifer, Threatened is a harsh word. And if you didn't like what was said, it's one thing. But if you were at school and you got into an argument with one of your friends, and they threatened you! That's an issue. But if they just said, Jennifer, I don't like you anymore. I don't want to talk to you anymore; I don't want to hear that; that's different. I don't want to listen to what you say, but if someone threatens you. What do you think the school would do? Or if you threatened somebody else. Or if somebody went to the principal and said Jennifer threatened me, you would be kicked out of school, or they would do something to you. Wouldn't they? What would they do?

Jennifer: Not necessarily, not if they don't have, well, they might ask me what happened. But that's, Mom, that's totally different no one said, oh I don't like you, it's not that

Martha: If you don't like what was said or you don't like the questions that were asked

Jennifer: Yeah, that's different than saying I don't like you. Totally different story.

Martha: Well, I'm trying to use a drastic comparison to the word threatened.

Jennifer: I know what threatened is!

Martha: Do you feel threatened in here?

Mr. Dawson: I need to know that.

Jennifer: Well Yeah

Martha: In what way?

Mr. Dawson: Yeah

Jennifer: (Frustrated) I already told you.

Mr. Dawson: That I could hurt you and your father in this custody battle. Is that what you're saying?

Jennifer: Yeah!

Mr. Dawson: how?

Jennifer: If you, I don't know, but it's what you said! You didn't basically, well kind of, you said if you don't cooperate that it will look bad on my Dad and me because it's up to you what you say. You said the court is gonna want feedback on what goes on, and you're gonna have to tell them. And if you have to say I don't cooperate or whatever, it's gonna look bad on my Dad and me, and we could get in trouble and there could be consequences to us, so yeah, that's a threat!

Mr. Dawson: Well, it's a fact; it's not a threat. I mean, I was sharing it with you to try and keep you going, like, ok, let's get real, let's get going on your treatment plan, quit resisting, that's a fact, that's not a threat! I will do it! It's not a threat; I'm obligated to it. I'm a court-appointed counselor! I have to be honest with them. I can't lie to them.

Jennifer: I'm not saying to lie.

Mr. Dawson: Well it's not a threat, it's a fact! Listen to this. (Clearing throat) You have the right to express your discomfort with me or with anything I say. Or deny answering any questions posed in the process of an assessment or therapy.

Martha: Honestly, do you want this to drag on and on and on and on for months and months and months?

Jennifer: What to drag on?

Martha: Counseling and, and, and all of this stuff, or do you want to get along and talk?

Jennifer: (Angrily) No, I don't want to get along with you and that's the end of it! It's not going to happen!

Martha: And that's why counseling is going to continue.

Jennifer: Nuuuuuu well, let counseling continue, I'm not paying for it. You are, so I guess you want to talk about

Martha: Me and Dad are.

Jennifer: Ok Dad is but, you say that you don't have money and that this was all because of money or whatever, funny you're spending a lot of it!

Martha: That's for you

Jennifer: Yeah well, continue Mom, be my guest. Doesn't mean everything is going to work out the way you want.

Martha: No, I'm sure, I don't know how anything is going to work out. That's all up to the judge.

Jennifer: Well then, I'm telling you ahead of time you're wasting your money because it's not, I'm not going to change my mind.

Mr. Dawson: Ok do we got this all cleared up now. Are you all clear about where I stand? Not threats, its facts. I'm obligated to answer, if they subpoena me to court or they ask me to write up anything, I'm going to write up what's been going on. Not a threat. Now you can choose to feel that way but I would, and you're a child, you're 14 years old. I would hesitate to say to any adult that distorts anything I say, I would hesitate to say that they need to be very careful and what they say about me. And it's not to you because you're 14. Because I'm not going to let my business or me or my license be threatened, that is a threat! When somebody takes a word that I say, takes something and distorts it, and turns it into something that isn't so that they can try to gain control over whatever they are trying to gain control over, I will not let that happen! No professional would.

Martha: And I don't even know what else that threat meant because your Dad called me up and said he's going to have John and me thrown in jail because of a threat.

Mr. Dawson: Did you know that?

Martha: Now, did I threaten you in any way? Why would your Dad say that to me?

Jennifer: Wait, what happened? What did you say?

Martha: He called me up and said if I keep it up, he is gonna have me thrown in jail, and John because we're threatening you in here. What am I doing to you, Jennifer, to threaten you in here? Am I doing anything to threaten you in here?

Mr. Dawson: Yeah, what is your Mom doing?

Jennifer: No.

Martha: I don't know what that was all about.

Jennifer: I don't know that that happened but....

Mr. Dawson: Well, see that's what I'm saying. I mean it's like these emotions are getting way out of control.

Jennifer: Well, but another thing, how am I supposed to believe that really happened when she lied about other stuff like that to get my Dad in trouble? How am I supposed to believe that really happened? She's lied about so many other things, and, like, about me and other things that I can't believe what she's saying right now really happened. So, just like....

Martha: How can you make that up?

Jennifer: But just like how could you make something like Dad was gonna kill me, made up?

(Silence)

Jennifer: Yeah, good question.

Martha: I was afraid that your Dad might do something, and I didn't know what he was capable of.

Jennifer: Mom, ok. Hold on, I'm not gonna argue, but like I said before, in the paper or you said, what happened. You said that Dad called you and told you that he threatened to kill me, you, and Todd right. Is that what happened?

Martha: To a degree.

Jennifer: Yes or no? What is to a degree? What do you mean to a degree?

Martha: Yeah

Jennifer: Ok so that happened; he told me that. Then why....

Mr. Dawson: Did you believe that his intent was to do that?

Martha: I didn't know what his intent was.

Jennifer: Ok, but....

Martha: He was saying so many things.

Jennifer: Ok, but now you heard her say that he actually told her that in a phone call.

Mr. Dawson: She said yes, she just said yes.

Jennifer: Yeah. Now in the paper, she wrote, "I feel or I believe that he might" he didn't tell her in the paper...

Martha: Uh

Jennifer: Ok wait, can I talk for a second? If she was that scared and he really told her that, she would have put 'Tom told me or threatened me on the phone that this was gonna happen.' Now she said that he was gonna supposedly kill me, her, and her boyfriend, but in the papers, she wrote, I believe he may harm not only me but my daughter.

Martha: Right.

Jennifer: May harm, I believe, so she thinks, that's what she wrote in the paper, she thinks that might happen.

Martha: Right.

Jennifer: Then why did you just say that he told you that? Think and told are two different things. You actually heard it, or you thought it might happen.

Martha: If I can't have you, nobody can.

Jennifer: Mom, where do I come in?

Martha: Jennifer, that's what I didn't know what he was capable of.

Jennifer: Ok but wait, ok she believed it, so now she believes it, there's a lie right there. Two minutes have gone by. First, he told her that! Now she believes it. She believed it might have happened. But then, yet in the paper, you didn't mention anything about your boyfriend. Why didn't you put that in?

Martha: It didn't have anything to do with him.

Jennifer: Oh, but you just said that he told you he was gonna kill him too.

Martha: That had nothing to do with it.

Jennifer: Why wasn't that mentioned in the paper then? Because you didn't want the courts to know that you had an affair isn't it?

Martha: Ha-ha...no.

Jennifer: Ok, ok.

Martha: Cause it's a domestic problem.

Jennifer: It doesn't matter but,

Martha: They don't put other people in the paper.

Jennifer: Ok, ok, whatever, but if that is true, why did you just say a couple minutes ago, and you even heard her, you agreed that you heard her, that she said he called her or if he called her or told her, whatever, that he spoke it. If somebody tells you something that means that, you actually heard them say those words. But now, in the paper and just a couple minutes after you clarified that, she felt it might have happened; she thought it. That's two different things.

Mr. Dawson: Wait a minute, ok.

Jennifer: So how am I supposed to believe that?

Mr. Dawson: Wait, wait, wait, wait, you're arguing; we're all under pressure right now in this room. We talked about something that was very upsetting. I'm upset, but I'm not as upset as I was a few minutes ago. And you're talking about an exact reporting and using the exact words like we're on trial, ok. But you're just as guilty as using the words I said and distorting them.

Jennifer: But I didn't distort anything ok, that's what I heard, but I said exactly what I heard. And I didn't change my story.

Mr. Dawson: You used the word threat.

Jennifer: Yeah that's what I felt, I felt threatened.

Mr. Dawson: Well, your mother felt threatened too.

Jennifer: Yeah, but there's a difference. You said those words to me, and I heard them. And I didn't change my story, I said that I heard them and that was that. I said exactly what happened, and I said the exact same story and I haven't changed my story, but yet first she heard them. She felt them or believed them, whatever and so there are two different stories. That's what I'm saying. How am I supposed to believe anything that comes out of her mouth if one little thing, a story that we are talking about, is two different stories when the conversation is happening all the time? If someone comes up to you and lies to you and then lies about something else, how do you believe what's the next thing they say? That's what I am trying to say, I can't believe what she is saying because of all the lies that happened.

Martha: Jennifer, when your Dad was on his killing spree! He was saying. . .

Jennifer: You act like there were 20, 30, Mom, twice!

Mr. Dawson: Let her finish!

Martha: when he was on his killing spree twice that you are aware of. One because he was removed from the house, and the other one was when he was committed. All the other times you don't know about!

Jennifer: Yeah ok.

Martha: Because that's something I didn't share with you. That's too much for a child

Jennifer: You shared everything else with me and told me all the details but that's not enough.

Martha: There was no way to get around not telling you why your Dad was removed from the house and why he was committed. He was saying a lot of things. Do I in my life ever think that he would hurt you? No! I. . .

Jennifer: Ok Mom, I don't mean to cut you off

Martha: Well then, let me finish.

Jennifer: Well, but this isn't what we're here for. We're not here for this, but I only brought that up to prove a point that you were lying and because that was brought up before, so yes, that's the only reason why I brought that up. And that is done with. Apparently, Dad's fine. He went to counseling and got help. (Starting to cry) Just like you said earlier, all those people that were in jail and did something terribly wrong. They still get to see their kids right! And be with their kids.

Mr. Dawson: They come there.

Jennifer: (starting to cry) Yeah exactly, so like that's done and over with. And he didn't do anything. Is he dead? Did he have a cut on him or something? No! And he's fine! And just like John said earlier, if you get the help or whatever, then you're able to be, Dad got the help!

Martha: So what about you? How come you're resisting the help here?

Jennifer: That's a different story.

Martha: No, it isn't.

Jennifer: Yes, it is!

Martha: No

Jennifer: No, it's a different story. That's a totally different story.

Martha: What's the story about then?

Jennifer: Because I don't want to talk to you and stuff, I have to talk to you.

Martha: Jennifer there's

Jennifer: There's a difference. I wanted to talk to my Dad. I wanted to be with my Dad……. I don't want to be with you, and I don't want to talk to you.

(Silence)

Mr. Dawson: Well, at least you're saying, you know she's communicating with you. It's not what's behind it, its anger and resentment; we talked about that.

Jennifer: Well I'm not going to change my mind, I'm just letting you know, but just like she stuck to her gun, I'm sticking to mine. Guess I did get something from you.

Martha: So what's that?

Jennifer: Sticking to what I think! And yeah, basically yeah, I guess I learned something from you, you don't change your mind and guess what, neither am I. So I guess that I don't know.

(Long silence)

Mr. Dawson: In the matter of whether somebody intends to do something as far as a professional, as far as me. If somebody said to me in this room here, a client, not you guys. You know I really want to whack that person out of existence. I want to get rid of him. In the next breath, they said I'm just expressing my anger. I would have a duty to warn that person what they are talking about. Whether they intended it or had a plan. You follow me?

Martha: I don't know what you are saying or where you are going with it.

Mr. Dawson: I am saying you did the right thing. If you had a feeling or if it was said to you, or not said to you, who cares! If there was a feeling or history of this behavior, you had a duty to protect and warn! You did the right thing. (Clearing throat) Just as I would have the same duty and responsibility. That's what I'm hearing, I'm hearing if somebody is afraid they got to express it. Just like you said, you felt threatened and you felt the need to express it. I can't fault you for it; I just wished you had passed it by me. And if an adult takes the information and they weren't present, they weren't here in the room, and they take that information and try to hurt me, I hold him accountable for it. Not now! Not this time! Do you see what I mean? Because I clarified, I clarified it. And uh, and I believe what the judge knows what my intent is. I believe they do! From what I know of the outcome............Are we having fun yet? He, he, he...Jeees! Ok next Monday I'm not going to see you because I won't be in town, but I will see you. Tonight's Thursday, a week from tonight, we'll be together again and the next session after that. I'm gonna talk with your mother about scheduling. So we're done. (Looks at Martha) I want you to stay.

Jennifer says nothing and leaves.

My blood was boiling listening to a child being interrogated by two adults as if she were behind enemy lines and forcing a prisoner to give up the opposition's strategy. This 14-year-old child would endure the same wartime tactics as a POW in a foreign country. I find the only difference is that she was in her own backyard, a seemingly safe haven. As I listen in to what they think is their own private torture chamber, being her only allied rescue team, I cannot move in and save her as I am surrounded by an elite force of the higher ranking officers of her captors. This brings me to the statement of the main interrogator, Mr. Dawson, "When somebody takes a word that I say, takes something and distorts it, and turns it into something that isn't so that they can try to gain control over whatever they are trying to gain control over, I will not let that happen! They are not present." There is no distortion and I am in that room, you "Son of a bitch!"

It was August 1, 2006. It was a record day with a temperature of over a hundred degrees. I had just worked a ten-hour shift. Jennifer had her last softball game that day. This day would determine first, second, and third place.

When I came home from work, Jennifer was ready to go to the game. I asked Jennifer, "Do you really have to play this game? I have a funny feeling again; something doesn't feel right. I do not feel comfortable when Mom is there."

"It is my last game," Jennifer said.

"Ok I understand," I replied.

I drove from Bridgeport to Hodgkin's Illinois where the game was going to be played. Every game, a parent was designated to bring drinks and treats for the players for after the game. This day was my turn. I had two cases of Gatorade and a box of assorted chips. I left the drinks in a cooler in my truck. I made several trips back and forth to get drinks for players because of the excessive heat. On one of my trips to my truck, I noticed in the parking lot a white SUV running with a man sitting in the driver's seat. I knew he had been sitting there for a long time with his vehicle running. Every trip back to my truck, he was still there. His vehicle was parked across the lot from my truck facing me and still running. I just thought it to be odd. During the game, I was standing behind the batter's cage watching the game. I saw a man that was standing about five feet from me wearing shorts. He was kind of watching the game but every time I turned toward him, he was looking right at me, and as soon as I turned back at him, he turned away. I decided to walk behind him to see if he would turn around to see where I was going. He turned around and looked at me. At one point, I decided to stand a few feet away from him and stare at him. He glanced at me a few times, but he stayed right where he was.

It was about halfway through the game, and Martha showed up. As usual, she sat on the opposing side's bleachers. It was about twenty minutes later I decided I did not want to be in the same place as Martha anymore. I went up to the dugout; I told Jennifer that I was sorry that I was going to leave. Jennifer said nothing. I went to my truck, drove up the road, and stopped at our new apartment. I brought a few things in, and I decided to walk back to the park. I parked my truck in a bar and grill parking lot next door to my apartment. I did not want Martha to drive by and see where Jennifer and I would be staying. I had headphones on, listening to music on my iPod as I was walking. I was a block away from the park when I noticed Martha driving in my direction. I kept my head down as if I did not see her. She was driving very slowly past me. I kept my head down as she passed. I was uncertain if she saw me or not.

I arrived at the park, and Jennifer's girlfriend Sandy ran up to me and said, "Jennifer got into an argument with her Mom in front of everyone, and she was crying."

I immediately searched the park for Jennifer. I found her and asked, "What happened?"

Jennifer said, "I was playing first base, and Mom was sitting on that side and I just could not play the game. Dad, I never get an out. I had three today, and I was missing balls. I just could not concentrate. Then, I walked up to Mom, and I said, "Why don't you leave? I do not want you here."Mom said I love you, Jennifer." And I said well, I hate you, you destroyed my life. Mom started laughing in my face and walked away. I was crying, I was yelling, and everyone saw what happened. My coaches ran up to me while I was crying to see if I was ok.

I said, "Jennifer, I am so sorry that I left."

Jennifer asked, "Dad can we stay and watch the next game?"

"Sure, Jennifer."

The second game was very uncomfortable. Jennifer's ex-friend's father, Rod, was there because his daughter was playing the second game. After the game, Jennifer and I walked up the road to where the truck was. We were approaching the parking lot, and as I got closer, I noticed the truck was gone. I said, "Jennifer, our truck is gone!"

"Are you sure Dad?"

"Yea I'm sure I parked it right here."

"Do you think Mom took it?"

I said, "You know that's possible. She saw me walking down the road right after I parked it here. Who else would have taken it?"

Jennifer said, "All of our stuff was in it."

I said, "That's it. I know she took it. Remember those men at the softball games. They are probably Rod's police friends waiting for an opportunity to take the truck. That's why Mom started showing up at your games. She didn't show up at games when the truck was visible from the field."

Jennifer and I started walking back down the road. Jennifer's friend Karen and her parents were driving past and stopped. We asked them to give us a ride to the Police station. I went into the police station with Karen's father; Jennifer stayed in the car with Karen and her mother.

There was a police officer sitting on the other side of a window opening. I told the police officer, "My truck was stolen, and I believed my wife took it. "Everything I owned was in the truck, we were moving into a new apartment and we were going to unload it after the game. The officer asked, what the license plate number is so I can fill out a stolen vehicle report. He went through a door as I waited in the hallway. The officer came back a few minutes later and asked, whose name is the truck in?

I replied, "Martha's."

The officer said, “Then Martha should be the person to report it, and if she took it, we cannot arrest her for stealing a vehicle in her name."

I said, ”What about my stuff she took that was in the truck? My wallet, cell phone, keys for my PO Box, credit cards, jewelry, GPS, blankets, tools, mail, Jennifer's iPod, Jennifer's clothes, my clothes. I can't think of everything."

The officer asked, what is her phone number? We will give her a call to see if she took the vehicle. The officer called, but Martha was not answering. He left a message on her voice mail, ”Hey Martha, this is a police officer, and I'm calling about your Tahoe; please call me back at this number.” The police officer told me, I suggest you take this matter up in court.

Karen's father drove us back by the apartment. I had a second car, but it was at least 15 miles away, and Jennifer and I had no way to get there. I started calling relatives to see if anyone could drive out to Hodgkin's to get us. I finally got a hold of Liz, but it would be a few hours before she could get there. Jennifer and I walked a couple of blocks by a restaurant where we sat on a bench by the bus stop waiting for Liz.

Liz arrived with her boyfriend and Jennifer, and I jumped into her car. We went downtown Chicago to a parking garage where I kept my car. I had my truck hidden there, but I need the truck to move. Just a few days before, Martha sent me an email about a few parking tickets I've received on the truck, saying she paid the tickets and she was deducting the cost of the tickets from the money she owed me. I lost that email.

The next day I sent Martha an email:

"I don't have access to the internet all the time. Is that why you took the truck? Jennifer and I were moving; everything I owned was in the truck. That address was where I was living, and I didn't get them intentionally. I have just sent a payment for the insurance, so you didn't have to pay it. I was also going to pay for the tickets. My brother went to pay for tickets he had and was going to pay for my tickets when they said they were already paid. So thanks, you have my cell phone, wallet, credit cards, jewelry in the ashtray, GPS, my bills, Jennifer's Ipod, and belongings. All items I gave a list to the police. The Judge told you I get one of the vehicles. Also listed in the MSA. I wonder if you will get contempt of court for not obeying a court order. Thank Rod Z. for Jennifer and me, I saw the people in the parking lot watching me."

Martha’s reply,

"Thank you for letting me know you're moving. I need the full address where Jennifer will be living and when this will take place. Since you purchased a car and don't care about where you park the truck (that is in my name), I could not continue to receive tickets and put my license in jeopardy. You created this problem, and I had no choice but to repo the truck and now have to deal with it. Since I happen to have your phone & wallet, because you left them in the truck, email is the only way for me to contact you. I will give you your phone & wallet tonight, 8/3/06, when you bring Jennifer to counseling. As to all the other items in the truck, we can make arrangements for you to get them after I receive the address where Jennifer will be living. Jennifer is welcome to come to the house at any time I am home to pick up clothing or anything else she needs.

You refer to the MSA (marriage settlement agreement), which is not a court order and not signed, so I am not in contempt of court.

Martha

Wow, I thought. Martha has so much power, as she clearly demonstrated in her ransom note, "You will get your things after you tell me where you live."

Was this for real, is this legal, or does this fall under Martha's protection of the domestic court? It was just too bad for Jennifer and me as our world had no rules, no consequences, or repercussions. All we had was survival.

August 3, 2006, Jennifer called Rachel Davis. Jennifer said, my Mom took my Dad's truck while I was playing softball and she left us stranded and all my clothes and stuff were in the truck. Jennifer said Rachel acted as if she were concerned, saying, "I will look into it."

Also, on August 3, 2006, Jennifer and Martha had a counseling session. I decided not to allow Jennifer to tape the session because I was not sure what evidence I left behind in the truck. I didn't want to take any chances. I dropped Jennifer off at counseling. I had time to spare, so I took a ride to a gas station to get water and a newspaper. On my way back I was approaching Mr. Dawson's block, and I noticed Jennifer running toward my car crying hysterically. Martha was a few feet behind Jennifer. Mr. Dawson was standing outside. He saw me coming and hurried into his house and shut the door behind him. I rolled down my window and yelled at Martha! "What are you doing to her?" Jennifer ran around the passenger side and jumped into the car. Martha was coming toward my window, and I yelled, "Stay away from me! Stay away; you're an animal." Martha came up to the car and handed me my wallet, and cell phone then turned and walked away. Jennifer and I drove off. Jennifer was still crying and was shouting, "I hate her, Dad! She is crazy! We got out ten minutes early, and Mom and I were waiting out in front because you weren't here, and that's when Mom said she took the truck. I started crying. She also said she could find out anything about you. She said you bought your car in March at Westbound Ford for five thousand dollars. I said, who got you that information, Rod? Mom said, don't worry about it. She said do you want me to call your father to see if he is coming?" I said, you have his cell phone Mom! She started laughing in my face while I was crying. She's mean, Dad, don't ever leave me again."

"I will never leave again, Jennifer!"

"I'm serious, Dad, don't ever leave me here."

"Ok Jennifer, I promise I will not ever leave you again."

August 4, 2006, 5:00pm, Jennifer and I discussed her calling her Mom to get her belongings in the truck. However, Jennifer had another plan. Friday after school, Jennifer called Martha, "Hi Mom, and its Jennifer. Can I come and visit you today?"

"Oh ok, Jennifer, I will be home at 5:00pm."

"Ok, I will have Dad drop me off."

"Alright Jennifer, I will be here."

I got off work at 4:30 PM. In addition, I went home to pick up Jennifer. We drove straight to the Countryside police station. Jennifer and I went into the station and spoke with a woman at the front desk. We told her our situation and that Jennifer needed to go to the house by her mother to get her things and that we would like police presence. The woman said she would have the Police meet us at the residence. Jennifer and I drove to the house, just blocks away. As soon as we arrived, there was a Policeman in front of the house. Within seconds, another Police officer pulled up to the house. I did not pull into the driveway. I parked on the street. Jennifer and I got out of the car. The two officers escorted Jennifer up to the front door and rang the doorbell. As I waited by my car, Martha opened the front door. To her surprise, she saw the police officers with Jennifer. Martha opened the screen door and said, "What is this?"

Jennifer then spoke up, "Give me mine and my dad's stuff you took from us; open the garage now!"

Martha hesitated with a confused look on her face.

One of the policemen stated, "Give this little girl her things; she has a right to her belongings." Martha, with a pissed-off look on her face, turned around, reached into the house and hit the remote in the house to open the garage door. The door opened, and Jennifer went inside. Martha came out on the front step and said to the officers, "This is not necessary, I talked to the courts, and they said the police should not be getting involved."

One officer replied," Mam, I just got a call to escort a little girl, and I am just doing my job."

The two officers stood a few feet from Martha the entire time. Jennifer went into the garage, and everything that was in the truck was boxed and bagged, stacked in the back of the garage. Jennifer grabbed some bags and brought them to the car. On her way back to the garage, she turned to me and said, "Dad, grab your stuff."

I caught up to Jennifer and walked toward the garage. As we were passing Martha, I kept my head down. She said nothing. She paused for a second and continued talking to the officers. Jennifer and I grabbed what we could. We had to grab what we needed first because I had a small car as opposed to the large Tahoe; not everything would fit. Once we had the car full, I thanked the officers, got in the car, and drove off.

We arrived back at the apartment and immediately started unloading our stuff inside. Once we were finished, we went through the stuff. Our mail and other papers were stacked neatly into a shoebox. All of our mail was opened except for junk mail. We had several bills that I knew were not opened and were now opened. As we were going through the stuff, I found the flash drive that I used to back up my book. I put it on the computer, and the file was gone. It was the first few thousand words of my book. I was not worried about that because I had an extra copy saved on a CD that I had hidden in my apartment and a copy stored on my laptop. I was just curious what she was thinking if she was the one who deleted it. I could not find the papers for my retirement fund. Martha did know the amount of the fund. It was about $8000.00. She was trying to get that information for over a year. Going through other papers, I noticed the first restraining order papers were missing the sheet that stated Martha felt that I would harm her and Jennifer. Papers were stapled together, and the last sheet was torn from the staple. As far as we could see, everything else was there. Most of the things we left behind were tools, fishing poles, tackle box, etc.

My reply to Martha's last email:

Martha, I was not referring to the MSA. Back in, I believe Dec, You asked the court to have the Tahoe because it was in your name. The Judge verbally denied your request. That is the reason why you put I promise not to claim the Tahoe in the MSA. Also, having your off-duty police friends follow and stalk Jennifer and me made her scared. They have been stalking us for several of Jennifer's baseball games. While Jennifer was playing her last baseball game, you had these police people take the Tahoe. It was 100 degrees outside, and we had to walk a mile, carrying baseball equipment and a large cooler. We were also 15 miles from home. The Tahoe had Jennifer's clothes and personal items as well as mine, my cell phone, wallet, Driver's license, credit cards, debit card, bills, P. O. Box keys etc. I had to cancel my cell phone, credit cards and was unable to get my mail. Because you had my bills, I was late making a few payments, and I will have to pay the penalty. And yes, I purchased another car because of your threat to take the truck, but that vehicle was also 15 miles away. We had three vehicles while together, and now you possess all. For your personal interest, you have left your child stranded in extreme heat. Your actions clearly demonstrate your lack of concern for Jennifer. I don't think having your police friends look up my personal information is legal. You cruelly announced to Jennifer that you were responsible for the theft of the truck. She was crying hysterically from that news. You told Jennifer you knew that I purchased a ford Taurus in March. Jennifer said I know Rod, who is a police officer, gave you that information, and you laughed in her face as she was crying. Your abuse of power is getting out of hand. Because of your constant threats and your friends stalking us, we are afraid of telling you where our new address will be. You could have taken your issue up in court rather than put our daughter in the middle. Rod is a police officer and has no right to get involved in my personal life. That is also an abuse of his power. Jennifer and I had to wait three days to get our personal belongings. I believe if we didn't have the police escort us to the house, you would not have returned my belongings. You clearly stated that I would not get my belongings until you have our new address. Another demonstration of your power! Jennifer and I live in fear, always looking over our shoulder not knowing who is following us and what you will do next.

Me

August 7, 2006. Session 11,

Mr. Dawson: Hi,

Jennifer: Hi,

Mr. Dawson: Come on in. Your Mom is here. She's in the office too. Martha: hi, no hi?

Jennifer: Silent.

Mr. Dawson: I know these sessions are stressful for you. I know they are. I want you to know it's not intentional, I don't intend like I don't wake up in the morning and go oh man, I'm just going to make it hard on Jennifer today, you know, I just want you to know that. What makes it difficult is um the content of what we talk about, your feelings about what's going on in your life, and that's good. I'm glad you're getting it out. I want you to, I want you to speak openly, respectfully, and I want you to get the information out or whatever you want to talk about as far as your feelings because that's an appropriate thing. I also want when you people talk, I want for you people to respect each other. So kind of imagine there is a glass wall in between the two of you, and there is a little opening in that wall and when one is talking, like you're in jail, you're listening. And then when the person has stopped, ask is it my turn yet, have you said everything you wanted to say. The session last week was a good one but a lot of arguing, and I didn't appreciate you guys arguing on the street last week. Whoever started that, whoever kept it going, please don't do that again because I have neighbors. The person across the street is an attorney, and she has a problem with anybody parking on that side of the street, let alone people arguing on the street in front of my house. She didn't say anything to me, but this is Hinsdale. Hinsdale is number ten on the scale of the social-economic scale. It's a high-end neighborhood, and people aren't going to put up with it. They will get me out of here, at least my business. Ok?

Martha: um huh,

Mr. Dawson: Because you know who's going to go? You guys, not me.

Martha: Ha, ha,

Mr. Dawson: Ha, ha.

Mr. Dawson: I understand your Mom told you about the truck; the truck got picked up. Was that a truck?

Martha: A Tahoe.

Mr. Dawson: Ok, Your mother told me that's what you were crying about out there. What was so painful about that? Did you love the truck? Like the dog?

Jennifer, crying: Well, I was at a softball game, and my Dad and I were walking back to the truck, and it wasn't there, and it had all our stuff in it cause we were going to move and um, yeah so all of our stuff in it and it wasn't there, and it was really hot out, and we had to walk all the way to the police station, and we were miles away from home because we had to go back to the city and we had to wait for a couple of hours for someone to pick us up. And like I said, it had all of our stuff in there, and like before the game and a couple of other games, me and my Dad noticed there were people watching us too. So that had something to do with it.

Mr. Dawson: Who was watching you?

Jennifer: I don't know like their names or anything like,

Mr. Dawson: Did you see them?

Jennifer: Not really, just like a quick glance because I was playing and stuff.

Mr. Dawson: So you didn't actually see these people?

Jennifer: No, not a good look.

Mr. Dawson: How about your Dad, who did he see?

Jennifer: Um I don't know if he got a good look either, but we saw people, but he probably did.

Mr. Dawson: Did you get your stuff back?

Jennifer: Well yeah.

Mr. Dawson: Tell me about this truck. Whose name was it in?

Martha: Everything was in my name, the loan, the title, insurance, and I was making the payments, license plate renewal. Then he started getting tickets on the truck, and after the fourth ticket, I just said enough is enough. I can't afford to be paying all these tickets, and if I didn't pay them, then my license was going to get suspended, and if I didn't pay for the loan, then the bank would have repossessed the truck.

Mr. Dawson: Oh my god! That's pretty serious stuff. And that means if they repo'd the truck, then you wouldn't have the truck anyway.

Martha: Right!

Jennifer: Well, it wasn't four tickets, it was only three, and it was just a parking ticket, and you can't get, you're not supposed to get your license suspended, and she paid them. My Dad was going to pay for the tickets, and he got down to the place. They told him that it was already paid, and my Dad was making payments for the truck and stuff, so she wasn't making the last few payments because my Dad recently, I don't know how long ago but sent money to make the payment on the truck, so he was paying for some of it too.

Mr. Dawson: Who is she?

Jennifer: What?

Mr. Dawson: Who is she?

Jennifer: My Mom.

Mr. Dawson: Good. Did your Dad give um, you know, a lot, so I'm going to treat you like an adult. You know a lot about what's going on. Did your Dad pay your Mom back for the tickets?

Jennifer, starting to cry: No, he was just going to pay them, and she is just going to write it down anyway for money that he owes her back, and she didn't pay him for all this other stuff and money that she has of his.

Mr. Dawson: How is it that he didn't pay your Mom back for the tickets that he created?

Jennifer: One, she is never by him; they are never anywhere, but two, she is just going to write it down to take it out of money he owes her, but she owes him money.

Mr. Dawson: Is it revengeful or dishonest?

Jennifer: No, she owes him money. She has a lot of his money that she never paid him, how come she didn't give him that money?

Martha: How do you know about all this money?

Jennifer: Because I was with you when you sold the van, and I know you didn't give it to Dad. And when you sold stuff at the garage sale, I was right there.

Martha: The money issues are between your Dad and me.

Jennifer: I was right there; apparently when I asked you where the truck was, you said that's between your Dad and me, why doesn't Dad know.

Martha: Pause: I sent him an email.

Jennifer: It didn't say where the truck was. It says, oh you're not getting your stuff back unless I find out the address of where Jennifer is at; that's what you put.

Martha: It's my right to know where you're living.

Jennifer: Angry: Um, You can't hold my stuff for ransom and Dad's too.

Martha: I put it in the email that you can get anything you want.

Jennifer: Yeah, my stuff, but you said we will make arrangements after I find out where you people live. So if I didn't come there with the cops, I probably wouldn't have gotten everything. We wouldn't have got Dad's stuff too.

Martha: I said anything you want, Jennifer.

Jennifer: Yeah, ok.

Martha: And you called me up, so I left work so I can be there for you, and you picked up your stuff.

Mr. Dawson: Where were you living?

Jennifer: In Bridgeport still.

Mr. Dawson: Where were you going to move to?

Jennifer: We don't know yet. I don't know the address of anything or where we were gonna go.

Mr. Dawson: I think what's probably going to be is your Dad is going to have to tell somebody in the court where you guys are moving to because you're a minor. He just can't take you and just disappear and not tell anybody where you are. You know what I mean. He is gonna have to tell somebody because he will be in contempt of court, and if that happens, he is going to be in trouble.

Jennifer: (Softly,) With what?

Mr. Dawson: What will he be in trouble about? Being in contempt of court.

Jennifer: (Softly) how is that a contempt of court?

Mr. Dawson: He has an obligation to tell your mother where you guys are going to, and contempt means, this is what it means in action, (Cocky), I don't care what you have to say judge, I'm not telling anybody. Your Dad will be in trouble if he holds that position. If he does that, so.

Martha: As far as the tickets, there were four. There are facts, there are records on it.

Jennifer: (mad) They were parking tickets, it was a Sox game, a couple were a cop didn't see his, there are little cards that you have to put in your windshield, and the cop didn't see it because the truck was the other way around and he was walking by, he didn't see it. So a couple tickets were for that. Then another one was he was parked in the wrong place for a Sox game during, and he didn't know you couldn't park there.

Jennifer: Mom, you don't go down there and know where we were parking, so stop laughing because everything is a joke to you. (As Jennifer starts to cry.)

Martha: I'm not laughing.

Jennifer: Cause everything is a joke to you.

Martha: No, it isn't Jennifer.

Jennifer: (Crying and sniffling) that's why you laughed in my face when you told me about taking Dad's truck, oh that's funny.

Martha: Jennifer, I didn't laugh at you. I wouldn't laugh at you.

Jennifer: (Cracking voice) Ok whatever, she's not going to admit it but, and we had to go to Bridgeport. How long, oh, she really cares, that's the second time I've been on the street from her, and she cares. (Sniffling)

Mr. Dawson: Were you out in front of my house?

Jennifer: No, the one time that she kicked me out and then, then. We were down at a softball game, Dad's truck was in Countryside, car, or whatever, and it was all the way down in Bridgeport. (Crying), how am I supposed to get down there, Mom? Did she think about that? No, (speaking fast) It's miles away; it was like a hundred degrees out, we were not going to walk all the way to Bridgeport.

Martha: Your uncle lives down the street.

Jennifer: We didn't have a phone.

Martha: Well then, how did a phone call come on my phone restricted and then another one?

Jennifer: Who said that was me?

Martha: Well.

Jennifer: You can't just assume it was me.

Mr. Dawson: I don't know if we can expect Jennifer to answer us as an adult in all these situations,

Martha: um hm.

Mr. Dawson. She has impressions of what she believes to be her truth, but the tickets are a fact; the tickets are dated. Um if I could express myself, if I got a ticket, I'm not going to try to get another one; I'm not going to keep getting tickets.

Jennifer: (getting angry) He wasn't trying to get a ticket.

Mr. Dawson: Hey, I'm just telling you, I'm not your Dad. I just wouldn't keep doing things to keep getting tickets.

Martha: They have due dates on them too.

Jennifer: Ok Mom, Dad was going to pay them. When he got there, they told him they were paid.

Martha: He went there to pay his tickets. He said his brother went to pay for the tickets.

Jennifer: Well,

Martha: well,

Mr. Dawson: That's ok, it's alright. What I want to make a point on is that, Can you tell me what was in your heart to allow your husband to have the car, or uh have the truck?

Martha: So that he could have transportation, to find a job and commute Jennifer and come and see her.

Mr. Dawson: What would you call that Jennifer?

Jennifer: Um,

Mr. Dawson: Is that mean or good? Good or bad?

Jennifer: Bad because she took the truck.

Mr. Dawson: He had the truck all this time, not paying insurance, right!

Martha: Right.

Jennifer jumps in: He started to pay, oh my god. (Sniffling)

Martha: He did not pay anything.

Jennifer: Crackling voice, Ok!

Mr. Dawson: If there was a record of it, we'll produce it if you want.

Martha: If he paid it, let him show me a canceled check, or

Jennifer: That doesn't give you the right; even if he didn't, that doesn't give you the right to take his truck! If you want to um, so if he wanted to transport me and whatever, why was the truck gone?

Martha: He had a car,

Jennifer: That doesn't give you a right to take someone's truck.

Martha: If he keeps getting,

Jennifer: You threatened him before that you were going to take his truck.

Martha: He got three tickets that,

Jennifer: Mom, Stop changing the subject; I thought it was four tickets.

Martha: There was one in November.

Jennifer: Whatever! Like I said, we were down at a softball game; how are we supposed to get fifteen or twenty miles all the way down to Bridgeport? Did she think about that? No!

Mr. Dawson: Please ok, please listen. Your Mom's going through from what I understand uh your Mom is going through a divorce with your Dad because she doesn't want to be with him anymore, but she lets him have the Tahoe, is that what it is? She lets him have the Tahoe, she pays his insurance, and she makes the payments. Now I don't know how you look at it, the way I'm looking at it. I think she's going way beyond what she is supposed to be doing. For a person who is going through a divorce, but I think, I think she did it because she loves you. She wanted to make sure you go to school.

Jennifer: with a pouting voice, How was I supposed to get home if there wasn't......... a truck?

Mr. Dawson: You mean that night when it was repo'd?

Jennifer: Yeah, and still she's not supposed to take the truck because before you're not, Mom! Mom! You and Dad were supposed to get a truck. Dad paid for his truck when you guys were living together and he helped pay for your truck. So they were each supposed to get a truck.

Mr. Dawson: Well let me continue with my story, the way I see it, and I could be wrong. Four tickets on your truck! You're right! What are the consequences for four tickets? If you keep getting tickets, what happens then?

Martha: They suspend your license.

Jennifer: Not for parking.

Martha: How do you know?

Jennifer: I talked to Dad to see what was happening about parking.

Martha: My license would be suspended.

Mr. Dawson: Your license?

Martha: The tickets are in my name.

Jennifer: But you paid them.

Mr. Dawson: She has to.

Jennifer: I understand, but she's just going to take the money and write it down that Tom owes me this much money for parking tickets, that's what she is going to do, so he's gonna have to pay her back anyway, but yet she's not paying him for the stuff she owes him.

Martha: Jennifer, let the money situation be between your Dad and me.

Mr. Dawson: Yeah

Martha: Why are you worried about it?

Jennifer: (Sobbing) because I'm living with Dad and you took the truck that takes us places.

Mr. Dawson: But he has a car.

Jennifer: Shouts, So what!

Mr. Dawson: uh

Jennifer: Because she threatened him before that, she was going to take the truck. That's when he got the car, and she's getting other people involved. She shouldn't get other people involved.

Mr. Dawson: So you say your Mom was forcing...

Martha: Who is involved?

Jennifer: Rod Z.

Mr. Dawson: So you say that your Mom is forcing your Dad to do things he doesn't want to do, so he was going to keep the truck indefinitely, not get a car, and be independent.

Jennifer: (sniffling) that was his truck!

Mr. Dawson: No, it was your Mom's truck! The one that she had repossessed was hers.

Jennifer: (Angry and crying) they bought when they were still a long time ago before the divorce.

Mr. Dawson: But it was in her name.

Jennifer: It doesn't matter, it was his truck, they paid for it just like when they got her truck they both paid for it, it doesn't matter, (Sobbing) and my point is, it's ok that we didn't get home that night. We were a long way from home: once again, she doesn't care. But it's ok.

Mr. Dawson: You know who could have taken you home?

Jennifer: (Sniffling) Who?

Mr. Dawson: Your Mom!

Jennifer: Yeah ok!! Like she,

Mr. Dawson: She would have!

Jennifer: Yeah, that's why she doesn't answer the cop's phone calls right.

Martha: Ooohhhhhh! So you did call my phone!

Jennifer :(Shouting) the cops did, I didn't. And they didn't call you restricted, they left a voicemail.

Martha: There was no voicemail on my phone.

Jennifer: Ok, that's what the cop said. So the cops are lying now, right!

Martha: There was no voicemail!

Jennifer: Ok!

Mr. Dawson: I'm going to give you a story that has to do with me: I'm going to give you a story that has to do with a car. I want your judgment; I want your judgment too. It's just not one-sided because I'm listening to both of you. Ah, during my divorce, ah we had two cars. She had a Camaro, a nice red one, fast! And I had a Toyota Tercel. But during the divorce, going through this divorce, nothing was finalized yet. She said you can have the Tercel, which was in both our names, which this truck wasn't, but ours was in both our names. So I uh, it had a lot of mileage on it. It had eighty-five thousand miles on it, and I was still going out to Morris, IL. I thought I have to trade this in and get another car because I was living in Joliet, which was not too far from Morris. So when I went to trade it in, I got this Honda. I don't know if you have ever seen it, but I still have it. I couldn't make a deal with the guy because I had the title, but she had her name on it, and my name was on it. So do you know what she did and I need your judgment on this. She wouldn't sign off on the title. So I had this deal, I had this sweet deal, I had a great deal! I had a car that I was about to buy, but I couldn't buy it because she had her signature on it. We're going through a divorce, and she says I'm not signing off on it.

Martha: Why?

Mr. Dawson. Well, I just, why? I'm going to tell you why but was that a good thing or a bad thing?

Jennifer: (Softly) Bad.

Mr. Dawson: How come?

Jennifer: because you both were paying for the car or whatever both had the car and,

Mr. Dawson: I was thinking....

Jennifer: Ok well, you guys both,

Mr. Dawson: So I called her up, and she went into this big control thing, well what are you buying, why you are doing this, what you doing that Dada Dada, and then finally the salesman are called her because I wasn't making any headway. So he got her to come in and sign off on it. But she gave me the car. She gave it to me, but it had two signatures on the title. In your mother's situation, it was titled in her name. In the state of Illinois, when they run her plates, whenever that car gets a ticket, it shows her name. So every time it comes up with a ticket or some kind of street violation, it comes up Martha .... So she's the one who's penalized. If the truck had been impounded, she would have had to pay the fine because it's her truck.

She had no choice like I had no choice: I couldn't sell that car, the car that I wanted to trade in unless somebody cooperated. Your Mom had no choice but to pay those tickets. Otherwise, she would have lost her license. She couldn't have got to work.

Martha: Do you think if I would have asked your Dad, and maybe this is not a fair question to you. To give me the truck back or get a loan and buy it out so the title could be in his name, he would do either of the two?

Jennifer: What?

Mr. Dawson: That's probably not a fair question. It's a very technical question.

Jennifer: I didn't even understand what you said.

Mr. Dawson: Your Mom was asking a question. Let me try to break it down.

Do you think your Dad, if your mother would have come to your Dad and said, look, you know I can't support my car and the Tahoe,

Jennifer: Uh, her car is already paid off, which my Dad helped pay for.

Mr. Dawson: The question would have been, Tom do you think, would you want to take over the payments and refinance and put it in your name, you take the truck! And it's an unfair question to ask you because how would you know what your Dad would do because you're not your Dad. But we do know that there were four tickets issued on that truck, and your Mom was, she was backed into a corner, she had no other way to go out. She had to pay them.

Jennifer: Ok, that doesn't give her the right to take away his truck and then look through the stuff: we found mail that wasn't open that was opened. We are missing a key.

Martha: Everything was in there.

Jennifer: You deleted one of Dad's files that were on a flash drive.

Martha: Everything that was in the truck was in bags or in boxes.

Jennifer: And his tackle box is gone, and then,

Martha: It's in the garage!

Mr. Dawson: She really had, she had a legal right to take back what was hers.

Jennifer: Not,

Mr. Dawson: Don't you think?

Jennifer: No!

Mr. Dawson: It was hers, why couldn't she take it back.

Jennifer: (Getting angry) because they were each supposed to get a truck, that's what they were told.

Mr. Dawson: Who told him that?

Jennifer: The Judge!

Martha: The judge didn't say it: we wrote it in the marital settlement agreement,

Jennifer: Ok!

Martha: It was never signed or entered in court.

Jennifer: Still! And then, like I said, you deleted one of Dad's files on one of his flash drives that was gone!

Martha: Pause: No.

Jennifer: Ok! Alright!

Mr. Dawson: Alright, let's move on to something else then, ok. The last time we were together, you talked about: I want to give you an opportunity to talk about your feelings because you told me already about your Mom letting the guy move in. Right! Was that the issue? If I remember correctly, the last time we got together was last Thursday? You said right, Mom you know, the guy was living in the house: I came back for my clothes, you know, something about tire tracks. Do you want to talk to your Mom about that?

Jennifer: Well, I did! I mentioned it to her, but she just said the realtor was coming.

Mr. Dawson: Oh! Living with him, that's it. It was, the thing you had a problem with was, if they got married and got together your mother expected you to live, all of you living together, the three of you, I think you had a problem with that.

Jennifer: Well Yeah, because it would be right before I was going away with my friends she told me, she's like! Oh, well when all of this divorce stuff is over he will get a house and he'll get a pool because he knows you like the pool and we'll have Daisy and stuff and it was already stuff I had with my Dad so she was basically trying to replace him.

Mr. Dawson: You'll do it! If you ever get divorced, you will replace Dad.

Jennifer: Yea but I wouldn't say that to my kid. (Sobbing) if I had a child with him I wouldn't be as mean as she is!

Mr. Dawson: I don't know if your mother is mean.

Jennifer: (sarcastically) Ok.

Mr. Dawson: I know she has done some insensitive things to you. I don't know, I wasn't there so I can't argue that but the reason I want you to read these books is because they talk about stuff like how when people go through divorces, They want to get the old one out of there, I'm done with you, history, gone. You can see the kids, you can have visitation but you're not a part of my life anymore, I got a new person in here, and that person is the one that she loves or he loves whoever it is and uh that's the way it is. That's just the way it is. It's not right for the kids but when the adults make the decisions they have all the power, they just do.

Martha: And it's not a replacement, your Dad will always be your Dad and I will always be your mother.

Jennifer: (Loudly) To tell your kid that you're gonna have a house with him and he'll buy you a pool and all that, yeah Mom that's replacing, because I had that with Dad. (Cocky) For someone who didn't want the pool you didn't care about having a pool with your boyfriend.

Mr. Dawson: What do you think your Mom was trying to do by telling you things? What do you think she was trying to do?

Jennifer: Try to bribe me to have me go with her.

Mr. Dawson: What were you trying to do, Martha?

Martha: Make it easy for her, and let her know she would still have the same things she has now.

Jennifer: (Crying) Ok, that's making it easy, Oh you're going to go live with another man, Oh Mom ok, just so you know, not tomorrow, but next time you go by Granny and Pupa, Pupa is not going to be there, it's gonna be another guy, and you're just supposed to get along with him right! And like everything, they're gonna have all the same things just with another guy; how would you feel? (Sobbing)

Mr. Dawson: Me as an adult, my Dad, died about ten years ago from cancer you know, and within about three years, my Mom hooked up with another guy,

Jennifer: That's different, that's overtime, you shouldn't cheat on her marriage.

Mr. Dawson: Is that the issue? Cheating?

Jennifer: Yeah And didn't do it right away, three years that's time.

Mr. Dawson: On a scale of zero to ten, how much do you love your Dad?

Jennifer: What being highest, Ten?

Mr. Dawson: Ten Yeah,

Jennifer: Over ten!

Mr. Dawson: Probably about twelve or fifteen, so anything that looks like a threat to your father or, anything that looks like he's out of the picture or you know he's not as important would be, would make you feel what?

Jennifer: Mad!

Mr. Dawson: Yeah, because you love your Dad that much right!

Jennifer: Silent

Mr. Dawson: Yeah

Mr. Dawson: But your Mom doesn't love him!

Jennifer: I didn't say she had to love him, but she didn't have to throw him away and expect me to move in with her boyfriend and get all the things that I already had.

Martha: Jennifer, my boyfriend doesn't live with me.

Jennifer: Ok!

Martha: And he wouldn't move in after we just get divorced.

Jennifer: Ok!

Martha: You can't do that,

Jennifer: Funny Mom, just like you said before, not if I'm not there, if I'm not there you can do whatever you want, that's what you told me before, you're not here Jennifer. So he could be here.

Martha: Yeah!

Jennifer: Yeah, so he was!

Martha: He could be at the house. He doesn't live with me,

Jennifer: Ok, he stayed over plenty of times.

Martha: How do you know that? I got to hear this one!

Jennifer: Um, like I said before the tire tracks that were in there, they weren't from your truck and I know you, you don't park the furthest away from the door in a snowstorm, like you would do that.

Martha: That day the realtor came over and got to the house first.

Jennifer: Yeah ok, they pulled up all the way in the garage then right! Because the tire tracks didn't stop it went all the way to the garage, like it went through the garage.

Martha: You said it was a car with small tires right!

Jennifer: Yeah, it was a small well it didn't match your truck!

Martha: So you're a private eye. Because you want to know what, he has a truck bigger than mine and his tires are bigger than mine, so now what.

Jennifer: Ok whatever Mom, you didn't answer your phone and your cell phone and Mom, people see!

Martha: Oh, what, who sees?

Jennifer: I don't have to tell you that! People walking by and stuff that have told me things and Dad things.

Martha: So I'm being watched!

Jennifer: No you're not being watched, I don't have people watching you like you do watching me and Dad!

Martha: I don't have anybody watching you.

Jennifer: Ok, two trucks that have been following me and Dad and guys that have been at our softball games and saying stuff.

Martha: If your Dad and you think somebody is following you and you see a truck write down the plate and report it to the police.

Jennifer: Ok and what about Rod Mom looking up stuff for you?

Martha: Rod is not looking up anything!

Jennifer: Ok, Ok! You're not going to admit it!

Martha: Rod had nothing to do with the repo! Absolutely nothing!

Jennifer: Ok! Then who drove the truck Mom?

Martha: I did!

Jennifer: Then who was in your car?

Martha: I parked it away!

Jennifer: Ok and you walked all the way back to get the truck.

Martha: I never said I went back home and parked it

Jennifer: No, I know, you weren't home because we drove past to see if the truck was there.

Martha: How do you know if my truck was in the garage?

Jennifer: And then where was Dad's truck Mom? You're telling me you drove your truck home and put it in the garage and walked all the way back to Hodgkins?

Martha: Nope! I didn't say I drove!

Jennifer: Yea ok Mom that's why people were watching us and all of a sudden, they were gone. Ok, Mom! Mom!

Martha: Get the plates!

Jennifer: It's rod! Rod is looking up stuff for you and then, now there's all of a sudden guy's watching, following me and Dad and sitting at softball games and stuff.

Martha: Then you need to report them, write their description down, and go to the police.

Jennifer crying: Mom! Why else would they say something? Someone had to tell them something and it wasn't me and Dad, Oh yeah come watch us and say stuff to us or whatever and follow us in your truck! That makes perfect sense it had to have been you!

Martha: I don't think so!

Jennifer: Ok!

Mr. Dawson: You know what I would have done Jennifer? If I thought someone was following me, I would go up to them! I'd go up and say, If I really. . .

Jennifer: And how are we supposed to know if they are going to hurt us or not?

Mr. Dawson: Silent...

Martha: And that's why you take their description down and go to the police.

Jennifer (crying) why don't you just tell them to stop Mom!

Martha: Jennifer I am not having anyone follow you, neither is Rod.

Jennifer: (Sobbing) Ok Mom, ok! Whatever I don't believe, you because apparently, they said stuff to Dad too, and it would only be stuff that you could have told them. . .

Martha: Who are they?

Jennifer: Screaming while crying: I don't know who they are, if I knew who they were, I would tell you!

Mr. Dawson: Jennifer if you haven't seen them, how do you know anybody was there?

Jennifer: (crying and sniffling) I saw them! They have been standing, if they stand so far away or something Mom, I don't stare right at them and be oh hi! I don't study them. I had to play softball, and then if we were driving they stand there and then after we go a while they'll come by. I can't get a really good look at them, it's not like I'm this close where I can see everything and know your height, your hair, your eyes, everything you look like.

Mr. Dawson: Could it be they're part of the crowd and they're there for their kids?

Jennifer sniffling: No! I have been playing softball since I was little. I know all the girls on softball and me and my Dad know what their parents look like and who they are, Oh that's so and so's parents because my Dad has coached. They're standing in the back with no kids around just staring at me and my Dad. If they were there for their kids, they wouldn't be staring at us.

Mr. Dawson: Alright I'm going to ask you a question, I'm going to throw something out here, if it's possible, is it possible that your Dad has done something along the way where, where somebody other than the police! Anybody! Somebody could be after him?

Jennifer: (sniffling) No!

Mr. Dawson: has he done anything along the way like hooked up with the wrong people, desperation is there any possible way that could have happened?

Jennifer: No! No! Because. . .

Mr. Dawson: Let's say I was buying drugs, I am buying drugs from people and I haven't paid them. I haven't paid them and they are following me.

Jennifer: No because they're mentioning about the divorce. One time I and Dad were walking and a guy walked by, back off the custody battle! Explain that Mom! Who would have told them that?

Martha: I have no idea!

Jennifer: Yeah ok, play stupid!

Martha: Well then, if someone was that close to him he should have had a description.

Jennifer: Mom if someone is walking by and you don't know they are gonna say something and as soon as they walk past they just say something and you're walking in a different direction then what do you see Mom? The back of them. You don't get a description!

Mr. Dawson: Were they young or were they old?

Jennifer: I don't know! I wasn't paying attention because all of a sudden someone walks by, you don't know, if they said something like that who's gonna tell them that?

Martha: Who heard them say that?

Jennifer: (loudly) Me and Dad were right there!

Mr. Dawson: Were there any other witnesses around?

Jennifer: No because we were walking to go to the truck to come to counseling.

Mr. Dawson looks at Martha: Back off the custody?

Martha: Well I don't know what to tell ya!

Jennifer: Yeah ok!

Mr. Dawson: The way you put it, it sounds like these guys were going to jump on your Dad.

Jennifer: Exactly and how are we supposed to, now we got to watch our back, we don't know if they are going to hurt me, hurt him. We don't know what's going on and how else would they know there is a custody battle going on? You know, and stuff like that and telling my Dad to back off!

Mr. Dawson: You know how many people there were?

Jennifer: What? I don't know because there's been different people. (Sniffling)

Mr. Dawson: Alright, that's scary!

Jennifer: Well yeah maybe you, I don't even believe that you wouldn't say anything but maybe Rod told some of his friends to do it and you just don't know about it or something but I know you know. .

Martha: Jennifer I am not having anyone follow you!

Jennifer: Ok!

Mr. Dawson: How does your Dad feel about this?

Martha: And, and neither is Rod!

Jennifer: Ok!

Mr. Dawson: When these things are going on how does your Dad feel about all this?

Jennifer: Well of course we're scared watching our backs not knowing who's gonna be where and what's going to happen! But I don't know,

Martha: Do you think I would do anything for you to get hurt Jennifer?

Jennifer: Ah, you threw me on the street a couple of times and anything to get hurt, do you know what could have happened to me and Dad when we were waiting for a ride, how long were we out there when you took the truck? Oh, no you didn't think about that. You didn't think about me when you kicked me out how far I had to walk by myself down dark streets so getting hurt. . .

Mr. Dawson: How did you get back home?

Jennifer: We had to wait for my Aunt to pick me up. By the time we got a hold of her we were waiting two three hours..

We knew she had the truck because she would have reported it stolen if we told her that the truck was gone.

Mr. Dawson: I'm going to change the subject ok! I'm going to give these back to you. We are going to discuss this before we stop. Martha why don't you just start with ah, where did we leave off? Were we on the unhealthy side? Wherever you want to pick up. Just pick it up.

Martha: Fair and consistent discipline.

Mr. Dawson: Ok, go ahead, flush it out, talk about it.

Martha: Well we had rules and Jennifer knew growing up what the rules were, she knew if she didn't do what she was supposed to she would be punished and...

Mr. Dawson: What did punishment mean?

Martha: Well time out or go to her room.

Mr. Dawson: How old was she then? Are you saying from the...

Martha: All the time.

Mr. Dawson: When did you start, when did you start to employ boundaries or discipline with Jennifer. These rules that you're talking about.

Martha: Oh early on probably two.

Mr. Dawson: What was it like when she was two years old?

Martha: Fun.

Mr. Dawson: Fun!

Martha: um- hmm

Mr. Dawson: What would she do that would get her in trouble?

Martha: I remember coming home from work one time and I was at school or something. I got home. It was probably after work and Tom was there and he fell asleep and she got baby powder and she had snow all over the house, she was powdering the house up all over. And it was hard to discipline her because it was funny but you know I told her that wasn't what she was supposed to be doing. She did it with lotion one time too: she made a mountain with lotion, poured it out all over. But it was just one time and she knew that wasn't what she was supposed to be doing. Playing with toys instead of things like that.

Mr. Dawson: Do you remember that? By any chance, I know you were too young, only two years old. (Jennifer shakes her head). Consistent you talk about consistent discipline.

Martha: Uh-hmm

Mr. Dawson: Except when she was 14. What made the difference? Discipline, discipline at that time when she was two seemed to be and I'm feeling it too, I'm putting myself in a position, you're seeing the humor of it but you also see that kind of thing is the powder, the snow all over the house not something you want to continue doing. How did she get a hold of the powder anyway?

Martha: I don't know.

Mr. Dawson: Maybe she went into the bathroom, who knows right!

Martha: um-hmm

Mr. Dawson: But when she was 14 and you guys were going through a period of time from what I remember you telling me of this, this battle. Some of it, some of it is adolescent behavior you know it's like it just is. You behaved in a way from what you've told me what Jennifer has told me, it wasn't consistent, it seemed uh very emotional.

Martha: Um-hmm

Mr. Dawson: When you started, can you remember when that started to shift? Not that particular Night or day, when it started to become inconsistent. Can you remember that happening and I know that's a hard question and what caused that to happen?

Martha: Well I don't know, probably the first time when I was scared that I didn't know what happened when she didn't get home from school. She didn't call because she had the rule to always call and let me know if she was going to be at our house or one of her friends because, they took turns going by whoever's house after school and I told her if she didn't call me that I would take her phone away but I let it slide once and, then the next time I mean I was worried I didn't know where she was and...

Mr. Dawson: What happened? How old was she at that time and how come she didn't call, did you ever find out?

Martha: She forgot.

Mr. Dawson: How old was she then?

Martha: 14.

Mr. Dawson: She was 14?

Martha: Um-hmm

Mr. Dawson: She forgot to call you, which happens right! How upset were you?

Martha: Uh when I called her phone and she didn't answer then I got more worried and I said the reason you have a phone is me to get a hold of you so I know you're ok.

Mr. Dawson: Were there any consequences for not calling?

Martha: um-hmm

Mr. Dawson: Because she forgot, she forgot to call. And I think it was handled appropriately because you did finally how, when did you, when did you finally come home that night or that day? Was it night or day?

Martha: No, it was after school.

Mr. Dawson: After school. How long did it take you to get home? Do you remember that? Was she with her friends? Was Jennifer with her friends?

Martha: Probably.

Mr. Dawson: Yeah. But it sounds like you were still, like you were still consistent, you were emotional, like over emotional like the night, the night that you chased her around the house. That was an extreme.

Martha: Um-hmm

Mr. Dawson: You know! So was something like that you chasing her around, do you think that was, how, how did you get to that point where you were just out of control, it's really what you were. How did you get to that point?

Martha: I don't know it was probably all emotions built up and holding things in and Jennifer not wanting to talk to me, and I thought she was going to call her Dad and leave.

Mr. Dawson: Hmm.

Martha: So I didn't want her to, I wanted to take the phone away from her.

Mr. Dawson: (talking to Martha) You know you've been, you've been consistent in that story with me, every time you tell me that story, you say the same thing over and over again. Consistent. And you know what that makes it? That makes you trustworthy because you're not changing your stories. It's always been the same story. So I trust that, that you're being consistent with me. Ok your turn.

Jennifer: Um, I circled family fun and relaxation.

Mr. Dawson: Did ya?

Jennifer: Um, well we always have nights where we like to rent movies or something and then we'd always like to sit down and watch a movie together and um there'd be times like where we would sometimes go downstairs and play pool or ping-pong and stuff.

Mr. Dawson: Those were fun times for you.

Jennifer: Or go bike riding, too.

Mr. Dawson: How did you feel about yourself when those things were going on? How did you feel about your place in the family when those things happened, family fun biking together? How did you feel?

Jennifer: Happy!

Mr. Dawson: How about secure? Was it a surprise to realize that your Mom and Dad were going to get a divorce? Big surprise! How come?

Jennifer: Cause like we didn't see any signs of them being...

Mr. Dawson: You didn't see them?

Jennifer: Like we didn't see any like,

Mr. Dawson: What do you mean we? Who is we?

Jennifer: Like me and my Dad, we didn't see anything wrong and like any signs of them wanting to.

Mr. Dawson: The issue of your Mom cheating on your father is very, very, very, important to you. You really see that as a bad thing, really a bad thing, a wrong thing...................... Do you want to talk about that?

Jennifer: Sure, um well I just don't like think it's right for you, for someone to cheat on someone after (Starting to cry) you made a promise in church or anything you know so, yeah that's like I don't know, I'm just like really against that and um,

Mr. Dawson: That's not something you would do.

Jennifer: Yeah, and like if anything you get a divorce because you're unhappy or something and like later on you know, look for someone or something..................................

Mr. Dawson: But maybe that's not everybody else's value, maybe it's not their, maybe it's not the way, maybe you're, maybe you're above as far as your standard of living, and your morals and values, maybe yours are above most kinds of people.... They really are! You know those, we've talked about your favorite things, I love talking about the things you like to talk about. You know, like violin and different programs and, if you watch any of these, well most, most, would you agree that most programs you see on TV are about relationships that are dysfunctional and, and those relationships somebody is having an affair with. How do you think that is so interesting? Hmm?

Jennifer: I don't know!

Mr. Dawson: Why do you think that is? Guess! You're an A/B student I know you are! Why do you suppose that happened? Why do you think, why do you think these, these, like Days of our Lives, do you ever watch those Soap Opera's? Days of our Lives or All my Children, why do you think they go on for centuries? Honest to god you can turn it on today: same people have the same conflicts doing the same things. Why do you think they keep going on and on? Why do you think they keep going on and on?

Martha: Because it's real life!

Mr. Dawson: This is what people do. This is what people do.

Jennifer: It doesn't make it right.

Mr. Dawson: That's right! It doesn't make it right but this is what people do.

Jennifer: Yeah well, it doesn't mean that people should go out and do what they see.

Martha: It doesn't, it's not like you plan it Jennifer, sometimes it's life takes a turn.

Jennifer: Yeah well you don't get a boyfriend and cheat on your marriage...

Mr. Dawson: So that's a value, you have an uh, it's a moral ethical value.

Martha: And I didn't think it would ever happen.

Mr. Dawson: But I think it's strongly tied in what you think about your Dad. Do you know that when you talk about occurrences you use the word we. Like that with your Dad, just that way! And anything that happens to your Dad happens to you. The truck, the checks, and the money you were supposed to have for your college fund. If it happens to you, if your Dad's hurt, you're hurt. Is that a fair appraisement? Yeah, you love your Dad....................

Martha: And you should Jennifer, he's your Dad.

Mr. Dawson: Yeah, you should, I'm not saying you're wrong, not to be mad at your Mom because she cheated on your father. I'm not saying that you're wrong. That's the way you see it and that's what happened and your Mom did that and she admits it, right?

Martha: Um-hmm

Jennifer: Now she admits it! She has never admitted that before that, that's why everything happened.

Mr. Dawson: No, that's not why everything happened: she's admitting that she had an affair from what I understand. Do you know what an affair is?

Jennifer: Yeah,

Mr. Dawson: What is it? I just want to know what you think it is.

Jennifer: When you go behind a spouse with someone else and they don't know about it, like your husband or wife doesn't know that you're involved with someone else.

Mr. Dawson: So your Mom admits to you that's why she's in counseling that's why I am helping, I know, I can see that I am helping your Mom. Remember I was telling you that I was working on your Mom, working with your Mom, and I'm working with you too. And she was openly telling you, that's what happened. And all my job is to help people get in touch with the truth. My job is to help them get in touch with who they are. Not to say they're bad or good you know, or to say you shouldn't have done that to your daughter. She did it, she did it, and she did it.

Martha: If everybody was happy in a marriage things like that wouldn't happen. So there are things that lead people to do things.

Mr. Dawson: Average people.

Jennifer: So leading you to cheat.

Mr. Dawson: Yes!

Jennifer: Mom, you were the one always coming home and starting arguments for the littlest, stupidest, stuff. For like little things and then you would yell at me for little things, Oh clean this, I don't get help around here bla, bla, bla, and

Mr. Dawson: What feelings do you think your Mom was expressing when she was doing that?

Jennifer: I don't know!

Mr. Dawson: uh, would frustration have something to do with it?

Martha: Probably! I mean Jennifer we would do laundry together and

Jennifer: I didn't always do laundry, once in a while I would.

Martha: Once in a while, and I appreciate your help and I always told you that and you would complain because we would fold your Dad's clothes and he would tell you to put them away and you would say why do I have to put them away, he could put his own clothes away. Yeah because everyone was putting their own clothes away, and then Dad did put his clothes away..........

Mr. Dawson: And we can expect Jennifer from now on, and she has been doing this for a long time, because she's that way with her Dad, she's gonna protect him.

Martha: Um-hmm

Mr. Dawson: And that's normal for her, that's where she is right now, that's normal for her to behave that way. And we do not want to attack her father but we want to express the truth of this behavior you know, just as I am doing it with your Mom. I said tonight,

Jennifer: High,

Mr. Dawson: If you would agree with me, what she did that night when she chased you around was not normal, it was insane, so I'm being fair on both ends. When I talk about your Dad's behavior I'm also talking about your Moms. I'm not siding with anybody. Also your behavior hasn't been, hasn't been rational all the time either.

Jennifer: Like what?

Mr. Dawson: Oh, I don't want to bring it up again, we already crossed that bridge. You know, I think it's gone , history, we're cool, you and I are cool, we're , we're this way, straight I don't care about what happened, it's gone. But nobody's normal, I'm not even normal. I'm just doing better because I've been working on myself but I'm not a normal guy! You know, think about how abnormal it would be if some guys were following me, for me to go up to them, would that be a normal thing to do, your Mom's right! I could get shot, knifed, get hurt, but you know something! The neighborhood I came from, where I grew up on 61st and Damen, you know where that is by Lynden high school. I jumped a lot. And I made a decision along the way, I'm not backing down. Even if it means you have to kill me! I'm not backing down! I'm not going to run, am I going to run from a fight I'm not backing down, from anybody. I had a reputation, the resource development institute, it was all black, all black! I was the only white token guy there. Another guy was there, the second token guy. Dawson took no, he didn't take any prisoners. Ha-ha,

Martha: Hmm-hmm-hmm-hmm

Mr. Dawson: This was back when I was younger, more buff, now I'm older and a little sluggish. (Cough) You walk around, you walk around, you see people walking up and down the street, there's nobody normal.......... People in this neighborhood just because it's high end, you know what's in this neighborhood? I know about it because I've treated some guys along the way because they're felons at other places. There're dealing co, there're dealing cocaine in this, this area here. And there are lots of people in this area that's having affairs outside of their relationships, I don't. I'm like you, I don't believe in it. If I have a problem with uh my wife, and I don't think we can straighten it out. Getting with somebody else is not going to make it better. It's just going to make it worse for me, but that's how I live my life. Can I judge these people? Do I want to live like that? No but I'm not going to judge them. It's just the way it is. So at this point, our time is up. I want to pick, I want to pick this up next time. We're going to go back to this, next time will be Thursday.

Jennifer: Is it only from seven to eight on Thursday?

Martha: Yeah.

Mr. Dawson: Right, right, I've adjusted it: I've adjusted it twice a week, you and your Mom, you and your Mom twice a week is that better? Do you want to say anything? What did you pick up about tonight? What did you pick up last week? Ha, ha- ha-ha-ha two weeks ago? What did you pick up uh tonight Martha?

Martha: Last week nothing, this week I think we communicated a lot better because we listened to what each other had to say.

Mr. Dawson: And that's what I'm looking for and as we practice this along the way, again nobody's right, nobody's wrong, everybody has got their feelings and the way they live. It's not going to change anything but at least we can listen, we can say ok I'm going to listen and we can agree to disagree. And we know you love your father to death! I think you would die for him! Would you take a bullet for him? If somebody put a gun to your head and they just said we're going to kill your Dad but we're gonna kill you first because that's the choice. We won't kill him, we're gonna kill you. Would you do that? You would. I know I would do that for Jamie. I'd put my life, I'd put myself in front of her. I'd give my life up for her. And there is nothing wrong with that, but if she ran up a big bill on me, she ran up some debt, threatened my license or my ability to practice as a clinician, or my ability to drive my car. You know what I would do? I'd protect me. I wouldn't take a bullet! She'd have to go! I would take my car back. I would have her arrested. I would do anything to protect myself because you know why? Because the contract we had with each other, marriage is a contract ok, and if that contract is broken, a contract is an agreement on a piece of paper. I'll honor you know I'll do you know I'll respect you, if she breaks that contract, there's no more marriage, I don't care what they put on that piece of paper, as far as I'm concerned it's over with. They break that con, if she emotionally abuses me, if she hits me, if she overspends the money that we make together, she does something nuts. Runs up bills you know, takes my car you know, does drugs, it's over with. Because I'm not going any farther, I'm not going to try to change her. I'm just going to say, you need to find somebody else down the street, not me, that's it. I might give her a chance you know I mean, I mean, these are radical you know, if she got into, if she got into uh, I wouldn't take hitting she'd be gone, because once they hit you, they're gonna hit you again. But if she got into a substance abuse problem, I'd have to say get help, I'm gonna watch you for six months get into AA/NA. We'll see what happens. But if she picked up again drinking and drugging that would be it. Because I don't want to deal with that. Get the point! What am I saying?

Jennifer: I understand, I don't feel comfortable repeating stuff, I, I do understand.

Mr. Dawson: All right, do you want to go? Your Moms got to pay me so I don't need to, thank you,

Martha: Um-hmm

Mr. Dawson: All right, I'll see you Thursday Jennifer. Alright Martha,

Martha: Ok, thank you. (Follows Jennifer outside) Here,

Jennifer: What? What's that?

Martha: Give that to your Dad.

Jennifer: Oh, he's going to kill you!

(Jennifer refuses to take an envelope from Martha) (Martha walks toward my car)

Me: (Rolled down the window) Get away from me, Get away from me,

Martha: I got to give this to your Dad. (Martha throws an envelope on the front seat)

Me: Animal!

Jennifer turns off the tape. I said, what was that about? Jennifer said I don't know. Jennifer opened the envelope, child support! Ha-ha

I said she must be scared about the truck. Jennifer and I laughed. All of a sudden, she willingly gave me child support after I was fighting to get it for six months. On the bottom of the check, Martha wrote Voluntary Child Support. Jennifer and I were driving down 55th street toward home. We were about fifty feet from the block where our house was located, and Jennifer said, "Turn, turn Dad!" As I was turning, there was a blue SUV in front of us also turning down that street, it braked in front of me and proceeded to turn into our driveway. Jennifer and I looked into the driveway and Martha was standing in the driveway on her cell phone, and the garage door was opening, her vehicle parked on the right side of the driveway. Martha looked right at us. Jennifer said, "How did she get here before us?"

The blue SUV suddenly avoided the turn into the driveway and went straight. The SUV was driving the speed limit down the street, 25 miles per hour, which I noticed was Wisconsin plates. I said, "It has Wisconsin plates."

Jennifer said, "Mom's boyfriend lives in Wisconsin." The blue vehicle came to the stop sign at the end of the street. He put on his blinker and made a left turn.

At the next short block, he made another left turn. I did as well. He was still driving about 25 miles per hour. At the end of this street, to my surprise, he made a right turn. It was a left turn to go back toward Martha. I made a right as well. The blue SUV went one short block and turned into Long John Silver's parking lot. I turned into the alley just past Long John Silver's. I got about 30 feet into the alley, and the Blue SUV was coming out of the back exit of the lot and came to a stop with his headlights facing us from the passenger's side of my car. A little blinded by the headlights facing us, we looked over and saw Martha's boyfriend, Todd, for the first time. Jennifer and I were just staring at him. As Todd was staring back at us, he was slightly slouched over, and he had a smile on his face. Jennifer said, "That's her boyfriend, he's ugly, he looks old" We looked at each other and busted out laughing. I balled my fist, waving it in front of my face as I stared down Todd and screamed, "Stay the hell out of my house, you son of a bitch!" and then we pulled away. I really doubted that he heard me, but I was hoping he got the message. Jennifer and I went to Panda Express to eat dinner. As we got out of the car, Jennifer called her mother. She was saying, "Mom, I thought you said Todd doesn't live there!"

Martha said, "He can be here, Jennifer, because you don't live here."

Jennifer said, "Get Todd out of my house!"

I said Jennifer, just hang up.

Martha asked, "Jennifer, are you scared?" Jennifer laughed and said, "Of what?"

Martha said, "Being in the car with your Dad."

Jennifer said, "Ok Mom, you're still a liar." Jennifer hung up.

We went to the restaurant to eat. While eating, Jennifer and I were still chuckling about Martha's new man. Jennifer and I were both expecting some young, good-looking stud. This guy was supposed to be my age, but he looked more like Martha's father. Jennifer that evening said, "Dad remember a few months before this all happened and we were watching the O.C. on TV, and Mom just came out and said, "If I ever get married again, it will be for money, not for love?"

"Yes, I remember that." I just looked at her and said, "Where is that coming from," and she just ignored me.

Looking back, I would remember certain things that were clues as to Martha's affair. I recall a time when Martha changed the style of her underwear. I jokingly said, "Martha, changing your style of underwear is a sign of cheating. "She looked at me and said, "Where did you hear that from?"

I laughed and walked away. I did not believe she would cheat, so it was no big deal. She started working late more and more often. On the 4th of July weekend 2005, she kept insisting I go away with my daughter. She was also suggesting I have a vasectomy, so we did not have to use contraceptives. 5 months prior to Martha asking for a divorce, the savings account did not grow one nickel with a combined $6000.00 a month income and bills being around $2000.00 a month. Martha was starting arguments for the littlest things. Many times, I recall Jennifer coming into my computer room complaining about her Mom constantly yelling at her. The strange thing was our sex life never changed. Martha never turned me away until the night before her news.

On August 9, 2006, I received an envelope from Martha's attorney. It was a Petition for Order of Protection.

AFFIDAVIT IN SUPPORT OF

PETITION FOR ORDER OF PROTECTION

MARTHA FRAWLEY, under penalties of perjury deposes and states as follows:

- I am the Petitioner in the above-entitled cause.
- If called upon, I could testify competently as to the matters contained herein.
- I give this affidavit based upon my own personal knowledge.
- This matter is currently pending and undetermined.
- The respondent, Thomas Frawley ("THOMAS"), and I have one child, namely Jennifer, currently fourteen (14) years old.
- On August 3, 2005, a plenary Order of Protection was entered against THOMAS due to his repeated threats against me and his suicide attempts. In that Order of Protection, Jennifer and myself were protected.
- Since February 1, 2006, Jennifer has been living with THOMAS.
- On Monday, August 7, 2006, at 7:00 p.m., I had a counseling session with my daughter, Jennifer, which went well. As Jennifer and I were leaving the counseling session at approximately 8:05 p.m., THOMAS was parked outside the counselor's residence waiting to take Jennifer home. I had a child support check to give THOMAS, therefore started walking towards his vehicle. As I was approaching and before I even said anything to THOMAS, he had the windows rolled down and began yelling at me, "Get the fuck away from me, you fucking asshole!" THOMAS continued yelling vulgarities at me, all the while in Jennifer's presence. I gave THOMAS the check through his car window and got in my

vehicle. Jennifer then got in THOMAS's car, and they pulled away. I waited in the driveway for a few minutes until they were gone.

- When I was driving home, I called my friend, Todd Scum, to meet me because I was afraid of THOMAS. Increasingly over the past months, THOMAS's paranoia has gotten worse. He has continually verbally threatened and abused me. THOMAS has accused me of stalking him, which is entirely untrue. Todd met me a few blocks away from my house and followed me in his own car to my house. As I pulled into my driveway at approximately 8:30 p.m., I saw Todd turning on my street to come to meet me. Immediately behind Todd was another vehicle, which I recognized to be THOMAS's car. I was on the phone with Todd at this time, he stated that a champagne Ford Taurus was following him, and he identified the license plate number to me. I confirmed the plate number, make, and model of the vehicle immediately as THOMAS' car. Jennifer was in THOMAS's vehicle during this entire stalking incident. Todd decided to keep driving his vehicle rather than pull into my driveway, hoping to avoid an altercation with THOMAS. Todd continued to drive around the neighborhood with THOMAS staying on his tail. Todd pulled into the local Long John Silver parking lot. Immediately upon pulling into the parking lot, THOMAS also pulled in and tried to block Todd's car with his own. THOMAS was screaming at Todd; however, Todd could not hear what THOMAS was saying because Todd had his window rolled up. Again, Jennifer was still in the vehicle with THOMAS. Todd was able to avoid THOMAS' barricade and drove to my house. I had Todd park his car in my garage.
- Todd and I went into my house whereupon Jennifer called me at approximately 8:45 p.m. Jennifer began yelling at me, "Get that man out of my house"! The entire time I was on the phone with Jennifer, I could hear THOMAS in the background also yelling, "Get out of my house!" Jennifer immediately repeated into the phone what her father was yelling.
- At approximately 9:00 P.M.., Todd and I went to the police station and filed a report about THOMAS' stalking.
- On August 6, 2006, Thomas e-mailed me, accusing my friend, Rod, who is an ATF special agent, of using his police powers to follow THOMAS and find out information about him.
- I am currently living in fear of THOMAS because I do not know what he might do next. He has made repeated threats to me in the past, has threatened to commit suicide several times, and made at least one attempt to commit suicide. THOMAS was committed to the

psychiatric ward of a hospital against his will. I feel that THOMAS will physically harm me.

- Unless an Order of Protection is entered against Thomas, he will continue to stalk and harass me and will continue to involve our daughter, Jennifer, in his malicious behavior.
- The current whereabouts of a handgun are still unknown.

FURTHER AFFIANT SAYETH NAUGHT.

Martha Frawley

Martha Frawley

Did the court actually read this affidavit? First of all, Martha stated that she called her friend Todd Scum to meet her because she was afraid. She then states that he met her a few blocks away then followed her to the house. Then she states that she saw him turning onto her street to come to meet her. Two different descriptions. There were two police cars parked a block away in the very direction we were driving. They were parked and occupied by officers right by the stop sign. Todd would stop right next to the police cars. He continued driving. The stalking incident lasted about 3 minutes. With Martha stating this all started at 8:30pm, she waits 30 minutes to go to the police station. My guess was she had to get her story straight. Her friend lived over three hours away in another state. Let's see, counseling ended at 8:05pm, and on her way home, she was so scared her friend made a 3-hour trip in 25minutes. I was being accused of stalking a man from another state in the neighborhood in which I lived. A man that was living in my house as my daughter and I were living like gypsies. I was starting to learn that you could go to the cook county court and tell contradicting stories on paper; they will actually file it. Martha's claim in an earlier counseling session that I had five, six, seven, suicide attempts and now stated in her affidavit of only one. If the courts actually read this serious accusation as well as all of the numerous others, they would find that the "one attempt" contradicts the "two" mentioned in earlier statements. Hence, she never tells the same story. Just look at her statement, "Increasingly over the past months, THOMAS' paranoia has gotten worse. He has continually verbally threatened and abused me," where are the police reports of me threatening her, and most of all, "I abused her." A serious accusation that went unreported. What a joke in this three-ring circus as the clowns working in the "Family Court System" to actually believe and act upon affidavits that even my 14-year-old child can pick apart the inconsistencies. That the people that call themselves professionals are made fools out of by a psychopathic, sociopath, narcissistic person.

In addition, Martha was filing a Petition for a So-called Dr.

MARTHA FRAWLEY,)

Petitioner,)

And)

THOMAS FRAWLEY,) COURTROOM 1623

Respondent,)

MOTION FOR THE APPOINTMENT OF JOSEPH ROSS, M. D.

AS 604(b) EVALUATOR

NOW COMES, Petitioner, MARTHA FRAWLEY, by and through her attorneys, Burnburg & Gordon, P. C. And pursuant to 720 ILCS 5/604(b),

And in support thereof states as follows:

- The above-entitled case is pending and undetermined at this time.
- MARTHA and THOMAS FRAWLEY (" Thomas") have one minor child, namely Jennifer, age 14. Currently residing with Thomas.
- The court-appointed child's representative is Rachel Davis, Esq. Jennifer's therapist is John Dawson.
- As Jennifer's well-being is an issue in this case, it is imperative that a professional be appointed by this court to conduct an evaluation of the parties and the minor child to determine the best interest of the minor child with regard to the issues of parental custody, visitation, and other pertinent matters.
- In order to properly adjudicate the custody issues in this cause, which is in the best interest of the child, MARTHA, requests that Joseph Ross, M.D. be appointed as a 604(b) evaluator in this matter.
- Section 604(b) of the Illinois Marriage and Dissolution of Marriage Act provides in pertinent part:

The court may seek the advice of professional personnel whether or not employed by the court on a regular basis. The advice given shall be in writing and made available by the court to counsel. Counsel may examine, as a witness, any professional consulted by the court, designated as the court's witness.

Dr. Ross is uniquely suited and well qualified to conduct a custody evaluation in this cause. Dr. Ross's curriculum vitae is attached hereto and incorporated hereby as Exhibit "A."

- THOMAS is an able-bodied man, gainfully employed, and can contribute to the 604(b) expenses. MARTHA is currently employed with Through-View and is capable of contributing to the 604(b) expenses.

WHEREFORE, Petitioner, MARTHA FRAWLEY, prays that this court:

- That Joseph Ross, M.D. be appointed as the court's 604(b) examiner in the above cause.
- That the parties and each of them be ordered to fully cooperate on an expedited basis with Joseph Ross, M.D., to enable him to expeditiously complete his 604(b) examination in this cause.
- That the parties be required to pay Joseph Ross: fees incurred for the completion of his 604(b) examination.
- For such further and different relief as this court deems just.

Respectfully Submitted,

MARTHA FRAWLEY

What in the hell was this about now? A medical doctor to check Jennifer out. And the blows keep coming.

On this same day, August 9, I also received a letter from Mrs. Davis requiring me to sign a release of my records from my counselor. I never signed those papers; however: I sent Mrs. Davis a letter with my counselor's phone number and said my counselor will give her whatever she needed as well as my side of the story. Mrs. Davis never contacted my counselor.

Session 12:

Before this session, I told Jennifer, "Do not talk about following Martha's boyfriend by the house."

Jennifer said, "Dad, you know they are going to talk about it."

I said, "Well, be careful what you say; they will twist things to hurt us. Say what you want, Jennifer, but just don't say we followed him. "I knew they were going to drill Jennifer about that night, and there was nothing I could do to stop this interrogation.

Mr. Dawson: I can read your face. I can read you. Let me guess, I'll do a comedy act. Johnny Carson, did you ever watch that?

Martha: rarely.

Mr. Dawson: He had a little skit where his sidekick, Jim Mc Mahon, I think his name was.

Martha: The football player?

Mr. Dawson: no, the other guy. Jim something, his last name was Mc Mahon, and uh ha ha, Johnny Carson would put this turban on top of his head, and Mc Mahon would hand him an envelope, and he would put it on his forehead like this and Johnny was supposed to guess what was inside of it. But he would answer what was on the inside of it with a statement or question.

Martha: So what's on her mind?

Mr. Dawson: I think that, that what I read, is you're unhappy about the baseball season being over with, and you not participating in it the way you wanted to. I think you're holding your feelings about that, and you can talk about it because it could be a good thing if you did. Just bring it out because it will hurt you if you hold it in. It's like I went through this whole season, if I'm going to put myself in a position, I went through this whole season and my Mom kept me from playing for this whole thing that's been going on. That's what I see. What do you think?

Jennifer: I don't know...

Mr. Dawson: Well, am I close?

Martha: She might be thinking that, but I think there is a lot more going on.

Mr. Dawson: Why is there something else going on?

(Martha nods her head) There is, oh? Well, I missed the boat, did I miss the boat, he-he-he, there's a feeling here, there's some kind of a feeling going on.

(Mr. Dawson and Martha laughs) there's a feeling, but I thought it was associated with baseball because it was important to you. I call it baseball, what is it?

Martha: Softball.

Mr. Dawson: Softball, I used to play both when I was a kid but not for a league.

Martha: Well, she could talk about softball if she wants to first, of course.

Mr. Dawson: If you want to. Is there anything you want to talk to me about?

(Jennifer shakes her head no)

Nothing, nothing at all? OK. (Mr. Dawson looks over to Martha): Do you want to tell me something?

Martha: I actually want to talk to Jennifer about it.

Mr. Dawson: Oh, ok. Go ahead.

Martha: When we left the session Monday, I went to give her Dad the temporary, well voluntary child support check, and he started swearing at me.

Mr. Dawson: ohhhhh.

Jennifer (defensive): He didn't swear at you. You apparently did not hear what he said. He didn't swear.

Martha: Yes, he did.

Jennifer (cocky): Ok.

Jennifer: He did not swear Mom, I was right there.

Martha: What did he say?

Jennifer: He said, "Get away from me", and then he just repeated it.

Martha: He said, "You fucking asshole."

Jennifer: That's not what he said. That is not what he said.

Martha: I was right by the window, Jennifer.

Jennifer: Uh well apparently, you heard wrong, Mom. That's not what he said. Oh my god!

Martha: Yeah, it was.

Jennifer: No, it wasn't; he never swore!

Martha: Ok, I mean, did he tell you why he was so mad.

Jennifer: What?

Martha: Why was he so mad?

Jennifer: About what? What are you talking about?

Martha: When he started yelling.

Jennifer: He said get away from me. What, cause he doesn't want you by him.

Martha: Ok.

Jennifer: And apparently, you're still scared of him, so I don't know why you're walking up to him anyway.

Martha: I know I'm gonna mail checks from now on.

Jennifer: Yeah ok, yeah, now! Because people, whatever.

Martha: Well, and what was the thought going through your head when he started chasing or following Todd by the house?

Jennifer: One, we didn't chase him: we turned down the block, and went that way. . .

Mr. Dawson: Who's Todd?

Jennifer: Her boyfriend! And you know how she said, Oh he doesn't live with me, Jennifer. When we turned down the block, guess who was pulling into the garage? Or towards the garage into the driveway? (Sarcastic) her boyfriend.

Martha: He is coming to see me; he doesn't live with me.

Jennifer: Oh yeah, he's coming to see you. What is he going to visit for a couple of hours, was that it? I don't think so, Mom, he lives in Wisconsin.

Martha: I know!

Jennifer: yeah so, no! He wasn't coming to visit when he had to work, so...

Martha: Living with someone and coming to see someone are two different stories.

Jennifer (sarcastic): Oh, ok. Ok whatever.

Martha: Why would you turn down the block, zooming up right on his bumper? What were you thinking when your Dad did that?

Jennifer: First, we were turning. I had told Dad to turn down the block.

Martha: Why?

Jennifer: I don't have to tell you why. I told Dad to turn. That's none of your business why I told Dad to turn.

Martha: Why?

Jennifer: Cause Dad doesn't, if Dad doesn't have to go by the house, then he's not going to. You think he wants to get anywhere close to you.

Martha: Then why would you go down the block?

Jennifer: Mom, that's none of your business. I told Dad to turn down the block, and we did, and he was going to pull; he happened to be there. We didn't think he was coming. We didn't know you were home like we knew her boyfriend was coming over.

Martha: Jennifer, I waited here before I left so you and your Dad....

Jennifer: Yeah

Martha: were in front of me....

Jennifer: Yeah, that's why, yeah, how were you already parked? We didn't know. We didn't know that you were in front of us and already at the house when we turned, and he happened to be there, and he went to pull in the driveway, and he went down the street. As soon as he turned, he turned again down Ashland....

Martha: And you followed him.

Jennifer: No, we went straight....

Martha: Your Dad followed him.

Jennifer: Mom, I was in the car; you wanna tell me.

Martha: Where did you end up?

Jennifer: We went straight to go home.

Martha: You went into Long John Silver's parking lot.

Jennifer: No, we did not.

Martha: Yes, you did.

Jennifer: You weren't there. How would you know? I was sitting in the car.

Martha: I was right in the driveway Jennifer.

Jennifer: Ok, whatever.

Martha: Ok, well, I was just wondering if you were scared when your Dad was chasing him.

Jennifer: (laughing) No, I wasn't scared. Why would I be scared?

Mr. Dawson: Did he get out of the car?

Martha: No!

Jennifer: No!

Martha: He didn't pull in the driveway because he did, he was avoiding an altercation that might have taken place if he would have.

Mr. Dawson: An altercation from??

Martha: Tom

Jennifer: Ok

Mr. Dawson: So Todd didn't get out of the car, what was Todd? Go back to the beginning, what did Todd, Tom do? At your house? Tell me again.

Martha: Followed him.

Jennifer: We didn't follow him; we turned down the street, and he happened to be there.

Martha: There is no reason that Tom and Jennifer...

Mr. Dawson: Were you, tell me the incidents, were you walking into the house?

Martha: I pulled into my driveway, and Todd pulled up behind me to park in the driveway. He was going to park in the garage, so his truck isn't seen, and um Tom comes zooming behind him down the street.

Jennifer: We didn't come zooming, Mom...

Mr. Dawson: Just let your Mom, just let her talk.

Martha: I was in my driveway and you know where our house is.

Mr. Dawson: Um-hm

Martha: People see it right off of 55th, so as soon as Todd turned and he was coming towards my driveway, that's when Tom all of a sudden pulled up right behind him, so Ted decided. .

Mr. Dawson: In the street? In the public street?

Martha: Yeah. And I was on the Phone with Todd when all of this was happening, and I said, I think Tom is behind you, so he goes, I'm going to keep going so that nothing happens. Avoid an altercation.

Mr. Dawson: So he kept going.

Martha: Yeah, he kept going and Tom followed him a few blocks into long John Silver's and I closed the garage and I backed out and I followed them so,

Mr. Dawson: What were they, what was the Long John Silver's parking lot about? Is that where Todd went?

Martha: Yeah, he pulled in after he went around a few blocks, and then he just pulled in and came back to the house.

Mr. Dawson: Did Tom follow him in to

Martha: To Long John Silver's.

Jennifer: No

Martha: by the alley part.

Jennifer: No, you are telling me where I went. I was in the car.

Martha: Why did you come down the block? There is no reason if...

Jennifer: Mom I don't have to tell you why I went down the block cause I have a reason for it, but I don't have to tell you that.

Martha: To follow Todd.

Jennifer: No! No! Like I knew, it was Todd. Like I said, Dad, there is Todd, let's go follow him.

Martha: Why did you call me on the phone right after, after,

Jennifer: Because then we figured out it was him when he went to pull in the driveway and started going, what are we supposed to do stop and back up right into 55th, and we weren't zooming down the street because if you got out Mom, there were cops, police officers right on that block where Todd turned.

Martha: Yeah, I know they were right there

Jennifer: So then, we weren't zooming. Dad would have got a ticket. Todd turned, and we went straight.

Martha: You stayed right behind him.

Jennifer: Mom, you weren't there.

Martha: Ok Jennifer, so why did you pull down the street then.

Mr. Dawson: What did Todd say?

Martha: Huh

Mr. Dawson: What did Todd say?

Martha: That he followed him.

Mr. Dawson: Ok, Why would he lie?

Jennifer: I don't know.

Mr. Dawson: Why would he say that Tom followed him?

Jennifer: Maybe because when we turned down the street, and we started going down the street. He went back into the street after almost pulling into the driveway; where else are we supposed to go? Yeah ok, we followed him. Where else are we supposed to go? Were we supposed to stop, go in the driveway and go back? Just because he is there.

Mr. Dawson: Why would he say your Dad was following him into Long John Silver's?

Jennifer: I don't know, I'm not him.

Mr. Dawson: What do you think?

Jennifer: I don't know why would people lie in general?

Martha: You were following him.

Jennifer: Mom, when we turned, he was already going in the driveway.

Martha: He never made it in the driveway.

Jennifer: He was

Martha: Cause your Dad was behind him.

Jennifer: Oh my god!

Martha: I saw it, I was there!

Jennifer: I was in the car. That was supposedly following him and speeding down the street……. No, that's not what happened. We were turning down the block, and as Todd was going to pull in the driveway, that's when we came, and he pulled out. Mom, I saw what happened.

Martha: Just like your Dad didn't yell outside here.

Jennifer: Mom, you know what, yes, he did yell, but he did not swear at you.

Martha: Yeah, he did.

Jennifer: No, he didn't.

Martha: He didn't yell now he

Jennifer: I didn't say he didn't yell, I said he didn't swear at you. He did not say that, he said get away from me. Once again, I was right there. And like I'm supposed to believe you.

Mr. Dawson: Hm. One time when I brought my kids home uh, the uh, the ex was already, you know, involved with someone else. And the guy was drinking and came out to the car, and he tried to engage me into a fight. I didn't get out of the car; I knew he was a nutcase…. And then he gets off, whatever happened, you know, whatever happened, you were in the car, you were in your Dad's car and you had to have feelings about seeing Todd, driving behind Todd, wherever you ended up. You had to have feelings about that, and what's unfair, just like the guy trying to get me involved in a fistfight with him. What's unfair is the kids are pawns and victims of adult insanity.

Jennifer: My Dad didn't; I told my Dad to pull down the street. We didn't know my Mom was home yet, because like she said, we left here before she did. We pulled down the street. We didn't know it was him at first until he pulled in and when we saw the license plate, it said Wisconsin plates, so um that would only make sense for it being him.

Mr. Dawson: You know what really makes sense to me? I'm only giving you reality; I'm not trying to make you wrong or right or whatever. I'm not trying to make your Dad wrong or right, according to your mother and according to that um document court document. Your Dad had threatened to kill him.

Jennifer: What court document?

Martha: Um-hm

Mr. Dawson: Do you know that? Your Dad had threatened to kill him so. .

Jennifer: Getting angry Oh! In that court document, it did not say that.

Martha: Yes, it did.

Jennifer: No, it didn't.

Martha: Yeah, it did.

Jennifer: No, it didn't.

Mr. Dawson: How come your Dad...

Martha: I pulled it out and read it again.

Mr. Dawson: how come your Dad...

Jennifer: Because you read it, I'm supposed to believe you read it.

Martha: Well I wish I would have brought it with me.

Mr. Dawson: You know.... .

Jennifer: I wish I would have brought it.

Martha: It's in the same paper that I had here.

Jennifer: Yeah, you know what, you know what? I'm going to ask Dad if he will let me bring it.

Martha: It says if I ever see the man you're with, I'll kill him. Those were his exact words.

Jennifer: That, you said before, ok one, what does this have to do with Dad? This counseling isn't supposed to be about him, but two,

Martha: because your Dad was following him on his bumper, following him down the street...

Mr. Dawson: You know it seems to be, it seems to be an issue for you....

Jennifer: Ok just like you have people follow Dad, and you followed Dad when he was at our last softball game you followed Dad down the street.

Mr. Dawson: So, So in all things being logical to use our minds to use our brains intellectually. Your saying, in fact, that statement was made....

Martha: Yeah.

Mr. Dawson: Would Todd be frightened If he was behind him, and would he be frightened if he was followed into Long John Silver's? Would he be frightened? And would Todd have the right, and he didn't do it, would he have a right to file a report against your Dad which would not look good in court.

Jennifer: My Dad didn't do anything.

Mr. Dawson: He followed him.

Jennifer: (Starting to cry) he did not follow him.

Mr. Dawson: And nobody knows his intent.

Martha: So why don't you say why you went down the street?

Jennifer: Mom, because I don't have to tell you about it.

Mr. Dawson: It's not going to do you any good to be cute with us.

Jennifer: I am not trying to be.

Mr. Dawson: Then why don't you be honest?

Jennifer: I am being honest, I don't have to tell her what I do with my life outside of...

Martha: Yes, you do.

Jennifer: No, not anymore.

Mr. Dawson: Anyway just, not you, you hadn't done anything but all those who are involved be forewarned that kind of stuff, like if that guy had just kept coming up to my car, I would tell him I wouldn't get out. By the way, I did bring the police one time because they were hiding my kids out somewhere. I was supposed to pick my kids up; I had visitation. They weren't there; he was there. The policeman went in, and I went in with the policeman and um the policeman told him, hey look, produce the kids, tell us where they are at. People can't fool with the law. The law is very, it's something people can't do, and they just can't do what they want to do because that's our society so....

Martha: And what about where you live? How come you don't give me your address?

Jennifer: Um, why don't you have Rod look it up because he is very good at that.

Martha: Rod has nothing to do with anything, Jennifer.

Jennifer: Ok,

Martha: You are my child, and I have a right to know where you live or what your address is.

Mr. Dawson: You know I'm just trying to help you remember what I said last week. Your Dad is really setting himself out there.

Jennifer: My Dad is not doing anything, this is

Martha: He is...

Jennifer: This isn't supposed to be about Dad.

Martha: I am supposed to know where you live.

Jennifer: Why don't you, instead of taking things into your own hands, take it to the judge?

Martha: It's going to the judge tomorrow.

Jennifer: Good, good, I'm glad.

Mr. Dawson: Are there any other issues you guys want to talk about? Because I can tell you the judge is going to win. The judge is going to win.

Martha: Um yeah, there is.

Mr. Dawson: Well, there is another one, Ha, ha, ha, ha, that's what I am here for

Martha: (boldly) about the papers for court tomorrow, for the evaluator.

Jennifer: Yeah

Martha: Why did you read the papers?

Jennifer :(sarcastic) Um, because Dad was telling me that I had to go to some doctor, so apparently I have to know where I am going.

Martha: Oh, but he is not supposed to discuss that stuff with you. You are supposed to talk to your attorney.

Jennifer: (cocky) Just like you're not supposed to discuss stuff about court but you do it anyway.

Mr. Dawson. If I were in court, if you're in court tomorrow, I would, I would uh, and you might want to make a note of this some time.

Jennifer: I don't...

Mr. Dawson: The evaluator is supposed to make contact, and if I was the evaluator, I would not want to have any part of that interview biased by anyone else. In other words, prepare for the interview like you say this, you make sure you say that. It's supposed to be purely scientific. Nobody is supposed to be involved in it at all. The evaluator makes the contact, and they make the appointment. They might do it through your Dad but, nobody is supposed to be....

Jennifer: Ok but I didn't read the paper. Dad just told me that I have to go to something and I didn't know what it was, that's why didn't I call you and ask you what it was for?

Martha: And yeah!

Mr. Dawson: Tom is not supposed to share that with Jennifer?

Jennifer: Well, He can't tell me where I am supposed to go, what I have to do?

Martha: You're not going anywhere yet.

Jennifer: Well I would like to know what I may have to go to.

Mr. Dawson: What did it say? What was in the letter?

Jennifer: I don't know, I didn't read it.

Mr. Dawson: Did you get your letter?

Martha: Umhmm, my attorney sent me a copy.

Mr. Dawson: I mean since you don't know what the letter is, and you know the letter, and you know what's in the letter and you can share it with me if you want or not and at this point since I want it to be purely scientific. No bias. Do you know what I mean by biased?

Jennifer: Yeah, no!

Mr. Dawson: No, oh. Uh like if I asked you if you have seen this movie and what you think about it and I tell you what I think about it then I am influencing your opinion about the movie. Instead of just asking, what did you think about the movie and just wait for the answer, I influence you, we, we all influence each other. So what was your question, you wanted to know how Jennifer knew about....

Martha: Yeah since, she called me up with a lot of questions.

Jennifer: Yeah, I was asking...

Martha: What is this doctor going to do, what is this all about?

Jennifer: (mad) Yeah, I didn't know what it was about.

Martha: Are you lying, I said maybe you should call your attorney and she can explain it to you. She said well why you can't explain it to me.

Mr. Dawson: Well that's their job, yeah. Do you communicate with her?

Jennifer: What?

Mr. Dawson: Do you communicate with your attorney?

Jennifer: Yeah sometimes.

Mr. Dawson: Sometimes?

Jennifer: Yeah!

Mr. Dawson: I probably communicate with her more than you do. Or have.

Hm.

Martha: And then after the incident that night you called me up screaming, tell that man to get out of my house.

Jennifer: (boldly) yeah, that's right!

Martha: Jennifer

Mr. Dawson: What man? Oh

Martha: When Todd was there.

Mr. Dawson: Oh.

Jennifer: That's right!

Martha: Her Dad was yelling in the background, get out, tell. .

Jennifer: That's not what he said, Oh my god that's not what Dad said in the background.

Martha: (sarcastic) Oh I must just be hearing all kinds...

Jennifer: You must be or you must be twisting things.

Martha: What was he yelling then, in the background?

Jennifer: One he wasn't yelling anything, he didn't say anything until after I said something and he was like, he said um, all we are doing is going home from counseling and we see him, that's all he said.

Martha: You were screaming and he was screaming.

Jennifer: He wasn't screaming. Once again, you weren't there and that's the one thing he said.

Martha: (Arguing back and forth with Jennifer) you were screaming. I could hear him in the background.

Jennifer: You're right I was. You're right I was screaming. Am I lying, I'm admitting it. You're right I don't have anything to hide, I'm not lying.

Mr. Dawson: I want you to talk about that, yes she has a lot of feelings about it being in her house. What's the, what, how do you feel uh that it's a violation, you know cause you don't live there anymore you know what I mean.

Jennifer: (yelling) Yeah but it doesn't matter, I grew up there. Me, my Mom and my Dad all lived at that house. I would feel pretty funny spending however many 18 years or however many years we spent in that house since I was five so, what is that years we were in that house and you spent it with your husband and then bringing another guy in. I would feel pretty freaked out and weird. That's pretty strange if you ask me. (Crying) but she doesn't, she doesn't care that it was my house or my Dad's house or anything she doesn't care.

Mr. Dawson: But you don't live there any longer.

Jennifer: (crying and sniffling) It doesn't matter, my stuff is still there. All my things are still there and I grew up there. It doesn't matter.

Mr. Dawson: Does this have anything to do with the reality that it is over between your Dad and your Mom?

Jennifer: No! No! I don't care, they are over.

Jennifer was brutally interrogated by two adults. Jennifer knew she had to deny us following that man, but she was correct, it wasn't a chase, and we weren't expecting to see him, it wasn't planned, it wasn't stalking. Also, the fact that Jennifer knew they were drilling her to make statements that the counselor could report to the courts and forcibly take her from the life she seeks and is defending. It's like she is a defendant in a trial, and she is under cross-examination. So basically, this is what Court appointed family counseling is, a child on trial for their freedom. The only difference between this dark secret world and the real world is there are no spectators, there is no court reporter, and certainly, no defense appointed for the minor defendant to shout out objection. You are badgering the witness. She has rights. Buckets of tears in that room, and I can only witness through the keyhole and say nothing with the duct tape placed around my mouth and the threat of going to jail for exposing the high authorities that control this torture. The very people I should report it to will imprison me as they rob the innocence of a young and tortured soul.

I was starting to learn this chess game that Jennifer and I were pawns in. I knew Martha would use this new attack in court to cover up her taking my truck without a court order.

On August 11, 2006, I went to court for the Order of protection. I was very nervous. I walked into the courtroom and looked around for Martha. In the courtroom, there were seats that looked like juror seats. Usually, only attorneys sit there awaiting their call. Well, Martha was sitting in one of those seats. Sitting alongside her was her boyfriend, Todd. As soon as they saw me, they turned their heads toward the front of the room. A few minutes after that, Mr. Burnburg walked in and went over and sat by Martha.

Shortly afterward Mrs. Davis entered the courtroom and sat on the same side as Martha and Mr. Burnburg. I was trying to get Mrs. Davis's attention by waving a piece of paper. She finally looked over, and I motioned her to come talk to me. As she walked towards me, she pointed to the doors for me to meet her in the hallway. Once we were in the hallway, I told her, "These accusations by Martha are ridiculous. This was retaliation for Martha taking my truck a few days earlier. "I handed her a printout of the email that Martha sent claiming she took the truck. She took the paper and said "I will read it," then turned and walked back into the courtroom. I went back into the courtroom and sat down, waiting for my name to be called. When they finally called my name, I approached the judge's bench. Martha approached the bench along with her attorney and her boyfriend. Mrs. Dawson stood in the middle. Mr. Burnburg started out by saying, "Martha is filing a petition for an order of protection due to a high-speed chase by Thomas with his child in the car."

Before I could say anything in my defense, the judge replied, "You will have to take this to a hearing judge on the 12th floor."

Mr. Burnburg also stated, "Martha will also be filing a petition for a Dr. Joseph Ross to evaluate Thomas and Jennifer."

Judge Nobal said, "We will have a hearing next month as far as the doctor."

Mrs. Davis spoke up, "Well, Your honor, the counselor refuses to counsel the child any further if they are going to continue to go to the police. We have to get a new counselor now."

I looked at Rachel and though what the hell are you talking about.

The judge answered, ``there was a problem with the counselor's being picked by the wife through her insurance, well you look into the new counselor through the insurance."

Oh my god, I thought, another counselor and a Doctor. I was screaming inside. How much more torture can I possibly endure. How much more can Jennifer handle before they mentally break her down. With these thoughts scrambling all around in my mind, I have yet to answer for the stalking charge.

Judge Nobal said, "Go to room 1206 to see the hearing judge immediately."

We exited the courtroom and I stopped Mrs. Davis. I asked, do you know what this doctor was about and the reasoning behind it.

Mr. Davis replied, "He's an evaluator, it's kind of like a counselor."

I asked her, "Do you know this doctor?"

She replied, "Yes, he's really good."

I turned away and went up to the 12th floor. I walked in about the same time that Mrs. Davis did. I sat to the right and Mrs. Davis went to the front left of the courtroom and sat next to Mr. Burnburg. Sitting next to Mr. Burnburg, was Martha and her boyfriend. Martha and Todd's backs were facing me. Martha and Todd would not look in my direction. I was looking in their direction, and I noticed Todd leaning over and talking to Mr. Burnburg and Mr. Davis.

Mr. Burnburg got up and walked toward me and asked me, ``Can you step into the hallway?"

"Yes," I replied. I followed him out the door. We went over to a bench and sat down.

Mr. Frawley, we want an order of protection for two years or just for until the divorce is final."

I said, "She could have 40 years; I don't want to be around her; this is a lie. We live in the same town. What do I do if we are in the same restaurant or store?"

He answered, "If Martha is there first, then you must leave. You're going to mess up that child, Tom."

I said angrily, "I don't care what you think. You do not know my child. "You don't care about my daughter; this is just your Job. She is fine."

Mr. Burnburg changed the subject, "I want you to sign the papers for Dr. Ross and sign papers to lower the price of the house."

I looked at him and asked, if I accept the restraining order, does that mean we do not have to discuss what happened in court?

"That's right Mr. Frawley, you go up in front of the judge, you accept the order, and it's over, you leave, we all leave."

"You know what? Give Martha her Order of Protection for however long she wants, I will sign the price reduction and sign the papers for Dr. Ross. I am not afraid of this doctor because I have nothing to hide."

Mr. Burnburg said, let's go back inside. I'm in a hurry, I have another case in a different courtroom. When the judge calls us, we will go up and say we agree to the orders.

We went back into the courtroom. I sat down, and Mr. Burnburg walked over and sat by Martha, leaned over, and whispered to her. I decided to give them what they wanted. I did not care about lowering the price of the house. I needed the money. By giving them what they wanted, I avoided the courts believing that I put my daughter in any danger.

The judge called us up. Only Mr. Burnburg, Mrs. Davis, and I went up to the bench.

Mr. Burnburg stated, "Your Honor, we agree on the Order of Protection until the divorce is final. The judge was an elderly man. He looked over and asked me, "Do you agree to the restraining order?"

"Yes, Your Honor," I replied.

He asked, "Are you sure?"

I said, "Yes, I am sure."

He said, "Ok," and he signed the orders.

I turned around and I could see Martha and Todd facing me. I walked toward the back of the courtroom, and as I passed them, Martha stared at me. Todd kept his head down. I exited the room and headed home. I could tell by the look on Martha's face she was furious because she couldn't tell her twisted side of events.

I couldn't believe that Mrs. Davis was not defending her client. It seemed that Martha was her client, and she was an evident part of their team. Mrs. Davis did not have day-to-day contact with Jennifer nor did she ever produce one affidavit or petition on her client Jennifer's behalf. A mouth full of vomit as I would receive monthly statements of my half of the money owed for the representation of Jennifer Frawley. Wasn't it her job to speak for Jennifer, even if she had to lie like the other attorneys in order to represent and show loyalty to her client? I felt Mrs. Davis was just a weak link caught under Donald Burnburg's possessive spell. Maybe they've worked together before, and they are friends. That's usually how the corrupt political system worked. I could only speculate on that, but something was not making sense.

I turned my focus back to Jennifer. I was working on Jennifer's first counselor Debby, writing a letter on Jennifer's behalf. I have been calling for a couple of weeks, but no returned phone calls. Finally, Debra called. She apologized for not returning my call sooner. I was just happy to hear from her. I explained to her that Martha was claiming that Jennifer did not like her, also that Martha and her attorney were claiming that Jennifer had missed sessions with her. I told her about Martha's manipulation and lying to gain control of Jennifer. I said there are two sides to every story, and that was just mine. I said, what I am asking you to do is Just write a letter stating that Jennifer attended regularly and if she cooperated or not. I said I am not asking you to do anything for me, just Jennifer. Debra said she would gladly write a letter on Jennifer's behalf. I said thank you that I appreciate it, and Jennifer will as well. She said it would take about a week. I said no problem: I have a few weeks before court.

August 12, 2006,

I was leaving my apartment about 6:00 pm, and as I was getting into my car, my building manager Tim stopped me. "Hey Tom, do you have a minute?"

"Sure Tim, what is up?"

"Yeah, Tom I was sitting at the bar next door yesterday, and this lady came in the bar and started yelling at the woman bartender. She was saying, “My daughter is Jennifer Frawley, and I hear that she lives above this bar with her father, Tom. Somebody better tell me what apartment they live in."

The woman bartender said, "I don't know who you are talking about, lady, I do not know Tom or Jennifer."

Martha said, "If I find out my daughter is living above a bar, someone is going to be in trouble."

"She then left. I figured it was your wife, Tom. I just laughed, knowing where you live. I sat there and watched. I didn't say a word."

"No kidding Tim, Thanks for informing me."

"No Problem, Tom. I understand; I was divorced a year ago."

August 13, 2006, Email I sent Martha:

Martha, I was warned by my landlord about domestic problems when I moved in. It was brought to my attention that you went into a bar screaming at a woman who works there, saying that Jennifer and I reside above the bar. The building manager was informed by the owner of the bar. My address is 6*** East Ave. It is a white 2-bedroom house. Our house is not completely furnished because you have everything Jennifer and I own. Once I have the house furnished, I will even allow you to go inside to assure you that Jennifer is well taken care of. I agreed to stay away from you and where you live. My wish is that you do the same.

Tom

August 15, 2006, Email from Martha:

Tom,

I don't know what you are talking about because I have never stepped foot into that bar.

Martha

On August 17, 2006, I received the letter from Debra Clancy, Jennifer's first counselor.

This was her actual letter.

To Whom It May Concern:

I had met with Jennifer Frawley for several counseling sessions. She regularly attended from January through May 2006. I found her to be a well-adjusted and pleasant young woman. She had developed a positive rapport with me during those sessions. Unfortunately, due to an apparent conflict with her mother's perception of events, Jennifer was reassigned to another counselor, with whom they have joint sessions. I had offered joint sessions with her mother to Jennifer, and she explained that she was uncomfortable with this. I found this understandable due to the circumstances at that time in conjunction with the fact that Jennifer appeared to need time to grieve the loss of the family relationship. As a part of the process, she has expressed feelings of sadness and anger. Due to these feelings and the sensitivity of the circumstances between the parents at the time, I had expressed to both mother and father the effect that these circumstances were having on Jennifer's well-being. I had also expressed my hope that they both attempt to keep these circumstances as stable as possible during the divorce proceedings in order to allow Jennifer to express her feelings in a healthy and assertive manner as she experienced them. It was my opinion that Jennifer should be allowed to grieve this loss according to her own time frame and be allowed to express her emotions as she experienced them. It was also my opinion that if given adequate time to grieve and heal from this experience that she would build positive relationships with each parent individually. I have taken every opportunity to express these opinions to both Jennifer's mother and father in the hopes of helping Jennifer through the grief process in order to allow her the opportunity to have stronger and healthier relationships with both parents at the conclusion of treatment. Unfortunately, the treatment was cut short, and her case was transferred to another provider.

If I can be of additional assistance, please feel free to contact me at 708-***-****. I am available by phone Monday through Friday from 9 am to 9 pm, and Saturdays from 10 am to 6 pm.

Sincerely,

Debra Clancy

Debra Clancy, MA, LCPC

August 24, 2006, I received a letter From Mr. Burnburg. It was a letter of agreement for Dr. Joseph Ross.

LETTER OF AGREEMENT

- Effective date

This contract shall be effective August 22, 2006, and shall expire on August 22, 2007.

- Intent

Thomas Frawley and Martha Frawley, hereafter known as "The Contractors," seek the services of Joseph Ross, M. D., hereafter known as "The Provider" to provide a 604 (b) psychiatric, custody, and visitation evaluation. The exam shall include interviews of Thomas Frawley and Martha Frawley, parents of Jennifer Frawley, and whomever else Dr. Kraus deems necessary on behalf of The Contractors. The Provider will make available a report of the evaluation of the contractors, as well as testify in court, if necessary. As full consideration, The Contractor shall make payments to The Provider, based on a fee rate schedule.

It is understood that none of the persons interviewed during the course of the evaluation process are the patients of The Provider.

- Services

The Provider agrees to provide an evaluation to make available to counsel a copy of the evaluation report after its completion. Additionally, The Provider will make available to all parties a report of the evaluation, as well as testify in court, if necessary.

- Consideration

As consideration for services rendered, the contractors agree to pay Joseph Ross M.D. the following fee rate: $ 400.00 per hour for services of the provider, with fractions thereof being separated into the nearest quarter of an hour, rounding upwards to the nearest quarter-hour.

- Payment Terms

A retainer of $8,000 shall be made prior to commencement of work by The Provider. Payment for services provided will first be deducted from this amount prior to any future billing. The Provider shall have the right to withhold documentation and services if terms of payment are not met. Billing by The Provider for the evaluation should not exceed $15,000 without prior authorization from The Contractors to do additional work.

Deposition, testimony, court, and/or other court-ordered appearances and time spent on-site waiting to testify shall be billed at the rate of $2,000 per half day. Court-ordered testimony is billed separately from evaluation services and will require an additional retainer prior to the court date(s). Cancellations for scheduled deposition or testimony must be made with at least 48-hour notice to receive a refund.

Payments should be made in the name of Joseph P Ross, MD.

- Breach of Contract, Jurisdiction, Notice of Termination

This Agreement shall be deemed to have been breached if one of the parties fails to perform any material act mandated by this Agreement.

This Agreement is governed by the Laws of the State of Illinois and The United States of America, Notice under this agreement, shall be sent to The Provider at the address provided above and contractors as follows:

I showed my sister Anne this letter. Anne worked in a hospital for over twenty years. Upon further research, Anne called me and said, "Tom, something is fishy about this. Dr. Ross works out of a hospital. Tom, I may be wrong, but I think this Doctor will check to see if you molested your daughter. It just doesn't seem right, especially the amount of money that is involved. That amount of money is usually for medical testing."

I didn't know what to make of this news but there was one thing I was sure of, that Martha would stoop as low as she had to, to win. Another counselor, this time a Doctor. How much more could she possibly put her own daughter through? How could the courts let this madness continue? When would it be enough? One thought came to mind. Several more months of reports and court dates, the flow of money would extend to the Cook County Court System.

August 27, 2006, Martha left a voicemail on my cell phone. It said, "Tom, I would like to work something out outside of court. Did you see the price of the new counselor? I did not know it was going to cost fifteen thousand dollars. Do you really want to put Jennifer's destiny in the hands of someone else? Give me a call."

Martha was surely an idiot. Her attorney's goal is to stay on as long as he can or until she is out of money. It goes with the territory. You control the rules, and you stay ahead of the game, but you will pay. For me, I was at their mercy fighting for my life as well as my daughter's, becoming sacrificed pawns in a game of greed. Yet, I refused to give up. My focus was not about money but about how I could out-think them.

August 28, 2006, Court date:

I exited the elevator on the 16th floor. As I was walking toward the courtroom, I could see Martha sitting on a bench by herself. I kept walking past and entered the courtroom. I looked for my name on a list that is posted in the courtroom. Once I recognized my name, I went up to a woman who sits next to the judge's desk to sign in. In my possession were several copies of the letter from Debra Clancy. My plans were to give a copy to Mr. Burnburg and Rachel Davis just five minutes before court starts. Something that they often have done to me, providing them little time to respond. I also had a check for $150 for Rachel.

I sat down and waited for my name to be called. Once my name was called, I stood up and stated the other parties were not here yet. The judge said, we will call your name later. I went out into the hallway, and Martha was still alone. I waited in the hall for almost fifteen more minutes when I saw a woman attorney approaching Martha. I knew who she was because she had substituted for Mr. Burnburg once before. I could see Martha showing the woman some pictures. I had no idea what they were, nor was I concerned. Then Mrs. Davis came from around the corner and stopped by Martha and her attorney. While they were all talking, Rachel looked over at me with a kind of smile. Rachel was talking to Martha for one or two minutes and suddenly turned around and went toward the elevators. After a few minutes of talking, they got up and headed toward me. I immediately said, where Rachel is going?" The woman attorney answered, "She has court in another room. She will not be in our room today." Then Martha said, "Tom, Jennifer needs to talk to me; I'm her mother, you know. She needs two parents."

I replied angrily, "She does not need two parents; she is just fine with me. You abused her! I shouted! You're not going to get away with it."

Just then, the woman attorney turned away and went into the courtroom. Martha followed right behind her. I walked right behind Martha, still talking to the back of her head. I uttered, "You and John Dawson abused and interrogated my child. I have evidence; I am going to prove it."

Right as we were called, I gave a copy of Debra's letter to the woman attorney. She was trying to read it as she approached the bench. The judge asked, what is going on? " Where is Mrs. Davis?"

"She will not be here today," expressed Martha's attorney. The judge said, "What else is going on?

I jumped right in and said, "Your honor, I would like counseling for my daughter stopped! I looked in Martha's direction, pointed, and said they said my daughter did not like counselors and she missed sessions with the first counselor. I have a letter from the counselor that my wife claimed my daughter did not like or attend."

The judge said, "Let me see it." I gave it to her, she looked over at Martha's attorney and said, "Did you know about this?"

The woman replied, "I just got it."

The judge then read the letter, and she gave it back to me. She looked over to Martha, "What do you have to say about that?"

Martha said, "He is the one who didn't like the counselor; that's why we obtained a different one."

I boldly stated, "That's a lie! I was the one who called Debra Clancy to inform her there was a new counselor. I liked that counselor."

The judge said, "Well, maybe we will use counselor number one again."

I said, "That's fine by me." Martha stayed silent and looked over at me with hatred in her eyes.

The judge said, "We will wait until Mrs. Davis returns and see what she has to say. Ok, see you on September 11.

August 28 evening after court email from Martha:

Tom,

FYI - I have removed you from my insurance plans. I also left a message for Jaime Frazier, your counselor, to submit claims through your insurance and send bills to you because I do not have any money to pay her.

Martha

September 11, 2006 court date: Martha was not present.

I was standing in the hallway. I looked around and did not see Martha anywhere. Moments later, Mr. Burnburg walked up to me and asked, "Are you going to sign the papers for Dr. Ross?"

"I said no!"

"Why not?"

"Because the amount of money this Dr. Ross requires is outrageous. I cannot afford to pay that."

"Mr. Burnburg said," What about a home equity loan?"

I said, "And how am I supposed to pay that?"

He said, ”Give me two of your most recent pay stubs."

I said, ”I will not pay that kind of money."

He replied, ”Well, you could fight it if you want."

He then went into the courtroom. I went in behind him and sat down. A few moments later, Rachel Davis walked in. She walked over by Mr. Burnburg and sat down next to him. We were called, and Mr. Burnburg, Mrs. Davis, and I all approached the Judge's bench.

The judge asked, ”What is new in this case?"

Mr. Burnburg started with, "Mr. Frawley does not want to pay for Dr.Ross."

The judge turned to me and asked, ”Why is that?"

I said, ”Your Honor, This doctor is going to cost up to fifteen thousand dollars, and I cannot afford that."

The judge said, ”Mr. Frawley, that is the going rate for such Doctors. Some can cost up to forty thousand dollars. The judge looked over at Mr. Burnburg and said, what about their home? Do they have equity?"

"Mr. Burnburg said, ”Plenty!"

The judge turned to me and said, ”I know you could use that money for something else like your daughter's college fund and other things, but that is just the way this works."

I said, ”Am I going to have to spend my daughter's college money?"

She said, ”Yes."

The Judge said, ”then that is what we will do."

Mr. Burnburg stated, “Mr. Frawley is going to submit his last two pay stubs as soon as possible to me so Martha can apply for the home equity loan."

The judge looked over at Rachel and said, “Mrs. Davis, what is going on with the new counselor?"

Rachel said, ”I have not had time to take care of that yet."

The judge replied, ”Well let's get that taken care of. This child needs to get back into counseling."

"I will take care of it," Rachel said. I left the courthouse in disbelief.

IN THE CIRCUIT COURT OF COOK COUNTY, ILLINOIS

Martha Frawley)

v.) No. 06D ****

Thomas Frawley)

ORDER

This cause coming to be heard for status respondent pro se present, counsel for petitioner, and the child's representative present and the court going fully advised in the promises wherefore it is hereby ordered

1. This matter is continued to 9-20-06 at 9:30 am for status on selection of a new therapist for the minor child.

2. Thomas Frawley shall immediately furnish his two most recent paycheck stubs to counsel for Martha Frawley. Thomas Frawley shall sign all documents necessary to enable the parties to obtain a home equity loan secured by the marital residence at **** S. Catherine Countryside, Illinois. The amount of the loan shall be not less than $15,000.

3. $8,000. Of the loan shall be used to pay the 604 (b) examiners retainer (Dr. Joseph Ross) or, if already paid by Martha Frawley to reimburse Martha for the advance payment of the $8,000 retainer.

4. The balance of the line of credit/home equity loan shall be used to make the monthly payments on this loan. Said payments shall be made without further court order. Any other usage of this loan shall be only by written agreement signed by both parties or pursuant to subsequent court order.

Entered:

Dated:____9/11/06____________

ENTERED

Judge Mary Nobal

Judge SEP 11 2006________

Circuit Court-****

September 16, 2006 email from Martha:

Tom,

I would like to resolve the divorce between us. Do you really want to pay someone to determine the destiny of Jennifer, or should we come to an agreement? Dr. Ross is going to cost us a minimum of $15,000. I would rather put my ½ of that money towards college for Jennifer. I don't know how you want to spend yours, but I think that you could use the money for other things. We both raised Jennifer to be the bright child that she has grown to be, and I don't want to cause her any more misery. I know she doesn't want to go to counseling or talk to the evaluator. I don't want to continue dragging this on, especially for her sake. I love her and want what's best for her. If she is happy living with you, I can live with this and give you custody/residency, but I do want visitation. It's only right. I am and always will be her mother. I took it upon myself to update the Dissolution of Marriage and would like to know if you have any changes. If we can come to an agreement, I will forward the document to my attorney.

Martha

September 19, prepared Jennifer for what might happen with the doctor. I sat Jennifer down. Jennifer, about that Dr. I am not sure what that is about, considering it is at a hospital they may want to test you for molestation.

From who, dad?

Most likely me, my sister said it could be that, and I've heard of cases where parents were falsely accused of this to win custody. So I am just preparing you for that.

Jennifer starting to cry: You never did anything, Dad.

I know Jennifer, I don't understand this either, but I have a plan. Your Mom loves money. I'm going to call their bluff, I'm just praying it doesn't backfire.

I just can't imagine what this Dr. is. What does he do for 15,000 dollars? What does he do that a family counselor does not? Will he say I molested my daughter? Will he put her through the tests? I can only wonder as again he is hired by Martha's side. How many counselors and Doctors must my child face for Martha to get the results she wants? Why don't I have a say in anything? Too many unanswered questions on my side but only one answer on Martha's, to whatever it takes to get her from him no matter how much it hurts our child. I want her soul.

September 20, 2006 court date:

I exited the elevator on the 16th floor. I see Martha immediately sitting by the windows. I kept my head down, walked past to go sign in with the court clerk. Afterward, I went back out in the hallway and sat on a bench just outside. Moments later, Mr. Burnburg came over and sat next to me. He asked, "What do you want to do?"

I said, "We are going to see this Doctor Ross. From what I have learned about the law, if a person falsely accuses someone of molestation or any type of crime, they can go to jail. She will be jailed for perjury, and I will sue her for slander.

He said, "Martha does not want to go to Doctor Ross."

"Why not, I asked.

"She wants to settle."

"Oh, now she wants to settle because she backed herself into a corner, " I replied.

"Tom, I have to go to another courtroom right now, but I will be back to talk more." Mr. Burnburg walked over to Martha. I followed and walked up to Martha, looked her in the eyes, and said, here are my last two pay stubs." I turned around and walked back over to the bench, and sat back down.

Mr. Burnburg headed toward the elevators. After a few minutes, I walked around the corner, and I see Martha sitting talking on the phone. I sat down about 10 feet from Martha. As soon as she hung up her phone, I walked over to her.

I said, "I have a deal for you; I will let you have the house, the money, everything if you give me Jennifer."

Martha just stared at me with no emotions.

"You know Martha, I have nothing but time. Every time I walk into that courtroom, it costs me nothing. Your attorney is going to get rich off you; I will drag this on as long as I can."

"I know Tom," she said sarcastically.

I said, "If not, we will go see this famous Doctor of yours."

Martha replied, "They will put Jennifer in a boarding school or a foster home."

"Why would they do that to her, Martha? Jennifer did not do anything wrong. Furthermore, how would you know the outcome? Why is it that I do not know anything?"

"I ask questions, Tom. Jennifer is not normal."

"You are not normal, Martha. What are you going to put your own daughter through? Are they going to check to see if she has been sexually molested? Is that what you are accusing me of now? Why does Dr. Ross work out of a hospital?"

"Whatever happens, it is going to be your fault, Tom."

"Martha, we will go see this Doctor. We have nothing to hide. You are responsible for all of this. You are evil! Bye!"

"Tom, get away from me."

I looked into Martha's eyes, turned around, and walked away. I went around the corner toward our courtroom and sat on the bench. Ten minutes passed and Mr. Burnburg returned. He came up to me and asked, "What are we going to do?"

I boldly stated, "We are going to see Doctor Ross."

Mr. Burnburg said, "Martha does not want to pay Dr. Ross.

"Oh well, this is what she ordered."

"Mr. Burnburg said, "Let me go talk to her." Mr. Burnburg went over to Martha, sat down, and began talking to her. Their conversation lasted just a few minutes. He came back over to me and asked if I would join him over by Martha. We went over and sat down. Mr. Burnburg said, "listen, I know you and Martha would like to get this over with. This is our offer. You get full custody of Jennifer. There will be no doctor, Martha owes you nothing, you owe her nothing, you split the house 50/50, you can have whatever you want from the house, Jennifer will not be forced to see her mother."

Martha, "Yeah Tom, I will not force Jennifer to see me. If she does not want to see me, oh well."

Mr. Burnburg stated, 'The only stipulation is the child will have to continue counseling. Neither you nor Martha will be able to call the new counselor as a witness for court. This counselor will have nothing to do with the court. The new counselor will probably include you in some sessions. You and Martha will be on your own."

I replied, "You know Mr. Burnburg, I cannot force you to like me; it is something you have to earn. That is what Martha wants from counseling."

Mr. Burnburg utters, "I hope you like me."

I laughed! "What about my Tahoe? I want Martha to replace it. Mr. Burnburg said, Martha sold the vehicle to CarMax, and she had to pay $1,600 because the vehicle was worth less than the amount owed."

"I do not care, she will have to replace my vehicle."

Mr. Burnburg stated, the court will not give you replacement value. They give less than it's worth."

"Oh well, it is better than nothing," I said.

Martha looked at me and said, "Tom, how many cars did I buy you?"

"You bought me cars; oh, that's right, I did not work, I didn't work 2 jobs most of my life, I did not put hundreds of dollars in the drawer for you to take cash on your business trips. You just bought me everything, right!"

Martha looked at me with no reply and a dumbfounded look on her face.

"Why is my car in the MSA? I asked. That car is not marital property. I purchased it after Martha filed for divorce."

"Yes, it is," Martha and Mr. Burnburg both said.

"So if I won a million dollars today, Martha would get half."Mr. Burnburg and Martha said, "Yeah!"

I boldly stated, "You people think I am stupid. "They stared at me for a second without saying a word.

I stated, "As long as Jennifer is not forced to see her Mother, we have a deal but I want sole custody."

Mr. Burnburg said, "Just so you know, the attorneys and courts will not have anything to do with the new counselor, and you nor Martha can use this counselor for the future as a witness in court. I will draw up the new MSA and have it ready for you in about a week. If you want, you can just leave, and I will see the judge to say there is a possible settlement."

Just then, Rachel walked up and said, "I take it they did not settle the case."

Mr. Burnburg said, "I think we have."

Rachel said, "Oh," wait here for a second Mr. Frawley. I have a court order for you.

September 26, 2006 email from Martha:

Tom,

I received a copy of the court order in the mail yesterday and noticed the counselor's phone # was not included. I called Rachel's office and then Jerry, the counselor. Jerry said he wants to see Jennifer and me together this Friday, Sept. 29th, at 7:00 PM.

Martha

I received a voicemail that same evening from Rachel Davis's secretary, Mr. Frawley this is the number for the new counselor ***-555-**** His name is Jerry Kozak. There is an appointment for Jennifer on Friday, September 29. I will be sending the papers out today.

I called the new counselor. He did not answer, so I left a voicemail.

About 30 minutes later, Jerry called back. He said, "Hi Mr. Frawley, this is Jerry Kozak, the new counselor. Jennifer has an appointment on Friday at 7:00 pm. Are there any questions about my background that you would like to know?"

"I replied, yes there is; who hired you? Martha did through her insurance, and then I talked to Rachel Davis. She filled me in on what was going on."

"I said ok, no, I do not have any more questions. See you Friday."

I hung up.

Amazing how no one asks me what is going on.

My reply to Martha's email:

Amazing how everything works with your schedule, I have not been notified of any appointment. .... Politics as usual.

Martha re:

If you would have called, then you could have made the appointment. The date/time was from the counselor. I notified you with the email and also left a message on Jennifer's phone.

Me re:

Your first email was a good one! You people make me laugh!!!! Before you tell a story Martha, make sure everyone has the same one. . . . .

Martha re:

I don't know what you're talking about, you people. . .

What about you? You tell me to pick a date/time so you can come and do a walk-thru and say ok, then you don't show up or call. What's up with that? Why don't you cut out your games?

I thought you wanted to get this over with? It's all time and money.

Me re:

We were coming, and at the last minute, Jennifer broke down and said I could never go back in that house, and it was tough for me as well. Why didn't I call . . . . . would you have cared or understood? It's just time for me, its money to you. Keep the laughs coming.

September 29, 2006 Email I sent to Martha:

I was just wondering, you sent me an email on the 26th saying you received papers from Rachel on the 25th, I received papers today, the 29th, 4 days after you. The day of counseling. I was called by Rachel's secretary, the 26th the postmark said the 27Th. You were the first one to tell me about counseling, I just want to say thank you,

Amazing how Rachel did not call me and ask if I would like to get a counselor through my insurance. I have also noticed one of the emails Martha sent me had Rachel Davis on the C.C.

September 29, 2006 7:00 pm.

I took Jennifer to her first counseling session with the new counselor Jerry.

His office was above a bank. Jennifer and I went inside, up a flight of stairs and his office was on the left. It had a glass door and a huge window. We could see Martha sitting in the waiting area. The waiting area was small, consisting of only 3 chairs. Jennifer and I walked in and sat in chairs opposite Martha. I never looked at Martha. She was vapor to me. I also brought along my laptop. I pulled it out of the case, put it on my lap, and turned it on. By the time it booted up, Jerry came out of his office. Jerry was in his late 50s to early '60s. He was soft-spoken and reminded me of Mr. Rogers from Mr. Rogers Neighborhood. He walked up to me and shook my hand, and said, 'come on in Martha, and Jennifer.' They went into his office, and he closed the door.

I would use this hour to write my story. I would take my laptop with me everywhere. It was my life. After the hour was up, Martha came out the door first, walked through the waiting room, and out the other door. Jennifer came out seconds later, and we left. Once we were in the car, I asked, "Jennifer, So how did it go?"

"Ok Dad, He seems to believe me."

"Well Jennifer, I want you to keep a journal just in case."

"Ok Dad, no problem."

Counselor # 3 session 1: (Jennifer's journal)

With Mom

Jerry told me that we were there because of a conflict between me not talking to my Mom, and he also said that Rachel will kind of know what is going on in the sessions. He asked me if I was in counseling before, and I told him that I had gone to two counselors before him. He asked me what I thought about them, and I told him that I liked the first counselor, and I told him that I liked her because she listened to what I said and she thought I was handling like a normal teenager and gave me advice. Jerry then asked me why I didn't like the second counselor. He told me what happened to me and just was for my Mom. Jerry said I don't think you are so tough. I told him that this is counselor #3. He then said that he was hired to help me and my Mom talk, and that was his goal. He asked me if I wanted to be in counseling, and I told him that I honestly didn't. He then asked me to tell him some of what happened between my Mom and me. I told him that there was a time when my Mom asked me what I wanted for my birthday, and she told me don't ask for my Dad because that's not going to happen. I also told him that she had said when all the divorce stuff is over, we are going to get a house and a pool with her boyfriend and then go on a vacation. Another thing was when I had a wedding picture of my parents in my bedroom, and she came in and said, what are you doing with that picture up because that's never going to happen again. The last thing I said was that she kicked me out.

After the session, Jerry came out of his office and said, "Tom, we will see you next Friday at 7:00pm."

Jennifer and I walked out to the car. When we got inside, Jennifer said, "Oh my god Dad. I have to go to counseling every Friday for at least a year. Tell them we do things on Friday. I said, "I can't Jennifer. I cannot interfere. Remember last time they were going to put me in Jail."

"I know Dad, but I hate this, Mom is going to keep me in counseling forever."

"When I get my money from Mom, I will get an outside attorney to help you, Jennifer. Right now, we just have to cooperate. I'm sorry Jennifer, they have all the control. In three years you will be 18, and then no one can tell you what to do anymore. For now, we have to do what they say."

"I know, Dad."

Jennifer would have to relive telling what her mother has done to her to another counselor.

October 6, 2006 Counselor #3 Session 2 (Jennifer's Journal)

With Mom

Jerry asked me to repeat the things that I said last week and explain what happened. I told him about my birthday, the vacation, the picture, and her kicking me out. I also added about her stealing my Dad's truck at one of my softball games. He said part of the problem with my Mom, and I was because she really didn't seem to let me have a relationship with my Dad and that since I was close with him before and my Mom was blocking him from me. I said yes that it was part of it and I told him that the other thing was what she said and did to me too, like what she said about the picture and for my birthday. I also said that she lies a lot. He asked me to tell him how, so I said that there was a time when she told me my Dad wanted all of my college funds, and I believed her. I didn't talk to my Dad because since I believed her, I was mad at my Dad. On a visitation night, I confronted my Dad about it, and he said it wasn't true, so I asked him if I could see the papers that really said what was going on, and he said no. I told him then I will still be mad. He showed me, and it said the opposite, that it was my Mom and not my Dad. I then knew my Mom was lying, so I didn't trust her. My Mom said that it's not true that she could bring papers in, that said it was true. Jerry said that he would like to see the papers. I then said that I would bring in papers that said it was true, and Jerry said no, don't bring them in. So I said, oh she can bring papers to prove her point, and I can't. Jerry said that is a good point and that neither of us could bring papers in because it would just turn out to be like court, and he apologized and said that would have been unfair.

October 13, 2006

This session, Jerry would see Martha alone. Jennifer did not have to attend.

On Sunday, October 15, 2006, while writing about the taped sessions with Mr. Dawson, I was getting very upset at what I was writing. Thoughts were racing through my mind. Even though Jennifer was not going to see this man again, I could not get what Mr. Dawson had done to my child out of my mind. The fact that Martha was very aware of what was happening in those sessions, nevertheless, playing a part. These thoughts are rolling around in my mind. I decided to have Jennifer call Mr. Dawson on Monday to request copies of her records. I was curious as to how they would reflect the tapes. From what I understood of the contract that Jennifer signed with Mr. Dawson, one of the papers stated that Jennifer has a right to her records upon request.

Jennifer came home for dinner after a day out with friends. I said, "Jennifer, I need you to call Mr. Dawson tomorrow and ask him for a copy of your records."

Jennifer said, "Ok, Dad."

Monday was Columbus Day, and Jennifer was off school. I went to work at 5:30 that morning. At about 11:30 AM, I called Jennifer. I told her, "Call Mr. Dawson. "Tell him you want a copy of your records, and if he asks why, do not answer, just say I need a copy of my records. If he does not answer, leave a message."

Jennifer said, "Ok, I will talk to you later."

At 12 noon, I came home to have lunch with Jennifer. I walked in and said, "Hi Jenn!"

She said, "Hi Dad, Oh I called John Davis and left him a message. I said, hi John, this is Jennifer. I called to ask you for my records. Can you give me a call back to let me know when I could get them? He called back two minutes later. He said Oh, about your records, you know that storm last Monday? Well, my basement flooded, and all the records were destroyed except for the people I have seen recently. Therefore, you can't get your records. How is everything, Jennifer? Did you start your new counseling? Yes, good, I said ok bye! And I hung up."

I looked at Jennifer and said sarcastically, "The records were destroyed in a flood."

Jennifer said, "Yeah, right Dad. Oh, and right after Mr. Dawson called, Mom called, I didn't answer. A minute later my phone rang again, and I did not recognize the number, so I answered. It was Mom, she said Jennifer, Jennifer, and I hung up. She called again from her work number."

I said, really!"

Jennifer said, "You know John called her."

I said," Yeah, I'm sure he did." Jennifer was very aware of what was going on around her. Jennifer and I were a team. More often than not, Jennifer kept me in line. She would often tell me, "Stop emailing Mom! You are going to say something, they will twist things around, and you will get in trouble. Why do you let her get to you? Be like me Dad, I don't answer her, so I don't get aggravated.

"Jennifer was definitely tougher than I was.

As far as the new counselor Jerry, it seemed that we finally had a counselor who was an honest person and believed Jennifer. He did not seem like a person who could be bought, and based on the first few sessions, Martha was on the defensive side. He was very talkative and friendly with me. Jennifer felt the same way.

October 15, 2006, I called Martha:

"Martha, I am taking Jennifer to the hospital; she is very sick. Her throat is swollen, and it hurts when she tries to eat."

"Tom, why would I go to the hospital? I know you and Jennifer do not want me there."

"That's true Martha, we really don't want to see you, but you are her mother. That's why I'm calling you. Whatever Martha, I have to go, bye!"

I hung up.

Later that evening, Martha left this voice mail:

"Tom, I'm calling to see how Jennifer is doing. Call me back."

I did not call her back.

October 16, 2006, Email I sent to Martha:

Martha,

I called you yesterday to tell you that I was taking Jennifer to the hospital. Do not call me and leave me messages like you were concerned. If you were concerned, you would have gone to the hospital. I called you tonight to tell you how Jennifer was doing, and you did not answer my call. You go to court, and you act like a concerned mother, but your actions show otherwise when we're out of court. Just as Jennifer said, your act only works on an audience. Please do not reply to this email; your lies are getting old.

October 17, 2006

Martha RE:

Tom,

It's your games, not mine. Like I told you on Sunday, I knew Jennifer was not herself as soon as I saw her at counseling on Friday. Why would you wait 4 days to take Jennifer in if she was not eating or feeling well? I would have come to the hospital, but you told me not to, that you and Jennifer did not want me there. You were taking her to be seen by a Dr., something you should have done on Friday or Saturday, but you waited until Sunday and took her to the emergency room instead. On Sunday, I tried calling you/Jennifer 6 times with no response from either of you. I had to call the hospital to find out if it was serious, but they said she was seen and released. On Monday, I assumed Jennifer would be off school, and I tried calling her 3 times. I didn't want to call her early and wake her.

Monday night, when you called, I didn't answer because I thought you were calling because you received the revised MSA from Donald. You decided to call me to let me know she was doing better. Thank you 1 day later.

Martha

I often wondered if Martha read what she wrote...

October 20, 2006

Counselor # 3 Session 3 (Jennifer's journal)

With Mom

Jerry said that he wanted to talk more about the situations that I had talked about the week before. He told my Mom that he just wanted her to sit there and listen. I then explained how I felt about those situations because that's what Jerry asked me. I told him that I felt mad, scared, and hurt. After I talked for a while about the situations from the previous week and I told him my feelings, he turned to my Mom. He then explained that he wanted her to repeat everything that I said and how I felt without justifying or explaining why she did what she did because she is an adult, and she has to show me that she understands what I said. My Mom started to say that she understands that I felt hurt, but she then started to explain and justify things, so Jerry stopped her and said, no, you can't do that. He then told her to try again, and she kept it short and simple by just saying she understands my feelings on the things she did and that she understands why I felt that way.

October 23, 2006, Rachel Davis left a voicemail on my phone while I was at work. "Hi Tom, this is Rachel Davis. There is a group I would like to get Jennifer into. I think it would do her a world of good. So if you call this person, her name is Janis Reno, and this is her number 555-***-

*** I called Rachel's number, and her secretary answered. I asked, "Can I speak to Rachel?"

"She is not available now. Can I take a message?"

"Yes, can you tell her that Tom Frawley called?"

"Oh, wait a minute."Moments later, Rachel said, "Hi Tom, did you get my message?"

"Yes, I did, but it was broken up. What is this about anyway?"

Rachel replied, "I have a woman doctor that I would like Jennifer to see. She is really good, and I know her."

I angrily stated, "Why would Jennifer need to see this doctor?"

"Because Jennifer doesn't talk to her mother."

I said, "Jennifer does not talk to her mother because of what her mother has done to her. I know what this is about; it's because I told Martha I am going after her and John Dawson for abusing a child."

Rachel said, "You say that like he has physically hurt her."

"They emotionally abused her, and John Davis used his house as an interrogation room. That kind of abuse, Rachel. I know you think I am crazy, but when you are gone, and this is all over with, I am never going to let this counselor get away with what he has done to my child. I love my child to death and they are not going to get away with it! For fifteen hours that is all they have done was question her about court. He asked my daughter if she would take a bullet in her head for me?"

Rachel uttered, "I don't think you are crazy. I just thought it would help."

I said, "What is wrong with the new counselor? I like him, Jennifer likes him."

Rachel angrily stated, "Well, if you are happy and Jennifer is happy with the new counselor, then just stay with him."

I said, "I do not want to bump heads with you or get in any trouble. I just do not want my daughter seeing doctors and counselors for the next four years. That will mess her up! She is fine, she is happy. She is an A student."

Rachel, somewhat upset, "I'm not bumping heads with you, Ok, stay with the court-appointed counselor."

I said, "I do not want to get in trouble."

Rachel said, "You're not going to get in trouble."

I said, "Thanks."

Rachel said, "Bye," and hung up.

As angry as I was, I was very careful while talking to Rachel. What the hell were she and Martha trying to do now? Another doctor, another counselor? Oh my god! I wanted to say you are a piece of crap, you were hired to protect a child, and you sent her to her abuse. You are an abuser, you continue to abuse, you are never going to stop abusing my child until she is 18 years old. I could only exhale and try to kindly fight off this bully because she still was in power.

The same day after work, I checked my email. I had an email from Mr. Burnburg:

Mr. Frawley, I would like to wrap up the settlement agreement before we go to court on Thursday. Kindly respond.

Donald Burnburg

My reply:

Very hard to do without papers.

Immediately after reading the email, I called Martha. To my surprise, Martha answered.

I said, “Martha?”

She answered, "Yeah."

"Where are the MSA papers?"

She replied, "You don't have them?"

"No, I do not."

She said, "Well, I received my papers on the 16th."

I said, ``Well, I do not have any papers."

Martha boldly stated, "I will email you a copy."

I asked, "So what is going on? Why is Rachel trying to have Jennifer see a doctor?"

Martha said, "I don't know what you are talking about."

"Yes, you do. Rachel works for you."

Martha said, "You hired her."

"The court-appointed her," I said. You people insult my intelligence. I see in court how she sits by you and talks to you. She agrees to every petition you file. She doesn't even talk to her own client."

"We are going to have to see Dr. Ross Tom."

"Dr. Ross, I said, Rachel gave me a woman's name."

Martha replied, "I don't know what she is talking about."

I said, "That's funny, her reason why she wants Jennifer to see that doctor is because Jennifer does not talk to you."

Martha stated, "I have not talked to Rachel for a long time."

"How would Rachel know that Jennifer is not talking to you? Ok Martha, I have a bill from Rachel with phone calls with you that I have to pay. You know what, Martha, all you do is lie!"

"Tom, they will put Jennifer in a boarding school or a home."

I said, "Why would they do that? Jennifer did not do anything wrong."

"It will be your fault, Tom!"

"Martha, you filed the petition to see this Doctor. You are going to do all this to your own daughter for this man. Is he that special to you for you to hurt your own daughter?"

Martha uttered, "I don't want to talk about that. I emailed you the MSA. You know Tom, the only thing I regret is Jennifer. Bye!" Martha hung up.

Within the hour, Martha called Jennifer.

Jennifer was out with her friends when she received the call. As soon as Jennifer answered, she asked Martha, "What's up with this new doctor, Mom?"

"Jennifer, I don't know, if you go through this, you are going to have four options. One you could come live with me, but I doubt that is going to happen. Or there is a chance that you will remain living with your Dad. Or there is a boarding school."

Jennifer angrily said, "What did I do wrong? I didn't murder anyone."

"The fourth option is an institution Jennifer, but I don't want that to happen."

"You know Mom, why don't you just leave me alone. I am happy when I am not talking to you. You don't deserve the last name Frawley!"

Martha laughed! "I don't want that last name. You know Jennifer, time is running out. Thursday is coming fast. Your Dad better sign those papers."

"Go tell Todd Mom or better yet, tell someone who cares!" Jennifer hung up.

Jennifer came home and told me what happened! She was angry, frustrated, scared, upset as well as fearful. I told Jennifer, call your attorney and tell her what just happened. I was angry as I sat on the front room floor in deep thought. Martha was cruelly using Jennifer as a tool to force me into submission. She knew Jennifer was my weakness. I just couldn't believe she would make our daughter suffer to get her way. The hardest part was that I couldn't understand why she would do this. What was fueling her hatred and torture? Was this the advice from her counsel? Did her family know what Jennifer may face? If so, what were their thoughts? Answers I did not have. A new massive battle for me to face in my quest to protect Jennifer.

Jennifer left to join her friends. When the door shut, the tears rolled down my face. My poor daughter was depending on me to protect her from her insane mother. I couldn't even protect myself. I was now faced with giving up my fight and sharing Jennifer with this nut job or throwing Jennifer into the hands of more corrupt counselors, doctors, or whatever the title these blood-sucking animals hide behind. I was fighting an army, going into a gun battle with just a knife. As I sat there crying in disbelief, the very thought of Jennifer suffering for reasons she had no control over, not understanding the consequences for both choices would be degrading. As usual, I could only wipe away my tears and deal with what was coming.

October 20, 2006

Counselor # 3 Session 4 (Jennifer's Journal)

Alone without Mom

Jerry said he really hasn't had a chance to get to know me, so he asked me how I liked school. I said that I liked it and that I was doing good. He then asked me if I was in any other extracurricular activities, and I said I was not yet, but I planned on trying out for softball. He asked if I played before, and I said that I have been playing since the third grade, but that was a slow pitch, and at school, it is a fast pitch, so it is going to be different. He asked me if I did sports last year and I said yes, badminton. I told him that we are ranked in it, and I was #2 in the singles and #1 in doubles. He asked me if I played any instruments, and I told him that I play the violin. He asked how long I have been playing, and I said since 3rd grade. After that, he asked me if I think people should be forgiven, and I said it depends on what they have done. He then asked me what I thought someone had to do to be forgiven. I said; first, they have to apologize and say what they are apologizing for and promise not to do it again. I don't know what else I said. He then told me his five steps of forgiveness.

October 24, 2006

My email to Martha'

No deal! Never.......

Martha RE:

Tom,

Just remember I tried to work with you. Since you cannot negotiate and come to a settlement, you are rolling the dice and leaving our daughter's faith in someone else's hands, not me. You say you want to end this, but you don't; you keep dragging it on and on.

The MSA was updated according to what you verbally agreed to when we were in court last month.

- You have full custody
- I pay child support
- I pay Jennifer's medical & dental

- We sell the house and split it 50/50
- No one owes each other anything

As I told you, time & time again counseling is not up to me, it is in Rachel's control. You were the one who asked to have a child representative, and Rachel has the final say over what happens with Jennifer and counseling, not me.

What is it that you don't agree on this time?

Martha

My reply:

First of all, you broke your verbal agreement. You said you would not force Jennifer to see you. In the new MSA. I shall force her.

Last night you told me, when the papers are signed, we will be done with Rachel. In the new MSA, Rachel will remain.

My MSA,

Jennifer will remain free of Counselors, Doctors, and lawyers. (Attorneys Discharged) She shall be free to choose when she wants to see you. However, I agree to have her complete the 26 sessions with Counselor # (3) Jerry. You nor I shall make the decision if counseling continues. (Jerry) alone shall make that decision. Based on his own reports and findings. No outside influence.

Child support shall be 20% of your gross income (The law) not net. You shall notify me immediately of any repairs needed on our home so that I can get a fair appraisal or make the repairs myself. I also want to go in the basement and confirm $5000 in water damage. Especially that I have the knowledge to make such repairs. I shall have the opportunity to make any future repairs to our home.

My Ford Taurus shall be taken out of the MSA. (Not marital property) (Insulting)

Amazing you have no control over Rachel yet she is listed in our settlement.

I told you time and time again I am not stupid. I can see your whole plan.

I do not fear any of your Doctors, Jennifer is an A student, and a perfectly happy young woman. She is content and living well. We have nothing to hide. Amazing why would someone put an A student who is happy and well and imprison them in a boarding school? Your handwriting is on that, not mine.

My new plans.

File a petition for mandatory Child support.

File a petition for the replacement of my Tahoe

File a Petition for money from the garage sale and van sold.

File a petition to prohibit you from making lone decisions on home repairs

File a petition for Jennifer and me to reside in our home until sold.

File a petition to get 3 estimates on repairs already made.

File a petition for a refund of tools I bought for my job.

File a Petition for you to come up with receipts for everything you sold.

File a petition for one-half of last year's tax returns.

File a petition for maintenance.

File a petition for the cost of my and Jennifer's attorneys.

I have the right in the Cook County Court Domestic Relations Division to file a petition for each court appearance and be heard the following month.

I will fight for Jennifer's freedom for as long as it takes. When I told you all I do is read. You said why I don't do something else with my life. JENNIFER IS MY LIFE!

See you in court Martha,

Tom

Email I sent Martha:

All you do is lie, nice try with the 401k. Illinois law 50/50. I will never let you rob me. Keep the MSAs coming? Attorneys are getting rich off you. I have nothing but time.

See ya tomorrow.

October 26, 2006,

I went to court and I got off the elevator on the sixteenth floor. As I was walking down the hallway, I saw Martha sitting alone. She looked up at me, so I turned my head and kept walking toward the courtroom. I then had to check-in and after doing so, I observed Rachel Davis pulling files out of her briefcase. I went to the back of the room and sat down. Rachel went over to the clerk, checked in, walked to the back of the courtroom, and went out the doors into the hallway. Moments later, Rachel came back into the courtroom and asked, "Tom could you step into the hallway for a minute?"

I followed her into the hallway, I walked up to Mrs. Davis and said, "What is up?

She said, "Mr. Frawley, I get all the emails you write to Martha, and I was wondering why you have a problem with me remaining as Jennifer's attorney?"

"Really? That is ironic, Martha insists that she does not talk to you. You work for Martha," I replied.

"I don't work for Martha," Rachel said.

I said, "Every court day you walk into the courtroom, you sit by Martha, you talk to her and you never talk to me unless I call you over by me."

"I didn't see you," Rachel said.

"You do not even know Jennifer. You have seen her once, and have only talked to her a few times in eight months. You want to keep Jennifer in counseling and want her to see a doctor. She is fine, she is an A student. Do you know about the phone conversations between Jennifer and Martha? I still make Jennifer call her every now and then. Just the other day, Martha told Jennifer what could happen to her if she were to see this doctor and she told her that time was running out. She also told Jennifer that she doesn't want the same last name. What do you think about that?""

Rachel replied, "That's why she needs to be in counseling. "

I said, "Who?"

She said, "Jennifer, so she can deal with those situations."

Oh my god, I thought, this woman is nuts!

Just then, Martha and Mr. Burnburg approached me.

Mr. Burnburg said, "What is the problem with Mrs. Davis remaining as the child's attorney?"

I said, "The problem is that all of you are still in control."

Mr. Burnburg said, "You think that Rachel is against you?"

I said, "Yes. When Martha pulled stunts like taking the Tahoe while Jennifer was in my presence, Rachel did nothing. But when I do something, she agrees to whatever you file against me and then files papers herself. You people actually think I am stupid. I don't mind keeping Jennifer with counselor number three. That's right you sent her to three counselors. I like number three. You wanted number three. No more!"

Rachel said, "I will not sign off on Jennifer. It is my job to protect her."

I yelled, "Protect Jennifer." What about what her mother has done to her? Don't you see what Martha has done to Jennifer?"

Rachel replied, "You mean when Jennifer thought she had been thrown out of the house?"

"Not just that, many things. You see, you don't even believe Jennifer."

Mr. Burnburg jumped in, "Mr. Frawley, Rachel is just going to be there to see that things are ok."

I replied, "You will keep my child in counseling until Martha gets her answer. She is never going to get that answer."

Mr. Burnburg said, "What answer?" at the same time as Martha when she said, "What's my answer, Tom?"

"For Jennifer to say I love you. They can't make her love you."

Rachel walked away and went into the courtroom. Mr. Burnburg told me, "I will be right back," and left Martha and me standing alone. I looked over at Martha and said, "You know, you didn't have to do it like this. Maybe we could have gotten along. You lied to get me thrown out of the house."

"I was scared," said Martha.

"I never threatened anybody but myself," I replied.

Martha said, "Yes you did, you were distraught. You probably didn't know what you were saying."

"All the things you have done to your own daughter, I feel sorry for you Martha. How does it feel knowing your own daughter will never love you like she once did?"

Martha replied, "She doesn't love me now, oh well, life goes on."

I said, "You were the world's greatest mother, and now you are garbage."

Martha just stared into space showing no emotions with every question.

I said, "You know Martha, you are a liar and so is your attorney and Rachel. I will never stop fighting until Jennifer is free. Free from all of you. I will die for her. I will go after Mr. Dawson until he is prosecuted. "

Martha replied, "Do whatever you want."

I said, "Oh you too, you participated in all of that and I can prove it."

Martha laughed and said, "If you have tapes, they are not admissible in court."

I said, "How about the news?"

With a grin on her face, she just stared at me for a second and said, "I am not on trial Tom, why don't you do something with your life."

I asked, "Why would you take the truck while Jennifer was with me? Why wouldn't you wait until I was alone?"

Martha stated, "Because the truck was in my name."

Mr. Burnburg came out and handed me a piece of paper. It was a court order not yet signed.

Martha Frawley)

)

v.) No. **** D*****

)

Thomas Frawley)

ORDER

This cause coming to be heard for status respondent pro se present, counsel for petitioner, and the child's representative present and the court going fully advised in the promises wherefore it is hereby ordered

1. Thomas Frawley shall have the temporary and permanent sole custody of the minor child Jennifer Frawley subject to the terms of the parties' custody appointment appeasement attached less to as Exhibit A.

2. This order and exhibit A shall be incorporated into any Dissolution of Marriage entered in the cause.

3. Rachel Davis shall be discharged upon entry of Judgment of Dissolution of Marriage.

Exhibit A

I said, "This paper says that Jennifer has to see Martha."

Mr. Burnburg pointed out that the papers state when visitation resumes. "We are giving you sole custody of Jennifer Mr. Frawley. We are also going to discharge Rachel Davis as counsel for Jennifer when the divorce is Final."

I held the papers in my hands with thoughts rolling through my head. I was under pressure as Mr. Burnburg, Martha, and Rachel Davis stared at me waiting for my decision. Jennifer would be stuck in counseling for at least a year but I have been fighting for joint custody of her for a year and a half. Now sole custody is staring me in the face. My heart was pounding. I looked at Mr. Burnburg, Rachel Davis, and Martha.

I said "Ok."

Mr. Burnburg said, do you agree to a trial by a judge for all your assets?

I said, "Yes."

Mr. Burnburg said, "You and Martha need to sign the bottom of this paper."

I signed the paper and handed it to Martha.

She signed it and we went back into the courtroom. It was just about empty. They were waiting for us. Judge Mary told us to come right up. We all approached the bench. Rachel to my right, Mr. Burnburg to her right, and then Martha to his right. Mr. Burnburg started out, "Your Honor, We are filing an order to give Mr. Frawley sole custody of the child, and in addition, the child's attorney will be discharged when the dissolution of marriage is final. Your honor, we attorneys do not agree with this but I feel for the best interest of my client's wishes, we go ahead with this order.

Judge Mary with a confused look on her face turned to Rachel and asked, ``what do you think about all of this?"

Rachel Stated, "Well Your Honor, Mr. Frawley seems to believe that I am working for Mrs. Frawley so I guess a new court-appointed attorney will have to be appointed when I am discharged."

Judge Mary stated, ”I find this highly unusual."

Mr. Burnburg said, ”I know Your Honor, but this is my client’s wishes."

Judge Mary turned to Martha and said, ”You’re ok with this Mrs. Frawley.?

Martha said, ”Yes."

She turned to me, "Do you agree with this Mr. Frawley?

"Yes, Your Honor."

Judge Mary said, ”Ok, then make copies and I will sign them."

That was it, the custody battle was over. My excitement was somewhat overpowered by confusion and anger. I stood there and watched as the attorneys gathered their paperwork, the writing in her agenda, I looked around the room, the police officer that stands guard alongside the judge’s bench, the woman sitting next to the judge recording the records, the people sitting in the back awaiting their case, attorneys sitting at tables preparing for their case, but I conclude my observation by facing the tall judge’s bench, the wooden plaque with gold trim bearing 2-inch letterer the honorable judge. The large room I’ve spent the last 15 months defending myself from accusations as serious as the possibility to commit murder. One of the possible victims being my daughter. With that said, why would a judge that ordered restraining orders, counseling, the threat of incarceration, based on affidavits from a person who is believed to be a victim of domestic violence, hand over a child that was seemingly in possible danger, to the person that was considered dangerous, without having one question for Martha? A bitter pill I would have to swallow, as I watched Martha walk out of the courtroom Scott free from crimes of perjury, mental cruelty, false imprisonment, theft, stalking, harassment, threatening, child abuse, abandonment, cruel and unusual punishment, mostly things I was accused of and punished for. How did that powerful human being as a judge feel absolutely nothing as she signs a court order to keep the child in psychotherapy, a punishing sentence to a young person she has never met, for the minimum of one year, at the request of Martha.

I went out into the hallway and waited for Mr. Burnburg to bring my copy of the court order. Once I had my papers, I left the courthouse, jumped into a cab, and headed for my car. On the way, I sent Jennifer a text message saying,

"You belong to me." Jennifer was in school but I knew she would check her phone at lunchtime.

She replied, "What do you mean?"

I replied I have sole custody of you. I will talk to you when you get home tonight."

When Jennifer arrived home after school, I filled her in on the details. I said, "Jennifer, I have sole custody but I traded with a year of counseling for you. We will be getting rid of Rachel as well."

Jennifer said, "A year of counseling Dad?"

"I know Jennifer but I think this new counselor is going to be fair." I hope that he will see that Mom is a liar, besides it will be harder for Mom to get custody of you again. This is the third time she has given you up."

"Well, I am happy that you have custody of me Dad."

"Me too Jennifer, let's go out to dinner and celebrate."

Basically, Martha traded her only child for $ 7,500, half of the $15,000 we would have paid for Dr. Ross. Martha all of a sudden wanted everything to end as soon as possible. I knew one of the reasons was money. I could only guess as for the other reason. My belief was Christmas day being Martha's birthday as she was expecting an engagement ring and she wanted our divorce over with so she could marry. It was all about her.

October 27, 2006

Counselor # 3 Session 5 (Jennifer's Journal)

With Mom

It started out with Jerry asking my Mom to explain what had happened when she went to court. She had said that she let my Dad have custody but that I have to stay in counseling. Jerry then said so you are stuck with me for a while. He also said that my Mom walked the talk by giving my Dad custody because that shows that she does want me to have a relationship with my Dad. Then he said that it is usually really hard for a man to lose his child and that it must be harder for a

Mom. He then told me that his goal is to come out of this with two parents. He asked me if I remember my last session with him when I was alone with him when we talked about forgiveness and I said yes. He then asked if I think people should be forgiven and I told him that it depends on the situation. He then asked me what it would take for me to forgive my Mom because she wants forgiveness. He said just something as a start. I told him a start would be a confession. He asked what kind to me or through the church. He said because there are different kinds of confession that I don't know if you're religious or not. He then asked what would be the littlest tiniest thing that takes a step forward in my Mom and my relationship and I said I don't know. He said just something small and I still said the same thing. He then told me that I was hard to read. He asked my Mom the same question. And she said for us to talk on the phone every day. Jerry said that is way too big. He told her to think of something even smaller. She said ok then every other day. And Jerry said that is still too big. Jerry then asked me how big that was and I asked him what he meant and he said well is what she is asking too big by a half a third? And I replied that it is too big as a whole. Jerry said he was thinking even smaller like me bringing in my grade report and giving it to her and that he will even cut me slack and that I can do it with an attitude. He asked me if I could do that or if I would be willing to. I said maybe. Then he asked me if that would be a step forward and I said NO. Jerry asked my Mom if it would be a step forward for her and she said yeah. He asked her why and she said because I would be giving her something that I do in my life, which is education. I told him that she already gets my grades and reports. Jerry told me I was missing the point and I said no I understand what I was just saying. Jerry then said that he thinks my Mom should write a letter to me taking responsibility for what she did and admitting to blocking me from my Dad and breaking up the family. He then told my Mom not to justify or make excuses for what she did wrong to me. Jerry asked me if I would be willing to coach her. I asked what he meant. He said that if she writes a rough draft of that letter that if I would read it and see if she needs more stuff and I said I might. Jerry then asked us if there is anything we wanted to talk about and we said no and he said to fill up some time he was going to tell us a story. After that, Jerry asked us again if there was anything we wanted to say and my Mom said yes. She said that my grandma and Aunt sent me something for my birthday and that I should call them and thank them. Larry said he agreed and then he said happy birthday and I thanked him. Jerry asked how we thought the session went and he asked me if I thought it went neutral, good, or bad and I said neutral.

October 31, 2006, was Jennifer's fifteenth birthday, it would be the first time in Jennifer's life that Martha would not see her on her birthday. For Martha, this day would be no different than any other. She made one call To Jennifer wishing her a happy birthday. She would not call again. Martha sent Jennifer a birthday card. Jennifer would not open the card. She mailed it back to Martha. As for me, I took Jennifer out to eat. For Jennifer's birthday, I told her I was taking her to Wisconsin dells, a water park resort along with seeing the beach boys in concert. My best friends were taking their children and asked if we would like to join them. I told Jennifer we were to go on November 10th.

November 1, 2006 Email to Martha:

I would like to take a walk through the house if possible. This time I will show. I want to see what is missing or sold. I have the papers from Gumphreys. SET JENNIFER FREE! And you keep everything in the house. Are you really going to keep our child in counseling for the rest of her teen life? Oh, did you see Jennifer's grades? A-pluses and B-pluses. Not signs of a messed up kid. . . . .

Have a nice day!

Martha's reply:

Let me know what day you want to come over to make your list of what you want. Friday, 11/3 @ 5:30 or Tuesday, 11/7 @ 5:30.

My reply:

Friday, are the police going to be there? If that's the case, forget it. At counseling, you sit within a few feet of me. In the 22 years, I've known you, I Never harmed you, nor will I ever and you know that. . . . . Let me know.

Martha re:

Yes, Countryside Police will be there to keep the peace. How could you say you never harmed me? I guess you don't remember hitting me and putting bruises on my body. I do because it happened to me. How about when you cut your fingers from grabbing the toaster - that was when you were attempting to throw it at me and your fingers got caught. I could go on. . .

Are you going to come or not?

Me re:

We had one fight in the '80s, I threw the toaster on the floor. You created this drama of me being dangerous to get people to feel sorry for you. You claim that you are afraid of me yet you are all alone at counseling with me (over a dozen times). NOT ONCE HAVE I EVEN MADE AN

ATTEMPT TO HARM YOU. I saw you in Kohl's a few weeks ago. Do you know what I did? I left the store, you were even with your sugar Daddy. I had many opportunities if I wanted to hurt you. It makes your story better. You lost your mind. I didn't plan to go by the house to argue with you or even say one word. Whatever Martha, You can cancel, I am not comfortable having the Police stand over me while I go through my home. I will be going to court anyway on 11/16 for the correct amount and mandatory child support.

As days passed, Martha's routine calls to Jennifer would remain unchanged. Jennifer let her cell phone fill up with voice mails. With her voicemail full, anyone calling her phone could not leave a voicemail. Martha would still call just once a day between five and seven o'clock. She would not call again for 24 hours.

Jennifer and I were vigilant every day. We both feared Martha's power. We were living just blocks away from Martha. Martha would miss out on Jennifer having her first boyfriend. Jennifer would tell me everything. She told me about their good times as well as their bad. I would give her advice and let her handle herself. By now she was one tough little girl. Jennifer was a normal child outside counseling and Martha. She hung with her friends as well as joined in on family functions, just my side of the family. Martha's family had not contacted Jennifer since Martha threw her out. Martha's mother called one time. Jennifer mostly argued with her grandmother because the call was about Martha, not about her. Every day I drove Jennifer crazy. I would say, Jennifer, you could call your Mom if you want. Jennifer would get angry with me and say, "Why do you tell me that every day? I don't want to talk to her."

I said, "Jennifer I am going to tell you that every day whether you like it or not. I want all the choices as far as your mother to be yours. I don't want you five years from now saying you kept me from my mother. I just want you to know I will back any choice you make for your happiness."

Martha was still paying her so-called voluntary child support. Two checks a month. Always different amounts one check would be around $262.20 and the other $320.35. It was definitely helping. Financially I was afloat. I was paying my bills and not charging anything on my charge cards. I had a debit card, I would only use that. I was still working six days a week.

Jennifer was able to join her winter bowling league that she has been on for years with her best friend Karen. Karen and her family were a huge help. Jennifer was always with Karen. Every day Jennifer would walk to Karen's house in the morning to catch the bus with Karen. After school she would stay by Karen's until I came home from work. If I had somewhere to go or something to do Jennifer would spend the night with Karen. I always knew where Jennifer was and who she was with. With Jennifer being a typical teenager I had to schedule my time with her. It didn't always work out that way but I wanted her to be a kid. Martha on the other hand was just blocks away and we were always worried if someone was watching us, or what Martha was up to.

Often I would think of running away. Somewhere where they could not find Jennifer and me. We just wanted to be left alone. Even though they were just notions in my head, Jennifer's life and friends were here. I sometimes asked Jennifer what she thought about living somewhere else. Her answer was, "Do I want to, no, but I will go with you Dad." For Jennifer's happiness, I would sacrifice my own. Just blocks away a man lived in my home with all the luxuries in the world as Jennifer and I lived in a small apartment with no furniture, no beds, and lugging clothes to the laundromat. As I was paying rent, I was paying the principal, taxes, and repairs on that home. Martha worked just a few blocks from my company. I could literally see her company from the parking lot of mine. I would sometimes see her at stoplights. With the restraining order, I had a leash and boundaries. I would stay blocks away from my home. When going to our local shopping malls I was always looking over my shoulder. If I went to local restaurants or bars I would have to look around to see if Martha was there. According to a restraining order, if I walked into a place and Martha was there, I was to leave. I feared running into her. All she had to do was say I was following or stalking her, I would be arrested and lose Jennifer. A man that lived a state away, moved into my town, moved into my home after my daughter was thrown out in the street, and he and Martha are protected by the law.

November 3, 2006, on this evening Jennifer and I decided to go for one of our nightly walks. Jenn was going to go see her friend in Hodgkins and I was going to stop at a local bar called Murphy's for a few beers. It was a little chilly outside and we threw on our hooded sweatshirts. Once we were ready, we went out the door, down our steel spiral staircase, across the deck toward the gate. It was about a 6-foot solid wood gate that you couldn't see in or out. The gate was on the side of the bar and grill parking lot. I walked out first with Jennifer right behind me. I took about 2 steps when all of a sudden I felt a blow to the back of my head. My legs went numb and I fell to the ground face first. I heard Jennifer scream, Daddy! Daddy! Within seconds someone jumped on top of me with their knees on my back. He started hitting me, punching me in the back of my head and the side of my face. My vision was blurred as several punches landed in my eyes. I could hear Jennifer behind me screaming, let me go! Let me go! . Hearing Jennifer screaming, I was struggling to get up as I was covering my face with my hands to defend myself from the continuous blows. I managed to get to my feet while still being struck. I was trying to turn around to fight back when all of a sudden there was a quick sharp burning sensation in the lower right side of my back. Then another, and another. My body became numb and I collapsed to the ground face-first as my hands were reaching around gripping my back where the pain was. It was excruciating pain. It started to feel wet. I slowly pulled my hand around to my face to look at my hand. It was red, my whole hand was full of blood. I suddenly realized I was stabbed with a knife. I could hear Jennifer screaming but I couldn't get up. The punches stopped. Laying there motionless as if I were paralyzed, I heard a car door shut and the sound of squealing wheels. I yelled out! Jennifer! Jennifer! Are you alright? It was silent, no answer. I started to crawl on the ground to turn my body around to see if Jennifer was hurt. I couldn't see, my vision was blurry. My eyes were almost swollen shut. My shirt was heavy and soaked with blood. I crawled dragging my motionless legs toward the gate. Jennifer was gone. I couldn't see her anywhere. I dropped my head in the dirt and started crying out loud. These bastards took my daughter. I cried and I cried as I lay there helplessly in a pool of blood. I then reached around searching the ground for my cell phone. It was in my hand when I was struck in the back of the head. I couldn't find it. I started to crawl toward the street. I could only get a few feet of the 20-foot crawl to the street. I was getting weaker and unable to crawl. Stunned, confused, angry, and badly injured, I put my head in the dirt and I cried until I passed out. I don't know how long I was laying there when all of a sudden I felt a sharp pain again! This time in my chest. My body jumped up! I was in the sitting position. The pain in my back was suddenly gone. My head felt heavy and was facing downward. I slowly turned my head to the left, and then the right looking at the ground around me. I was sitting on the floor in my apartment when I realized, it was just a dream! My heart was pounding fast as I thought to myself. Just when I thought there was nothing left for Martha to take from me, she has taken my dreams. I looked across the room where Jennifer was sleeping on her blowup mattress. I grabbed my cover and went over and lay next to her and put my arm around her. I couldn't imagine life without her.

November 10, 2006, I was taking Jennifer to Wisconsin Dells for the weekend to see the Beach Boys in concert and to stay at an indoor water park resort. This was part of Jennifer's birthday gift. We were going with our best friends and their children. For me, it was a little strange at the beginning. This was a place that Martha and I have taken Jennifer for the past 10 years, nevertheless, we had a great time.

November 17, 2006,

Counselor # 3 Session 7

This session would consist of seeing Jennifer for the first half-hour and me for the second half-hour. At this point, I was still unsure of this counselor's intentions. When Jennifer's half-hour was up, she came out of the office along with Jerry. Jerry told me to come right in. I walked into his office and sat on a couch that was opposite a chair. Jerry said, "My goal is to try and get Jennifer to have a relationship with both of her parents."

I said, "Are you aware of the things that Martha has done to her own daughter?"

Jerry replied, "Yes, some things."

I said, "let me tell you something. To be honest, I really do not trust you. The second counselor who was chosen by Martha abused my child up until the point I went to the police. Then he quit. If I could, I would have him put in jail. Jennifer's attorney who I had hired through the court has talked to Jennifer only a few times in seven months. Martha wants Jennifer to just forget about what she has done to her. All of these people tell nothing but lies. I admit I had a suicide attempt in the past. I was married for 19 years and I had no clue this was coming. It was well over a year ago. I am fine now."

Jerry said, "I think that maybe the child is afraid of your depression and she does not want a relationship with her mother because she is afraid of you slipping back into depression and making another attempt of suicide."

I stated, "Jennifer has lived with her mother for five months after that. She does not fear that whatsoever. Martha is nuts, it was all the punishment that Martha has put her through that caused Jennifer to resent her mother. I like the old Martha, I do not know who the new Martha is. All of this is totally unlike her."

Jerry uttered, "Well I am going to get the old Martha back and I feel we can all have a good relationship again for the child's sake. Martha for her child has given her what she wanted for you to have custody of her. She has given you custody to show that she is willing to start somewhere."

I boldly stated, "Martha has given me custody because she did not want to spend any more money in court."

Jerry said, "The things Martha has done are part of a custody battle, custody battles get ugly. Now it is time to get the child into a relationship with both parents."

I said, "Interrogating her own child about court-related issues is a crime."

Jerry replied, "Well the courts want me to get the daughter and mother to talk and Martha, you and I, will all make the decision when counseling stops or if it needs to go on."

I looked at Jerry and said, "Whom do you work for?"

He smiled, twitching his body, changing sitting positions in his chair, hesitating to answer, "I work for myself."

I asked, "What is your goal?"

"To have this family talking again," he said.

"Well good luck Jerry. Jennifer refuses to talk to her mother because of all the cruel things her mother has done to her. Every day Jennifer and I wonder what Martha will do next. Are you aware that her mother threw her out in the street without a coat in February and she stole my vehicle when we were moving with everything Jennifer and I owned, while her child was in my presence?"

"Jennifer told me some of those things and I realize Martha needs to apologize."

I said, "Martha has done so many bad things to Jennifer."

Jerry stated, "Well Martha is not going to apologize for every little thing" as he counts on his fingers.

I boldly replied, "Oh so Jennifer is just supposed to forget as if nothing ever happened. It does not matter anyway, Martha will never admit she has done anything wrong. All she does is lie. What punishment will Jennifer receive if she does not have a relationship with her mother," I asked.

Jerry said, "There will be no punishment here."

"This is her punishment for not speaking to her mother because of the cruel things her mother has done, the child is forced into counseling. Jennifer is very happy, she is an A student."

"Mr. Frawley, I would like in the next session for you and Jennifer to be in here together to discuss Jennifer refusing to have a relationship with her mother because of the fear that you might slip into depression and make another attempt at suicide. You know I think the problem with the boyfriend is?"

I cut him off saying, "This has nothing to do with the boyfriend."

"Ok Tom, well that is enough for tonight."

I said, "Whatever" and walked out.

Jennifer's half-hour (Jennifer's Journal)

Alone for 30 minutes

Jerry first asked me if there was anything I wanted to start off talking about. And I said no. He then asked me how I thought counseling was going so far and I said it's nothing I haven't already been through. He asked me what I thought about and how I felt about my Mom agreeing to give my Dad custody and I said that I was glad my Dad got custody. Jerry asked if I wanted to reconcile and heal the hurt with my Mom and I said no. He then said well if you don't mind me asking why not? I told him because of all the things she put me through and he asked if those things were things we talked about in previous sessions and I said yes those are some. He said that my Mom wants to reconcile with me. He also said that in the papers it said that I have a year of counseling or it could be stopped when he, my Mom, and Dad agree to stop it. He also said that he thinks a healthy marriage in his eyes is to come out with 2 parents. He asked me if I believe there could be a change for the future and I said not for this, I don't see anything like that happening. He then asked me what I thought a healthy divorce was from my perspective and I told him that I really didn't know. He asked me if I knew anyone that is a kid that has a divorced family and I said that one of my friends does. He said well how is her relationship with her parents? I told him that she doesn't talk to her Dad because he did some stuff. He said ok well what would I consider that? Unhealthy divorce. He asked something like what went wrong and if any problems went on and I said no. I wasn't aware of them. I said it was just her boyfriend. He said that he deals with a lot of marriages and issues and when there is an affair there is a conflict that went on in the family before the person came into play. He also said I don't know if it was through work and I said it was. He said that is mostly where people meet for affairs. He said if there weren't certain needs met at home when they find this person at work that person seems to meet their needs and their relationship grows. He said that it's like the last straw on the camel's back and most likely the new person (affair) is usually the last straw. That's all he could say in general.

It was after this session I decided to have Jennifer record the sessions. It was the statement, "I think the child refuses to talk to her Mom because she fears that you (me) will slip into depression and make another attempt at suicide."

I could respect the fact that this man's job was to repair a broken relationship with a mother and daughter. However, common sense tells me that in order to do that Martha would have to admit all the terrible things she has done to her daughter. She would have to be truly sorry for what she has done. Not point the finger in the other direction or justify and make excuses.

Although this counselor was not as arrogant and had a kinder approach as opposed to Mr. Dawson, I felt his intentions were the same. Blame me, justify Martha's actions, make excuses for her, just sweep it under the carpet and get Martha what she is paying for.

November 25, 2006

Counselor #3 Session 8

Once again I would have to prepare Jennifer. I told Jennifer, "They want to take you away from me. They are going to try to play with your mind. They want you to say that you are afraid of me getting depressed and attempting another suicide."

Jennifer laughed!

"Jennifer, it is not funny, I am serious."

She said, "I know Dad but that is crazy."

"I know Jennifer but that is what they are going to try to prove to the courts. You go in there and you tell the truth like you have done a hundred times. Just don't let them put a word in your mouth."

Jennifer and I were about a block away from the counselor's office. Like a routine, I hit record, switch the hold button to on, and give Jennifer the recorder. She would put it under her shirt and we would go into the counselor's office.

Jerry: Oh, hi Jennifer.

Jennifer: Hello!

Jerry: So how was your thanksgiving?

Jennifer: Good.

Jerry: Is there anything you would like to talk about uh till your Mom comes?

Jennifer: No.

Jerry: No, ok. Um what place is your bowling team in? We will talk about the important stuff first.

Jennifer: Um, I don't know, I think like 7th.

Jerry: Out of about how many teams.

Jennifer: Fourteen.

Jerry: Oh, ok, so you are about the middle of the deck. And is it all male or uh all-girl league?

Jennifer: No. Mixed.

Jerry: Mixed league oh, I think your Mom is here. Hi, Martha, come on in. We just started. I figured you would be here any minute so we were just uh catching up on the bowling talk.

Martha: So how is it going?

Jennifer: (softly) fine.

Jerry: We know she did not bowl a 300 game but can we share that with your Mom? Ha, ha, ha, ha,

Martha: What did you bowl?

Jennifer: Ok, like 175.

Martha: That's good. What is your average this year? You don't know?

Better than last year? Worse? Hard thing you know. Who is on your team this year?

Jennifer: People.

Martha: Ok.

Jerry: Are you sure? Ha, ha, ha, ha.

Martha: Girls, boys?

Jennifer: People...

Jerry: Ok, Well let's talk about some other things. You know I would like um you know to be able to let you guys have kind of some of that you know just kind of hi how are ya you know that kind of talk. Uh but um I'm afraid if we do that uh right now it's not going to go anywhere. Um so um actually I had a couple of thoughts about how we might use our time today. Um so let me run that by you.

Martha: Ok.

Jerry: Um one thing I thought that maybe would be good for us to talk about is that uh I know that uh Tom agree to um you know what the um residential and custody arrangement is going to be and that uh it would be incorporated into the divorce agreement you in the distant future. Um, I guess technically it's a temporary order until it's entered into the divorce agreement. So I thought that maybe one thing we can talk about is um not only what that is cause I know you already know that, but um you know like what your thinking was and um and then um, I also thought another thing we can do, I know you wrote a letter. If we could kind of go over the letter and hopefully that letter will be helpful in healing for you Jennifer. So um you know that's probably a full agenda for today I think. So um does that make sense to the two of you?

Martha: Um hm.

Jerry: Ok, if you have any other ideas say so. No, ok. Well, why don't we go at it in that order? So why don't you tell me a little bit about what you're thinking about. I think it's probably important to you to be able to say a little bit about that.

Martha: Um rather than going through an evaluator and more counseling and talking with yet another person and the potential that Jennifer would not have been able to be with her Dad that I agreed to give him full custody so that she could.

Jerry: Because you knew that, that's what she was asking for.

Martha: And that's what he wanted too. I didn't like the alternatives that were given and that the potential she wouldn't be with him, not that she would have been with me either but I just couldn't, I couldn't roll the dice for something like that.

Jerry: Ok and you were also realizing too uh you told me that uh you realize it had become probably something that's just going to drive the two of you farther apart.

Martha: Um-hm

Jerry: Right. Ok, could you say a little bit about that, because you also hope this could kind of be a healing gesture you know in a way for Jennifer, right?

Martha: Right, that could have dragged on for probably another year back and forth with counseling and plus another evaluator, a meeting with Jennifer, me and Jennifer, me by myself, Tom by himself, Tom and Jennifer, it would have just prolonged things for another year at least.

Jerry: Yeah, probably, and uh my experience with the whole evaluation process is extremely hard on everybody and um so it not only would have dragged on but it would have been very difficult on everybody too. Ok, and um Martha it's fair to say that um in agreement to this that one of the things you were hoping is that um you know by being gracious in this regard that um it would maybe take one source of tension out of your relationship with Jennifer.

Martha: Um-hm, putting some finality to stuff and this is the way it will be moving forward, all the fighting back and forth and going back and forth to court and...

Jerry: Yeah, yeah, in my perspective on the two is that um in a way this could be a transition time um you know for your family um because the way I look at it is you are still a family, you are a divorced family but you are still a family and uh sometimes having um you know uh the court stuff behind uh can be a transition. Uh because some of the anger and the hurt you know can uh start to heal so I'm hopeful that this can be kind of a transition for your family. Um I'm also thinking too that you know one of the things that the two of you have talked about at our session is the fact that Mom had done some things that made you feel that she was trying to prevent you from having a relationship with your Dad, right we've talked about that and in a way you know, the way I look at this is this is a very tangible sign. That-uh you want Jennifer to have a relationship with her Dad and that you accept that's very important for her and you know uh for you to uh you know you and Tom agree to this. This is a sign, a very tangible sign, and a very hard thing to do too uh that recognizes the importance of her relationship with her Dad and whatever mistakes she made in the past uh this is kind of a way of trying to make good on past mistakes. Would you say?

Martha: Um-hm

Jerry: Maybe you could put that in your own words Martha because they are just my words right now.

Martha: He wanted her to be with him, Jennifer wanted to be? with him. It's not what I want but, you know so we can start to talk to each other and see each other, it's something that's going to you know let's move on moving forward and...

Jerry: So it's a very hard thing for you to do.

Martha: Um-hm

Jerry: Um and you know you might even fear that you're going to lose Jennifer um. .

Martha: I can't lose her any more than I already have.

Jerry: ok, ok, ok, but you're hoping that this could be a transition. Ok, and do you view this in a way that you can kind of prove to her that you want her to have a relationship with her Dad and that you accept it as super important to her?

Martha: Um Hm

Jerry: Can you put that into your own words because I think that's important that Jennifer hears it from you.

Martha: If I didn't want her to have a relationship with her Dad I would have kept going through court back and forth and battling but I know she needs him, he needs her, but I need her too.

Jerry: Sure, and as I have said um you know to both of you and to Tom you know my goal is always for kids to come out of a divorce with uh two parents they can be close to and um I talk about a happy divorced families ah that's my picture of a healthy divorce family is to help you come away from this divorce with you know two parents whom you can love that's kind of um what I uh view as my objective you know and um actually uh you know that uh cause I met some with Tom. Tom wants Jennifer to come out of this with two parents she could love too because he and I talked about it. Um………. Let us maybe shift gears now and maybe we can go to the second part of what I felt we can talk about. Is that ok?

Martha: Um-hm

Jerry: Unless either of you has more you want to say about this. Ok.

You have written a letter I know. You got it with you today?

Martha: Um'hm

Jerry: Ok and um……before you read it hang on just a second Martha um I want to say a little more about it. This is a letter that um you know you Mom has written on the spirit of helping you to heal over you know what's happened in your family and um you know you talked some in our first few sessions about uh things that happened that were a problem for you and made the whole divorce process more difficult and you know so this letter is kind of your attempt, uh to apologize for some things that you regret right? And um we talked about it that maybe this can be you know the beginning of something. Right? Do you want to say any more about it before you read it or just get into reading it?

Martha: Just read it. Jennifer, I know you are angry with me and I understand why you feel that way. (Crying) To begin I am wholeheartedly sorry for all the pain and sorrow that I caused you by asking for a divorce and I know I hurt you and I'm sorry. I stayed married to your Dad for your sake and happiness and wellbeing and I understand that in your eyes that when I asked your Dad for a divorce that I changed life as you knew it. I was asking for a divorce from your Dad, not you. But I understand how it affected you and the way of life you were used to. It must have been really hard for you to begin to live life without two parents in the house together with you and for that I'm sorry. I want you to know that you will always have two parents and I will always be here for you. I think about you always and miss you very much. The events that led up to your Dad being removed from the house I totally understand why you feel that I was keeping you from seeing your Dad and breaking up a relationship you had with him. I was afraid and as your mother naturally I wanted to protect you.......... and I wish I could change the way things happened. I wanted to shelter you from what was happening and I'm sorry this hurt you. It's the last thing in the world I ever wanted to do. I'm sorry for telling you to take down the wedding pictures and other memorabilia that I took down from the house, I didn't want the constant reminders I didn't take into consideration how it would affect you. I understand how difficult it was for you to deal with it and I'm sorry. Last year on your birthday I asked you what you wanted and I told you the one thing you couldn't have was me and your Dad back together was a terrible thing for me to say. I should have never put your birthday and divorce in the same context. Your birthday should be a happy occasion and I'm sorry I said this to you. Since Christmas leading up to February 1, both you and your Dad continually expressed that you wanted to live with him. On February 1st granny came over to be with us because I was going out of town the next morning. We were arguing when she arrived and she could not believe what she was hearing. Even though you kept saying you want to live with your Dad I wasn't sure if you really wanted to go so I without thinking called your bluff and told you to pack your bags and go with your Dad. I didn't know what else to do to make you happy. I understand that you felt like I was kicking you out but it was never my intention. That was the worst day of my life. As your mother, I would do anything to protect you. I never want anything to happen to you or anyone to hurt you and after thinking about what happened on this day I realized that I'm the one who hurt you. I hope you never feel this pain again. I am truly sorry for the actions that occurred on this day.

I have never been through anything this painful in my life. I understand that you are hurt and angry. Sometimes you don't get to rehearse things in life and they just happen. I'm so sorry for all the pain. I wish I could take it all away, take it all away. If I could, I would take all your pain and put it on me. Jennifer, I love you more than you could ever imagine and I miss you so much. From the day you were born you were always number one in my life and you always will be. I will always put you before anything and anyone and I always will. I understand that you feel .... incidents up to this point.

Sometimes life takes twists and turns and it can bring hurt and pain but it can also bring good. I love you more than life itself. I'm sorry you have to go through all of this. I want the healing to begin and for you to be back in my life. Some days I read the letters that you used to write to me and cry myself to sleep thinking about you and how it hurts, your pain that you are feeling believe me I'm feeling it too. I miss the days that we played games, cuddled on the couch and watched TV. Reading and especially talking every day and night. I miss waking up to you in the morning and tucking you in, hugging you, and kissing you goodnight. I miss and love you very much. I'm sorry I caused you all this pain..............If you ever need anything I am here for you. I wish someday you would find it in your heart to forgive me. Even if it's a little every day. I love you with all my heart.

Jerry: What's your reaction to your Mom's letter Jennifer?

Jennifer: (sniffling) Um................ um like she had, in a way I'm kind of still upset because she couldn't do something on her own you know, you brought up the idea of the letter but like she wrote it and stuff but um so that kind of, it would have been better if she thought of it herself. Um yeah, I don't know there was some stuff missing that like caused a lot too so everything wasn't in there.

Jerry: Well we will talk about both of those things but let's talk about the first one........................... . Here is how I'm looking at it um......See that way I look at it my job is I'm supposed to try and facilitate change. I mean that's the only reason anybody comes here because there are some changes that they want to see happen. And sometimes I get people to think about things in ways sometimes uh I get them to do something they might not have thought of or how to do. Um so when something happens because I had some roll in it of course you know what I'm thinking, that's good. Because that's what people come here for. And I always know whoever I work with, don't get caught up in if a change happens. Don't get caught up in the fact that it happened because you came here and do minimize its significance because I might have had some role, minor role in bringing it out because if you do then you can't really enjoy and celebrate the changes that are happening. A change is no less significant, this is and really important in my view of what I'm going to say right now. A change is no less significant because I suggested it, or you asked for it. It's no less significant that it happened. Some people kind of get into this thing, well, if I asked for it or you asked for it and it happens it doesn't mean as much because it wasn't spontaneous. A change is a change and umm if the only change is worthwhile to you is that kind of change that happens spontaneously, then most of the changes that happen in your life you won't be able to appreciate. Does that help at all? (Jennifer nods head) Ok. So what your Mom, did, uh even though um I might have had some minor role, you know it is every bit of significant um because you know your Mom did something I think that was hard to do, you know hard for people to you know say you're sorry. And your Mom obviously listened to the things you were talking about. Does that help you at all with the first part of it? (Jennifer nods head) And does that make sense to you

Martha? (Martha nods head) Ok, let's deal with the second half of what was said now. In essence, you said it was a good start but that there were things missing, right? Now Martha I want you to hear this in a particular way. Um in a way um I'm gonna ask you to just kind of listen and in a certain sense consider Jennifer as your consultant. You know what I mean? And I just want you to hear what comes next as um kind of like uh important information upon how to improve to what I think is an excellent start. Ok. So, go ahead, what were you getting at?

Jennifer: Well like um certain situations that really hurt too that weren't in there and um, Yeah, so there's just like that.

Jerry: Um, let's talk a little bit about those certain situations cause it sounds like what you're telling me that if some additional situations were included in this letter, that would be a lot better.

Jennifer: In a way.

Jerry: Ok, ummm, can you say what those situations are that you're getting at?

Jennifer: Um, there were like the one time where like she chased me around the house to get my phone away from me because she didn't want me to talk to my Dad, and um when after I was living with my Dad recently in August like she came to one of my softball games and she took my Dad's truck. Um, so yeah those, and I can't think of any off the top of my head like besides those. Those were two big things that like, yeah.

Jerry: Ok. So, uh just to put it in shorthand, the cell phone incident thing, and the truck incident.

Jennifer: Yea. And then also like the night where um, when I was with my Dad on February first like when that all happened and I was sitting with my Dad at the restaurant at like right after when he just had picked me up and she called and said that um, that since he wasn't, cause she asked if he was going to bring me home and he said no, just to get clothes and she said well I'm gonna call the cops and tell them that you kidnapped her. Yeah, that too.

Jerry: I'm not sure I'm clear on the chronology, let me just ask you um, you were at a restaurant with your Dad and you said you're gonna come home and get clothes.

Jennifer: Yea because it was that night of February 1st.

Jerry: Ok but was it before the incident between you and your Mom?

Jennifer: No, after. Cause then when I got to my friend's house he picked me up from there and we were sitting down at the restaurant and or Yeah, and she called and asked if he was going to bring me home and he said just to get clothes and then she said well then I'm going to call the cops and say that you kidnapped her.

Jerry: Ok, ok, so these three uh events you know, the cell phone, the truck, and uh February 1st just is kind of a shorthand way to...to refer to them. Ok those are things that you would like in an apology letter.

Jennifer: Yeah.

Jerry: Ok, ok, Martha can you take uh what Jennifer has said under her advisement.

Martha: Um-hm

Jerry: Ok...Jennifer what was it like for you to hear your Mom's uh letter?

Jennifer: I don't know... not that different I guess. . Like I don't know.

Jerry: It was a little different otherwise we wouldn't have talked about um that it would have been better you know if I hadn't suggested it. If it wasn't different we wouldn't have had that conversation....... um......Did it help your hurt at all?

Jennifer: No.

Jerry: A little bit? Ok. Um... Did it touch you at all?

Jennifer: Um...maybe a little like saying what we used to do.... like before the divorce and everything but like. No besides that, Not really......

Jerry: Ok, alright, um.......... This, this is just you know my opinion nobody else's just mine but I think it touched more than you recognized .... and um your eyes told that story and um...you know my sense is that the reason you don't want to say that it touched ya, is because you know there is more healing to do. It's just my opinion. Um what was it like for you to not only write the letter but actually read the letter to Jennifer today?

Martha: Hard.

Jerry: Hard, I'll bet it was. Um..... Reconciling a relationship is always hard work. Can you say more about what was hard about it,, let, let, excuse me for saying one more thing....... when people do something hard. Uh, in my business that's often a good thing. Um...and you did something that was really hard. I think for three reasons. One, you were hoping to heal Jennifer. Two, you were hoping to help heal your relationship. And three you were uh hoping uh that Jennifer would like you back in her life. Um and you know that you did something that was hard to accomplish those three things um that's good. But can you say more about what it was like?

Martha: That's not something you can just sit down and write in five minutes, it took quite a while to get it where I wanted it to be.

Jerry: I'LL bet it did, I'll bet it took hours.

Martha: And then just thinking about everything, for the last year and a half. It was hard.

Jerry: Um-hm, Um-hm, but.......... but hopefully were you know even though we are talking about things that happened in the past hopefully for the both of you were talking about them in a healing way. Um you know whenever I talk about the past to people it's because I want to take those events and you know help them.... vent to get past them, see them in a little bit different way.... you know I think um...you've done like two wonderful things. You know, I think writing a letter, I think was a wonderful thing and I think the decision you made not to pursue further court battle you know, I think that was a good thing too. Both of those things I think was very loving, very loving things.... Um...Would you be able to incorporate some of those things from the three uh things that Jennifer talked about today into...your letter? And would you be able to do it by next week or would you need more time to do it?

Martha: I could do it by next week.

Jerry: Ok and then what I'm going to suggest is that we schedule a time for the two of you to come back next week to continue our work together and uh we'll go back to Friday ok, I'm going to get my book. ....

Jennifer: Can I add one more thing, I just thought about it cause it was another like um, the when my Dad first got kicked out of the house um.... Cause, it was because my Mom had said that he was going to kill me.

(starting to cry) and that hurt really bad because my Dad's not like that and like, I know that he would never do anything to hurt me and so that hurt really bad hearing that, and knowing that's why like he was partly gone. (Sniffling)......

Jerry: Ok, ok, I'm glad you added that one in so then there are really four things...

Jennifer: That I could think of right now yeah.

Jerry: the truck, February 1st, and um that's around when uh your Dad was asked to leave............ Alright, 7:00 next Friday.

December 1, 2006

Counselor # 3 Session 9

Jerry: Welcome, how are you doing Jennifer?

Jennifer: Good.

Jerry: Hello Tom how are you?

Me: Good.

Jerry: Did you have trouble with traffic today?

Me: No.

Jerry: It was a nasty day weather-wise.

(Martha was already sitting in Jerry's office. Jennifer and Jerry went into the office and closed the door.)

Jerry: Hi Jennifer, how are you?

Jennifer: Good.

Jerry: What does your shirt say?

Jennifer: Michigan.

Jerry: Michigan, Who do you know from Michigan?

Jennifer: No one.

Jerry: No one. Ok, well did you have school today?

Jennifer: Yeah.

Jerry Yeah. Too bad a lot of kids were off. You know what, that woke me up. Uh, my wife works nights, she wasn't home. I got up about 6:30 and I heard a loud yoo-hoo

Martha: Um-hm.

Jerry: And I went to my bedroom door to find out that my kids have a snow day. Ha, ha, ha. Yeah, Yeah Willow Central was off. You go to LT?

Jennifer: shook her head.

Jerry: Yeah you guys were one of the few schools that had school. I suppose you and all your friends were complaining. No?

Jennifer: No not really.

Jerry: How unusual if I were in your shoes and I have seen snow like this, I would be praying for more. Ha, ha, ha, so anyway. Ok, well uh um we have something on um our plan for today. Uh you had given Mom uh three more things that you wanted to see included in her letter as I recall and uh Martha you said you would go more at it.

Martha: Um-hm

Jerry: And uh that you would have it today. So um you know what I would suggest maybe is that uh we reread it. Yeah and um you reread the whole thing uh and uh you added to it I know so uh go ahead.

Martha: I added the parts in here where they kind of fit in.

Jerry: Ok, good.

Martha: It's not all.... .

Jerry: Good.

Martha: Jennifer I know you are angry with me and I understand why you feel that way. To begin I am whole-heartedly sorry for all the pain and sorrow that I caused you by asking for a divorce and I know I hurt you and I'm sorry. I stayed married to your Dad for your sake and happiness and well-being, and I understand that in your eyes that when I asked your Dad for a divorce that I changed life as you knew it. I was asking for a divorce from your Dad, not you. But I understand how it also affected you and the way of life you were used to. It must have been really hard for you to begin to live life without two parents in the house together with you and for that I'm sorry. I want you to know that you will always have two parents and I will always be here for you. I think about you always and miss you very much. The events that led up to your Dad being removed from the house I totally understand why you felt that I was keeping you from seeing your Dad and breaking up a relationship you had with him. When I was meeting with my attorney we went to court to get an emergency order of protection because your Dad was not thinking with a sane mind. Under normal circumstances, I don't think your Dad would ever hurt you. Before I went to my attorney he was making many threats and saying things that a person in their right mind wouldn't say. Jennifer sometimes parents say things to one another and don't discuss it with their children because it would hurt too much. Some things are better kept between parents and not shared with the children. Unfortunately from this divorce, you have been exposed to too much and I'm sorry for the things I told you. But this time I thought that I had to tell you something especially that your Dad was removed from the house. I was scared and didn't know what he was going to do. I received many calls within a few hours from your Dad from different places, scary, sad, mad, and depressed. I also received different calls from Aunt Sandy crying, Granny worried and upset Aunt Anne yelling and upset. .... Many times when you hear about families going through a divorce and the husband and the wife end up killing their spouse and the children. Jennifer, I haven't been so scared in my life. Your Dad knew you were the most important person in my life. In our relationship, he knew there was nothing he could do to hurt me except through you. I was afraid and as your mother naturally I wanted to protect you.......... . And I wish I could change the way things happened. I wanted to shelter you from what was happening and I'm sorry this hurt you. It's the last thing in the world I ever wanted to do. I'm sorry for telling you to take down the wedding pictures and other memorabilia that I took down from the house, I didn't want the constant reminders I didn't take into consideration how it would affect you. I understand how difficult it was for you to deal with it and I'm sorry. Last year on your birthday I asked you what you wanted and I told you the one thing you couldn't have was me and your Dad back together was a terrible thing for me to say. I should have never put your birthday and divorce in the same context. Your birthday should be a happy occasion and I'm sorry I said this to you. When we were arguing I wanted to take your cell phone away because I didn't want you to call your Dad and tell him to pick you up. When you started running I chased you because I didn't want you to leave the house. I wanted you to stay with me. You said in your whole life you never saw me so mad that you were afraid because you didn't know what I was going to do and that you thought I might hit you. I have not and would not hit you, you are my daughter, and I love you. In the past, we always talked about everything. During this time I understand how you may have felt that you were losing the relationship we always had. We had a bubble as your Dad would call it and it was breaking. I felt my heart tearing apart because I didn't want you to leave the house in the angry state you were in. I have never given up on you and I never will. I now understand why you were afraid because it's not like you to act that way. I'm so sorry and I hope that one day we could get back to talking about things the way we used to. I miss not talking to you. Throughout your life, we talked like best friends. Since Christmas leading up to February 1, both you and your Dad continually expressed that you wanted to live with him. On February 1st granny came over to be with us because I was going out of town the next morning. We were arguing when she arrived and she could not believe what she was hearing. Even though you kept saying you want to live with your Dad I wasn't sure if you really wanted to go so I without thinking called your bluff and told you to pack your bags and go with your Dad. I didn't know what else to do to make you happy. After you left the house and went with your Dad I couldn't believe you actually left because of how close we were and all the talks we used to have. In the past whenever we talked about divorce you always said Mom I want to stay with you. I called your Dad to see if he was going to bring you home because I wanted you to come back. He said no and I told him I was going to call the police because I didn't know what else to do. When I called my attorney at home he knew that both you and your Dad expressed that you wanted to live with him and he told me since I was going out of town to let you go with your Dad. I didn't want you to go. I wanted you to live with me. It hurt so bad to let you go and I didn't think that letting you go with your Dad I would never get to see you again. I understand that you felt like I was kicking you out but it was never my intention. That was the worst day of my life. As your mother, I would do anything to protect you. I never want anything to happen to you or anyone to hurt you and after thinking about what happened on this day I realized that I'm the one who hurt you. I hope you never feel this pain again. I am eternally sorry for the actions that occurred on this day. In August when I took the truck I did not realize that you were not going to be able to get into your apartment or get a ride. The truck was parked next door to where you were moving. I didn't know that your Dad's keys, wallet and cell phone were in the truck. I returned these items as soon as I could. If you would have called I would have picked you up and given you a ride and I'm sorry that things happened this way.

I have never been through anything this painful in my life. I understand that you are hurt and angry. Sometimes you don't get to rehearse things in life and they just happen. I'm so sorry for all the pain. I wish I could take it all away, take it all away. If I could, I would take all your pain and put it on me. Jennifer, I love you more than you could ever imagine and I miss you so much. From the day you were born you were always number one in my life and you always will be. I will always put you before anything and anyone and I always will. I understand that you feel this is not true because of the incidents up to this point.

Sometimes life takes twists and turns and it can bring hurt and pain but it can also bring good. I love you more than life itself. I'm sorry you have to go through all of this. I want the healing to begin and for you to be back in my life. Some days I read the letters that you used to write to me and cry myself to sleep thinking about you and how it hurts, your pain that you are feeling believe me I'm feeling it too. I miss the days that we played games, cuddled on the couch, and watched TV. Reading and especially talking every day and night. I miss waking up to you in the morning and tucking you in, hugging you, and kissing you goodnight. I miss and love you very much. I'm sorry I caused you all this pain...............If you ever need anything I am here for you. I wish someday you would find it in your heart to forgive me. Even if it's a little every day. I love you with all my heart.

Jerry: What was that like for you to hear again Jenn?

Jennifer: Um no different I still have the same feelings cause like she still didn't admit that she kicked me out when she did cause she didn't say pack a bag and get out she told me or and go with your Dad, she told me to get in the house pack a bag and get out and like she um……there still, there are so many things that happened that a letter itself couldn't you know…. . I don't even um, that a letter itself can't say all that and I like I said, I still, I feel the same way as I do because she explains a lot of the stuff that she did in there and you know you can't just she, it's hard for her to just say you are sorry and she has to explain why she did things and half of the stuff it's not even like true. Because um how she said if I was scared of her that one night um cause I never saw her like that before, that's just, I don't remember exactly what she said but um……. . I don't remember exactly what she said but she said something about how she would never do something like hit me or anything like that. Well, that's exactly what I thought when I heard that she said my Dad was going to kill me. Just like she said she would never do something like that, neither would he, so all that stuff that, I still feel the same way and no I, the letter doesn't really help because there are so many things… that she's done and that has happened that like I said a letter itself can't tell and explain.

Jerry: Um-hm, ok, let me digest for a second uh what you said um. . You know that when there is a divorce um…people perceive things in different ways right?

Jennifer: Sure.

Jerry: And so um…. . What you consider the truth is your belief but you know there is a difference between beliefs and facts. Now all I'm saying is that uh you know if three people look at the same event there are three different, people will describe the event in three different ways…and uh. . That doesn't mean um one is true and you know one is false necessarily. Um…I'll tell you some of what I think happened in your family. Um…I think your Mom and your Dad were very fearful and I think your Mom and your Dad were both very fearful about losing you. Now I've been doing this for almost 30 years going back to 1978. Um but one of the things I've learned is that. . Um when parents are fearful about losing their children……. . Those are the nastiest fights they have and…. you were fearful too. Fear is like going on a rampage in your family…cause you were fearful uh that you were going to lose your Dad and your Mom did some things that we've already talked about which made you fear like she was trying to interfere in your relationship with your Dad and expunge him……from your life. So you were fearful too. So your family was a family system, which uh fear was running rampant.... . Your Mom had her fears of losing you...your Dad had fears of losing you. You had fears of ummm you know losing your Dad uh because the things your Mom did and because of uh...the, the serious bout of depression and uh the suicidal gesture that your Dad made . . . so your family system had like they're running ramped......Now when people are fearful.... like if you're fearful or you're anxious what do you do? You make a question right! Um when people are fearful and they're you know like they are losing something. They get controlling....... over to try and maintain you might say, what they fear they are going to lose.... . And um I think you want to see what happened in your family and um...you know, different light. That might be a lens that you want to use that you know, there was fear that was uh you know, that was ramped in your family and um I don't know um...it's my believe.... that sometimes when people are fearful uhhhh they do things that are out of character.... . And what else, maybe even cut them a little slack uh but I do think.... your family was a family that you know fear was really running, running rampant.... and it uh my opinion. Does that make any sense to you?

Jennifer: Umm somewhat.

Jerry: Ok, ok, and if you look at...what happened between you and your Mom.... . is the actions of a person who was afraid......you, you know it makes a little sense...for that matter uh for you, if you look at uh things that Jennifer did...through the lens of fear. Um you know that's a way you know for...you to look at things. And then generally um in our legal system. . as much as the legal system tries to avoid it um the legal system generally pumps up the parents fear of losing access to the child...uh because it tends to get very adversarial.... and um matter of fact years ago I was involved with a project with the Wake county court a county in northern Illinois. Uh the court system made a lot of interference and made them fight a lot harder over kids. Uh and I haven't gone through that lately except to mention that uh there was uh that source of fear being injected into your family system too. You know and uh if your Dad were in this room you know I'm sure he would say he had fears of losing you too. And uh in a way.... . If you understand everybody's action through the lens of what a fearful person does it kind of makes sense. You know, you did what a fearful person does.... your Dad you know was afraid of losing you. Here are a few things, um which you feared losing contact with your Dad, with what we talked about. Um Tom was I'm sure fearful of losing his relationship with you. And you know that uh fear that was affecting everybody and now when people are afraid... We know quite a bit about it, when people are afraid or anxious there are kind of like two competing tendencies you might say, one tendency is toward flight, to run. And the other is to fight, to contend you know, to hurt you. And uh I think um you know the fear uh probably fueled a lot of those tendencies in uh you know your, your family...........Um anyway does that make sense to you guys?

Martha: Um-hmm

Jerry: Um.......... . Run by me if you would, Jennifer what was missing in the letter?

Jennifer: A lot of things...

Jerry: Run it by me again.

Jennifer: What I said before, um that there were so many more things that I could easily write down and make a long thing kind of like she did just not in a letter like almost like a list of things that she did and, and all the stuff where a letter doesn't even come

The recorder started beeping and shut off about 26 minutes into the 60-minute session. Jennifer said her heart was pounding, she said Larry was rattling on so she was sure that he did not hear the beeping sound. As far as Martha, Jennifer was unsure because she did not look in her direction.

Jennifer's journal, rest of session 9

Jerry told me to write my list and bring that in so we would just read each thing and discuss them. I said ok. Jerry said that we have 2 more weeks and then we would be off the following weeks because he was going to be off. He then said he would like to do something a little more fun on the second week before we are off for Christmas. He said he would like us to bring in cookies or brownies and we could just eat and talk or we could just eat it could be for however long. Jerry asked if we were willing to do that. My Mom said yes and I said not really. He said he would still like to do that. Jerry said that I imagine that my Mom is not there. I said yeah. He said that usually, that is because you see it from your parents. Jerry said that he had another idea that he wanted to run by me and he was like oh boy. My Mom was giggling and he asked if she knew what he was getting at. She said she had no idea. He then said ok, well I think you and Tom should say hi to each other when you come in and only that, you don't have to talk about the snow or anything. Jerry then said that could be a good way to show me and he asked her if she would be willing to do that and she said I guess. Jerry said he would run it by my Dad.

While I was waiting in the waiting room I fell asleep with my headphones on listening to music on my laptop. Then next thing I knew someone was poking me. It was Jennifer. I jumped up half asleep. I could see Martha walking past me toward the door. I kept my head down. Martha stopped just to the left of me and said bye. I said nothing as she stood there for several seconds. Jerry came out to the waiting area and said, "Tom can you step in here for a bit."

I said, "Sure," as I turned to Jennifer, and said, "pack up the computer stuff," and I went into jerry's office.

Jerry said, "Have a seat," as he sat down in his chair. Jerry said, "Tom, I would like to run something by you if you don't mind."

I said, "Go right ahead."

"Tom, I have noticed that you and Martha treat each other like ghosts. I said, "Yeah."

Jerry uttered, "Um I was wondering if you and Martha could say hello to each other when you are here."

I said, "No that is not going to happen."

"For Jennifer's sake," he replied.

"No, Jennifer understands why I do not speak to her mother just like Jennifer has her own reasons why she does not talk to her mother. As for me, she has had me thrown out of my home using Jennifer as a pawn in her lie about me killing my own child. She has taken everything I owned, 2 vehicles, my money, I could go on."

Jerry said, "Well I was just thinking about Jennifer."

"You do not care about Jennifer, you could care less what her mother has done to her. That poor little human being has been thrown in the street, Interrogated by a counselor, telling her that these things did not happen to her and that she needs to change her story to how he sees it. That is messed up. Jerry you said that it was a good thing that Martha has given me custody of Jennifer. You must have been at court right."

Jerry said, "What?"

"Well, you must have been at court that day because you know everything that happened."

"Well no, I was not there," Jerry said.

"Then how do you know what happened? Just from what Martha and Rachel have told you?"

Jerry said, "Yes, Martha wanted to spare Jennifer from going through an evaluator."

"Well let me tell you something Jerry, Martha was the one who hired that evaluator and when she saw what it was going to cost her, she wanted to stop the process but I said let's do this. She knew the only way to avoid paying $15,000.00 was to give me Jennifer. So you see it was about money."

"Well, the courts ordered me to get the child and mother to be a family again."

I said, "That's funny I was told the courts would not be involved with this counseling."

Jerry stated again, "Well the courts ordered this counseling."

I said, "Rachel ordered this counseling, she works for Martha, and you work for them. You gave yourself away when we talked last time."

"How did I give myself away, Tom?"

"Let's just say you did Jerry, I do not mean any disrespect toward you, but after everything I have been through with Martha's control and manipulation I do not trust anybody and Jennifer does not trust anybody especially adults. I am the only adult she trusts."

Jerry said, "Well Tom I appreciate your honesty and no disrespect taken here. What do you think my intentions are?"

"To take Jennifer away from me."

"I don't want to take Jennifer away from you, they already gave you Jennifer and I hope I can prove to you down the line that is not my intention."

"We will see, I said. Martha is nuts and I will not talk to her. Sorry but that's the way it is. She has done this to herself."

"Well let's talk about scheduling Tom, I will be here the next two Fridays and the 2 Fridays after that I will be getting some R and R. Ok well I'll see you next week."

"Ok bye," I said.

December 5, 2006 Trial

I took the day off work because I was told it could be an all-day trial. I drove downtown and parked by Fred's garage. Fred had one of his employees Andy drive me to the courthouse. I went inside and stood in line by the metal detectors. The line was moving very slowly because the detectors were going off as office people passed through. People had to go through several times removing more items such as watches, coins etc. When I finally got through the metal detectors I went to the elevator and went up to the sixteenth floor. I went to the courtroom that I usually went to on every court date. I did not see Martha or Mr. Burnburg. There was also a different judge on the bench. I went back in the hallway and asked a man that looked like an attorney, "How do I find out what courtroom I am supposed to be in for a trial?"

He said, "Go to the eighth floor to the clerk's office and they should know where you are supposed to be."

To get to the eighth floor you had to take the elevator to the seventh and then an escalator up to the eighth. I hurried to the eighth floor to find out where I was supposed to be because by now I am fifteen minutes late. I gave the woman at the counter my case number and he told me I had to be on the 21st floor, But to get there I had to go to the seventeenth floor, get off the elevator and take another elevator to the 21st floor. I hurried back down the escalator to floor seven. I took an elevator up to the seventeenth floor. I went around a hallway to catch the elevators: up to the 21st floor where I see dozens of people waiting to catch elevators. I overheard some people talking that something happened in the courthouse and that's why security was so tight and the elevators were slow. After waiting another fifteen minutes I finally caught an elevator to the 21st floor. I went down the hallway and saw a glass door that said room 2103 a. The doors were locked. I sat on the bench for about five minutes not knowing what to do. I walked around the floor and down the hallway, I noticed a woman sitting at a desk. I told her I was supposed to be in room 2103 and that the doors were locked. The woman told me that I had to go through her office in order to get to that courtroom. I hurried to the courtroom as for now I am over 30 minutes late. I walked into the courtroom and I saw Mr. Burnburg sitting at a table with Martha sitting beside him. Mr. Burnburg stood up, walked toward me and asked, "Can I speak to you in the hallway? We went out into the hallway and sat on a bench as Martha followed along. I sat on the bench, Mr. Burnburg sat to my left with Martha sitting behind him.

Mr. Burnburg angrily stated, "You are late!"

"Yes I am," I replied, "There was something going on in the building and security was slow and elevators were slow as well."

"I don't believe you," Mr. Burnburg said.

"I don't care if you believe me, this is not school, I don't have to answer you, who do you think you are?"

Mr. Burnburg said, "I would like some respect."

I angrily replied,   "You show me some respect, I am not afraid of you."

"I know you're not afraid of me, Mr. Frawley. Let's have some respect here."

"I don't respect anyone that has hurt my daughter," I replied.

"I didn't do anything to your daughter Mr. Frawley."

"You will soon find out what you have done to my daughter."

"Is that a threat Mr. Frawley, are you threatening me?"

"Did I say you were going to be harmed; I said you will find out what has happened to my daughter that's all."

"I don't even know your daughter Mr. Frawley."

"Exactly,"   I said.

Mr. Burnburg pulled out some papers and put one in front of me. He said,   "If you sign this paper there will be irreconcilable differences. If you do not, we will charge you with mental cruelty."

"I thought this trial was about our assets."

"It's for everything Mr. Frawley, you agreed."

"I don't believe it, you tricked me," I will not sign any papers until Jennifer is free."

"Then we will file for mental cruelty," Mr. Burnburg boldly stated."

"What are they going to do to me," I asked.

"Nothing," Mr. Burnburg said.

"Whatever, do what you want?"

"What do you want from the house, Mr. Frawley?"

"All I want is Jennifer's bedroom set, her piano, and my TV. Also sheets of uncut money."

Martha sitting behind Mr. Burnburg looked at me and laughed.

"What is so funny I asked? Everything is funny to you. Martha turned her head and said nothing.

"Mr. Burnburg said so you're not going to sign the papers."

"Nope."

"Well I'll see you in the courtroom he said, come on Martha."

Mr. Burnburg and Martha I got up and walked down the hallway. I got up right behind them and went straight to the courtroom. We went back into the courtroom and right as I got through the doorway I looked up at the judge, I couldn't believe my eyes. It was the same female judge that I faced for the contempt of court charge. She told us all to come up and sit at the table that was set just below the bench. The clerk told Martha and "Please stand and raise your right hand, do you swear to tell the truth and nothing but the truth so help me, god?"

I said, "I do."

Martha, "I Do."

We sat down, and the Judge asked, "Would any of you like to waive your right to have a court reporter?"

Mr. Burnburg said, "It does not matter to us."

I stated, "I would like to have a reporter."

As usual Mr. Burnburg started right in, "Your Honor, we are filing this divorce on the grounds of mental cruelty."

The Judge said, "Begin."

Mr. Burnburg looked over to Martha And said, "Martha you and Tom did not get along, and he would yell at you until you cried. Is that correct?"

Martha said, "Yes."

Mr. Burnburg, "It was so bad you could not sleep at night, is that correct?"

Martha, "Yes."

Mr. Burnburg, "Tom verbally and mentally abused you, is that correct?"

Martha, "Yes."

Mr. Burnburg, "It was so bad that you couldn't eat and lost weight, is that correct?"

Martha, "Yes."

Mr. Burnburg, "And now that you have been separated for the last year and a half you gained that weight back, is that correct?"

Martha smiled, "Yes."

The judge said, "That works for me, now let's get to the assets."

Mr. Burnburg said, "I have a list of assets and bills that we can go through as one by one and I'm sure Mr. Frawley is going to have a problem with some of these things."

Mr. Burnburg handed me a piece of paper that he called exhibit A.

Exhibit A:

CD	$24,883.39
Charter one	$ 14,000.00
Van sold	$ 3,000.00
Total money	$ 41,883.39
Joint bills	$ 27,731.10
Balance	$ 14,152.29
50/50	$7,076.15
Tom bills	$ 13,777. 24

Balanced, owes Martha	$ -6,697. 10
Bills owed by both 50/ 50	
Mortgage principle 7/ 05-10/ 06	$3,476. 64
Property tax-Oct ' 05, Mar " 06, Aug '06	$6,599.79
State farm homeowners 9/05-11/06	$964.64
Basement sewer back up	$1,699.01
Air condition unit & install July, '06	$3,600.00
Swimming pool	$4,045.63
Circuit city TV	$1,211.60
Furniture	$1,157.74
Credit card	$1,001.75
Jennifer orthodontist 8/05-8-10-06	$2,560.00

Jennifer-John counselor 5/9/06	$1,170.00
Jennifer-doctor	$214.30
Jennifer-dentist	30.00
Total	$27,731.10

Tom's bills paid w/CD & bank money	
Tahoe payments 7/05-7/06	$5,146.70
Tahoe insurance 12/ 05-6/06	$371.91
Tahoe tickets 11/05 & 6/06	$225.00
Tahoe plates 12/06	$78.00
Tom-counselor 8/05	$888.07
Hospital 7/27/05	$1,391.52
Hospital 7/05-8/05	$210.00
Medical 1/23/06	$130.00
Medical 3/13/06	$195.00
Life insurance-July, '05	$39.10
Life insurance Oct 05	$24.87
7/16/2005 – Cash from bank	$2,500.00
8/29/2005- Cash from bank	$1,000.00
8/29/2005- Cash from bank	$1,000.00
12/25/2005- Cash	$300.00
Cell phones-July, '05	$273.07
Total	$13,777.24
Voluntary child support	$1,977.50
Water/sewerage	$378.04
	PETITIONER'S
	EXHIBIT

I took a few moments to look over the paperwork. I was very nervous and put my pen in my mouth. The bailiff would remind me several times to take the pen out of my mouth. I had a hard time studying in the numbers because my real fear was Martha fighting for Jennifer again. I looked down and the (air conditioning unit installed July, '06) I looked up and said, "Your Honor I have a problem with the cost of the air conditioning unit."

"And what would that be Mr. Frawley," the judge asked.

"Your honor, I was in construction for many years and worked with people in the air conditioning business. That is double of what it would have cost me and I could even save more money because I know how to install it myself."

"Well Mr. Frawley, I just had an air conditioner installed in my home and it cost a lot more."

I looked at the judge and I had no words. I thought to myself, it is December and it is cold outside and she just had an air conditioner installed in her home. I wonder how big a judge's house is, the square foot."

"What else," the judge asked.

Mr. Burnburg said, ``Your Honor, Martha has a check for $5,000.00 from the insurance company for flood damages in her basement, and we would like to have Mr. Frawley sign it."

I looked over at Martha and asked, "Were the repairs made?"

"No," Martha said.

I said, "Your Honor She will just have her father or a fly-by-night guy do the repairs and pocket the rest of the money."

The judge replied, "Even insurance companies hire fly-by-night guys that is the way it is."

I said "Your Honor, I am a carpenter, Plummer, and an electrician, I practically built that house. Martha can have people repair the house and inflate the bills. Can't I do the repairs on my home?"

"No! "You are not going in that house, you have a restraining order."

"What else? She asked.

I replied, "Your honor we had three vehicles in our marriage and Martha took all three. She stole the third vehicle from me and sold it."

"How much did you get for it," the judge asked Martha.

Martha, "I had to pay $1,600.00 that was still owed on the vehicle, I have been making payments for the last six months."

I looked at Martha and said, "I have paid half of your $20,000 truck Martha."

"You bought another car, Tom."

"I bought it after the filing of divorce, that has nothing to do with marital assets."

"Yes, it does," the judge said. How much is your car worth Mr. Frawley?"

"$5,000.00. I replied,

The judge, "How much is your car worth Martha?"

"Ummm about $6,000.00, " Martha replied.

"Well Mr. Frawley, you keep your car, and Martha, you keep yours."

I said, "Your honor, you mean to tell me I have to pay Martha $5,000.00 for a truck I don't even have."

"People get away with things in a divorce Mr. Frawley. She got away with things, and you got away with things."

"I didn't get away with anything, your honor."

"That's just how it goes," she said.

What else?

I stated, "Your honor 8 29 2005, cash from the bank, $1,000, she has that twice."

"You withdrew twice that day, Tom," Martha said.

Frustrated, I said, "Your honor, you cannot withdraw a thousand dollars twice in the same day at that bank." Looked over at Martha and said, "And you know it."

The judge said, "I will take the second $1000.00 off."

Wow I thought, did I hear that right? One for me!

"What else," the judge asked?

I said, Your Honor as far as the child support, can you make that mandatory because she plays games sometimes she pays, and sometimes she doesn't. She had only recently In August started paying child support."

Martha said, "Your Honor, I had Jennifer for six months and Tom didn't pay and then he had her for six months and I didn't pay. After six months, I started paying."

I looked over at Martha and said, "I gave you money, you can easily say that because I gave you cash, and you know it. When I stopped paying you, I was giving Jennifer money, and I was also buying her clothes and whatever else she needed while she was living with you."

Martha looked at me for a moment, turned towards the judge and put her head down. She had nothing else to say.

The judge said, "Yes, I will make it mandatory."

Mr. Burnburg Said, "Your Honor I have marked the income with the itemized deductions and the cost of living. Tom has one in front of him also. I believe it was exhibit B. I have lost that piece of paper but it was a breakdown of taxes and pretax is in Martha's column. It stated Martha made $51,000 a year and that I made $30,000 a year. They had some breakdown where in the end with Martha giving me child support she ended up making less money for the year. Martha was currently paying me almost $700.00 a month. This breakdown reduced it to $520.00 a month.

I looked over at Martha and said, "In your last MSA, you were offering over $700.00 a month based on your income.

Mr. Burnburg stated, "Well, she didn't do the deductions for that."

The judge looked over the paper and said, "This is the correct amount and that's what Martha will pay." I sat there, put my pen in my mouth and just shook my head. At this point, that bailiff did not tell me to take the pen out of my mouth anymore.

I couldn't believe what was happening. Martha's attorney was committing perjury. In many other petitions, he wrote Martha's income of 60,000.

"What else," the judge said?

I said. "Your honor, Martha did not account for the 2005 tax returns on this piece of paper. I feel I deserve half."

"How much was your tax returns Martha," the judge asked.

"Ummmm about $1,000."

The judge looked at me and said, "I will give you half, $500.00."

Another lie, we would have returns of a few thousand dollars.

"OK let's move on to the assets in the home," the Judge said.

Mr. Burnburg stood up and read the list. Mr. Frawley would like his TV, Jennifer's bedroom set, Jennifer's piano, and sheets of money."

"Is that correct Mr. Frawley?"

"Yes, it is your honor."

Mr. Burnburg stated, ”Your Honor, we would like to add a new two-year restraining order against Mr. Frawley for Martha. He has threatened her in the past and Martha feels he may still harm her."

"Yes, we can add the new restraining order,” the judge replied. Any questions Mr. Frawley?"

I Looked at the judge and said, "No."

"Do you have a closing argument Mr. Burnburg," the judge asked.

"Yes your honor, Tom and Martha both have pension plans and Tom claims his is worth $8,000.00."

I replied, "It is worth that. I called them up and that’s what they told me."

Mr. Burnburg looked at me and said that’s not the actual payout."

"Yes, it is," I said. I called up the company that has my pension plan and told them my situation and they sent me this form that states $8,000 is the payout."

"What is your plan worth Martha," the judge asked?

"$7,000.00," Martha replied.

"She has a 401k, your honor," I stated.

The judge stated you both keep your own pension plans. Do you have a closing argument, Mr. Frawley?"

"Yes your honor, in all the years I have been married I put most of my money into my home and Martha put her money into her 401K. Since Martha will get half of the profit on the house I think it is only fair that I get half of the 401K."

The judge paused for a moment and said, "You are entitled to half of the 401K as far as the other two plans, each person keeps their own."

"Is there anything else," the judge inquired?

Mr. Burnburg stood up with a piece of paper and handed it to the judge and stated, ``your honor we would like to incorporate sole and permanent custody of the minor child Jennifer to Thomas Frawley in the divorce decree."

"Ok well, I guess that’s it."

Mr. Burnburg looked over at me and said, `` I will be back at 3:00 with the revised paperwork if you want to hang around."

I said, "No, I have to get back to work."

He said, "Fine, I'll send you a copy in the mail."

I asked, "Can I get a copy to look over to make sure everything is correct.?"

"No, the Judge said, you don't get to look it over, it is done, and that's it."

I turned around and walked toward the door and stopped by the female bailiff. I told her, "I am sorry about the pen thing." She replied, "That's ok, I understand you were nervous up there."

I said, "Thanks, have a nice day!"

She said, "You too."

I walked out the door and headed towards the elevators. I was finally divorced. I felt nothing, No sorrow, no sadness. Just relief. The court punishment was over.

Once I got home that day, I closely read their so-called exhibits.

Exhibit A, Bills owed, Martha had the amount of $6,599.79 property tax for a period of 17 months. We paid $3,200.00 a year. The true amount should have been $4,800.00. She got me for $1,799.79. The basement sewer backed up at $1,699, Martha stated on record she did not have repairs done yet I will have to pay $845.00 half of a made-up bill of $1,699.00, as she received the insurance check for $5,000.00. For such repairs. The air at $3,600.00 doubled the price with Martha gaining $1,800.00, if that is even true.

Under Tom's bills paid of course the Tahoe, 3 vehicles purchased in our marriage as I possessed none, I would have to pay Martha $5,596.62 for plates, insurance and a car payment for the Tahoe Martha sold. For Jaime Frazier $888.07. Jaime was paid through Martha's insurance with a co-pay of $13.00 each visit at 8 sessions amounted to $104.00. The cell phone bill, $273.07. I owe her 63.97 for life insurance on me, she could have stopped paying that, oh wait she was the beneficiary probably hoping I would die. And wow, I have to return her half of Child support 1,977.50. The fact that I had to pay ½ of mortgage, property taxes, and homeowners insurance while I was not living there as a strange man resided there for free.

This was absolutely insane. Never in our life did we have a bill that high for just one month. What a huge slap in my face as I would have to pay Martha's calls to her boyfriend. What Mr. Burnburg did was a slick attorney robbing me of over $11,000.00 not including what was sold from my home as well as child support money. The Judge agreed to it all. No investigations, no consequences.

People say I was crazy for not having an attorney for the trial. For all the money that I have lost to Martha, I would have paid it to an attorney anyway. I wanted the right to speak for myself and also my daughter. I depended on the seemingly 50/50 Illinois divorce law only to learn the reality of it is you have a 50/50 chance of winning or losing. However, Martha's love for money made her lose sight of the gold. It was I who won the gold. Jennifer was the gold. As Martha and her attorney laughed their way to the bank singing victory, without an attorney, I won sole custody of my daughter, something I was told would never happen. I had Jennifer's corrupt attorney removed, and got rid of an abusive counselor. However, my fight was still not over. I had to figure out a way to fight for Jennifer's freedom of counselors and Martha's evil power. Jennifer was still serving her 1 to 2-year sentence of psychotherapy at 52 sessions a year. She has already served over 37 sessions in 11 months.

Counselor #3 Session 10

Jerry: Hey Tom.

Me: What's up?

Jerry: How are you?

Me: Alright.

Jerry: Welcome Jennifer, Martha hi! Come on in guys.... . Is there anything that you want to start with today? Jennifer? No, anything that happened or that we talked about in uh the other sessions that you guys would like to talk about that you would like to start with?

Martha: No.

Jennifer: Shook her head.

Jerry: Well you guys make me work so hard just to get, just to get you talking. Ok, well um, when you guys were here last week I had asked you to do something.... and um I had asked you to make a list of things that were bothering you because uh you know you had written that letter and you said in essence Jennifer that uh well you know that other things that were bothering you too. Those things Mom mentioned weren't all there, and I asked you to make a list of the other things that were bothering you. Uh so that's kind of I guess what I'd like to uh talk about today and uh you know we're going to talk about the um not from the angle of uh you know like trying to explain everything like that but this is your chance to get it kind of out and uh off your chest and let Mom know what's bothering ya uh just to be heard in essence. Uh so um you know let's start with that then. Do you have it with you?

Jennifer: Um-hm.

Jerry: Is that a list or a letter or what?

Jennifer: It's a list but then at the end, I put like um, kind of a paragraph like about how I feel towards her and stuff like, cause like how she expressed, how she felt in her letter, I kind of wrote my own on how I felt, I feel towards her. Do you want me to just start reading down the list?

Jerry: Uh why don't you and then maybe we can...

Jennifer: Go back.

Jerry: Um item by item or let's see what on, what you got...

Jennifer: Well I just put everything including some of the things we already talked about.

Jerry: Ok.

Jennifer: Yeah,

1. Um for the first one was when she said my Dad was going to kill me.

2. Um the second, she took down family pictures.

3. The time where she asked what I wanted for my birthday and she told me that I couldn't have my Dad.

4. Um, she told me that my Dad was going to take my college fund.

5. She said that um, that I don't talk to her when I was living with my Dad, because he doesn't let me.

6. Um, the night where she kicked me out of the house.

7. Her boyfriend started staying at the house.

8. Um, she said my Dad was going to kidnap me the night she kicked me out.

9. She left me stranded when she took my Dad's truck at my softball game.

10. She laughed in my face at one of my softball games when I went up to her and told her how I felt.

11. Um, she also laughed in my face when she told me that she took the truck when we were out at the second counselor's house.

12. She claimed that I didn't go to counseling with the first counselor when I did.

13. Um, she changed her mind day to day about supervision when I was living with her and having supervision with my Dad.

14. She told me that her boyfriend was going to get me things I already had with my Dad like a pool, a house and other things like that.

15. She deleted some family pictures from my Dad's computer when we were both sitting in the basement right in front of me.

16. Um, well most of the time almost every day, she was working late so I had to make dinner for myself and I always ate by myself when I was living with her.

17. Um, the night when she chased me around the house for my cell phone.

18. Um a conversation where she told me that she didn't want the same last name.

19. Um, she basically like my last year of softball was gone and like taken away from me because I had to be in counseling on all the days that I had softball except for one.

20. Um, she said my Dad had seven suicide attempts, which isn't true, there. was only one.

21. She kept um, um when I was living with my Dad she kept mail that had my credit card in it so I couldn't um use that.

22. Um, she didn't, when I was living with her and she went out of town she didn't give me money for my King of Hearts dress for a dance at school when I was going shopping with my friends.

23. She told me that she could have or that she could have another man in the house because I wasn't there.

24. Um, she said that my Dad better sign papers or I would have to see an evaluator or maybe get put into a boarding school or home in one of our phone conversations.

25. She wouldn't let me see my Dad on some days where we ended up rescheduling to see him because I was at my cousin's house.

26. Um, basically every phone call that I had with her she only talked about something to do with the court.

27. Um, there was a time where I went to the house to get some of my stuff. She didn't answer the door when her car was outside or her phone.

28. When she took the truck um she kept my clothes from me and I couldn't get them back unless I saw her.

29. She threatened me by saying that if things didn't go back to the way they were I would be in counseling for a long time at the second counselor.

30. Um, she, this is the third counselor that I have been through.

31. And she sold things that were mine and my Dad's stuff like our ping-pong table and things like that when I was living with her.

32. Um she had people follow me and my Dad.

33. Basically gave my dog away to my Grandparents.

34. She lies about being afraid of my Dad because she goes up to him and stuff when she gave him a letter and that she said she was afraid of him.

35. She told me um the time where she told me to take down her and my Dad's wedding picture from my room because she didn't like it.

36. Um, she said that if I didn't live in the school district by August she would call the school and I don't live in the area so I couldn't go there when I was living with my Dad.

37. She accused me of stealing a necklace when I was at her house or when I was living with her. Yeah and um she accused me of stealing it when I didn't just because she couldn't find it and it was gone.

38. Uh she wouldn't let me stay with my Dad when she went out of town even though I asked.

39. Um, we would fight about her giving me lunch money a couple of times.

40. And she took my phone away from me and when she went out of town left me only 14 dollars when I was going to the mall with my friends, that was also along with that King of hearts dress.

And that's it, it's just the letter.

Jerry: That's a long list. Very long list. .... How would you like to use that list?

Jennifer: What do you mean?

Jerry: Um....... . If something were to happen now that you read that list and you felt good about it, what would that be?

Jennifer: I don't really understand what you are saying.

Jerry: Um....... I am trying to get a sense of what you would like to have happen.... You know, you know what I mean?

Jennifer: Ummm

Jerry: Like...how you know those were the hurts that you have right, ok was it kind of like helping the hurt?

Jennifer: Nothing really.

Jerry: That's pessimistic. You don't think there is anything that could help the pro....

Jennifer: No because like I said before it's way too much, it's so many things wrong, it wasn't just a couple.

Jerry: There are a lot of things on that list, there is no question about that...Um...hmm.... . I believe that you know people can hurt and can be healed though um.... that's just uh you know that's just a belief uh of mine...What else do you have there you got uh something that you wrote?

Jennifer: Um-hm like more about the kind of like...what I feel and my thoughts and what I think and that's basically what's on here.

Jerry: Ok, ok um.... let me ask you Martha these are things that you know they're uh are uh...problems that are dealing with her hurt. Do you have ideas about how to help with those things?

Martha: No I don't.

Jerry: Ok, do any of them surprise you or. .

Martha: Um-hm

Jerry: Some of this is new to you.

Martha: No it's not new it's just her perception.

Jerry: Ok, ok ok. What have you tried you know uh you know to heal the hurt Jennifer has?

Martha: I'm not trying to heal anything with no conversation, no contact other than counseling.

Jerry: For sure, for sure. And uh I think uh we could fairly say it's hard, even when there is a conversation about it in counseling, because I don't know that we've made much progress.... . Other than getting things out.... um ok...how do you believe forgiveness occurs?

Martha: Talking about things that are on your mind and changing your ways, the anger that you have....

Jerry: Ok, how do you believe forgiveness occurs?

Jennifer: Depends on the situation.

Jerry: Ok, are you interested in creating forgiveness between you and your Mom, feelings between you and your Mom?

Jennifer: No.

Jerry: No. Ok and um ......why is that?

Jennifer: Because um or like I said there is just so much... that has happened and even by this list like... even there is so many things where, how it's really, really, really, really hard to for even forgive and think about forgiving someone for all those things were as if it's just a couple of things that happened um... that it 'd be easier cause yeah it's a couple of mistakes but when you keep going and going and going and you can make something like this a list being that big and keep naming things and stuff...it's just... really hard to even think about forgiving someone for all that because apparently, you didn't want to change that if you kept on going throughout that...

Jerry: Hm, would you say that you know...what happened you know while your family was going through that very difficult period, would you say that it was unusual or typical.

Jennifer: Meaning...

Jerry: .... Um what happened between you and your Mom when your family was going through the divorce.... Would you say that the stuff that happened between you and your Mom was unusual or typical?

Jennifer: Um well it was unusual to how she's been in the past years but then it started to become like typical because she was like that all of the time then for like a long time and nothing changed, so it's like basically, she became like a whole new person like there was no, like yeah she became a whole new person.

Jerry: Ok, see another possibility, you have no choice about how you were thinking about things, of course, another possibility is that um you know um .... Your Mom that you remember all the years gone by.... uh is still your Mom. But obviously, there were things that really...were hurtful and painful to you...And um... it's not like one of those uhhhh.... is uh your true Mom, the one that is lovable. You know what I am getting at? Like the Mom that you remember from years gone by...uh you know is still there...uh to love and enjoy if you choose to. And you know it's possible that you know the stuff that happened ...um was kind of like um. . Atypical.

Do you know what atypical means? Unusual like out of the ordinary. Maybe even fueled by circumstances....... .

Jennifer: Um so well I don't know because like I said it's not there anymore...it's just gone and...yeah over, like there is no old Mom, she's gone so...

Jerry: Well um, what I would say is that probably the old Mom is there. That, that's just my belief and that um...there is stuff that happened where uh you might not be seeing the old Mom, you might not um...know that it's still there cause you guys don't really see each other except when you come here to see me right...Um so um. . I believe that uh you know the old Mom is still there that the things you enjoyed uh you could enjoy again, and I do believe it's possible for you to have uh, to come out of this with two parents and not have to pick uh you know one parent over the other. I mean you could live with your Dad and still have a good relationship with uh your Mom, I believe that's uh possible. ...Um............How would you like a little psychology lesson?" Do you like a psychology lesson?

Jennifer: What's that?

Jerry: Ha, ha, ha, ha, ha.

Martha: Ha, ha.

Jerry: Uh, I was going to say a little bit about um, kind of like, how we think about personality. In some quarters it is kind of like what happens in families just to give you kind of uh, a new way of thinking… about things if you want to…Would you be interested in this?

Jennifer: Not really because I'm still going to end up believing the same thing I already do and feel the same way.

Jerry: Well you might, you might, and if you do, you do. Um but uh, uh I'm just going to say a little bit about how we think about personality um because we got to do something when, when uh we're here and you know maybe this will be helpful and maybe it won't. If it's not helpful then you are no worse off now at this Moment right…Um see the way we think about personality is that everybody's personality is composed of certain uh parts or certain sides of themselves. Uh have, if you train your ear to listen to it people will talk about parts of themselves or sides of themselves all the time.

Have you ever heard anybody say that? You never heard anybody say part of me feels this way, part of me feels that way…. A side of me feels like this, a side of me feels like that…. you never heard that?

Jennifer: I don't know I might have.

Jerry: Ok have you ever used that just to talk about yourself like you know there's part of me that feels this way and a side of me that feels that way?

Jennifer: not that I remember.

Jerry: No, ok. Well the thinking is that um you know… that everybody's personality is uh composed of different sides or different parts of themself and uh there's kind of self that can kind of direct these parts. But sometimes parts get extreme and out of control and when parts get kind of extreme it crowds out other aspects of who people are. Like um, you know um…well let me give you an example. Like if I was uh, really concentrating on something and really focused on something, uh my wife and my kids can talk to me and I would go uh what…um. . the other day. I probably shouldn't tell you this but my wife was talking to me about she was going to a wake today, somebody died. She was telling me what time she was going and I was like uh kind of thinking about problems …you might say and uh, when she was done I asked her uh, so when are you going to the wake. She goes I just told you, weren't you listening. I said well I guess not. Uh but that was because there was like a side of me that was very task full…that was thinking. . About something else. Now I'm not normally the kind of guy that ignores the people close to him. Uh but, in that instance, I literally didn't hear what she was, what she was telling me.... And the point I'm making is that uh, sometimes you know parts of people get extreme and crowd out uh other aspects of you know who they are so, you know uh there's probably like a side of you, you know that says um I don't ever want to be close to Mom again...because of you know all those things that you just mentioned, um you know I think there's probably uh, uh, a side of you uh you know that misses the nurturing of the old times. And uh probably as your family was going through everything uh you know there was probably uh... a side of you uh that might of got uh you know extreme at times and you know your letter you know uh, which we went through the last couple of times you know you have expressed some regrets over you know some things that you have done.... . And um, in a way that's kind of what makes people so interesting is that uh they can be very different people at very different times. And uh the reason is because ah sometimes there are sides of people getting extreme and you know certain conditions....... . Does that make sense at all? ......

Jennifer: Um.... . Kind of sort of not really though.

Jerry: Kind of sort of, well it's, it's new. Does that make sense to you at all Martha?

Martha: Um-hm.

Jerry: Yeah, and uh, this, this is uh...um...normal by the way. You know that certain sides of people um you know get um extreme. Um and sometimes it can work to their disadvantage in uh relationships. Umm.... you know um...there is a side of me that's uh can be very competitive, like if I uh play racquetball. I got a friend who uh were pretty evenly matched...and uh you know when you play racquetball you're supposed to know where your opponent is cause it's a small area and you could take out their teeth with your racket and he one time hit me across the mouth with his racket, he was swinging at the ball. He didn't mean to take out my teeth but he literally, literally cracked my teeth. And uh so I had to go to the dentist and get you know caps but um he is one guy if we play racquetball, if he hits me with the ball I always make sure to hit him back. That's kind of real competitive, real competitive, the only person I'll do that to ha-ha, ha. Um but it's just my way of saying that uh sometimes uh parts of us get extreme and when parts of us get extreme uh we do um you know things we might not uh otherwise do. And um when parts of one person in the family system get extreme it tends to uh illicit parts of other people in the family system so you could bet...that if uh one person in the family system is extreme the others in the family system who also have some uh you know extreme parts going on.... Um... does any of that make sense or is it too psychobabble?

Jennifer: Huhh, it was a lot but ...not really.

Jerry: ok, I won't uh ???right now but at least it provides a way to you know kind of think about things...See the way I would think about it... is um like when you say to me uh, I don't want anything to do with my Mom because of all this stuff that happened uh that's uh, uh a side of you, that's apart of you, you know, and uh, that part of you is blocking um some other parts of you um that maybe don't want to risk getting hurt again. You know uh, that's you know kind of how I look at it......Um..............Are you aware of any sides of yourself that got kind of extreme you know as you went through this whole thing.

Martha: Um-hm.

Jerry: Yeah, what sides of yourself got extreme?

Martha: Well me and Jennifer arguing for one.

Jerry: Ok kind of a combative side of you...

Martha: And in the past, we talked about everything but of course?

Jerry: Yes everybody does but uh that combative side of you uh got to be kind of extreme.

Martha: Um-hm.

Jerry: Ok, and uh more extreme than was good for you and good for your relationship with Jennifer.

Martha: Um-hm.

Jerry: Ok, any other sides of you that uh you know got extreme?

Martha: Probably talking more about the court stuff that I shouldn't have discussed with her. It was between her Dad and me.

Jerry: Ok, ok so there was a side of you that you know kind of dragged Jennifer into stuff that she shouldn't have listened to as a child. Kind of put her in the middle. Ok and uh uh you know that's was the side of you that was, a part of you, a side of you that was scared.

Martha: Yep.

Jerry: You know now we can argue about whether uh you know that side was um um what's the word I'm looking for out of proportion, disproportionate going on or not but you know that was a part of you that was a side of you.

Martha: uh-huh.

Jerry: Ok and um that's kind of what I mean. I think nothing else you did from where you were thinking about human nature I guess. .... Um.... Are there any parts of your sides or yourself that you're aware of that might be .... Extreme?

Jennifer: No!

Jerry: No, ok. All parts by the way have positive intentions. This is actually a pretty healthy theory of it I, in that they all want to do something positive for a person.... but um when parts get too extreme they usually work against the person's best interest, that's uh also part of parts theory, so uh anyway there is more that you prepared.

Jennifer: Um-hm.

Jerry: Do you want to read the rest of that paper?

Jennifer: Um yeah and basically I just wrote like something kind of small but it's just like to tell her how I really feel and my feelings and so that she knows and stuff. Because this is how I feel it's basically how I'm gonna always feel and just to like say it and get it out there so she knows so...

Jerry: Are you ready to listen?

Martha: Um-hm.

Jerry: Ok

Jennifer: Um, with all these things that you have done there is really no way I could find a place in my heart to forgive you. It wouldn't have been so bad if you did a few things and said sorry for them and then never let them happen again but that obviously wasn't good enough and so it was you who brought us to this point because you kept on hurting me with being hateful not only to me but someone else that I love very much, my Dad. There is no excuse for all these things and I'm tired of all the lies. I don't want to hear any more about you being sorry and wishing that you can take things back because you are not sorry and there is obviously or there is absolutely no way you can take anything back. What was done is over so now you just have to live with that. I don't love you anymore and if you can't get that in your head then now we are on the third counselor so if you can't realize that by now it's pretty sad. Over the year's you taught me to stick to my own thoughts and feelings and stick with that and keep them there and now that's what I do and you can't accept it. Well that's too bad because I'm sticking to it and with me not speaking to you or seeing you again because there has just been too much. But you also taught me something else in this last year and a half and that was that I can't trust anyone. There is no one else but you to blame for everything that has happened.

Jerry: Is that it?

Jennifer: Yeah.

(The room is silent)

Jerry: .... Ok, do you want to say anything or sit with it on what Jennifer was saying?

Martha: Sit with it.

Jerry: Ok............ Um, that might be best because our goal is to help you know Jennifer to get her uh, to help her get her feelings out.

Martha: Um-hm.

Jerry: Did you really mean that you can't trust anyone?

Jennifer: Yeah.

Jerry: Really, wow um that's kind of low-blown universal, which is my way of thinking on a good way to live your life but um.... Do you trust that I want you to have a relationship with both Mom and Dad that I want you to come out of this with two parents?

Jennifer: Well you're a counselor so yeah you would but that's not what I meant by that and that was like I can't trust anyone because the reason why I can't because so many things have happened and so many lies and her going behind our family's back that makes me not want to get close to anything um because I don't know who I can trust because I did trust her and she broke that trust..................

Jerry: Yeah, part, part of the problem. . . you have to remember that you know and uh you know there have been regretful things that happened and you know your family, huh and um....... sometimes all sides of a person are part of the same person............ and um.... . You know I guess you know my thought for you would be that um you know you might consider that there were things which happened in an extraordinary period of time which were kind of out of the ordinary and um you know while it's true we can't um redo the past, we can certainly create a new future. That was kind of uh you know the spirit in which remember toward the end of our spirit last week um I said to you guys I want to talk a little bit about whether you know to do anything uh special for uh Christmas, remember that part of the session...and um I, you know said nothing big just bring some cookies or whatever and uh you know I even said you know we could invite your Dad if you wanted to be part of it um …. Um I don't think he does but um did you give any thought to whether you would like to uh do something like that next week when come?

Jennifer: I, I, have the same answer as last week, I still don't want to.

Jerry: Ok, is there anything at all that you want to happen next week that would be…. Good for you?

Jennifer: No.

Jerry: Ok, um if your Mom was to bring uh Christmas card could she uh bring you a Christmas card?

Jennifer: I wouldn't take it.

Jerry: You literally wouldn't take it.

Jennifer: No.

(The room is silent for several seconds)

Jerry: Well that's, that's sad…. um …. uh just because I know I had this belief that you know this could be uh you know uh a time of peace and a time healing and uh I thought that maybe we could take a tiny step in that direction but uh…um…………..you know obviously I can't make that happen…um……………………. k um, what we'll do is maybe we will stop then. . and uh what I would like to do is uh you know maybe spend the last uh five minutes or so alone with your Mom today… and uh then next time um uh which will be next week I'll spend the last few minutes of the session uh alone with you. Fair enough?

Jennifer: Um-hm.

Jerry: Ok, and uh we're going to get together next week, ok?

Jennifer: Um-hm.

Jerry: Alright I'll see you later.

Jennifer: Bye.

Martha: Bye.

Jennifer walked out.

December 14, 2006

My building manager called me and left a voicemail, "Tom, the police came here looking for you and I told them you live upstairs and I guess you were not home. Just giving you a heads up."

I checked with the local police and it was not them looking for me, my guess was the County Sheriff. Days later, I knocked on the building manager's door. I asked him, "What police were looking for me, was it the Cook County Sheriff's?"

"No, he replied. He was some other kind of officer, He had a white unmarked police car. I asked him if you were in trouble and he just said not yet."

"Can you describe him for me," I asked. He said he was a short Stocky bald man with black hair on the sides."

I assured him I did nothing wrong and did not understand why he was looking for me. He said, "No problem, I was just giving you a heads up, I know how it is."

I said "Goodbye," and went up to my apartment. Jennifer came home from school shortly after. I told her about the description that the building manager gave me. Jennifer said, "Dad that sounds like Rod Z. He drives a white car that looks like an unmarked police car that he keeps in his garage."

"Yes, it does Jennifer.

December 16, 2006

Counselor # 3 Session 11

As usual, Jennifer and I enter the counseling waiting area and Martha is sitting alone. Jennifer and I sat in the two remaining chairs, one across from Martha and the other to her right. I never looked at Martha or said a word. She was Vapor to me as well as Jennifer.

Jerry: Hi everybody, come on Martha, Jennifer, how is school?

Jennifer: Good.

Jerry: I'm going to make a quick detour and I'll be right with you ok.

(Martha and Jennifer go into Jerry's office)

Long silence as Jennifer and Martha sit in the office alone.

Jerry: Hello.

Martha: Hi.

Jerry: Got some bubble gum there? Yeah, what kind? Bubble yum, no that was a big hit when I was a kid because it blew big bubbles. That and Bazooka bubble gum.

Martha: Hmm, bubble yum yeah, or bubblelicious.

Jerry: We used to get it with uh baseball cards. Remember the little trading cards, it was big among the guys. Uh you used to get one piece of bubble gum with five baseball cards for five cents. Those were the good old days. Anyway, how would you guys like to use your session today?

(Silence)

Jerry: I see you got something, so you must have some thoughts.

Martha Um-hm

Jerry: You brought some Christmas cookies.

Martha: Um-hm.

Jerry: I will have one. Thank you.

Martha: These are the rice krispies. .

Jerry: Ohhhhh.

Martha: Peanut butter and. .

Jerry: Those sound pretty good. I'm going to get a little water to wash it down, I'll be right back.

Martha: There is no poison in there.

Jennifer: Hm you're funny..

Jerry: So you like to bake.

Martha: Um-hm

Jerry: Yeah, my wife likes to bake too......Hm, that was good. If I were you I'd reconsider. Ha, ha, ha.

Martha: I told her they are not poisoned.

Jerry: Ha, ha, ha.

Martha: Ha, ha.

Jerry: Oooh, these are good. You know, um, my favorite Christmas cookie is brown sugar cookies. Have you ever had brown sugar cookies?

Martha: Uh huh.

Jerry: Um, that's kind of my mother's specialty. Uh as the name applies a regular brown sugar and then you have powdered sugar on top. The longer you let them sit the harder they get an idea if you kind of let them melt in your mouth they're really good. ....so...

Martha: I have a card for you too...At least you can do is open it.

Jennifer: (shakes her head)

Martha: Why not?

Jennifer: Cause I don't want it.

Martha: Jennifer..... Why?

Jennifer: Cause I don't want anything from you.

Martha: Oh yeah...........You won't even open it, you at least have to read something out of there from your cousins.........This is from Kristy and Katy......(Martha gave Jennifer a picture of her two cousins and also a picture of Daisy with Santa.

Jerry: How old are your cousins?

Jennifer: 14 and 12.

Jerry: Ha, ha, ha, ha......A Doberman.

Martha: That's our dog.

Jerry: Um-hm.

Martha: Guess who was Santa.

Jerry: Who was Santa?

Martha: My brother, for the dogs, my sister had um a dog washing...

Jerry: Um-hm.

Martha: And my brother played Santa at the boutique.

Jerry: Where is her boutique?

Martha: Um it's in **** on 105th and Lange road.

Jerry: Oh, um-hm...hm...no kidding hm. I had a client one time who was a dog groomer and she often used to take care of uh dogs like for people who were working people who had dogs. It's actually big business now.

Martha: Um-hm.

Jerry: You know because you can't get home to take care of your dog. Um, that was good Martha.

Martha: Thank you.

Jerry: I don't want to talk with my mouth full so I'm going to let you guys wait for a second.............................. . Well I was thinking about how I might be able to help today.....................And I kind of thought Christmas is uh a happy time of year and one of the things people do around Christmas is they talk about uh, ah you know because there is so much tradition a Christmas past and stuff like that, so maybe we could talk about that a little bit. Um, what were your, what were your Christmas customs in the family?

Jennifer: Meaning.

Jerry: Well I could tell you my Christmas customs like every Christmas Eve you know uh, when my family gets together we have what you call, but we do something called the beginning which is like uh official less meal. . Did I say official

Martha: Um-hm

Jerry: I meant to say meatless, meatless meal. Um, which is really kind of nice. We have uh, like uh, uh different various kinds of shrimp. It's like uh Dijon, shrimp cocktail, shrimp. You can tell we like shrimp in my family. Uh cod, which is uh kind of like a fishy, not a fishy tasting fish.

Martha: Um-hm.

Jerry: And uh different kind of, in polish they are called??? Which are kind of like uh

Martha: Um-hm.

Jerry: Kind of like ravioli or something like that.

Martha: Holidays (Could not hear her)

Jerry: And then uh, we do a grab bag, uh because you got uh, well the family has grown over the years. I have 4 brothers and all of us have kids now. It's too difficult to buy gifts for everybody so we do uh a grab bag and uh all the kids, all the kids get gifts from the grab bag you know we don't exchange gifts anymore......Uh but that's kind of our Christmas eve, Christmas Eve tradition since we are Christians you know, uh

Martha: Um-hm.

Jerry: What are your Christmas customs in your family?

Jennifer: I don't know.

Jerry: Well from years gone by.

Jennifer: Just go by my family's house.

Jerry: Uh did you go, whose side did you go by?

Jennifer: Um...

Jerry: Your Mom's side your Dad's....

Jennifer: Yeah

Jerry: Whose?

Jennifer: her side.

Jerry: Your Mom's side, ok.... What do you guys do uh do you like to have some kind of, do you have family dinner or family banquet?

Jennifer: No.

Jerry: No, did you have a gift exchange?

Jennifer: Yeah.

Jerry: A grab bag or does everybody buy for everybody?

Jennifer: Everyone.

Jerry: everyone.

Jerry: Everyone, you've got kind of a smaller family than I would think. How many cousins do you have on that side?

Jennifer: Three.

Jerry: three...It's small enough where you can still do something like that. So that's kind of an every year thing.

Martha: Um-hm.

Jerry: And uh, how many brothers and sisters do you have Martha?

Martha: A brother who's a year older and a sister who is a year younger.

Jerry: Ok.

Martha: And I have Jennifer and two months later my sister had her daughter. .

Jerry: Ahhhh.

Martha: In January my brother had a son. .

Jerry: Oh ok.

Martha: They were like the three musketeers growing up.

Jerry: Ah gosh real close in age. Each of you only has one kid.

Martha: My sister has two daughters.

Jerry: Oh two daughters ok, ok hm,

Martha: So they are missing Jennifer...

Jerry: Um-hm

Martha: And they missed her last weekend at the doggie shop. .

Jerry: Um-hm,Um-hm. Hm, I'll bet they do. I'll bet they do...Do you miss them?

Jennifer: My cousins. .

Jerry: Um-hm, uh you were going to say something.

Martha: I think you need to be with them.

Jennifer: not through you....... .

Jerry: Well there is no reason it has got to be through you. No um.... . Do you talk to them at all like on the phone you know all kids have cell phones these days?

Jennifer: No.

Jerry: You guys do.

Jennifer: No.

Jerry: No.. Um .... . Is your Mom still alive? Yeah, I thought you mentioned your Mom and your Dad?

Martha: Um-hm

Jerry: Ok, well you're lucky to have both of them uh, both of them there. And are you close or have you been close with grandma and grandpa? Now or in the past I mean.

Jennifer: Um, not really.

Jerry: You haven't been close.

Jennifer: Not really, they were always with my other cousins.

Jerry: Yeah, um-hm. Hm. Ok.... . So was your celebration on Christmas Eve or Christmas?

Jennifer: Eve.

Jerry: christmas Eve. And then uh did you go to like night services and that sort of anything like that? No. And when did you open your gifts in your family, did you do it on Christmas Eve or Christmas day?

Jennifer: Day.

Jerry: Christmas day, ok. In the morning. Yeah, um.... and what was your tradition? Did you guys have a real tree, or did you have an artificial tree?

Jennifer: Artificial.

Jerry: Artificial, hm. It wasn't one of those old aluminum ones, was it? You wouldn't remember ha, ha, ha, your Mom remembers. .

Martha. Hmmm. We didn't have one but I recall...

Jerry: You know us, I had a couple of them, and they were screwy-looking things. They were made of aluminum and you shine a floodlight on them.... Yeah.

Martha: Yeah I remember that.

Jerry: Yeah the Vinyl trees were quite an improvement, quite an improvement............ . So what will you be doing for Christmas this year Martha, um are you going by your family?.

Martha: Christmas day.

Jerry: Christmas day...Oh good, good. So it's Christmas day, not Christmas eve....... Everybody, everybody will be there?

Martha: Um-hm. Yeah. We have pasta and we bring vegetables

Jerry: Ohh.

Martha: And things like that.

Jerry: Ok, are you of Italian ancestry?

Martha: Um-hm.

Jerry: Oh ok,

Martha: Loretta

Jerry: Ahh ok. That's Italian.

Martha: Yep.

Jerry: Um-hm. Hm. .... Yeah.

Martha: We are used to having ravioli

Jerry: Oh uh-huh. . That sounds good.

Martha: Sometimes we?????

Jerry: Um-hm. Ah, that is so festive.............................. . I think it will be kind of a bad Christmas because of all this.

Martha: Yep.

Jerry: And uh do you want to say why, what it will make it a bad Christmas for you, I think we know but uh you know people talk about their feelings. Go ahead.

Martha: Cause Jennifer won't be with me...or the family.

Jerry: Hm and that makes your heart really heavy doesn't it, sure..............What will this Christmas be like for you Jennifer?

Jennifer: Fine.

Jerry: Fine. Hm, is this the first year your family is a divorced family, so that will be different.

Jennifer: Well last year too.

Jerry: Well you guys were separated last year so, I guess uh everybody wasn't all together. What was last Christmas like?

Jennifer: Different.

Jerry: Different? Did it uh take some of the luster of Christmas for you, sometimes people say when they have something painful that they are going through around Christmas that it kind of uh you know take some of the shine off of Christmas for a couple of years.

Jennifer: Yeah last year it did.

Jerry: Did it last year, yeah. Kind of a sad, kind of a bad Christmas.... How did your family work it out last Christmas? Your Mom and your Dad weren't under the same roof anymore so uh you know that makes some complications obviously. How did your family work it out?

Jennifer: Um for the first week of break I was with my Mom and then Christmas Day and then for the second week I was with my Dad.

Jerry: Hm.... . Ok...yeah...For you what was sad, what was sad about. .

Jennifer: Um not having both parents for the holiday.

Jerry: Uh even though they, not having both parents and having the family together under one roof you know that's a loss in itself. Yeah and uh do you have any Christmas traditions on your Dad's side?

Jennifer: Well um I don't know this will be the first time I'm with him by myself.

Jerry: U-m-hm. So ok, ok. Yeah. Did you find coming up to this Christmas it wasn't as joyful as in the past.

Jennifer: No.

Jerry: No....................kay...Was there anything that could have made your Christmas last year better?

Jennifer: Well I guess not cause they were apart so no.

Jerry: Hm.... I met some families who are going through divorce the first year uh they still do a mini get-together you know the entire family, sometimes that kind of helps the kids. Not everybody can do that.. What, do you have any thoughts about what could make this Christmas a nice one for you?

Jennifer: Um well I'm going to be with my Dad, that's nice.

Jerry: That will be nice, sure, sure. Any other hopes or wishes?

Jennifer: No.

Jerry: Ok, Do you ever imagine reconciling with any portion of your mom's family? Reconciling isn't maybe the right word because you don't have the absent mind with your cousins I don't think, do you?

Jennifer: No.

Jerry: Ok, do you ever imagine getting together with them?

Jennifer: Who?

Jerry: Your cousins.

Jennifer: Um well no because like I said it will end up being through my Mom.

Jerry: Ooh, it wouldn't have to be. Why do you believe it would have to be through your Mom?

Jennifer: Because that's basically the only way I will be able to see them.

Jerry: Where do they live? Do they live in this area?

Jennifer: No.

Jerry: No out south?

Jennifer: I don't know.

Martha: About 45 minutes south.

Jerry: Um-hm. So you got no, no way to get there............. .

Martha: She does, do you want to go by Aunt Carrie and visit for a couple of days?

Jennifer: Um no!

Jerry: Or uh, what if she wanted to do something shorter like uh I don't know, meet at McDonalds for lunch or something like that. Would Aunt Carrie be willing to drive for that?

Martha: Um-hm.

Jerry: You know bring the girls to you know McDonald's out here. There's an option for you. But would Aunt Carrie give the girls time alone or would Aunt Carrie like uh hover there.

Martha: She would let the three of them be together.

Jerry: Well what would you want? Would you want to be alone with them or. .

Jennifer: Yeah.

Jerry: Ok alright.... Well, I think we opened one possibility for ya.......... What did you and your cousins do when you would get together?

I guess you are part of the video game generation that probably played video games.

Jennifer: Yeah, sometimes.

Jerry: Hm, yeah. Do you have a favorite?

Jennifer: No not really.

Jerry: Um, did you play some other games?

Jennifer: Ummm, we just do our little thing like I don't know different stuff. .

Jerry: How about mall madness did you ever play that game? That's fun but probably obsolete now I'm sure.......... . Do you have the desire to see anybody else from that side of the family besides your cousins?

Jennifer: No.

Jerry: Grandma no, just your cousins..Um when do you start your Christmas break?

Jennifer: Umm..... in a week from today.

Jerry: It's kind of funny the way Christmas breaks are this year.

Martha: Um-hm.

Jerry: My sons who are uh still in high school much rather have some time before the holidays rather than uh the time after. How do you feel about it?

Jennifer: I don't know, it doesn't matter.

Jerry: Yeah it doesn't matter. Yeah, my kids prefer to have time before so they can uh get into you know kind of the Christmas spirit. I don't think much is going to happen anyway because the last couple of days of school because a lot of kids will be traveling out of town.................. silence.................

Do you have a Christmas tree this year?

Martha: Um-hm.

Jerry: Good, good. I think you should try and make it as normal as possible...Silence........................ Well, let me ask you guys um.... I kind of thought that um you know maybe you would like you know a little bit of a pleasant session today. Maybe a little bit of a lighter one. Um, but um, that doesn't have to be if you guys want to talk about other things.........

Martha: I do.

Jerry: Good.

Martha: Jennifer you called me the other day and asked me about planning something and you wouldn't explain what that was......

Jennifer: Ok I was seeing what you were up to....

Martha: I don't know what you were referring to.

Jennifer: Well that's it.

Martha: What would I be planning that would hurt you?

Jennifer: I don't know, good question, that's why I was asking you.

Martha: You just called me up and said are you planning anything so help me god if anything happens and I don't know what that was .... .

Jennifer: That's why I was calling you to ask you....... .

Jerry: For the record are you planning anything?

Martha: Huh, no.

Jerry: Ok, ok well good, good that you called back. Um can I ask you what you were worried about?

Jennifer: Just asking a question.

Jerry: Um what was that you were saying, are you planning something?

Martha: So help me god if something happens are you going to hurt me again. And I don't know what she means by that. She didn't explain it.

Jennifer: I asked a question, it was a yes or no answer and you couldn't answer it. That was all.

Jerry: Well you owned up, you're not planning anything. You got your answer.

Jennifer: She could have just said it on the phone. She didn't have to drag it on.

Jerry: Ah, nothing wrong with trying to have a phone conversation. I do that with my kids ha, ha, ha. So you didn't answer on the phone.

Martha: I didn't know how to answer because I didn't know specifically what she was asking about. I figured I'll ask her Friday at counseling.

Jerry: Um-hm.

Martha: But I don't know about that comment, what your comment was about, so help me god if something happens, I don't know that was ....

Jennifer: Just asking a question that was all......

Jerry: Ok I think that is as far as that can go.

Martha: Um-hm.

Jerry: You know um, evidently, you were worried about something and hopefully, the answer helped you.................. Were you asking your Mom to find something for the two of you to do?

Jennifer: No.

Jerry: Ok anything else that you want to bring up?

(Silence) Well, you and I are going to spend a little time alone um because you and I had some time alone uh last time.

Martha: um-hm.

Jerry: So uh, we will spend maybe uh five or so more minutes together, and then you know you and I will spend time alone. Um .... Do you have a dog?

Jennifer: Not anymore.

Jerry: Not anymore, did ya? Yeah. What happened to your dog?

Jennifer: Went to my grandparents.

Jerry: What kind of dog was he?

Jennifer: Doberman.

Jerry: Doberman, is that the Doberman in the picture? Yeah, what was your dog's name?

Jennifer: Daisy.

Jerry: Daisy, ha, ha, ha. Wow, Daisy is such a dainty name for a Doberman.

Martha: She was dainty, she was a baby.

Jerry: You had Daisy since she was a puppy I gather? Yeah,

Martha: She was Jennifer's 10th birthday present.

Jerry: Um-hm. Oh who knows if you decide to get together with your cousins I don't know, can Daisy travel in a car I mean uh some dogs are not good travelers. May you go for a walk...Did Daisy do any tricks?

Jerry: Um-hm, Um-hm, Um-hm. Daisy uh???? And uh ah maybe that's another possibility you know a way to see daisy......I trust she would still remember you. How old is she now?

Martha: Five.

Jerry: Five....... . Silence.... .

Martha: Daisy would cuddle and sleep in the bed.

Jerry: That's a sign of a friendly dog......

Martha: Um-hm.

Jerry: Did she sleep with you in your bed? Yeah, did you actually let her sleep on the bed or...?

Jennifer: Um-hm.

Jerry: Really, She gives you a lick in the morning?

Jennifer: Sometimes.

Jerry: Yeah……. .

Martha: She likes getting under the covers too.

Jerry: Ha, ha, ha, gosh, but uh we never had dogs ha, ha, ha……. Is she a purebred dog or is she a mixed breed?

Martha: Pure.

Jerry: Pure………. . silence………………………………….well Martha I think that uh I'm going to spend a little time alone with Jennifer.

Martha: Ok.

Jerry: And um, I just want to remind ya I'll be gone in the next two weeks so we will not meet for the next two Fridays and uh we will be back on a regular schedule on uh the fifth.

Martha: Ok.

Jerry: At uh seven o'clock ok.

Martha: Ok. Did you figure it out?

Jerry: What is the copay?

Martha: Um-hm.

Jerry: You know it's going to be what you think it is because I'm going to be doing a statement at the end of uh, well probably next week so if we have any squaring up to do we will square up.

Martha: Ok.

Jerry: You had what you thought it was $13

Martha: 13 or 30 60 and 60 something like that.

Jerry: Yeah. You know, just make it an even 13 and you know.

Martha: Ok.

Jerry: When I run my statement at the end of the Month uh we'll square it up. Ok gotcha.

(Martha stood up put her coat on and walked over to Jennifer)

Martha :(Starting to cry) you have a nice Christmas Jennifer...

Jennifer: Don't, no, no, no, no,

Martha: I am going to hug you.

Jennifer: No you're not!

Martha: Jennifer.

Jennifer: No! No! I'm not going to take it..... .

Jerry: Martha I will see you in the next session.

(Martha left.)

Jerry: Tom I'm going to spend some time with Jennifer alone.

Me: Ok.

(Jerry) shuts the door.

December 23, 2006

Jennifer and I would go out to Michigan to spend Christmas with our best friends and their family. Jennifer would get to be with her adopted Pa and Gram, cousin's aunts and Uncles.

December 27, 2006, Jennifer was on the computer when Martha sent an email stating that I persuaded Jennifer to hate her. Jennifer opened this e-mail and immediately called Martha.

Jennifer said, "Mom quit blaming my Dad because I don't talk to you. It is your fault that I don't talk to you."

"You are not normal, Jennifer."

"No Mom, you're not normal."

"It is not normal for a child not to talk to a parent."

"Whatever Mom, I need my Social Security card and birth certificate."

"Are you doing something that you shouldn't be, do I need to know about something? What do you need it for, are you going out of the country?

"No Mom, are you going to give it to me?"

"What do you need it for?"

"I need it Mom, just put it in the mailbox and I will come and get it."

"Well I am out of town and I won't be home until Tuesday."

"Well, I need it as soon as possible. Jennifer hung up.

Martha called back telling Jennifer, "I have some of your mail."

Jennifer said, "What mail, Mom?"

"The pictures you put in the door."

"What pictures Mom?"

"Your school pictures."

"I didn't put them in the door. Those are Dad's pictures. Did you open them?"

"No Jennifer."

Jennifer hung up.

When I came home Jennifer told me about the calls. I said, "Why would the school send the pictures to your Mom?"

"I don't know Dad."

I told Jennifer "You should have told her what you needed her birth certificate for Drivers Ed."

She said, "Dad, she just kept assuming I was going out of the country."

"I know Jennifer but she will just give you a hard time if you don't tell her what you need it for."

"Ok Dad."

January 5, 2007 Counselor #3 Session 12

Jerry: Hey Jennifer

Jennifer: Hi.

Martha: Hi

Jerry: Hey Tom.

Me: Hi.

Jerry: So I was just telling your Mom we are official. We don't have our window hangings back up, our shades because they replaced the windows. So uh do you notice the difference?

Jennifer: No.

Jerry: Ha, ha, ha, ha. You probably weren't here long enough to know. Anyway actually in my last session I just discovered that uh, I was sitting here and I looked out. They were kind of selected in the way they painted; they didn't paint the bottom.

Martha: Ohh.

Jerry: But they obviously aren't done. So, anyway, welcome back. The first time I have seen you guys since uh before Christmas. Um, how was Christmas for each of you?

Jennifer: Good.

Jerry: good. OK, OK, yeah. What did you do?

Jennifer: I was with my Dad, Christmas.

Jerry: Well I knew that

Jennifer: Yeah.

Jerry: Yeah and uh, did you guys spend it at home or do anything special?

Jennifer: No, just me and my Dad.

Jerry: Hm, ok. And um New Years'? Did you spend New years at home or with friends, family?

Jennifer: family.

Jerry: OK uh, was there a celebration or dinner.... . And now you are looking forward to going back to school.

Jennifer: Uh kind of.

Jerry: yeah hmm, there's some uh comfort to going back to routine isn't there? I mean as much as you like your time off. Yeah uh do you like school?

Jennifer: sometimes.

Jerry: sometimes. It probably depends on what class we're talking about and how much work you've got. Yet, so uh you go to LT right.

Jennifer: Yeah.

Jerry: Yeah. So Monday is your first day back, Yeah ok. And how are the holidays for you Martha?

Martha: Nice.

Jerry: Um-hmm yeah, could have been better.

Martha: could've been better.

Jerry: Yeah, I'm sure. I'm sure. Well, how can I be helpful to you guys today? What would you like to talk about?

Martha: This mail that came, your pictures. I took one of the little ones.

Jennifer: Uh Yeah why?

Martha: I thought that you put them into the door for me.

Jennifer: No I told you I didn't.

Martha: Well.

Jennifer: Well Dad paid for them and I am sure he wants his pictures, he was giving those to his family.

Martha: Well I will get it back and I'll give it to you next week.

Jennifer: Is the permit and Social Security card in there?

Martha: I wanted to know what you wanted that for.

Jennifer: So you didn't bring it.

Martha: I do have it with me.

Jennifer: Well can I have it, I need it?

Martha: For?

Jennifer: Drivers Ed.

Martha: You need your birth certificate and Social Security card for drivers Ed?

Jennifer: Yeah.

Martha: You do?

Jerry: Hm.

Martha: Why did you need it as soon as possible a week ago when you were off school for two weeks?

Jennifer: How do you get your permit?

Martha: I don't know.

Jennifer: You have to go take a test and you need your birth certificate and Social Security card.

Martha: That's all you had to tell me when I asked.

Jennifer: You didn't ask, you just assumed I was going out of the country.

Martha: No I. .

Jennifer: Yeah, no you were like you're going somewhere that you're, or you're going somewhere should I know about something. That's exactly what you said.

Martha: I asked...

Jennifer: No, you did not.

Martha: What do you need it for?

Jennifer: No, you didn't.

Martha: Yeah I did.

Jennifer: You just assumed I was going out of the country because that was the first thing that you said, are you doing something that you shouldn't be doing? Do I need to know about something? That's all you kept saying.

Jerry: And did you answer? Um because you obviously had information about what you needed it for what you just shared now. Uh did you say that during the phone conversation?

Jennifer: No

Martha: No.

Jerry: No, ok.

Martha: She hung up on me.

Jerry: Ha, ha, ha, wasn't this much easier?

Martha: I know, that's why I ...

Jennifer: Isn't it much easier to ask instead of accusing at first.

Martha: I did ask Jennifer.

Jennifer: No you just accused first, assumed.

Martha: If you would have answered me then we wouldn't have had any trouble but here is a copy of both.

Jennifer: I can't have my real Social Security card if I need it for anything else? (Jennifer opens the envelope) ok, I take that as a no..... .

Jerry: Well you need the actual Social security card.

Jennifer: Well there is not, I might need it for other things but...

Jerry: Maybe you will but if you do that's an easy enough problem solved...you know, um... because just by talking about it, um you know it can be resolved. Uh you know if uh, you need it, for your social, for your driver's permit then bring it up again. Um this little conversation you guys had uh over the phone about the social security card. Um.... Can you think of something that each of you could have done differently?

Jennifer: No.

Jerry: No? Ok. Well, what you did just now was what you could have done differently ...because it would have worked as well in the original phone call uh..... . can you think of something you could have done differently?

Martha: Well I know I asked her why she needed it but she apparently doesn't have that same perception but I guess I could have asked her. But I did call her back and ask her what she needed it for.

Jerry: Ok,

Martha: But she hung up on me again.

Jerry: Ok, So I'm getting like...

Jennifer: No when you called me back you told me that you had some of my mail....

Martha: And then I asked you again what you needed the stuff for.

Jennifer: No, and then I asked you if you had opened the pictures and you were like yeah, or you said No that you didn't and I asked you if you took one and you said no.

Martha: Well I didn't until today.

Jennifer: Yeah, ok.

Martha: I thought you were doing something nice by putting them in the door.

Jennifer: I told you that I didn't.

Martha: I know that but

Jennifer: Why would I put a pi, whatever a whole packet.

Jerry: Hope brings...

Jennifer: She asked, I told her that I didn't.

Jerry: Well there is a different story that I get about what was said in the phone call about the um social security card, because you're saying uh that your Mom accused you of going out of town.

Jennifer: Pretty much.

Jerry: Right. And you're saying uh you asked why she needed it uh you might have been thinking about whether she was going to go out of town...but you don't remember saying it.

Martha: Well uh, yeah I did afterward after I asked her. I

Jerry: Ok so that

Martha: She just didn't answer so I was assuming she was going to do something and I wanted to know cause if they go out of state I'm supposed to be alerted of dates and where they are going.

Jerry: Right, right. So in a way um...it was kind of like the non-answer like why do you need it uh the kind of thing it kind of made you wonder all the more.

Martha: Yep.

Jerry: As if there were some secrecy.

Martha: because if she would have told me it was for drivers ed. it would have been nothing but she was upset because I was not home and I was out of town and she wanted it as soon as possible, put it in the mailbox and I'll come and get it.

Jerry: Um-hm.

Martha: I said well as soon as possible won't be until Tuesday when I get home I'm out of town.

Jerry: Um-hm. Ok, ok.

Martha: But what the urgency was a week ago, that's what kind of was throwing me.

Jerry: Um-hm, um-hm. How do kids get their uh permits now by the way?

Jennifer: You have to take a test at the DMV.

Jerry: Do you have to go to the DMV? Yeah. ...... at your school. I'm trying to remember when my kids went through it if they had to do that. I don't think we went to the DMV until they took their driver's license test.... Um....

Martha: Do you have to do that for a permit?

Jennifer: (frustrated) Yeah.

Jerry: Hm, k, alright. Um cause I know that umm the way it used to be is you would take your, are you taking drivers Ed at school?

Jennifer: I'm going to but I need to get my permit so I can take it.

Jerry: Ok alright. I don't really remember that clearly so uh, but you know, I think maybe uh you know the thing to take from this is that uh you know clear communication is uh good communication.... . Um....... What else do you guys want to talk about, have you had any other conversations during the break?

Martha: Um-hm.

Jennifer: When?

Martha: When you called me up and you were yelling about me accusing you saying that your Dad was telling you to hate me.

Jennifer: Oh yeah because she sends an email saying that um it's my Dad's fault that I don't like her and I don't talk to her, and it's not true.

Martha: I wish I would have brought a copy with me. Because that's not what he said clearly.

Jennifer: Ok.

Martha: It said that nobody can make me love her.... .

Jennifer: Yeah continue, what else did it say?

Martha: But there, someone can be persuaded or someone can influence you or something like that.

Jennifer: Yeah, so you're saying you can be influencing her. I'm not an idiot. And you also said why you don't persuade her... It's not his job to make me like you. If I have a problem with you then that's between me and you, it's not between him so you don't have to get him in the middle.

Martha: Jennifer it sparked because your Dad sent me an email first.

Jennifer: saying oh, she doesn't like you because I made her. No.

Martha: That should be between me and your Dad if he sent me an email.

Jennifer: Um, alright, I get emails through that too. So if I see something, sometimes I read things and it was from you. How do I, ok.

Jerry: Do you have your own email account? I'm not real savvy about this, your own uh email address or your own. .

Jennifer: I do but I don't use it.

Jerry: So all emails go into the mailbox you share with your Dad.

Jennifer: Yeah.

Jerry: Ok, ok, so you saw an email from your Mom and you opened it.

Jennifer: Yeah well it was already opened. But me, because me and my Dad were on his computer and it was there. So basically yeah I saw the email. Whatever she said, whatever she said.

Jerry: Um-hm. But your point is your Dad didn't show it to you, you saw an opened email from your Mom and you opened it and looked at it. Ok, ok.

Well, that is information for you.

Martha: Um-hm. You know.... that's good clarification....... .

Martha: If I want to send an email to you I send it to your Dad's email address.... .

Jennifer: Doesn't mean I'll always look at it. Now maybe I shouldn't look at your emails but...whatever that is beside the point.

Martha: What's beside the point?

Jennifer: Never mind.

Jerry: Well, well what's the point you want to make?

Jennifer: Well the point was, she was bringing up a conversation that I had between her on the phone because she was accusing my Dad of why, of me not liking her, that it's his fault. That's the point. The point isn't that she is going to send me an email or whatever or if I'll look at it or not.

Jerry: Um-hm, Well we want to create you know enough of a boundary around your relationship so that what happens between the two of you is uh decided you know uh by the two of you. We all agreed on that right. Do you agree with that?

Jennifer: What?

Jerry: I said um, are all three of us agreed that we want uh to have a relationship between you and your Mom, where you and your Mom are responsible for what happens between the two of you, and there should be enough of a boundary around the two of you so that the two of you are in charge of your own relationship...

Jennifer: Meaning that no one else can be blamed for something or, what do you mean by that?

Jerry: Um....... meaning that your relationship, the two of you shouldn't be overly influenced by what happened between Mom and Dad. It shouldn't be influenced by what happens between you and your Dad. That what happens between the two of you uh, should be somewhat independent of going on in other relationships in the family.... I'm losing you aren't I?

Jennifer: Yeah.

Jerry: I'm talking psycho-babble......How to explain that. See in a family we always say uh you know that, you know what let me get a piece of paper, a picture is worth a thousand words. Ok........................... . Ok this is kind of like a family diagram, Mom, Dad, Jennifer. This dotted line is a generational line. Ok, and in family systems what we say is there is a subsystem you know. One system is this subsystem ok. Now Mom and Dad are still a subsystem. They are just not a marital subsystem, they are a parental subsystem ok, and each of them is always parents to you. Ok, now you got a relationship with Dad, you got a relationship with Mom. Ok, kind of like simultaneously. And your relationship with your Dad is a subsystem, your relationship with your Mom is a subsystem and what I was trying to get at is what happened between you and your Mom, we want enough of a boundary around the two of you so that uh what happens between your Mom and your Dad, doesn't control what happens between the two of you. And what happens between you and your Dad doesn't control what happens between you and your Mom. We want enough of a boundary where the two of you can decide uh what you want your relationship to be like. Does that help at all?

Jennifer: Yeah.

Jerry: Ok. And um, in family systems there is a notion that is called triangulation. Uh and it's thought. It's thought that uh what happens in a family is when there is trouble with two people oftentimes uh that dyad, a dyad means two. It can't contain the tension a third person sometimes gets involved in, and um you know that's not considered uh good for anybody at all. But uh my only point is, I'm not trying to make a family therapist out of you. My point is there has got to be enough of a boundary around the two of you where uh the two of you have a relationship that is somewhat independent of goings on elsewhere within the family. And we're all three agreed that's what we want right. You're nodding your head. Are you nodding your head? Now that you know what I am talking about,

Jennifer: Yeah.

Jerry: Ok, good. Good. And in a way you know um.... . You guys should be able to have a conversation about driver's licenses.... That's just; I'm skipping social security cards, (looks at Martha) which you didn't know was part of the permit and driver's license process. You guys should be able to uh...have a conversation about that without you having to think that this has implications for being excluded from Jennifer's life. That's what a clear boundary looks like.

Martha: Um-hm.

Jerry: You should be able to um you know feel free to talk with Mom about anything without feeling like you got to defend your Dad. You know that's what a clear boundary looks like.... So uh that's what I was getting at......But um, to get back to the question you posed a minute ago um you want Jennifer to read um emails right.

Martha: Well I don't know, if I sent her one, I don't know if she is going to read it or not or if she is going to get it or not if it goes to her Dad's email address and I didn't know they shared an email together.

Jerry: Um-hm. Um-hm. Hm. Well, something to consider is that you know, the way a clear boundary would look is that sometimes uh you guys might have communication that would be shared with your Dad and sometimes you would have communication that wouldn't be. That's how a clear boundary looks depending on whether you are going to share it or not. You know um, a clear boundary, boundaries you know can be ridged which means totally exclusive uh where they can be enmeshed. And that means no sense of boundary. And if everybody knows of everybody else's communications that's kind of an enmeshed boundary and uh a clear boundary as opposed to a rigged or an enmeshed boundary and uh a clearer boundary as opposed to a ridged or an enmeshed boundary uh people can communicate and share with others uh if they choose to. So from this standpoint of a clear boundary if you want my opinion uh like your own email account would be better but that's just my opinion. You know and you would still be free to share if you want to or not, depending on if you wanted to.............. what else happened in this conversation where um you know you told your Mom not to accuse your Dad of interfering with your relationship with her. Was there more to that, that you guys want to tell me about? ....

(Silent)

Jerry: Ok, ok. But uh you know I got to give you a compliment. I mean something bothered you and you said it.... You called your Mom and you said it and I think it's a good thing. You know, would you say that's the case?

Martha: Yep.

Jerry: Ok... And uh you do want to know uh what Jennifer thinks.

Martha: Um-hm.

Jerry: How she feels, and should she protect you or shelter you from anything?

Martha: No.

Jerry: Ok, so if she feels that you've done something uh to criticize her Dad um...its ok for her to tell you.

Martha: Yes.

Jerry: Ok, because one of the things that bothered her early on is that she felt that uh you were um interfering in her relationship with her Dad. It's something we talked about weeks ago.

Martha: Um-hm.

Jerry: Ok, so if there is anything at all that happens that makes her feel like you're trying to interfere, We're all three agreed that she talks about it right.

Because I mean that's how things get clarified. So that was good that you made that call………. Ok. Ok. What else do you guys want to talk about today?

Martha: Nothing.

Jennifer: Nope.

Martha: Are you sure?

Jennifer: Yeah.

Jerry: Curious about something?

Jennifer: Me?

Jerry: I'm curious about something.

Jennifer: Oh.

Jerry: Yeah, we talked recently about uh…seeing your cousins. Uh did you see them over Christmas or talked to them or anything?

Jennifer: No.

Jerry: No, ok. Because we have talked about you knowing that your Mom didn't have to be involved in that. Remember that conversation?

Jennifer: Yeah.

Jerry: Ok I was just curious. Ok….

Martha: Well since you don't want to talk about anything I do want to tell you something so that you hear it from me and nobody else. Um Todd asked me to marry him and I said yes.

Jennifer: Oh I didn't see that coming.

Martha: I'm sure you saw it coming but I just wanted you to hear it…

Jennifer: Yeah. Ok like I care.

Martha: How does it make you feel? I don't know.

Jennifer: Ha ha, I don't care, that's your life, and have fun.

(Silence)

Jerry: So you're saying you're not surprised.

Jennifer: No.

Jerry: No, you thought this was going to happen...eventually.

Jennifer: Yeah.

Jerry: Ok, ok. It's good that you told Jennifer um because it's better if she hears it from you...Um.... if in the future...Jennifer wanted to see you would she have to see Todd?

Martha: No.

Jerry: Ok. If in the future, we're just talking hypothetically now... Jennifer wanted to have a relationship with you. . And um she could do that without having to see or talk to Todd or acknowledge him in any way?

Martha: Right.

Jerry: Ok. So that clear boundary thing you know that you guys have a relationship, which should exist independent of what's happening in other relationships. It's also true with respect to uh you know Todd.

Martha: Um-hm.

Jerry: You don't expect Todd, Jennifer, and Todd to have a relationship?

Martha: No.

Jerry: Or for Jennifer to recognize Todd uh in any way?

Martha: Not unless she chooses to, but I doubt that.

Jennifer: Yeah right.

Jerry: Ok.Ok . So that means that um I know there were times where you felt your Mom tried to push Todd on you.

Jennifer: Yeah.

Jerry: Right. And kind of tired, and sell you on the fact that, that uh he was a nice man or whatever.

Jennifer: Um-hm.

Jerry: And uh that was one of the things in one of our sessions that you told me uh you felt was um not only premature but may be disrespectful.

Jennifer: Um-hm.

Jerry: Right.

Jennifer: Yeah.

Jerry: Of your relationship with your father.

Jennifer: Yeah.

Jerry: Um I'm not sure if those were the words you used exactly but that was the . .

Jennifer: The point yeah.

Jerry: um so this is helpful then hopefully you know that would clarify that uh your relationship with Todd in no way has any expectations um for Jennifer.

Martha: Right.

Jerry: You know, not even to the point where you know, you have seen or met you know or uh recognize Todd. You know that's not an expectation that you have....... Ok. Does that help you with what you expect of what was coming to know that you don't have to...?

Jennifer: No cause, um no because I wouldn't even if, no-one can tell me if I have to like him or not or who I can like and everything so no.

Jerry: Well that is true, no one can make you like anyone. No one can make you have a good relationship with anyone. Uh nobody has that kind of uh power or control you know you're a free person. Ok. Ok.................Jennifer uh you know are there things that you'd like to say to your Mom uh about that decision or how you feel about that decision?

Jennifer: No.

Jerry: ok, sometimes kids have a hope I'm not saying this was necessarily the case with you uh... you could tell me if it was or not. But sometimes kids have a hope that their parents are going to get back together someday and I've seen hope for sometimes after the divorce. Uh did you have any of those hopes?

Jennifer: No.

Jerry: Or did you know it was over between your Mom and your Dad.

Jennifer: No not after everything, no I didn't have any hopes, I liked it better the way it was then.

Jerry: You liked it better the way it was when?

Jennifer: How it is now, just me and my Dad, her wherever, whatever she's doing....................

Jerry: Ok. Well in my business we say you cannot, not have a relationship with a person................ . You know that?

Jennifer: No.

Jerry: How would you, you just heard this for the first time. The double negative is intentional. The idea is that um....... With a parent, with someone who is important to ya. You cannot totally cease a relationship with a person because they have uh you know kind of uh an impact on you. You can have a choice about what kind of a relationship you have with a person but it's impossible not to have a relationship with a person. Even an angry relationship is a relationship. And uh even a cutoff relationship is a relationship. Um in thinking in family therapy circles as a matter of fact is that if somebody cuts off that relationship, that uh they are still very much emotionally tied to that person..... Because even in cutting off that relationship what it means is there is unfinished business and um I .... only say that to offer you the thought.... that um you know even if there was you know some way that you could totally come out with a relationship with your Mom. Uh you wouldn't really be cut off you would still have a relationship um...my father and my mother are both dead and in the grave and I still have a relationship with them...uh cut off could mean because somebody is six feet under you can't talk to them anymore, but I still have a relationship with them...and uh that's kind of uh um important concept in family therapy. And uh that's why we work with people... and when we feel like you cut off contact with a parent uh try and develop some understanding of your relationship with that parent um because that relationship does travel with you. Um the American Indians used to say um once you've met somebody you could never be the same..... because they were part of you and uh while I'm not into American Indian lore I think that's particularly true you know a parent and a child will always have a relationship because they have uh you know a bond..........

Martha: You know I'll always be here for you Jennifer, I'm your mother.

Jennifer: Whatever, doesn't mean I'm going to need you, I don't.......

Martha: Well if you ever do I'm here.

Jennifer: Well I won't. Just letting you know now, I haven't for the past year, I won't now or anytime soon...or ever...

Jerry: Ok, well and we always say you know that um..... with..... anger would that be fair to say that was an angry statement?

Jennifer: No, it's the truth.

Jerry: Well you know how you feel, that's truly how you feel you know I'm not disputing that uh... but you know in my business we always say that you know whenever there is anger there is a traveling companion and uh you know that's, that's hurt. You know sadness........ you want to say anything about the hurt and the sadness that you're feeling right now?

Jennifer: I don't feel anything. Like I said before...um...I don't have a Mom anymore, not this one and it's just too bad and that's just how it is.......

Martha: You know I'm still your Mom and I will always be your Mom.

Jennifer: No...no.

Jerry: My perspective on this bond is there is no way to dissolve you know the connection? That is my perspective that the two of you will always have a relationship. .... Tell you what, what I'd like to do for uh you know the rest of the session unless you guys you know you guys want to use the rest of the session um you know I spent some time alone with you in the last session, would you mind if I spend some time alone with your Mom today? Ok and uh if it's ok with you um maybe the next time we'll have you come back by yourself.

Jennifer: Sure.

Jerry: Is that ok with you?

Jennifer: Yeah.

Jerry: Ok, So then uh that will be next Friday. I'll ask your Dad if you can come at 6:00. Ok.

Jennifer: Ok. Bye...

Jerry: (tells me) we're done I'm going to spend some time with Martha can you come next Friday at 6:00

January 12, 2007 Counselor #3 Session 13 (Jennifer alone)

Jerry: Do you feel like you have made any progress, that you and your Mom have made any progress in reconciling your relationship or healing it?

Jennifer: No.

Jerry: No?

Jennifer: It's been just about a year since I've talked to, since the day I got kicked out and everything. This has been the third counselor and nothing changed, so I don't think that anything will change, actually, I know nothing is going to change. Because I can't, that's how I feel and she can't change that and neither can a counselor. Three counselors, that's a lot for a year and nothing changed.

Jerry: You're making me depressed Jennifer, ha ha ha.

Jennifer: It's the truth.

Jerry: I guess you're telling people (could not make out what was said). Yeah I know I'm the third person and uh gosh it has been what February something right.

Jennifer: February first.

Jerry: February first. Ok, so it's just under a year. Ok. Um, at least you got to talk to your Mom about what was bothering you, was it at least helpful to you?

Jennifer: No.

Jerry: If not, uh you know, healing of your relationship with your Mom, did it at least help you to kind of like vent and get it out?

Jennifer: No.

Jerry: No, hmm ok. Boy, I guess what you're telling me is I've done absolutely no good.

Jennifer: Pretty much.

Jerry: I hope it hasn't been a negative experience anyway because I wouldn't want to turn you off to counselors.

Jennifer: I've already been through three, it's not going to really make a difference.

Jerry: All right, ok, umm. Well, when you look at what's happened in your family, uh since your parents separated, got divorced, would you say uh your experience is different than most families?

Jennifer: What...

Jerry: Like uh harder on you in your family than most families?

Jennifer: No.

Jerry: No

Jennifer: It's not hard on me at all. I'm fine, doing good in school and everything else, I just have to come here with my Mom. That's the only thing that still bothers me because like I said, I'm not going to change my feelings and everything and like I said this is the third counselor and she still doesn't realize it.

Jerry: Um-hm, yeah, yeah she hopes to be able to repair you know uh her relationship with you. That's what I hope is to somehow repair that relationship because that's what counselors are supposed to do, is to help people you know repair their relationship but I realize that's ahh, that's a tall order. And I also realize that uh, there's nothing I can do to make it happen um you know I know that. Uh. . . . . You think there were any uh, you know I'm sure you had other friends or know other kids that have gone through a divorce. Do you think uh, what happened in your situation with your Mom was um unique in any way?

Jennifer: Yeah she did a lot more stuff than all more than the people that I know that went through a divorce.

Jerry: Um-hm.

Jennifer: She did a lot more things to push me away and that's her fault.

Jerry: Um-hm. Ok. Um, I'm just curious, is there room for forgiveness in your view of the world?

Jennifer: Not for her.

Jerry: Not for her? Ok. As a general principle, is there room for forgiveness?

Jennifer: Like I said before, it depends on the situation but if it's concerning her.

Jerry: Um-hm.

Jennifer: Because nothing like, yeah nothing like that has ever happened where someone keeps doing something like she did so like I said no there's not any room for forgiveness for her.

Jerry: Um-hm. Ok. Would you say that you know with regards to your feelings to your Mom that um, your hurt or your anger is the bigger of the two feelings?

Jennifer: Can you repeat that?

Jerry: Yeah. You say that regarding your feelings to your Mom and you know what happened between the two of you would you say that hurt or anger is the bigger of your two feelings?

Jennifer: Uh, both.

Jerry: Both. You feel it's harder to separate one or the other?

Jennifer: Yeah.

Jerry: Ok. Well, what's the biggest hurt that you have?

Jennifer: Um, I don't know. Pretty much everything that she's done, you can't just pick one there's just so many.

Jerry: Um-hm. Ok. Is there um like a top piragua?

Jennifer: Probably when she kicked me out.

Jerry: Was it what she said when she kicked you out?

Jennifer: Um, well that and doing it in general.

Jerry: What do you, what do you think should have happened at that point?

Jennifer: I don't know.

Jerry: I mean if you were a mother, uh you know god forbid if you should have to go through something like this. If you were a mother how do you think a mother should handle a situation like um you guys were going through that your family was going through?

Jennifer: Well I definitely wouldn't have kicked my kid out, but I would have just talked to my kid and let her make the choice if she wanted to go with her Dad then that's her choice. I'm not going to keep someone with me who doesn't want to be with me.

Jerry: Um-hm. Ok. Well and uh certainly your Mom was trying to keep you there and uh........ Just you know, what the information will do for you I don't know but a lot of times what happens is when people are going through a loss you know they have uh, you know very mixed feelings and um, I think that um when your Mom and your Dad separated my guess is that uh both of them were worried about uh losing you. And um because both of them were worried about losing you, and losing their relationship with you there were certain grief dynamics and grief feelings that happened. And believe it or not when people are dealing with loss, uh there is sadness but there is also anger and uh you know it's probably some of what came out between you and your Mom when you made the decision that you wanted to be, you wanted to be with your Dad.

Jennifer: That doesn't still make it right. . . To kick your child out. . . And do what she did. So she's supposed to take it out on them, no.

Jerry: The way, the way I look at it uh when people are angry they say things uh they say things they don't mean. Um and when you know people uh are hurt uh a lot of times they respond with anger and what they say in anger it doesn't represent uh you know their true feelings. You know it just represents, you know, the way they feel at a given Moment. And um, you know, what your Mom said, you know at that point probably didn't represent her true feelings.

Jennifer: Then she wouldn't have said it. Even though no matter how much you want to stick up for her or whatever, it's still not right and it's not going to change what happened or how I felt.

Jerry: Well, um. . . . . I'm giving you new ways to think about it you know and um, it's up to you whether you know you want to utilize or take these new ways of thinking about things. Um you know personally I believe uh you know that it's good for kids to come out of a divorce with two parents. I said that to you before you know a kid shouldn't have to lose one parent because there is a divorce. I also believe that um anger is not good for people to carry so that's why I am trying to give you some um you know different ways to think about it. See because I don't believe that what people say when they're angry is necessarily what they mean. And I don't know my guess is that there were probably uh there was probably a lot that happened that was kind of out of character. . . . Um. . . For your Mom you know. And you've said yourself because it felt like it wasn't your Mom anymore some of the things that you know uh you went through during that time were kind of like so far different from the way you knew your Mom up to the point of the divorce. That's what makes it so hard for you to accept. You remember saying that right?

Jennifer: Well, yeah it was hard because she did that but I still don't agree that if she, that if that's what she really felt she would have done it, she would have stopped herself. If she really was thinking about what she was doing, she would have stopped herself from saying get out and all that. But she didn't and there's nothing that could change that so that's just how I take it because that's what happened.

Jerry: Well, you know she said get out um you know that's the fact um. . . . But sometimes what a person says when they're angry doesn't represent their true feelings. Have you ever said anything when you've been angry that might have represented where you were at a moment in time but really didn't represent how you felt the majority of the time?

Jennifer: No.

Jerry: No? You never said anything that you regretted?

Jennifer: No.

Jerry: Really?

Jennifer: I say what's on my mind and how I feel and that's that.

Jerry: Yeah, but you never said anything you regretted later?

Jennifer: No.

Jerry: Really? Well give yourself time, you will. But um. . . . you do know by the way that uh when I talk with you about different ways to think about what happened between uh you and your Mom it's not because I think you should have a relationship with your Mom as an exclusion of your relationship with your Dad. You know that right?

Jennifer: Wait, what do you. . .

Jerry: In other words I want you to have a relationship with both your Mom and your Dad.

Jennifer: Ok, but it's not going to happen.

Jerry: I know that, I know that's what you're saying. I guess I just want to say I in no way uh want to jeopardize your relationship with your Dad or take it away from you. And I think the stuff that you talked about that your Mom made you feel like you had to pick her over your Dad. A big mistake she made. So, I just want to go on record of saying that, you get what I'm saying?

Jennifer: No.

Jerry: Ha ha ha, talking over your head, talking psychobabble to you huh? Yeah. Uh, what I'm saying is uh I think the things that your Mom did which made you feel like you had to pick her over your Dad. You know things we talked about like the picture thing, the birthday thing that was all stuff that made you feel like you couldn't have a relationship with your Dad right?

Jennifer: Yeah.

Jerry: Ok. And what I am saying is I think those were big mistakes that your Mom made.

Jennifer: Yeah.

Jerry: I'm just trying to go on record saying that those were big mistakes. Um, so um I don't think uh she's really right without fault. . . . . . What did she actually say in February when you were leaving? Do you remember the exact words?

Jennifer: Well, I was standing outside because we were arguing and I just stepped outside and was standing in the driveway because I just wanted to get away from it for a minute and then she opened the door and she told me to get in the house, pack a bag and get out.

Jerry: And when you were like uh standing there in the driveway, you wanted to get away from it, you've already made your decision that you wanted to be with your Dad right?

Jennifer: Yeah.

Jerry: And uh you had told her that earlier in the evening?

Jennifer: Yeah and before that.

Jerry: Um-Hm, hmm. Ok. . . . . . . Words hurt, I acknowledge that . . . . do you feel like your Mom did your Dad dirt by having an affair?

Jennifer: Say that again.

Jerry: Do you feel like your Mom did something terrible to your Dad by having an affair?

Jennifer: Um well yeah, but still she basically did it to me too. Cause I was in the family, so it's not all you know about my Dad though too. I was there, you know.

Jerry: Um-hm, ok. What do you mean by she did it to you too? What meaning do you give the fact that she had an affair, I mean uh could you say kind of like what meaning it had to you?

Jennifer: Well, um cause like, I take it if you're part of a family that's your family and if one person abandons that family for someone else and just dumps their family you know that's not right. So basically, it was him or me and she goes for him.

Jerry: So the way you think about it is that uh, your Mom abandoned you for him.

Jennifer: Yeah. But that's not the only reason that I'm not talking to her. It's everything else that just constantly happened at home when I was living with her, I lived with her for a while after it first happened and it wasn't until February that I went with my Dad because it got to the point I was sick and tired of it, yeah I finally decided I wanted to go with my Dad but then we got into that argument and that's when in February when she kicked me out. So it's not just that, it's everything she's done.

Jerry: Um-hm. Yeah, I understand it's not like there's just one thing. Uh but this is certainly an aspect that we haven't talked about which is that the way you experienced it you felt like she abandoned the family, your part of the family so and uh that's something we haven't talked about. But that's not all of it, um. . . . . When you say that she abandoned you, can you say anything like what meaning it had to you?

Jennifer: What do you mean by that?

Jerry: How do you think about it, what do you think it says about your Mom, anything like that?

Jennifer: Um, well like I said I don't think its right and I don't know I just don't think that it's right to leave your family you know. Um, basically that's it.

Jerry:. . . . . Can't argue with that. . . . . . . Although I'm sure that's a complex thing. But that's not all, you know that uh hurt you right, you know her involvement with another man. Um, what were some of the other things that happened during the time that you lived with her?

Jennifer: Well, like all the things we talked about like all those incidents and stuff like that and then there were just like, there was always an argument she would always have something to say and then it would always get into an argument and stuff like that and it wouldn't stop. Like she was like a whole different person. And yeah it led to all those incidents like the birthday and all that and then it just you know got way out of control.

Jerry: Um-hm. Hm. When you say your Mom became a whole different person, I mean how was she different from the mother you used to know?

Jennifer: Um, well like she kind of changed and I don't know it was just living with her and everything and how she acted. I don't know how to explain it but like I would have never pictured her kicking me out or doing everything that she did. You know it's not, I would have never pictured her like that. Like all of a sudden, she just changed instantly.

Jerry: Was she more argumentative than she has been in the past?

Jennifer: Yeah.

Jerry: Yeah.

Jennifer: Like every little thing turned into an argument.

Jerry: Give me some examples.

Jennifer: I don't even know I just like, I don't know she'd come home, like id have dinner, uh I don't know anything that she said would turn into an argument and stuff like with the whole picture thing and it led into an incident and stuff like that and other stuff and she'd be working late so I would sit down and have dinner by myself every night and I would cook for myself and things like that. She wouldn't be home, she would come home late and I don't know it's just like a bunch of things. It's so much to explain like I don't know how to explain everything. But like it's basically like all those incidents, almost every day was an argument.

Jerry: Were you home by yourself a lot?

Jennifer: Uh, yeah. She would work in the morning, I would get up for school and she'd still be sleeping and right when I'm about to leave, was when she gets up and then she would work until like six and then sometimes she would have to stay late so I'd be doing homework and by the time she'd get home she would be doing something whether it was more work or she would eat and I would watch TV or something after my homework was done and then I would go to bed.

Jerry: So you really didn't have much, even though you were living with your Mom you really didn't have much contact with her?

Jennifer: Yeah, pretty much. And then like when I did talk to her I said everything turned into an argument.

Jerry: Um-hm. Um-hm. Wow, had she worked long hours before that?

Jennifer: Uh

Jerry: Or I mean was she working more?

Jennifer: Yeah. Because usually she gets off work at like five and like she even does now, so I don't know. I mean there would be days once in a while where she would work late but it got to like every day I was coming home you know, even if I went to my friend's house after school I would still come home, then eat, and stuff like that.

Jerry: So you were eating alone a lot?

Jennifer: Yeah.

Jerry: It must have felt kind of lonely.

Jennifer: Yeah I guess.

Jerry: Understandable.......... . Did you believe that your Mom was at work or spending time with the other guy rather than coming home.

Jennifer: Who knows probably both..... .

Jerry: But it was a lonely time for you. Yeah, Yeah. What else was hard for you about that time? I mean um, let's talk about the arguments a little bit. Um prior to that have you and your Mom had an argumentative relationship or not?

Jennifer: Um not before like all of this happened like the divorce and everything no, but like I don't know, they just started and everything I don't really know it was so long ago but, I don't know she just got really to the point where every little thing was an argument and stuff. I don't know, it's just how it was.

Jerry: Um-hm. Hm. So you must have felt like you lost much of uh you know uh what you used to value about your relationship with your Mom.

Jennifer: Yeah.

Jerry: Are we talking like a hundred and eighty degree change?

Jennifer: Meaning like a big change or. .

Jerry: Yeah.

Jennifer: Yeah.

Jerry: That's the sense I get. Yeah hmm. How else did she change when your family was going through the divorce?

Jennifer: Um, I don't know.

Jerry:............Tough situation you went through. Um you know one way to think about these sessions is um you know um ......the purpose of the sessions you know uh was really to try and heal your relationship with your Mom but even if that doesn't happen you know you still might be able to get benefit out of this for yourself. Just in understanding what happened in your family.

Jennifer: Well I already know, it's nothing new.

Jerry: Well Yeah but I mean uh sometimes when things happen and we can fairly say what happened in your family was a traumatic experience, sometimes it's beneficial to just talk about it and um you know, who knows maybe some of the, maybe that's the benefit you get out of, out of coming here.

Jennifer: Uh I've already talked about it twice with the other two counselors so...

Jerry: Why would I be any different?

Jennifer: Exactly.

Jerry: Maybe I won't, maybe I won't but um...you know um.... You know I would like to at least have the hope that I could do something that would be beneficial for you. Um............Did, I'm just curious when your family was actually going through the separation and the divorce and uh things were deteriorating between you and your Mom. Um, did she try anything to try and mend your relationship?

Jennifer: What do you mean?

Jerry: Did she do anything to correct what was going wrong between the two of you?

Jennifer: No.

Jerry: You know like uh have any heart to heart talks or anything like that?

Jennifer: No.

Jerry: No. Hmm. And what were you telling yourself at the time was the reason your Mom had changed?

Jennifer: Well I figured it was because of her boyfriend.

Jerry:..... Hm, ok. And how do you figure he had changed her, what, how do you think he had influenced her?

Jennifer: Just because how she had changed like the arguments and everything. Everything was like a lie and stuff so I don't know, and how she started treating um like me and things like it was way different...

Jerry: Um-hm, hmm. So you figured this different person because she really was different, a big change that you were living with uh that was because of her boyfriend's influence............... Probably a stressful time, no doubt. ......How do you think she was influenced, being influenced by him?

Jennifer: I don't know, she just was different.

Jerry: Um-hm.

Jennifer: He could have probably told her anything and she would have believed it, I don't know.

Jerry: Cause you don't even know, you've never met him have you?

Jennifer: No.

(Silence)

Jerry: I didn't realize there had been so much arguing even about everyday things between you and your Mom but it sounds like it was, do I have it right?

Jennifer: Yeah.

Jerry: Hmm……. . Did you feel like she tried to make you like a little adult as you were going through this whole thing?

Jennifer: No.

Jerry: I mean like uh were you getting more responsibilities around the house to cook, to clean you know?

Jennifer: Well like I said before I was cooking dinner and stuff for myself and then I don't know, I don't really remember doing anything else sometimes I'd do the dishes but we had a dishwasher so I'd just load that, clean up the house sometimes.

Jerry: Um-hm. Who used to cook?

Jennifer: Uh

Jerry: I mean when the whole family was together?

Jennifer: My Mom and sometimes my Dad if he was home from work and stuff.

Jerry: So you had to cook for yourself when she wasn't home?

Jennifer: Yeah.

Jerry: Did you ever tell her at the time that it bothered you, that she wasn't home?

Jennifer: Um…I think I mentioned it once but she just said something like she had to work or something like that.

Jerry: Um-hm.

Jennifer: Because I said something like you're never home anymore or something like that. But I don't know. And she knew I was eating by myself because every time she'd come home I'd already be done or I would be finishing up eating and make something for herself and eat so.

Jerry: Um-hm. Boy, a lonely time. A lonely time. Did your family generally eat dinners together?

Jennifer: Yeah.

Jerry: Did you like, did you like that?

Jerry: Yeah most kids do, most kids do....... . You probably .... . ????

Jennifer: I guess.

Jerry: Lonely, sad, ok. .... Well, I want to thank you for your anger and thank you for uh telling me a little bit more about uh you know what your life was like and what happened between uh you and your Mom. Uh as your family went through the separation and divorce, um you know you shared some new things with me today. You know like the fact that just the fact that your Mom had a boyfriend, you felt that she kind of abandoned you, abandoned the family. You are part of the family and she abandoned you just by the fact that she got involved with another man. Uh that was something new that you never shared with me before. And uh also just you know the extent of uh kind of the loneliness and isolation you felt at the time uh because she was homeless.... then she had been before. Uh that was new and uh the other thing that you told me today that was new um you guys were arguing uh about little things too. Uh and that uh it wasn't only you know the bigger stuff that you told me about before like uh the birthday and the pictures that kind of thing. Uh but there were little things you were arguing about too, so uh it kind of rounded out my understanding a little bit today if nothing else. Anything else you want to tell me to kind of help me to understand your situation or your feelings?

Jennifer: No.

Jerry: No. .... Ok, alright. I will see you next Friday.

Like any business, these counselors are paid to do a job. They do just that. Their job is to get the customer what they want no matter what, becoming blind to the truth, ethics, and even compassion toward a young child. The only difference between these types of Counselors and the mob on the street is Counselors have the law on their side. The law protects them with confidentiality, therefore, keeping it a secret of the horrible manner in which they conduct themselves in their private torture chambers. If called upon in court they are considered highly credible rendering anyone who opposes them helpless, especially children. The sad part is the courts allow one of the two people in a heated battle to choose these predators. The person is allowed to make the choice through their insurance. They first call by phone and then set up an interview to meet face to face. The customer boasts of a huge court case and that the counselor will play an important role with many sessions worth thousands of dollars, in addition to allowing the counselor sole control of the frequencies of the sessions. The counselors knowing that the choice of who will get that large-paying case is the person sitting right in front of them. The counselors promise to deliver to make the sale as a child's soul is bought and sold.

January 19, 2007 Counselor #3 session 14

Jerry: Welcome, Let me give this to you while I'm thinking about it. You asked for a summary statement?

Martha: Yeah.

Jerry: So there you go, take care of that. That was all the sessions that we had.

Martha: Ok.

Jerry: Ok, So welcome. So as you know Jennifer and I met alone last week and uh there are a couple things that uh you know I think you know we should talk about uh. Two things that I think uh were kind of new but I thought maybe I could help you talk about. Um Martha um when Jennifer and I were talking. Uh Jennifer used the word abandoned and uh she really said that she felt like uh you had abandoned her, and uh we got into talking a little bit about what had happened uh to make her feel abandoned. And um one of the things she mentioned you guys already talked about which were circumstances uh actually about a year ago on the day that she left to live with her father. Um but there were two other things that she said which had led her to feel abandoned and as I was thinking you know what might be useful or helpful for today, I thought maybe it would be a good idea if we talked about what those two things were. That had uh you know kind of creative precipitated however you want to put this feeling of being abandoned. So that's how I thought maybe we could productively use our time today. Does that make sense to you guys? Ok, um one of the things that you told me and I'll let you talk about it in your own words Jennifer.

Jennifer: Um-hm.

Jerry: Uh what it meant to you that um Mom was involved with another man and uh you explained to me how it was you felt abandoned as a result of that. That was one of the things we've talked about. So do you think we can do some listening?

Martha: Um-hm.

Jerry: Ok, So go ahead.

Jennifer: So just. .

Jerry: just talk about it and explain you know what about that made you feel abandoned.

Jennifer: Um well what I said was that it made me feel abandoned because like we had a family and you just decided to leave because of another man, yeah so basically you abandoned me and for someone else, I believe that's what I said.

Jerry: That's about it yeah. And um you know you kind of said If you abandoned the family I'm part of the family you abandoned me, that's how you experienced it.

Jennifer: Yeah.

Jerry: Right. And um I don't know um do you want to ask any questions to understand more the feeling that Jennifer had as a result of that?

Martha: Well I'm going to say I'm divorcing her Dad and not her.......

Jerry: And you know that's how you were thinking about it but the way that you were thinking about it was that um Mom had made a decision as you put it to um, I don't know if you said to leave the family or break the family. Do you remember what you said in your exact words?

Jennifer: No I'm not sure exactly what I said but it was along those lines.

Jerry: Ok, and uh your slant on it was break the family, leave the family, leave me,

Jennifer: Yeah.

Jerry: That was your slant on it. And then you said that.... What happened during the period where Mom and Dad were separated also gave you a feeling of being abandoned....... You were home a lot

Jennifer: Yeah

Jerry: That kind of thing. Maybe you could share with Mom what you told me about that:

Jennifer: Um well said that after Dad left and stuff I was home alone a lot cause you were working late till like six and sometimes later if you had other things to do so yeah I was just by myself a lot and basically yeah eating dinner and stuff by myself.

Jerry: So it was a lonely existence...You even felt like Mom was working more at that time.

Jennifer: Yeah.

Jerry: Then before and you know uh that was kind of part of this feeling of being abandoned you had.

Jennifer: Yeah.

Jerry: And then um.... you also talked a little bit about what had started happening between you and your Mom during that period of time and you felt like uhhhh the new Mom was not the old Mom that you always knew, uh because you know there were a lot of arguments and stuff, so could you talk about that a little bit?

Jennifer: Um well we were just arguing more and stuff and that's really it like over little things, but basically everything was an argument.

Jerry: Right, right. And you know you said uh you know prior to that you and your Mom did not have an argumentative relationship. And so it was kind of like um everything you knew was you know kind of like gone.

Jennifer: Um-hm.

Jerry: That was the sense I got from what you were saying.

Jennifer: Yeah.

Jerry: So that's some of what um .... We talked about last week, there was this feeling of abandonment uh was very strong worded. Um could you understand the feeling that Jennifer was feeling Martha?

Martha: Yeah I guess, I mean she never talked about it now that she's mentioning it as far as work and stuff, I don't think there was really a change. I basically put in the same amount of hours that I always have.

Jerry: So, who knows um being that it was now a one-parent household and obviously would be for you a lonelier household, your Mom was working but can you say a little bit more to give

Jennifer a sense that you understand her feelings? Just to kind of give her a sense that you're like walking in her shoes a little bit.

Martha: I do understand that she would be alone because there was no one home if I was working so I can understand that. Feeling like she was left alone.

Jerry: Um-hm.

Martha: Um, of course, she was off of school before I would get off work, I tried to work it where she would be at our house with a friend or at a different house, one of her friends' houses. Stuff like that. I understand it was a whole change for her you know, for Jennifer because we used to all be together.

Jerry: Um-hm, typically you know before the separation did you come home to one parent or the other?

Jennifer: Um,

Jerry: Was somebody always home when you came home from school, I don't know like work schedules.

Jennifer: Sometimes depending on when my Dad got off, sometimes he got off, sometimes he'd be home.

Jerry: Um-hm, Um-hm. Ok so uh you had a lot more time alone.

Jennifer: Yeah.

Jerry: Ok, and uh, did you try to express your feelings of loneliness at the time?

Jennifer: I know I mentioned once about her working like a lot more and stuff but that was it.

Jerry: What do you remember?

Jennifer: I don't know, I just remember mentioning that she was working a lot more but I don't remember much after that.

Jerry: Ok uh, do you remember what happened after you mentioned it though. Did it change anymore for better or worse?

Jennifer: No. It stayed the same.

Jerry: Ok, alright, so uh that was the only time that you mentioned loneliness.

Jennifer: Yeah.

Jerry: Ok. Martha Um.... I think what's really important is that uh Jennifer gets a sense that you know you're walking in her shoes a little bit, kind of like understanding things from her perspective. Um could you ask, do you have any questions to ask her to try and understand um how she experienced events? Make the questions, not questions like to try and change how she feels but rather to understand how she feels...Or do you feel that you got it.

Martha: I mean like I said before she was alone more because of the absence of one of us being there, I can understand that but, I don't recall my work schedule changing that much where I would be gone more than I was typically before.

Jerry: Um-hm, ok, what about like do you understand Jennifer's thinking about your involvement with another man. Do you understand how it is she feels that was an abandonment of her?

Martha: Um-hm.

Jerry: Do you? Ok, tell her how you understand so that she can kind of get a sense that at least uh you can understand her experience of events.

Martha: Because she was always there and she was important to me. Maybe she felt that this person was replacing her and not just her Dad. It's not the case but, I can understand that, that's how she felt.

Jerry: You know that he displaced her, you can understand?

Martha: Um-hm.

Jerry: Ok, ok......And this was obviously an incredibly uh stressful tense time, painful because there were a lot of arguments and stuff and um your Mom seemed like a different person to you right.

Jennifer: Yeah.

Jerry: Ok, how she was different than you always knew.

Jennifer: Um well like I said before she was always working late, she used to get off at five but then like she would work at six and stuff so she was barely ever around um and then like I said there were arguments almost every day about like little things so yeah.

Jerry: Hmm.

Martha: What things Jennifer?

Jennifer: Just the littlest things, the littlest things you'd get mad about and you'd argue with me on them.

Martha: The first six months I don't remember us arguing.

Jennifer: Oh yes there was arguing.

Martha: Until about December.

Jennifer: No, no there was arguing before that....

Jerry: Ok, were you eating meals alone?

Jennifer: Yeah.

Jerry: Ok so you were like preparing your own meals and. .

Jennifer: Most of the time yeah.

Jerry: And how had been before that time?

Jennifer: Um usually she would cook when she got home from work and once in a while my Dad would cook if he got home before her...

Jerry: But typically before all this happened uh your family would have family meals.

Jerry: Ok, a lot of families now don't have that. Um but that was another huge change. I assume you like family meals and missed it when it stopped.

Jennifer: Yeah.

Jerry: And did you find that you were angry about the changes going on in your life?

Jennifer: Um I guess yeah.

Jerry: And uh you said you talked about being lonely at least one time that you recall.

Jennifer: Yeah.

Jerry: How did your anger get communicated?

Jennifer: What do you mean?

Jerry: Well we got an old saying that you cannot, not communicate. You're feeling something. It always gets communicated uh in some way either through what you say or what you do so that's what I'm wondering you know if you were angry how did you express it?

Jennifer: I don't know?

Jerry: Did you say it?

Jennifer: Well yeah, yeah, I told her but nothing changed. .

Jerry: What did you tell her you were angry about?

Jennifer: I just told her she was never home and stuff and she worked late. From what I remember she just said she didn't and it didn't change.

Jerry: Do you remember that conversation?

Martha: No.

Jerry: Ok, ok. But you were suddenly feeling lonely and angry about it. Ok. And were you feeling angry with your Mom about the fact that she had a relationship with another man?

Jennifer: Yeah because that's what I said before where I felt abandoned because she broke up the family.

Jerry: Ok, ok.... . And ... do you still feel, still feel angry about that? Mom's decision to be involved with another man because you view that as breaking up the family?

Jennifer: Yeah but I don't really care anymore she can do what she wants.

Jerry: Um-hm.

Jennifer: I'm fine how I am now.

Jerry: Yeah we talked about that.........Do you have some questions that you want to ask Jennifer you know what she is sharing to understand more Martha.

Martha: Well I mean as far as us talking and everything she used to sleep in the bed with us and sometimes when her Dad was not in the house, in the beginning, she and daisy still slept in the bed with me probably for about five months or so and then she went to her own room and then started sleeping in there by herself. We used to still talk every night and stuff just around December time things just changed.

Jennifer: (somewhat angry) No it definitely wasn't that long. I went to my room a lot sooner and no we still did not have talks. We did not have talks, we did not have talks ever since you mentioned the divorce and you know that's true because you've always said stuff to me about it. Oh you never talk to me anymore so no that's not true.

Jerry: So you think things began to really go downhill with your Mom when she mentioned divorce.

Jennifer: Well yeah that too.

Jerry: Ok and when do you recall your Mom mentioning divorce?

Jennifer: What do you, what do you mean?

Jerry: Well sometimes when parents separate you know uh the kids are hoping the parents are going to get back together and work things out and uh you know sometimes parents even tell the kids we're separated but they don't use the D-word, they don't use the divorce word until later on. So that's why I'm asking you when did Mom tell you that uh you know the divorce was coming?

Jennifer: When she told my Dad. But she mentioned, I think she said something to him first and then she came home and told me.

Jerry: Ok, but I mean was it like uh December, or was it like far in advance of December?

Jennifer: Before July I think it was.

Jerry: Ok, So uh quite a bit before. So you would say things began to deteriorate as early as you know July or

Jennifer: Yeah, because she even mentioned she would be like you never talk to me about anything anymore, so that's not true because I didn't. And so that's not true that five or six months or to December is when I stopped talking to her. That's not true. It happened a lot earlier than that and she knows that.

Jerry: So you have different recollections uh you know when things started to go south between the two of you but um you know, I think um what's important is that you felt pretty angry about the events that were happening, and you know kind of held Mom accountable, and you had a big hurt too because you were feeling abandoned .... . Right.

Jennifer: Yeah.

Jerry: Ok, and um lonely too. Ok. Did you try any things to try and heal your relationship with your Mom at that time?

Jennifer: No.

Jerry: Talk it out or anything like that? No, ok. And could you tell that Jennifer was really hurting struggling when your family was going through this.

Martha: Not in the beginning.

Jerry: Ok, and uh when did you start to notice that uh she was really struggling? With what was going on?

Martha: Um, Well there were a lot of things that happened along the way but I remember us talking about stuff probably around October, November.

Jerry: Ok, And when did you begin noticing in the fall that uh told you that Jennifer was in pain over what was going on? Over the changes in the family?

Martha: Well certain things that we used to talk about were starting to dwindle and that was kind of ......

Jerry: Ok, so the first thing you started to notice is that there wasn't as much conversation between the two of you.

Martha: Yeah.

Jerry: Yeah. Ok, and what, what did you make of that at the time? That you guys weren't talking as much?

Martha: Well I would ask her every day, do you want to talk about it, no, no, no.

Jerry: Um-hm.

Martha: ????

Jerry: Ok. And um that was pretty different because you guys used to talk about everything.

Martha: Um-hm.

Jerry: So what I see here is uh other change. Ok, and uh that's pretty much what you said too somehow what started happening between you and your Mom was like nothing you'd ever experienced.... Um.... Did you do any things to uh you know try and help Jennifer when you began noticing that she was having trouble coping with you know the changes.

Martha: I tried to talk to her, I tried to put her in counseling and she refused to go. Then she started to go a little bit...

Jerry: Ok. ....Ok and then from the fall on arguments became more uh frequent and more severe I gather.

Martha: I don't know if it was more frequent, it was just she wouldn't talk to me................

Jerry: Ok, and as you got quieter and talked to your Mom less, did your...hurt or goings on in the family, your anger did it grow stronger or, or not?

Jennifer: No, I was still mad about the same things...

Jerry: Um-hm, ok. When you held in the anger did it...get even bigger?

Jennifer: No.

Jerry: It certainly didn't diminish at all.... . What, I'm just curious Jennifer, earlier on was there anything that could have happened that might have avoided things getting as bad as they did?

Jennifer: No.

Jerry: Really, ok. So even if in the fall, you know you and your Mom were able to talk, you don't think it would have made any difference?

Jennifer: No. Cause she didn't.

Jerry: Make an effort to talk to you.

Jennifer: Well yeah. I guess.

Jerry: Gee I got kind of lost here. Ha, ha, ha, she did or she didn't make an effort to talk to you?

Jennifer: She didn't but I wouldn't have talked to her anyway. Cause like I said everything was an argument and stuff like that.

Jerry: And you're talking between the two of you obviously?

Jennifer: Yeah.

Jerry: Things were bad between Mom and Dad.

Jennifer: No between. .

Jerry: Yeah things were bad between the two of you.

Jennifer:? You said, my Mom and Dad.

Jerry: Right I just wanted to make sure you were talking between, we're on the same page...(Long silence).................Were you feeling at the time, were you feeling at the time that Mom deserved to be punished for what, for the decisions she made, cause of the way it affected the family?

Jennifer: Um.... What do you mean?

Jerry: Well obviously the decisions Mom made had a great impact on the family.... because you know your Dad left eventually Mom and Dad divorced um and what I'm wondering is whether you were thinking that Mom deserved to be punished because she had done a terrible thing?

Jennifer: Um.... meaning like I didn't talk to her because she deserved to be punished?

Jerry: You got it.

Jennifer: Um well if that's the way you want to put it I was just mad and stuff and like I said everything was an argument so I didn't talk to her so if that's.... how other words for how I'm saying it then yeah.

Jerry: .... Well then in a way those are two different things, you know sometimes people don't talk because they are trying to avoid an argument you know and, sometimes people don't talk because you're angry.... and... kind of like withholding attention or affection is kind of uh the way that they punish the person they are angry with. And you know that's why I asked the question, did you feel Mom deserved to be punished for the decision that she made to um be involved with another man?

Jennifer: Yes. I guess its part of what I was mad for, so.

Jerry: That's hugely what, what you were mad for.

Jennifer: Yeah but it was, like that's what started it but it was everything else too, that made it worse. It wasn't just that.

Martha: I don't remember arguing, it being that bad because we still did things' your friends still came over.

Jennifer: Yeah my friends still came over but what did that have to do with you?

Martha: I'm just saying.

Jennifer: No, yeah, we definitely did.

Martha: It was pretty much fine until...

Jennifer: No, no,

Martha: December

Jennifer: No, it wasn't, you would get mad over the littlest things if something wasn't cleaned up or anything and you would just.... go off.

Yeah, yes you were.

Jerry: Were you feeling irritable at that period of time, do you remember being irritable? When people are undergoing stress uh generally they are irritable. At least I am.

Martha: Well as far as keeping the house clean and everything, the house didn't go on the market until January and that's when we had to keep it clean for showings and stuff like that.

Jennifer: Before that.

Martha: I don't remember

Jennifer: Well of course you wouldn't remember.

Martha: I used to clean up, we used to do things together.

Jennifer: No you were always working, yeah or on the phone with Todd.

Martha: I called Todd after you went to bed.

Jennifer: Oh yeah..... Ok.

Jerry: Do you remember that there were times Mom was at home and the two of you could have been talking or whatever and she was talking to Todd.

Jennifer: I know that she was talking to Todd whenever she, I wasn't in the room or something. I'm not completely stupid. And I know she talked to him at night after I went to my room. She doesn't, if she wants to hide stuff she's not very good at it apparently.

Jerry: Did you feel Mom was putting attention into Todd that could have been better shared with you?

Jerry: Well like I said again I felt abandoned and I was pushed aside so that's just how it was. You get used to it after a while.

(Silence)

Jerry: So in a way, you feel like Mom's involvement with Todd really ate up time that kind of pushed you to the side, right?

Jennifer: Yeah.

Jerry: Ok, well that's another aspect of why you felt abandoned…. . You know because like you felt like time…. that might have been yours you know was uh going to Todd…

Martha: Well I don't understand that because we usually talked after we went to bed. He pretty much knew if I was with Jennifer he wouldn't call unless it was something he absolutely wanted to talk about. Like if he was with his son I wouldn't call him so we tried to be aware of that. But typically

Jennifer: No, cause your phone rang and rang and rang all the time so no that's not even true. And whenever we went to places it would ring too……I, I'm not two, I'm aware of what goes on especially when I'm there.

Martha: If you were there then we wouldn't talk because I was with you.

Jennifer: Yeah, I'd be in the vicinity that we were in and yes you would. Even if I wasn't sleeping so no.

Jerry: So there were a lot of intrusions.

Jennifer: What's that mean?

Jerry: Um, an intrusion is an interruption. Calls from Todd interrupted uh what might have happened between you and your Mom got in the way.

Jennifer: Not really there was nothing going on. But I knew he would be calling.

Jerry: Ok, even if there was nothing going on between you and your Mom and that call came and you suspected it was Todd, How would you feel

Jennifer: No, I knew it was Todd.

Jerry: You knew it was Todd, How did you feel?

Jennifer: I don't know, Like I said you get used to it.

Jerry: So sometimes you would tell yourself you didn't care.

Jennifer: Yeah.

Jerry: What does it matter?

Jennifer: What else is new?

Jerry: Ok, um and other times would you feel like that anger?

Jerry: Would you feel angry the day that Mom was talking with him?

Jennifer: Yeah.

Jerry: And can you say anything about what those calls would mean to you?

Jennifer: No not really, basically everything I've already said that.... someone else is calling or whatever um you get used to it.

Jerry: If you don't mind my asking, did you see Todd as a home breaker?

Jennifer: What do you mean by that?

Jerry: Uh a family destroyer.

Jennifer: I guess if you want to put it that way.

Jerry: I mean did you see Todd in that light?

Jennifer: Um yeah but then I would see her the same way because he had a family too with kids so.

Jerry: Ok, so that every time there was a call that would probably be an event that would spark up uh you know your hurt and your anger.

Right.

Jennifer: Um not really, I didn't do anything about it or say anything?

Jerry: Well, you know I mean uh that could be true. I mean a lot of times when people are saying it doesn't matter, that it's just a face that they wear to the outside...

Jennifer: No, it doesn't matter.

Jerry: At the time it might have.

Jennifer: Like I said you get used to it.

(Long silence)

Jerry: You know a lot of times when parents' divorce even after the divorce uh it's actually really common that uh kids feel the attention that's going toward a new romantic interest is taking time from them so uh you know the feeling that you were losing some of your Mom to Todd, that would be a pretty common feeling in my experience of working with kids you know who have been through a divorce. Let me give you a chance to uh react to what Jennifer had been, do you have any reaction to that Martha? Can you understand the feeling and what it was like for Jennifer?

Martha: I can understand it but I didn't realize that she felt that way because she didn't talk to me about it.........Jennifer has always been number one to me and she always will be and I'll always be here for her no matter what.

Jerry: You might have been really kind of a dutiful kid.

Jennifer: What's that?

Jerry: Well I have seen situations like where um when parents are going through a divorce kids do their best not to rock the boat. You know they don't want to make things worse. They kind of even sit on a lot of their feelings uh because they don't want to further burden one parent or the other. And um you might have held in quite a bit of your feelings at the time. Maybe you were even afraid.... that uh... you know if you were to talk to your Mom about your feelings it would have just um I don't know led to an argument.... you know. Like if you would have told her you were angry with her or how you felt with Todd.

Jennifer: It wouldn't have changed her mind.

Jerry: Probably not, probably not. You know arguably it would have given the two of you a chance to uh, allow things from getting as bad as they got.

Jennifer: There wasn't only that like I said before, it had nothing to do with that but like I said if I did say anything it wouldn't have changed her mind so why waste my breath.

(Silence)

Jerry: Well you're talking to a social worker ha, ha, ha, so you probably know the answer that you're going to get. Uh, because it's just good to express your feelings. You know you probably knew you were going to get that answer didn't you.

Jennifer: Yeah third one.

Jerry: Huh.

Jennifer: Third one yeah.

Jerry: I know, I know we all read the same books you know. Uh but um.... that's just kind of like argue on the world if you talk about your feelings it's better even if it doesn't change anything. But I don't dispute your point if you were to tell Mom you were angry about her uh, the choices she was making um it's probably unlikely if it would have changed her choices, true.

Martha: True.

Jerry: Were there other things that happened that resulted in you feeling abandoned or angry.

Jennifer: Nothing that we haven't talked about.

Jerry: Ok................................ . Well let me kind of uh run an idea by you guys what I would like to do next. Um .... You and I met alone last week.

Jennifer: Um-hm.

Jerry: And what I would like to do is uh, I would like to meet alone with your Mom next week.

Jennifer: Fine.

Jerry: Uh because I would like to talk to your Mom a little bit about you know what you shared with her today. So uh that would mean you got uh a week off. Is that ok with you?

Jennifer: Yeah.

Jerry: And uh and that means that you will be back in two weeks, and uh that will be at the same time.

Jennifer: Ok.

Martha: In two weeks I will be out of town.

Jerry: Well, let's alter the plan a little bit. Let's plan on the two of you coming back next week. I would like to give you kind of an assignment if you would like to take it on.

Martha: Ok.

Jerry: I wonder if you just would uh kind of prepare a summary of what Jennifer has said today. And kind of summarize her feelings just so she has a sense that you know that you understand them. And uh the summary should be uh without any editorial comments because I think what's important is that Jennifer has a sense that uh she be heard and understood when she talks about her experiences of what happened in the family. Uh, would you take that on as an assignment?

Martha: Um-hm.

Jerry: And you could put it in letter form. And um what I would say is uh you know don't get hung up on um details like when things started to deteriorate whether it was in the fall or whether it was July uh I think what we want to do is give Jennifer a sense that your hearing and understanding you know her experiences ok and then um I'll do a session with you some other time. Ok.

Martha: Um-hm.

Jennifer: Is that it?

Jerry: Yeah.

This was getting me sick to my stomach, this bastard asked Jennifer the same questions over and over and over again. How many times must this little girl answer the same questions? Did he not get the answers that he wanted the first dozen times? Jennifer, your anger, about your anger, as he continuously explains what he thinks Jennifer was feeling or even thinking. How about discussing her mother's anger, how about explaining to her mother how Jennifer was feeling. How about asking Martha the same question over and over again. Considering all of the rotten and mean things Martha has done, Jennifer would barely speak in these dissecting of a brain sessions as it is as clear as glass how many times Martha would speak as if she were on the sideline of a head-to-head game. I could only look through the window and watch my daughter fend for herself all alone with no one on her sideline.

January 26, 2007 Counselor # 3 session 15

Jerry: Um is there anything either of you want to start with today?

(Silent)

Jerry: Ok, well I have kind of given you an assignment.

Martha: I know.

Jerry: And um you know maybe, well we certainly want to uh get to that. Is there anything you want to talk about today?

Martha: Well do you want to talk about the summary first or other stuff.

Jerry: Well uh why don't we talk about other stuff?

Martha: Well Jennifer I just want you to know I love you with all my heart and I thought about everything we talked about last week so I didn't write anything but it's all in my head and it's in my heart. And I'm always going to be here for you. I just kind of wanted to let you know that, I know I talked about me and Todd getting married and we're going to do it sooner than later so I just wanted to let you know before it happened. We are going to get married next week when we are in Los Vegas for the trade show. I just wanted to kind of let you know.

Jennifer: Ok like I said before, do I care............. No.

Martha: Well I think you should hear it from me rather than anybody else.

Jennifer: (chuckling) I don't care.

Jerry: Ok, uh well that's absolutely true she should hear it from you. Um do you have any feelings or comments about it?

Jennifer: No.

Jerry: No. Surprised, not surprised?

Jennifer: No.

Jerry: No, No you're surprised or no you're not surprised?

Jennifer: Not surprised.

Jerry: Not surprised, ok. It's not exactly a shocker.

Jennifer: No.

Jerry: OK, do you have anything you want to say about it or any reaction to it?

Jennifer: No, I could care less.

Jerry: Any more you want to say about it?

Martha: Well I don't think any time would be a good time and

Jennifer: I, I don't care you're wasting your breath.

Martha: You know I don't think so Jennifer.

Jennifer: Ha-ha, I do.

Jerry: Well...you know all you can do I think Martha is take care of your side of the street and um you know you can't be in control of any kind of reaction or non-reaction that you get from Jennifer uh but you know you told her and um I gather you want her to know that it doesn't mean that uh you love her the less. And I would assume that what you have said in the past stands for the future. Which is that uh, if ever Jennifer wants to have uh contact with you in any form that it doesn't have to include Todd.

Martha: Right.

Jerry: Right.

Martha: Um-hm.

Jerry: Ok. It could just be

Martha: The two of us.

Jerry: The two of you, ok.

Jennifer: (whispers) It's not going to happen.

Jerry: Pardon.

Jennifer: I said that's not going to happen.

Jerry: Well, maybe not but at least you should know what you're uh, what your options are. There may have been a time where you tried to push, you know, too fast.... for Jennifer right. Like tried to encourage her to have a relationship with him.

Martha: No, not really.

Jennifer: Yeah.

Martha: I talked about how she could still have the same things and we could do things together but I never forced her to meet him or anything like that.

Jennifer: Yeah.

Jerry: You never forced her to meet him but did you feel like Mom like

Jennifer: (frustrated) Yeah...

Jerry: Force that on you

Jennifer: Yeah. ,

Jerry: How did that happen?

Jennifer: because she told me. She said oh well you could um, you'll have to meet him and I could show you a picture of him and um we could get a pool, have our dog, it will be just like how everything else was, we'll go on vacations and stuff once this is all over with. I don't want to go on a vacation with him.

Jerry: Um-hm so even like painting the picture

Jennifer: Yeah. Like it was already done, she had her mind set so once again is that a surprise, no!

Jerry: but what I'm getting is even painting kind of a word picture of the three of you together felt like uh pushing you.

Jennifer: Yeah but now she could paint her picture of her, the two together because huh I'm not having anything to do with him nor either, definitely not her.

Jerry: Ok Well I know that um.... . You Mom is giving permission to not have anything to do with Todd. You know that it's not part of the package.

Jennifer: I don't need her permission, she can't control what I think and what I do.

Jerry: Well she's accepting that is that a better word.

Jennifer: Um, meaning accepting that I don't want to talk to Todd.

Jerry: Yeah.

Jennifer: Like she knew, she already knew that wasn't going to happen to begin with.

Jerry: Well but sometimes parents don't accept it but I, I mean in a way we are arguing over, over words. The effect is the same. Nobody can make you have a pleasant relationship with anybody uh you know nobody can compel or make it happen. Um......Jennifer shared some new things, right and you've been thinking about those and you said you'd make mental notes about it I have asked you to write a letter or formulate kind of a response to it uh to give Jennifer a sense that uh you've heard and understood what she was saying and you know about the abandonment thing. Um, so you want to say a little bit about it.

Martha: Ok, Um as far as you feeling abandoned when I wasn't coming home from work at a normal time, I could understand that you feel like that because there was no one in the house um and.... possibly taking time away from you talking to Todd I know you're angry. You see and hear things and I understand that you felt like I was pushing you away, it was not my intention. You mean more to me than anything in the world and nothing will ever change that. But I can understand how it made you feel Jennifer. I think if we would have talked about things maybe it wouldn't have been as bad. Um I hope we can talk about things in the sessions here and put them on the table and hopefully move forward.

Jerry: Ok, What is your reaction to what Mom said?

Jennifer: Um no I'm not, number one as she likes to call it um her frame of words because she wouldn't have done everything she had did to me if that was true and nothing's going to happen moving forward. A counseling session you should know by now probably like forty or the fiftieth that I've been to. Nothing had changed, nothing is going to change, I said everything I needed to say and even like you said, no one can tell you earlier just in this thing when we were talking about Todd, no one can tell you who to like and um who you can have a relationship with but yet I'm sitting here.... Trying to get, having someone trying to get me to have a relationship with my Mom which isn't going to happen, but if no one can do that, then why am I sitting in counseling for the third time.

Jerry: Well because the Judge ordered you to be here and that's the long and the short of it uh based on a belief that kids should have a relationship with both parents and um you know all mental health professionals will tell you uh that uh a good thing is to have a relationship with both parents. Uh you know nobody can make that happen but um you know their reference and opportunity to give the best possible outcome to a divorce.

Jennifer: Yeah but the third opportunity, like I said I've been to already like forty sessions and nothing has changed and nothing is going to change.

Jerry: Well you've only been to fifteen with me.

Jennifer: Yeah, including the other ones that couldn't do it either.

Jerry: Um-hm, yeah, yeah. And uh you know I'm realistic I've been doing this for thirty years so I'm realistic I like to know that uh for me um you know it's an uphill struggle you know I've been asked by the court uh to provide family counseling to you. So I'll do it to the best of my ability. But you know I don't know.... . If I'll have any greater luck than the last people. But I mean that's why you are here. Cause the Judge said you had to be.

Martha: Jennifer unfortunately you had to go to different counselors because of situations and things that took place. It's a lot of repetition in the beginning so the new counselor gets to know you and your situation and tries to help you.

Jennifer: Uh no when I went to Debbie, I got stopped for who knows what, nothing happened with that. John Dawson didn't want to counsel us anymore.

Martha: Right for unfortunate reasons

Jennifer: Yeah like? Because maybe he realized that I don't want to talk to you and that maybe yeah I was serious when I said it.

Martha: And part of the counselor's job is to help the relationship.

Jennifer: Yeah, it's not helping.

Martha: An hour every week.

Jennifer: It's not helping.

Jerry: Well I mean uh you know you may come to the end of the court-ordered counseling and say Jerry uh counseling was a failure and hasn't helped. But uh you know the fact is the court has ordered you to be here you know. Uh so why are you here you know like why.

Jennifer: Well I know that's why. But it's just a matter of how long I have to be in here when I know it's not helping and it's not going to help.

Jerry: Uh the court order said uh a minimum of one year uh and that the counseling ends when uh both parents and the counselor agree that it should end. That's what the court order said so how long? Um you know that's what the court order says you know for me to say you guys don't need to come uh I would have to see you know uh ....A healthy relationship. You know, restored between you and your Mom. Uh you know I would not be uh against you know I mean if we got to the point where uh you know the two of you could uh.... uh I don't know go to Starbucks or go to Bakers square or bowl a game or something like that. I wouldn't be against saying do that instead of coming to a session you know. Uh so long as you could have a pleasant time together during that hour if we got to that point. Where you could spend an hour together without me then I would say you know you don't have to go.

Jennifer: (getting angry) So basically what you're saying is that I'm going to be in here until I'm out of high school because I know like I said, that I'm not going to be in a relationship with her, but you said that um we can't get this stopped until you see a relationship happening.

Jerry: That's what it would take to get me to say that you don't have to come anymore. Ok and uh you know the judge's order says that you have to come for a minimum of one year or until uh both parents ....I couldn't say the work was done until the two of you reestablished uh a relationship as long as, as long relationships are cut off uh in my business a cut off is unfinished business usually.... . There is a relationship cut off. Um you know based on the judge's order you know you have to remember too Jennifer um .... The court came to me and said would you work with these people and I said yes, and then the judge wrote the order. The judge has ordered that you have to be here so that's kind of the line. I know that it isn't your choice, you know I know that uh you know you wouldn't be here.

Martha: I know what you mean, who would choose to.

Jerry: Well it varies, it varies, you know I have some teenagers who come here because their parents bring them and I have other kids and teenagers that I work with, some of them want to be here and find it helpful. Um a lot of times when the court orders somebody to be here they're not willing uh clients. In a way, it's kind of like uh running a store and having somebody in your store that is not really a customer. In a way that's kind of what you are, you know what I sell so to speak. It is change, and change of relationships are the things I sell you know in a way you're not interested in what I sell. You're only here because the court says you gotta be.........You know and the way I look at it, the only way, the only way I could help you by doing what I do which is uh you know family therapy much of the time. This is kind of how family therapy works. Families sitting in here talking.

Martha: You know Jennifer, sometimes there may be things that you don't want to talk to me about or your Dad and you want a third person's opinion.

Jennifer: No I could tell my Dad whatever I want, see that's something me and him have, that's called trust.

Martha: And that's a good thing, Jennifer.

Jennifer: Yeah.

Jerry: Alright, when you and I get alone the reason that we meet alone is to use my effort, give you an opportunity to learn about what this divorce has been uh, been like for you. That's why I helped you. Uh talk with your Mom about your feeling about when she got involved with Todd, she left you and even though you know from an adults perspective uh your Mom might have been leaving your Dad, sometimes from a child's perspective it feels like, it feels different..

Martha: Divorce is not an easy thing Jennifer.

Jennifer: I don't care......I know what you're going to say, it's not nothing new. Yeah it's not easy whatever (starting to cry) I don't care, I honestly don't anymore.... and if that's why you think there are tears running down my face you're wrong. (Crying) If you want to know why it's because that every Friday for the next two and a half or more years, three years where do I have to be? I have to be sitting right here (sniffling) somewhere I don't want to be wasting my time when I could be with my friends or other family or with my Dad, but no, I have to be sitting here, trying to fix a relationship with something that's not going to happen. It's not going to happen. And if it takes you that long to realize it, it's pretty sad.

Jerry: Well what you said isn't exactly true though

Jennifer: No, it's true.

Jerry: Well, here's what I'm going to say, I mean uh there may be times where uh .... I might meet with your Mom alone and there will be occasions where you might have a week off. There will be times where I'll be on vacation so

Jennifer: Ok, that's not my point. It's how many years until I'm out of high school is how long I have to be coming here. I'm only a sophomore which means I have two years before I go to college(loudly) And I'm not coming here when I go to college. That's for sure...and ok so I get one week off every how many months or vacation. That's, there are four weeks in a month in 12 months. That's a lot of sessions even with a couple off every year. So no. And I know she's thinking oh she's just upset about the divorce, no, I don't care anymore. The fact is I haven't cared for a long time but she thinks that I get upset over it, no! I get upset because I constantly have to go to counseling for something that's not going to be changed. And I know I have to do everything that she wants to do (still crying) so everything works out perfect for her life. My life isn't perfect, nobody's is but you know hers has to be. Ok, whatever my parents got divorced I'm over it, I don't care, I'm happy. I'm with my Dad, I'm happy but I don't want to talk to her and that's, that is my point. You guys want to know how I feel you're hearing it, that's how I feel I don't care anymore.... I, I, I don't... and that's that, but the fact that I have to come here for the third time ...It, It's ridiculing that I have to come every Friday or if I get a couple times off until I'm out of high school. . . So if she thinks she hasn't done enough, how much of my life of that do I get back? How many hours in so many years do I get back trying to heal a relationship that's not going to be healed. None of it.

Martha: Jennifer I love you and I'll do anything

Jennifer: No! No! No! You don't understand.

Martha: As long as it takes I will never give up on you.

Jennifer: Ok you know what, I gave up on you a long time ago, when I got kicked out of my house it was done…And you can't change that no matter how hard you try. If I were to go to five more counselors…it's not going to change. Just like you don't change your mind, what makes you think I'm gonna change mine. I guess I learned one thing from you… (sniffling)…

Jerry: Well if nothing else, you're able to express your feelings………. and um I guess the way I look at expressing your feelings is uh you know always, always a healthy thing. …Um…. . I was going to say this although I don't think it will be helpful to you. That uh, Na that's a big stretch it will never happen forget it…. . Um but at least you get to express your feelings.

Jennifer: It's still not going to change anything.

Jerry: By the way for what it is worth, I don't think it's her fault that you know, you don't want to come here. Um you know um for what it's worth to you, I don't take it as a sign of disrespect you know I just take it that uh you feel there has been huge damage done to your relationship and uh that's uh what you're communicating………. . Um ………. . Is there more you wanted to say?

Jennifer: No.

Jerry: Ok……. (Silent)……. . This hasn't been, I mean you're coming here once a week has been as frequent as your previous counselor right.

Jennifer: I know I actually went

Jerry: Three times a week

Jennifer: Yeah and then they narrowed it down to two. But, but still, it doesn't matter.

Jerry: Yeah but I mean at least this, this is a more uh, you gained uh two hours a week.

Jennifer: It doesn't make a difference I still have to come every week and everything like that.

Martha: One hour a week Jennifer is

Jennifer: Is not going to kill me?

Martha: No, it's not.

Jennifer: Actually it is, it might not kill you.... but it is.

Jerry: Well...in a way uh you know from an adult perspective an hour a week is uh small investment you know and this is a situation that uh you feel uncomfortable with coming here..... Do you feel uncomfortable coming?

Or just feel that you're wasting time?

Jennifer: I know I'm wasting my time....... (Silence)............

Jerry: So in a way the only goal you have in coming here, the only thing that you want to get out of coming here is not to have to come in a certain sense.

Jennifer: Exactly.

Jerry: Your only goal for coming is not to come.

Jennifer: Pretty Much.

Jerry: Yeah, and you know what that's actually a lot of times when people are ordered into counseling by the court that's their only goal is uh you know how not to come.... Um.... But the problem that a person has uh in your situation and it had been ordered by the court is that um..... there has got to be some change in order to you know get to the point of uh not coming...........I would like nothing better honestly than for the two of you not to need me anymore. Uh that actually is always my goal where people don't need my services cause they're better so uh in a certain sense I share your goal I want to make it possible for you not to have to come...

Jennifer: I don't need a counselor anymore but it's not my choice, once again it's hers.

Jerry: Well it's the court's choice, there is a court order.

Jennifer: Well that too but like you said, if she wanted basically she could talk to you and stop it you guys get to decide.

Martha: No I couldn't

Jennifer: Yeah you could. It said even in the paper, it's or until both parents and the counselor get to decide.

Jerry: It's, it's a minimum, what it says it's a minimum of one year.

Jennifer: Ok but you even said I'm going to be in here longer than a year basically because nothing is going to happen.

Jerry: Well

Martha: Unless you have a change of heart Jennifer.

Jennifer: I'm not going to have a change of heart.

Martha: I love you and if I. . .

Jennifer: I don't love you, I don't love you.

Jerry: Well I don't have um.... you know any magic power that's going to force you to change you know but uh the order does say one year or until one year after the divorce dissolution, which is what November or something.

Martha: December.

Jerry: Right ok or until the uh both parents and the counselor agree...that it is no longer needed.................you know, honestly there is no counselor worth his soul that would say uh it's no longer needed. Uh.... you know based on what's happened between you and your Mom you know..................... but you know.... maybe the thing to do is um.... maybe to give you the rest of the session off and uh you won't be here anyway next week. Maybe you and I could meet alone next week and I'll spend the rest of the time with your Mom. And uh at least we can shorten your visit today. ......And I'll see you next week by yourself which may be more tolerable for you because you will be by yourself...... Ok.

Jennifer: I guess so.

Jerry: Let me tell your Dad. (Jerry comes to the waiting room) Tom I'm going to spend the rest of the session with Martha and I'll see you next week.

Me: Um I will be out of town next week.

Jerry: Ok then let's plan on getting together in two weeks and that will be at 7:00 and that will be for you and your Mom ok?

Me: Ok bye.

We go outside Jennifer: (crying hard)" I'm going to have to be in counseling till I'm out of friggen high school because basically he already said it's a minimum of a year or until I decide and my change won't be, or until I see a change or something good happens. That's bull s**t! I don't care anymore...."

"That's ok, don't worry about it. I was supposed to let you drive,

"Dad, I don't care. I'm not talking the rest of the sessions. I don't care what they say."

"There you go, what are they going to do to you, they cannot force you to speak."

I'm done. I can't say any more than I said today if she doesn't realize shit by then. I don't care anymore they could think I'm a bitch that's good for you, that's not going to change me."

Jennifer shut the tape off.

I told Jennifer, "Don't swear so much, I understand how you feel. I need time to think about what we are going to do. I'll think of something."

After listening to this session, oh my god I thought. Martha was going to hold her own daughter prisoner until she has a relationship with her. Would she really want a fake relationship? She should save the counseling money and hold a gun against her Daughter's head, take her on vacations against her will as I call this a legalized kidnapping. At this point I am furious. This is a court-ordered abuse of a child. I would now spend every waking moment thinking of a way to free my innocent child. I knew I would have taken some kind of action due to the fact there are no accessible people in power that can stop this nightmare. I find it absolutely mind-blowing that I must not commit a crime trying to stop one.

It was amazing how outside of this insanity, Jennifer stayed a normal kid, playing sports, being an honor student, acting like the happiest kid in the world, as her Mother's torture was hidden behind her smile.

For myself as well, I too was very good at hiding a tortured soul behind a funny happy person that enjoyed life to the fullest. What else could people like us do, no one believes the unbelievable. Jennifer and I would consider this our powerful way to show not only the people that torture us but the surrounding people in our lives, that they couldn't break us.

February 16, 2006 Counselor #3 session 16 (Jennifer alone)

Jerry: Hi Jennifer.

Jennifer: Hello.

Jerry: How are you?

Jennifer: Good.

Jerry: Well how can I be helpful to you today? I mean this is a time for you, obviously, your Mom is not going to be here today so uh this is the time for you to get what you want out of the session.

Jennifer: Nothing really.

Jerry: Yeah, gosh I know you really don't want to be here but basically, the court has said you got to be here. So...um I don't know if you want to tell me anything uh about the divorce and kind of just get things off your chest, things that have bothered you, that kind of thing. Some of the times when you and I have met alone

Jennifer: Um, no I think I pretty much said that all I wanted to say already like in the last session.

Jerry: Um-hm, ok. Ok yeah. Um.......... let me ask you um, you know sometimes when you know there is a divorce in the family or something that happens, sometimes in a way parents and kids, they can't uh agree on a common story of events. You know what I mean uh, and that's kind of the case with you and your Mom. Right. You have one version of events, your Mom has a different version of events and um you know that may never uhhhh that may not be something we can change.

Jennifer: Um well no because I know she's not like I said admit to the stuff that she did and when like her excuses change like she has told a different story, different stories in here than she has told other counselors and stuff so I ,I don't even know anymore, so I don't really care.

Jerry: Um-hm, hm. Well and you know what I'm saying is that um.... that happens it's not all that uncommon that uh when something bad happens in a family people have very different versions about what happened. You know we may not be able to change that. Now I've been thinking a little bit. I mean really the only thing you want to get out of coming here the truth be told is not to have to come here. Right.

Jennifer: Yeah.

Jerry: And um you're only here because the Judge said you have to be here, I know that. Um......sometimes when bad things happen in the family people can't figure out an agreed common version of events. Uh they just kind of negotiate what their relationship is going to be like.... . and um I don't know have you ever thought about um you know basically you are here because you won't do visitation with your Mom, that's why the court is making you come here, right.

Jennifer: I guess, I wasn't in the courtroom but all I know is that I have to have counseling.

Jerry: Right. That's why you are here. I mean have you ever given any thought to the fact that you don't want to come here? You know maybe we could talk about how to do some visitations that might be halfway decent?

Jennifer: No, because I don't want to see her or spend time with her or anything.

Jerry: Ok, we'll, do you understand where I am coming from, and I am just trying to give you another alternative.

Jennifer: Yeah but I don't want to see her. She knows that and it's just how it is.

Jerry: ok well I'm just trying to open up some other possibilities for you but uh you're not interested, you're not interested. I just thought it might be uh preferable to have to come here.........I mean um.... should I go farther with this idea or is it like no-win forget it.

Jennifer: Forget it.

Jerry: Forget it, ok consider it forgotten. Ok well you mentioned before that um your Moms story has changed from time to time with different counselors, I know I'm the third one. Uh, how has her story changed?

Jennifer: Just with everything, everything's different, I can't even keep up with her, it's ridiculous. It's like I don't know, sometimes she will say that what she did and stuff um to me that she's never done it or that didn't happen or next time It's oh I'm taking things the wrong way or yeah I said that but I didn't mean it that way and things like that but she never oh yeah I'm sorry, I said it, it's no I would never do anything like that. I don't know, it just changes. I don't even know how to explain it but um her stories just are never, I don't think I've ever heard her tell one story the same...the whole time.

Jerry: Um-hm. Well, she said she is sorry for hurting you. That she said.

Jennifer: Yeah but I don't buy it one bit.

Jerry: Uh why is that?

Jennifer: Because I just don't believe her.

Jerry: You don't believe she is sorry?

Jennifer: No. Saying something and meaning it are two different things, but it doesn't, I don't really care even if she does mean it, I don't care I'm not going to accept her apology it's not going to make a difference.

Jerry: Um hm, Ok. Well, was one of the hardest things about, you know the divorce for you the fact that uh it happened because of the infidelity?

Jennifer: What do, what do you mean?

Jerry: Well you know what infidelity is right.

Jennifer: No.

Jerry: An affair.

Jennifer: Oh. No, she did what she wanted to do, no one can tell her what to do. She just shouldn't have done what she did to me, and she did so that's...her fault.

Jerry: Yeah last time you talked about how she had abandoned you. What else happened that was uh really hard on you?

Jennifer: Nothing really that's just that's it. Just everything she had done.

(Silence......)

Jerry: Were there any times, I don't know how many times we've met about 15 times I think probably close to that um I mean counseling wise you guys were here together with your Mom and by yourself. Were there any times that you thought anything good was happening?

Jennifer: No

Jerry: No. Have you gotten any benefit from any of the sessions?

Jennifer: No. It's still the same, I don't talk to her, I'm not going to talk to her, and that's how it is.

Jerry: Hm............Is there any way that I could make these sessions any better for you?

Jennifer: No because like I said before, I have to come so it doesn't really make a difference.

Jerry: Um hm,, ok. But I mean if you had some way that I could make it better for you I'll be open to hearing from you. But uh you know, I just want you to know that...ok.... well it's been about a year now that you have been with your Dad, cause it was February of last year when you moved out right, February something.

Jennifer: February 1st.

Jerry: February 1st ok. So a little over a year. Um how did it work for you, has it been a good change for you?

Jennifer: Yeah.

Jerry: Ok. Uh is it better for you than living whatever tension you were living in?

Jennifer: Yeah.

Jerry: Ok....... . Well at least something good has happened. Um what's been good about it for you?

Jennifer: I don't have to be with my Mom.

Jerry: What else has been good about it?

Jennifer: Um I would spend time with my Dad.

Jerry: Uh I don't know your Dad very well. We just talked a couple of times. What do you like about being with him?

Jennifer: I don't know, he's funny. Fun to be with, I always have a good time.

Jerry: Does he have a good sense of humor?

Jennifer: Yeah.

Jerry: That's good ha, ha, ha. Did he get you to be a bear fan?

Jennifer: Yeah.

Jerry: Kind of sort of.

Jennifer: Yeah.

Jerry: Did you watch the game?

Jennifer: Yeah.

I lost the rest of this session

February 19, 2007, I woke up at 5:00am because it was cold in my apartment. I could also hear cars going by as if a window were open. I was sleeping on the floor about 2 feet from my front room window. I had a picture window in the center and a small window to the right and the left of the picture window. I always slept by the left window. I had mini blinds that were closed at all times. I got up from the floor and walked over to the window that I was sleeping by, pulled the blinds out of the way, and to my surprise the top inside window was all the way down. I pulled the window up and locked the latch. I thought this to be odd because that was the third time in six months that I had to close that window. I got ready for work and left for work at 5:30am.

Throughout the day I was constantly thinking about that window. We had a quarry close by and they were always blasting. I thought maybe the constant shaking of the house could have caused the window to fall down. I arrived home that evening at about 4:45pm. Jennifer was home early after a day of shopping with her friend Karen. I asked Jennifer, "Did you have a window open yesterday?"

"Yeah Dad, but not that window, I had the bottom window on the other side opened." I started to investigate the window once again. I was shaking the window trying to simulate the house shaking from the blasting of the quarry. The window did not move at all nor did the latch unlock. I unlocked the latch and raised the bottom window. Just as I had the bottom window all the way opened the top window came crashing down on my left thumb. I let out a yell running through the house jumping up and down in extreme pain. Jennifer was in the kitchen cooking and came running into the front room to see what the matter was. "What happened Dad?'

"The window came down on my thumb."

As she and I looked down at my thumb it was bleeding from my thumbnail. After several minutes I regained my composure and continued investigating. I lifted the top window and held it up with one hand. I looked down and saw something shiny in-between the storm window and the inside window. It was a butter knife. I also noticed the outside bottom storm window was half-opened. I knew this butter knife was not there before because in that particular window I had an air conditioner back in August. I had wood on that flat surface and would have noticed the knife. I closed the windows and locked the latch. I took the knife and pushed it down in-between the two windows by the latch. It fit perfectly. I pulled the knife out and I stood there motionless with notions running through my head. I thought oh my god, someone has been in my apartment and not just once. I walked through the apartment to see if anything was missing. I had three computers, two were laptops. I had a jewelry box with diamond rings and gold chains. Nothing at all was missing. What could they have wanted? Who could it be? Was Martha behind it? Not having any answer I walked into the kitchen where Jennifer was standing with her back toward me. I tapped her on the shoulder and whispered, "Someone has been in our apartment. I want you to turn the radio up and start gathering anything that has to do with the book." We are going to take them to a disclosed location. Jennifer, used to living by Martha's sneaky attacks, showed no fear and started gathering Items putting them in bags and boxes. I helped as well. On trips between the apartment and the car, I had a few conversations with Jennifer. I told her, "While we are in the apartment or in the car do not talk about the book, counseling, Martha, or anything that has to do with that part of our life. Do not talk about these subjects while on your cell phone as well. Do not talk to your friends about anything over the phone. Tell them in person. We will talk more when we get to where we are going." We loaded up the car and headed far into the city. My daughter knew as well as me, Martha was capable of anything.

The Court system basically gave Martha a license to steal, stalk, punish, torture, lie, the total control to make my and Jennifer's life a living hell. To the world, she feared me, to me and my daughter and we feared her. Martha knew we feared her. She knew I was capable of boxing, wrestling, and some martial arts. Though she thought I still possessed a gun, she knew I was not a killer. All these weapons were no match against Martha's team of police, attorneys, counselors, and judges. Jennifer and I were in our own little world surrounded by bad people waiting for us to come out and give up. We both vowed, they would have to take us. We will never let these evil people beat us.

With nowhere to run and nowhere to hide I decided to play the game. I was going out of town the following weekend with Ray, Dianna, and our children. I put a small note at the bottom of the frequently opened window, only to be noticed once someone reaches the top of a ladder on the outside. The note said, "Smile for the cameras for the second time!". Realizing the window was usually opened after we returned from a weekend away I would try and surprise the secret visitor.

February 28, 2007, I was going through my bills and I realized I was missing a few. I called one of my credit cards that I did not have a bill for. The automated system said my bill was past due and I had late fees applied. I called customer service and was told that my bill was mailed to my PO Box on time. I was also waiting for an insurance card for Jennifer to be insured on my car. I was told it was mailed over two weeks ago. I purchased a wireless internet card over a month ago and had not received the first bill. When I called customer service that bill was overdue with late fees as well. As Jennifer once said in one of her counseling sessions, you get used to it. With bad things happening all the time, something new was not a surprise. The only thing we could do is counteract. One thing I was sure of, someone was intercepting my mail at the post office. Back in August when Martha took my truck, there was a PO BOX key in it. She could have made a copy. Even though the key said do not duplicate it was not a special key. It looked no different than a house key. Coincidentally after the taking of the truck Martha obtained a PO Box in the same post office. Her PO BOX was just a few feet from mine. At this point, I decided to go to the post office. I filled out a card to have any mail going to my apartment stopped and go directly to the post office. I waited in line to speak to a clerk. A man in his 40's called me to his counter. I gave him the change of address card. I then said, "I have a problem with missing mail from my PO BOX. I believe my ex-wife may have a key and is taking some of my mail."

His reply to me was, "Oh, we have a lot of domestic problems like that here. I could have your locks changed if you like." I said, "Is that not a federal crime to take other people's mail?"

"Sir we have a lot of domestic things like that, I can change your locks."

I replied, "Oh yea that's right, the domestic law."

Frustrated as usual, that was my only option and I agreed. I knew it was Martha because she had done this before with mail that was going to my home. Holding back bills so they will be late costing me money that I didn't have at the same time ruining my credit.

Jennifer and I knew Martha was never going to stop the punishment.

March 2, 2007, Counselor # 3 session 17

Jerry: Come on in. Well, it has been a long since the three of us have been together because you were in Las Vegas for one week, and you were married. Then there was the week that I couldn't make it which was the ninth. The two of you were alone one time so really this is the first time in several weeks uh that you guys have come and are here together. So, um how would you like to start today? Do either of you guys have something you want to start with? God, you guys make it hard on me.

Martha: Well your concert was nice last night.

Jennifer: Whatever.

Jerry: What was the concert, a musical concert? Violin, cool, school I presume?

Jennifer: (nods her head)

Jerry: What tunes did you play?

Jennifer: Um we played a double concerto and then I was on a solo part.

Jerry: Oh, good and you were pleased with your performance I take it.

Jennifer: Um yeah it sounds good.

Jerry: Well, Good. And I gathered you enjoyed it too.

Martha: Um-hm.

Jerry: Ok.

Martha: And why are you rolling your eyes?

Jennifer: Because I hate when you come to my concerts.

Martha: Well I will continue to come, Jennifer:

Jennifer: You also continue to make me and Dad look like fools...because you're good at that. You think me and all my friends are blind?

Martha: What are you talking about?

Jennifer: That you walk in there and you have to give Dad, stare him down and give him dirty looks. Do you think we are blind? Don't even deny it, Don't even deny it.

Martha: Why would I give him a dirty look? There is no reason for me to do that.

Jennifer: Ok, but you did. I'm not blind, I'm not blind and I'm not the only one who saw it.

Martha: Ok.

Jennifer: So I would appreciate it if you don't come anymore.

Martha: I will come, you're my daughter and that's a way for me to see you.

Jennifer: Alright, no actually one, no I'm not your daughter and you want to start with oh you need to get over that and face that, right back at you. Using your own words quote unquote......

Jerry: Well, one thing that is a fact is that mothers and daughters do have a blood bond.

Jennifer: I don't care, it doesn't make a difference.

Jerry: Well uh in my world it does.

Jennifer: Yeah but, it's not, it's mine and her world right now.

Jerry: Yeah but what I'm saying is that because mothers and daughters have a blood bond you cannot say we are no longer parent and child. You always, you always got that bond.

Jennifer: You just did.

Jerry: You can decide how close or how distant you are

Jennifer: Well she's soon to find out. I'm in here all through high school. After that, you think I'm staying close to you? So don't plan on seeing me again because that's not going to happen. It's coming around a lot sooner than you think. It will seem like a long time for me because I have to sit in here but…. .

Jerry: How would you even know who your Mom was looking at, by the way, I'm just curious.

Jennifer: One there wasn't a lot of people there, to begin with, and two, she sits right behind him and gets up, who else would she give a dirty look to. ? She wasn't looking up on stage, she was sitting right behind him, she got up, she gave him a dirty look and she went and sat in a different spot.

Jerry: Well I guess the way, the way I would look at it, if I was in a divorced family, uh parents are always uncomfortable to be in the same place together.

Jennifer: So give him a dirty look.

Jerry: Well

Jennifer: Let's just make a big scene about it.

Jerry: Well

Jennifer: Why don't you just not come, it will make everyone's lives including mine especially a lot easier.

Jerry: But what I'm

Jennifer: Ok keep being like that.

Jerry: But what I'm getting at is that um you know with the dirty look it's just people being uncomfortable around each other. You know what I mean?

Martha: That's why I just got up and walked away.

Jennifer: What's, what's a dirty look, so it's supposed to mean absolutely nothing, so everyone can go around giving dirty looks.

Martha: How did I look at him, Jennifer?

Jennifer: You, oh my god you know what, I'm not even going to argue with you because you know what you did.

Martha: I walked in, I sat down and when I noticed he was there

Jennifer: You have to make a scene, I'm not whatever, whatever, whatever I'm not even going to argue with you anymore because you know it.

Martha: No, I

Jennifer: Ok yeah, I know, I know, I know you're always right. Whatever you're perfect I know.

Jerry: Well nobody in this room is perfect.

Jennifer: Oh she thinks she is pretty much close to it.

Martha: No.

Jennifer: Yeah ok.

Martha: It's not what I think.

Jennifer: I'm sure.

Jerry: Do we agree that I'm not perfect ha, ha, ha. Ok, you guys don't want to hear about me. Um, you know the way I look at it I mean you always have your choice you know how you want to think about things...and one of the things we know is that there are certain ways of thinking that create certain feelings. And um we know that you know probably the most effective way to alter feelings is to take a look at how you are thinking. And I don't know that I want to, all I'm saying is that in a situation like that when both parents go to an event uh it's oftentimes uh a very uncomfortable thing you know for both of the parents. It's just another lens that you could look at, you can look at things through.

Jennifer: Ok but it, it's not what happened and I know she gave him a dirty look, I'm not the only one who saw it. I have other people that saw it and even said something to me about it.

Jerry: Well

Jennifer: So what, everyone else is blind but she's not? No, I don't think so.

Jerry: All I am saying, all I'm saying is you know uh I wasn't there I can't see what kind of expressions people have on their face but sometimes uh you know there is great discomfort when uh you know parents go to an event like that. I mean honestly um your family system is a stressful one to be...around even for somebody outside the family you know such as myself because I can feel the anger in your family. All I'm saying is I'm an outsider you know you guys are insiders to the system, so it would be very uncomfortable for everybody just another you know lens to look at it through.

Jennifer: Well if there is that much discomfort then why does she come?

Jerry: Um...

Martha: For you Jennifer....... You are my daughter. I love you, I care about you.

Jennifer: Yeah ok, keep telling yourself that. You think I'm hearing it, I'm not.

Martha: That's what's in my heart, Jennifer.

Jennifer: Yeah, I'm sure.

Jerry: Well you may be telling yourself and saying out loud that you know I'm no longer your daughter but uh (looking at Martha) the reason you came is you know for reasons of love...and uh you know I believe that. Now,

Jennifer: I Don't

Jerry: (looking at Jennifer) you may not want to accept that love nor recognize your bond with your Mom...(looking at Martha) but you know you're the only one who knows what's going on in your heart and uh you know it was love, I'm sure that took you there.

Jennifer: No.

Martha: What else would I be going there Jennifer if I didn't care?

Jennifer: Who knows.... who knows.

Martha: Well. What reason would I go? If I didn't care about you and wanted to see you?

Jennifer: Who knows, If you had no reason to give Dad a dirty look, why would you do it, if you know I don't want you to go why do you come?

Martha: Because I love you.

Jennifer: Yeah. Like I said, don't believe it. You could tell me 50 million more times, I'm still not going to believe it.

Martha: I would still tell you every day if

Jennifer: Every day is going to end pretty soon so you might as well save all your pictures and everything else because you're not going, It's not going to happen anymore. I'm not going to hear it every day. Like I said college is coming around pretty soon...and if you think I'm going to stay anywhere near you...or you're going to know where I'm at, think again because it's not going to happen.........

Jerry: Well you're a freshman.

Jennifer: Sophomore.

Jerry: A lot can happen in a short time if you want it to, and if you don't want it to you can be exactly where you are at, you know, in a year or two.

Jennifer: In a short period of time, Yeah it's already been two almost three years. Nothing's happened. A short period of time is less than three years nothing is going to happen. Nothing is going to change if it didn't change for almost three years.

Martha: Two years.

Jennifer: two, yeah it's going to be three years.

Jerry: its one year since you left

Jennifer: Well yeah, it's not since everything started.

Martha: It will be two years in July.

Jennifer: I'll be going on my third birthday.

Jerry: Jennifer I'm just curious, what do you think is the start of it all?

Jennifer: What do you mean?

Jerry: Well you said it's been three years since it started.

Jennifer: Almost three years.

Jerry: Ok, but when you say started it all, what started it all? When did things begin to go downhill? In your life and in your family?

Jennifer: When she became nuts!

Jerry: And when you say when your Mom became nuts, what does nuts mean?

Jennifer: Nuts, she changed, a different person.

Jerry: Ok, and um what changes did you start noticing about your Mom three years, let's not get hung up on whether it's 2 ½ or 3 but let's say 3. What changes did you begin noticing in your Mom way back then?

Jennifer: Um, I don't know everything we've already talked about and how she just like, like I said there are so many arguments and stuff like that. She was just different.

Jerry: Ok, uh, and when you say arguments, who were the arguments between, she and your Dad

Jennifer: No, between me and her.

Jerry: Ok and were there more arguments between her and your Dad?

Jennifer: I don't know. I know some but I don't know

Jerry: Not all arguments are in front of kids

Jennifer: What's so funny? What's so funny? You see, it's a joke to her and she knows that nothing is going to happen. We're only coming here so that she can claim that she is going to see me, and she is claiming to try to get me to like her, but it's not going to happen.

Jerry: It may not.

Jennifer: No, It's not.

Martha: I don't think it's a joke at all, Jennifer.

Jennifer: Yeah, ok, keep laughing then.

Martha: Well, when something is said that totally doesn't make sense

Jennifer: Oh my god, you want to talk about not making sense, Oh my god, you of all people should not be talking about that.

Martha: What are you referring to?

Jennifer: Oh my goodness, you are so ridiculous, it's not even funny (starting to cry), and you know it. Go ahead, laugh again, I see you smirking.

Martha: I don't know what you are talking about?

Jennifer: (crying) No, because this is a waste of my time, and you know it.

Martha: No, it's not.

Jennifer: Yes, it is! (Crying harder and yelling) If I could, and Dad wouldn't get in trouble, I swear to god I would walk out of here right now; you are so lucky... (sniffling) that you could control everything about him and me. So lucky because I swear to god I would get up and walk out of here right now. (Sniffling)

Jerry: Ok, ok, let me ask you a question, Jennifer.... . When you uh say that things were breaking different, arguments increased. Now we're talking about three years ago, ok. What else was different? When you say that Mom changed. Can you say what other changes there were?

Jennifer: It was just everything. She was a lot meaner, everything was an argument, everything..........

Jerry: So your love changed greatly.

Jennifer: Yeah, sure.

Jerry: And was that a sad time for you beginning like 2 ½, 3 years ago whenever?

Jennifer: Uh I don't know. It was just different.

Jerry: Ok.......... . What.... What hopes did you have for your family at that point? Now you would have been about twelve, right.

Jennifer: 14, I was thirteen.

Jerry: You're 15 now. What was your family like before all these changes?

Jennifer: Normal.

Jerry: Um-hm, and what was normal like for your family?

Jennifer: Fine.

Jerry: Uh, yeah, but can you say more about what it was like for you?

Jennifer: No, it was just normal.

Jerry: Ok was um, who were.... . Was there fighting going on between Mom and Dad?

Jennifer: No

Jerry: No, ok. When did you have any inclination that things were going bad in the family?

Jennifer: I didn't.

Jerry: You didn't, ok. Well, at some point, you realized that things were going bad.

Jennifer: No.

Jerry: No?

Jennifer: I didn't know anything until she came up to me; Jennifer I'm divorcing your father.

Jerry: Ok so you thought things were ok until then ok. Now, where does that fall? Was that like the beginning of this three year period or

Jennifer: I guess yeah.

Jerry: Ok, alright, and you know we've talked about, uh you know, some of the anger you have for your Mom. Um, would you say?

Jennifer: It's not anger. I just don't want to hear or deal with her anymore....

Jerry: Well, anger, hurt.

Jennifer: (getting upset) No, I'm fine, but no one can understand that (crying) I'm, I'm like five years old to everyone and I can't make up my own mind. I'm a sophomore in high school, but I'm too stupid to figure out what's going on with her, and I'm too stupid to make my own decisions about what I want to do. .... that's what it is....

Jerry: Well, what...you know what you are saying is actually one of the things that uh you resent the decisions that adults are making that affect other lives, that's a pretty common sentiment that I heard from other kids.

Jennifer: Well, it's true.

Jerry: It is.

Jennifer: It's too bad no one listens.

Jerry: Decisions when parents choose to get divorced, decisions are being made that affect kids. And there is no getting around that; that is true. Um.... see in a way.... in a way, you decided that you're going to deal with your hurt and anger, you know, is in a way to kind of cut off your relationship with your mom.

Jennifer: It's been cut off, it's just she doesn't get it.

Jerry: I know it's been cut off. I mean that's why you guys are here. And um .... You know I have what feels like a Herculean task of trying to heal your relationship with your Mom.

Jennifer: (softly) Good luck cause it's not going to happen.........

Jerry: Well, I know it's a Herculean task, Jennifer.... Um............what are you most upset about? I mean we've talked about some of the things that have happened and upset you. But are you most upset about the fact that your Mom did things that hurt you, that your Mom did things that caused your Dad pain that your Mom busted up the family, what are you most upset about?

Jennifer: Just everything she did to me.

Jerry: Ok, is there stuff beyond what we talked about that you want to mention?

Jennifer: No, not that I could think of right now.

Jerry: Ok.... Do you feel that your Mom brought any shame on the family?

Jennifer: What does that mean?

Jerry: Uh embarrassment. Shame, embarrassment. Sometimes when people go through a divorce, uh they have a sense of shame or embarrassment, and they feel, you know um...one or the other parent, or sometimes both parents brought some shame on them.

Jennifer: I don't know.

Jerry: Ok.... just checking............ since we've been meeting.... um has your anger and the hurt that you feel about the stuff that happened between you and your Mom, uh has it been alleviated at all?

Jennifer: What does that mean?

Jerry: Has it gotten any better?

Jennifer: Wait, what?

Jerry: Has your hurt and anger over the divorce gotten any better...since we've been meeting back in September?

Jennifer: It's been fine like I said before I don't care anymore. I don't care. It's just when I come here that's when it all just .... hour a week the only time that is something that I don't want to do and I hate, everything else I'm fine.... I'm fine, I don't care. She thinks I care and that's a big deal, whatever it's not.... .

Jerry: Well for what it's worth to you, you know what I'm thinking is that um you know there is going to be times when I continue to meet with you and your Mom alone and I would think um those sessions are probably easier for you.

Jennifer: I still have to come so.

Jerry: Yeah, I grant ya but hopefully, those sessions are a little easier for you.... um .... if you were to get closer to your Mom, how would that be a problem?

Jennifer: It's not going to happen so...it doesn't make a difference.

Jerry: Ok, but do you feel like you would get hurt again or uh do you fear..... Um I don't know it would be hard on your Dad?

Jerry: I don't fear nothing, it's just not going to happen.

Jerry: Ok..... And what else, it may not happen for many, many years. I suspect that at some point, you two will be able to reconcile.

Jennifer: Nope.

Jerry: Um but, I know there is uh no way that I'm going to convince you of that. Do you ever believe in mercy?

Jennifer: What's that?

Jerry: You know what mercy is, like if somebody does something wrong to you and you have mercy and forgiveness.

Jennifer: Not for her.

Jerry: But as a general principle.

Jennifer: Sometimes.

Jerry: Sometimes ok, ok. And.... What do you think needs to happen for forgiveness to take place?

Jennifer: Well, nothing because I know it's referring to her, and it's not going to happen. So it's, it's no point to it.

Jerry: Well, in general. Can we talk about it in general?

Jennifer: But I know it's referring to her, so it doesn't matter. I'm not going to forgive her, and that's too bad it's not going to happen.

Jerry: And nobody can make you want to forgive. You know that, right.

Jennifer: Yeah.

Jerry: There is nothing that I could say that could make you forgive.... um but we could talk about the option of forgiveness, recognizing that's your choice whether you forgive not tomorrow or ever for that matter.... So what do you think has to happen for forgiveness to occur, in general, it doesn't have to be...

Jennifer: Same answer as before.....

Jerry: Do you know anyone who is good at forgiving?

Jennifer: No.

Jerry..................Because I mean you know forgiveness is a matter that all religions talk about. I read something recently. Uh, in a poll that was taken in America. 95% of people pray for forgiveness at some point............and um you know, just for your own information. Forgiveness sometimes is a gift to the forgiver......because it can free a person of pain they carry with them.

Jennifer: Like I said before, I don't carry any....... .

Jerry: Is there any way that your Mom can rebuild trust for you, Jennifer?

Jennifer: No.

Jerry: Not even some small

Jennifer: Nope.

(Long silence)

Martha: Is that a cross you're wearing around your neck? I can't see the whole thing, is it?

Jennifer: Yeah.

Martha: And what does that symbolize?

Jennifer: A gift from my Dad, that's what it symbolizes. It symbolizes something between Dad and me that you have no business that you need to know.

Martha: The cross itself.

Jennifer: Is that why I am wearing it?

Martha: It's a Christian thing.

Jennifer: So....

Martha: So god is all-forgiving; that's what you're displaying in my eyes by wearing a cross.

Jennifer: Doesn't mean that's what I mean...and since when do you become miss godly religious? Yeah, when was the last time that you went to church?

Martha: It doesn't matter. You don't have to go to church to pray or believe in God or anything like that.

Jennifer: Ok, never in your life have you said anything like that, but all of a sudden, now it's in your benefit, and you have to say something.

Martha: No.

Jennifer: Yeah.

Saturday, March 3, 2007, at about 12:30pm, Jennifer called her mother to see if she could get some of her things from the house. Martha agreed, and Jennifer said that she will come the next day.

On Sunday, March 4, 2007, at 11:30am, Jennifer called Martha to see if she was home for her to get her things. Martha answered and asked for Jennifer to give her a half-hour for her to take a shower. Martha also told Jennifer her dog Daisy was there and then asked if her father was coming in because if he is, I will have to have the police here. Jennifer said, no, my Dad is not going in the house, but I am bringing a friend with me. A half-hour later, Jennifer and I stopped to pick up Jenny to go along with Jennifer. Jennifer, now driving with her permit, pulled into the driveway but did not pull all the way up to the house at my request. Jennifer and Jenny got out of the car, went up to the door, and rang the bell. Seconds later, Martha opened the door and let the girls inside. It seemed like an eternity as I waited in the car. Jennifer and Jenny finally came out with their first trip of stuff along with our dog Daisy. She then went inside again. Jennifer came outside from her second trip in the house, and as I was helping her and Jenny put boxes into the back seat, Jennifer blurted out," She has a nerve; she had a picture out of her and her boyfriend at their wedding. Like I wanted to see that." I said nothing and shook my head. After Jennifer finished getting her things, we said goodbye to Daisy and drove away.

As Jennifer was driving, she angrily gave me the details of Martha's demeanor inside. When Martha opened the door, Jennifer headed straight for her bedroom. At that point, Martha's only words were I put boxes in your room, I didn't get a chance to get a lot of things ready. Martha did not say hello to Jenny. Jennifer said she noticed two pictures on the floor standing up against the wall, one in front of the other. The one visible she thought to be her grandmother. Once inside her room, Jennifer and Jenny started putting DVD movies into empty boxes on the floor. Moments later, Martha came to the room and stood in the doorway, and asked, "Do you need any more boxes?"

"I don't know at the Moment," Jennifer replied. Jennifer then went into her closet and started grabbing clothes. Martha asked, "Do you need a bag?"

"Yes," Jennifer said.

Martha returned with a bag and stood over Jennifer. Jennifer said, "Don't hover over me."

Martha said, "Jennifer!"

Jennifer said sarcastically. "It's my stuff. Don't hover over me, you can leave now."

Martha said, "You know, you're not very nice."

"Well you're not very nice kicking your kid out."

"I didn't kick you out Jennifer, and that's why you don't talk to granny, she was here, and she knows I didn't throw you out."

"Yes Mom, she was here and she did nothing when her grandchild was thrown out. She called me up, saying other things didn't happen to me when she wasn't even here. Whatever, Mom shut up."

"Shut up, don't tell me to shut up, Jennifer."

"Whatever," Jennifer said.

Martha walked away. As Jennifer was walking toward the front door with the full boxes, she noticed the picture of her grandmother was now moved to the side, revealing the picture that was behind it. It was Martha and her new husband. Martha was sitting at the dining room table just feet away. On Jennifer's last trip, she walked out the door saying nothing to her mother, nor did her mother say anything.

I could not understand why Martha would want Jennifer to see that picture of the people who destroyed her life. What were her intentions? Martha was definitely cold-blooded. Her only child, who wants nothing to do with her, has not been in her life or in that house in over a year. She came by to remove some of what was left of Martha's memories of her child, and she decides to display her new life, caring only about herself. How does a woman live in a house that has ten years of memories with her husband of 19 years and only child, live there with her new husband with all of the furniture, especially her child's, and not feel anything. How does she walk into her daughter's bedroom with all of her furniture, stuffed animals, bed, and pictures still on the wall? I guess you would have to have a conscience.

Jennifer called Martha later that day and said, "What was that with the picture about?"

What picture Jennifer? "Oh that, you're very observant." Jennifer hung up.

March 9, 2007, counselor # 3 session 18

Jennifer and I walked into the waiting room, and Martha was sitting in one of the three chairs. As usual, I would sit opposite Martha, never looking up at her or in her direction. With Martha present, Jennifer and I said very little.

Jerry: Well, how would you guys like to start it today?

Martha: I have your new medical and dental insurance cards.

Jerry: Um excuse me, did any of that change? Is there anything pertinent to me?

Martha: Oh, I could let you take a copy of it. I didn't bring a copy with me.

Jerry: Why don't you just bring a copy the next time? So um anyway um what would you guys like to talk about? Do you have something you would like to talk about, Martha?

Martha: Not really.

Jerry: Ok. Well, actually what I would like is I would like you guys to start thinking about what you would like to talk about when you come here. Um because in a way, uh I kind of feel like uh we've gotten too dependent on me, like gearing on something to talk about. And as long as we are doing that, I don't know; these sessions may not be as useful as you would like them to be.

Martha: Ok. Well, just so you know, Jennifer came by the house to pick up some of her stuff on Sunday.

Jerry: Um-hm

Martha: And if there is anything else that you need, Jennifer, I'm at home. You're welcome to get some more.

Jerry: Ok, I trust that went smoothly.

Martha: Yes, it did.

Jerry: You didn't lasso her?

Martha: Yeah

Jerry: Ha, ha, ha.

Jennifer: Oh no, she only had to move a picture to show me a picture of her and um her new husband. Yeah.

Jerry: Your Mom showed you a picture of her new husband?

Jennifer: Yeah. She had to show me their wedding picture. She felt that was necessary, apparently.

Martha: It was sitting on the floor, one is his Mom Jennifer. They were just sitting on the floor, and the wedding picture was behind it.

Jennifer: And she moved the front one just so the one of her and her wedding could be out. How that's necessary.

Martha: They were next to each other and when I heard Jennifer was coming, I put one in front of the other, then I figured I'll just put it back how it was.

Jennifer: Yeah

Jerry: But so in other words, at first you hid it because you were afraid it would be offensive to Jennifer, but then before Jennifer came, you decided not

Jennifer: No, after. I walked in, and only the one was there. There was one covered. When I went to walk back out, she removed it.

Jerry: Ok, so let me see if I got this, so the wedding picture was covered,

Jennifer: Yeah

Jerry: And before you left, your Mom uncovered it.

Jennifer: Yeah.

Jerry: And uh, I'm just curious why did you do that? And I want to hear how you felt about it.

Martha: I don't know, I just thought maybe she was curious cause I saw her look down at the one by itself so

Jennifer: Oh yes, I'm curious to see

Martha: What was behind it?

Jennifer: Yeah ok, if I was curious, I would have asked. Did I ask? No.

Martha: But you called me about it afterward.

Jennifer: Yeah, because you moved it and that wasn't right.

Martha: Why

Jennifer: Why, Why! (Getting angry and loud) do you think I want to see a picture of you? One, I don't want to see a picture of you or you at all. Two, let alone a picture of you and Todd.

Jerry: So I gather you weren't pleased.

Jennifer: No! She just likes to be smart and but yet she's nice, you know she's just like the best person in the world, I know. (Sarcastically) Like I said, we are here, but she keeps going on, doesn't she. That's proof right there. You brought that upon yourself....... so that's showing that it goes nowhere. It's just a waste of my time, like I said before.

Jerry: What did it prove to you, though?

Jennifer: What does what prove to me?

Jerry: That your Mom

Jennifer: That she showed a picture?

Jerry: Yeah.

Jennifer: That she is still psycho and never going to change. That's what it proves.

Martha: So that's what I am, psycho?

Jennifer: Do you want me to put it in nice terms?

Martha: (Silent)

Jennifer: That's what I thought.

Jerry: So, uh I'm just curious what was your thinking about exposing the picture?

Martha: Well I'm living there and I figured why I should hide something because Jennifer decides to come and get some stuff. So, that's what made me move it back to where it was.

Jerry: Ok.

Martha: I'm not going to, I shouldn't have to scurry around and hide things and move things because Jennifer was coming over and while she was over, I just kind of realized, you know what, I'm not going to hide stuff from her. This is part of my life, and you know.

Jerry: Ok, so in a way, you were kind of making a statement to Jennifer even though it would aggravate her. That uh this is part of your life, your identity.

Martha: Um-hm.

Jerry: And you decided to make that statement even though you knew it would aggravate her.

Martha: Yep.

Jennifer: I have two things to say about that. One, you're living there, I thought the house is supposed to be going for sale.

Martha: It is for sale. It's in the paper every week

Jennifer: That's a lie. I know that right there.

Martha: Oh you do.

Jerry: What paper?

Martha: Country life.

Jerry: Now you have the assignment to get the country life.

Jennifer: Oh no I do. I don't need her to tell me what to do, but I know it's not been there...sometimes.

Jerry: If we bring a copy in.

Jennifer: It's probably going to be in there now. The times I've checked, it hasn't been there every week. But two supposedly since you live there and that's your "identity" then why while I was living there you had to take down pictures of my family. I lived there, that's my identity; why do you have to take them down? You got to hide something from someone else? Hmm.

Martha: I didn't want to look at them.

Jennifer: So. Were you the only one in the house? Didn't think so.

Jerry: But you know

Jennifer: Do you want to play? Two can play that way

Martha: That was

Jennifer: No you're right. Once again

Jerry: But

Jennifer: There is another check on your wrong list.

Jerry: But two things, um you asked your Mom when you lived there why did she take down the picture or tell you to turn it the other way because that was part of your identity when you lived there right.

Jennifer: Yeah.

Jerry: Ok. And um, in a way, the way you felt when you had to cover up that picture that's the way Jennifer felt when you told her you wanted her to take down that picture..... Does that make sense?

Martha: Um-hm Well then why were the pictures that you wanted so desperately, they are still in your room? Do you not want them anymore?

Jennifer: Why do I want to look at you?

Martha: Then I can get rid of them?

Jennifer: Don't touch stuff in my room, that's my property. Whose property is it? Don't touch any of my stuff. Did I go to your room and touch your stuff? I didn't think so.

Martha: Jennifer

Jennifer: I didn't think so.

Martha: Do you not want them?

Jennifer: Don't touch my stuff. I don't want to look at a picture of you, that's for sure.

Martha: Well then, what would matter?

Jennifer: Just don't touch my stuff, it's not yours. Don't touch it. Do I go through your stuff ? No.

Jerry: I think Martha, regarding what pictures and whatever is in uh the room, I think you ought to accept that Jennifer decides what she wants to do with them.

Martha: Well, all her stuff has been sitting there since she left.

Jerry: Ok, ok, so you can kind of understand that

Martha: Um-hm

Jerry: Um the way you felt about recognizing life through pictures and that's kind of why you revealed the wedding picture. That is how strongly Jennifer felt about being able to represent the family as she remembered it when you asked her to take that picture down.

Martha: Well and I didn't ask her to take it down I just remember taking it down from the front room and she could have it in her room or whatever she wanted.

Jennifer: Did she say that no.

Martha: Yeah those pictures are in your room.

Jennifer: Those pictures aren't in my room.

Martha: Whatever you wanted, you could have:

Jennifer: No. You just said that you asked me if I wanted the pictures before.

Martha: The one you asked about was the wedding one.

Jennifer: Then. Whatever..... Wait, why would you be putting pictures up anyway if you're just going to take it down when the house sells.

Martha: Cause I'm still there. They are not on the wall.

Jennifer: Oh but you were going to put them up. Did you not say that? Hm, I got you, I know what you're, and I'm not brain dead.

Martha: What do you got, Jennifer?

Jennifer: Nothing.

Martha: Because your way of thinking is different from my way of thinking and I like to know what's on your mind.

Jennifer: Absolutely nothing, don't worry about it, don't worry about it. Like I said, you think I'm a little kid and so does everyone else. But I'm not. I'm a lot smarter than you think.

Jerry: Do you think I believe you're a little kid?

Jennifer: I don't know, it sure seems like it. But along with everyone else, it's nothing new.

Jerry: I don't think you're a little kid. I think you're a fifteen-year-old young woman who uh...

Jennifer: is not smart enough to see what's happening right in front of my face, yeah, I know.

Jerry: No, that's not what I was going to say. What I was going to say is...

Jennifer: You don't have to say it to think it. You guys, like I said before

Jerry: I'm the only one who knows what's going on between my ears, Jennifer.

Jennifer: That's true, but things you do sends me clues. I'm not like I said

Jerry: Well, everything, if you think about everything I have said and done, I've been consistent about one thing. I told you from day number one um my job is to help you have a relationship, to come out of this divorce with a relationship with both parents.

Jennifer: And I've said from day one it's not going to happen but

Jerry: Yes, I know you have.

Jennifer: I know I don't get a say in anything. (Starting to cry) It's my life, but I don't get any choices I know.

Jerry: Well, I mean

Martha: You have choices, you're with your Dad and you don't see me.

Jennifer: Yeah, but no, no, (loudly) I come here every Friday, but I don't see you. What am I blind? That's what I thought.

Martha: Outside of counseling.

Jennifer: How is that a big choice? Why do you think I'm coming here? So I can try to see you. So you get time to see no, no,

Martha: The Judge and the attorneys

Jennifer: Let me ask you a question then, why couldn't I go in and say it? I'm old enough. Why couldn't I go say it then? You don't have an answer to that, do you?

Jennifer: Cause you run everything.

Martha: You can't go into the courtroom. It's between Parents.

Jennifer: Bull crap, I looked it up online. I was at a friend's house, and we looked up my rights. (loudly) you want to tell me, you want to tell me, do you know how far I wanted to get away from you. I had friends helping me with research. I'm old enough but yet I can't go. ……

Jerry: Jennifer Um,

Jennifer: So don't tell me.

Jerry: The reality is that uh, in cases like yours, the court looked to mental health people like me to help families because there is a strong belief that kids should come out of a divorce with

Jennifer: Too bad they didn't know everything that went on.

Jerry: Both parents, well, like I said, there is a strong belief. But to get back to what I was trying to say before, we kind of got off track. Um, I do not believe you're a little kid, you know I believe that uh you're a very strong-willed uh fifteen-year-old young woman. I believe that you have been through a very nasty situation. And um…I think you're very intelligent, not like uh a naive young little kid. I also believe that sometimes you see things in terms of black and white…and I think uh it's not a good way to look at complex situations. I'll tell you that, that's my belief. And that's why sometimes I try and help you see uh shades of gray. You know, although I did stop doing that today, I want that to be known.

Jennifer: I just look at facts, I don't look at anything else. I know what happened to me and that's that.

Jerry: Yeah well, see that's where you and I have uh I think, an honest disagreement, you know. Uh history that is uh occurrences plus meanings, and I know you don't buy that

Jennifer: No, because its facts, you learned stuff that happened in history well, what happened to me happened, I was there. I know; it got done to me.

Jerry: Well, uh like I said, I think there are facts and I think there is meaning something you derive from facts…but anyway, um let me ask you…. um each time you guys come together, I like to spend a little time alone with one of you. Last time I spent some time alone with you, um today I'm going to spend a little time alone with your Mom. For our next two visits, I would like you to come to one and Martha, I would like you to come to one.

I lost the rest of this session

The pictures in Jennifer's room that Martha desperately focused on getting rid of were a wedding picture of Jennifer's mother and father. Martha was showing her true colors right in the presence of the seemingly good counselor. Did Jerry not see this, or did he choose not to see it?

As the soldiers overseas were risking their lives fighting a war to assure we remain a free country, I found myself utterly baffled as my daughter and I were being protected abroad: we were fighting in our own backyard for our freedom against the very people that possessed the sole power to protect us. We would fight our war without weapons or soldiers on our side. Without these necessities, we've become more like POWs, held in confinement. Although our prison was far greater in size than ones in the war abroad, the rules were similar. We do what we are told; we submit to the punishment rather than face the consequences. Held in this surreal captivity, we endure our punishment and torture, sharing the same thoughts of real POWs, to escape without harm. To find the people that are on our side. I have found only one difference between these two wars, there are people looking for prisoners abroad. An entire country backing them. I take nothing from our soldiers overseas; they face a greater danger than I or my daughter, the possibility of death. I often wondered, though, is a life living in hell and fear better than being dead and feeling nothing. I don't know the answers to that, nor am I willing to find out. Who am I to make such an audacious comparison to soldiers risking their lives? I guess it would be the irrepressible notions haunting my soul.

March 17, 2007, I joined a once a month bowling league that I started a few years back. The league consisted mostly of my friends, including Rod Z. This particular night, I was bowling against Rod Z's team, which included his wife. I figured they were not going to show up, and I believe they figured the same because we did not speak to each other. Usually, when I see these people, I would put my head down and just walk by. I arrived at the bowling alley a little early along with Jennifer and her friend Jenny. I looked for the name of my team on the TV screens on the bowling lanes. Once I've found it, I put my ball on the ball return and headed for the bar to get a beer. I went back to sit just behind our lanes with Jennifer and Jenny. We were sitting there talking when all of a sudden, Jennifer said, "Dad, Rod is here."I turned around and looked in that direction. Rod was standing in the lane, putting his ball on the ball return. He looked up and saw me looking at him. He looked as surprised as me. Shortly after, my brother Jim and his girlfriend Caroline arrived. We were on the same team. I walked up to the lanes to take some practice shots. As I approached the lane on the left, Rod was returning from the right. Just as he passed me, I said, "What's up, Rod?" It seemed like he hesitated for a second and then kept walking. I wasn't sure if he heard me or not, I thought nothing of it. I threw two balls during my practice shot. I was heading back to my seat when I heard Rod's voice,

"Tom, can I talk to you for a minute?"

I turned, looked at Rod and said, "Sure and started walking toward him. I sat down next to him and said,

"What's up?"

"Tom, I just want you to know I had nothing to do with taking your truck. I couldn't believe it when I found out Martha did it that day at the game."

"Well rod, I am going to be honest with you. Every time you were at the same games, I would see you make a call from your cell phone, and Martha would show up minutes later."

Rod said, "You mean at my daughter's games, you know my business. I get calls all the time."

"What about those men following my daughter and me."

"Why didn't you get their license plate, Tom?"

"They were standing in the park. I know all the parents; these men were alone and watching my daughter and me."

"Tom, they were not the guys I work with, and I heard you were accusing me of going by your apartment."

"Well Rod, my landlord told me about a police officer in a vest with your exact description and a white unmarked car. You own an unmarked white car, Rod. How do you explain that?"

"How long ago did that happen, Tom?"

"A few months ago"

"I got rid of that car back in October. Tom, you know what I do for a living. Do you think I would show up at your apartment knowing if you saw me, you would recognize me?"

"I really don't know Rod. Martha said you can find out anything about me. How did she know where I bought my car from?"

"All she told me was you had a gold car because you like that color, and it said Westbound Ford by the plate."

"Yeah Rod, but how did she know how much money I paid for it? How do you get that information?"

"I don't have any idea, I don't hardly talk to Martha anymore. She lives in Wisconsin most of the time."

"Well Rod, I just want to be left alone. I didn't do anything to anybody. Martha is nuts. She is the one who said you get her information. I don't have any animosity toward you. If you say you didn't do anything, I'll take your word for it. Ok let's bowl." Ron and I shook hands.

I had fun that night. Nothing else was said about Martha except, halfway through the night, a woman on Rod's team came up to me and said, "Tom, I know Martha too, but you and Jennifer need to let it go and move on. I had a husband before, and you just need to move on."

"I am moving on, but thanks."

This woman was always nice to Jennifer and me but I knew she was in Martha's circle of friends. I have heard many times that Martha was telling people that I was the one who was trying to hang on to her. I also knew that these people only knew Martha's side of the story. They had no idea what my daughter and I have been through, and I wasn't about to tell them. It made me wonder though if they read my book, what they would think then. What words could they possibly say to my child and me? Would they believe my story? I found it interesting when people tell a story that is fiction, and it gets bigger, better, and more exciting. The people around them are convinced. They know no other side. They choose not to know. With the attention of their small audience, the storyteller gets so caught up they are forced to live the part. As for Rod's story, I wanted to believe him, he was a nice guy, and he was once my friend. But I kept reading his story over again in my mind looking for mistakes. First of all, when getting the story, I keep people talking for as long as I can. The more they say, the more I learn. I read it back over and over again. I separate the chapters. Now my questions. The men following me only made appearances at games Rod attended. Coincidental? Could be. The white car and Rod's description coincidental again? Rod asks first, when the policeman in the white car went by my apartment. After getting that information, he informed me he got rid of his white car two months before, assuring it could not be him. Why would Martha give Rod a description of my car? Rod stated he hardly talks to Martha anymore, but in the same sentence, he knows where she lives most of the time. It was only my thoughts, for I had no proof. However, I got two things out of that. Although Martha has never directly said Rod was helping her, by saying that, she would lose Rod's trust. A little friction on her side of the fence. I had no idea that Martha was living out of state most of the time as she holds my daughter and me prisoner in Illinois.

I told Jennifer about that conversation with Rod. Jennifer's only reply was, "Dad, I saw Rod's wife dropping the kids off at the bowling alley a few weeks ago, and she was driving the white car."

"Are you sure, Jennifer?"

"Yeah Dad, that's the same white car they had for years."

"Maybe they got a new one, Jennifer."

"No Dad, I was in that car a hundred times, I know that car."

"I don't know, Jennifer."

Carrie bowled in that league and was there that night as well. We never spoke or came within feet of each other. Jennifer did not speak to her as well. At times I would look over at her, and she would be staring at me. Her facial expressions were not of hate, more like sadness, curiosity. Although I wasn't sure, I wondered what she was thinking. Did she want to say something to me but was afraid. I wanted to talk to her so bad. I wanted to tell her what her sister was doing to her child, hoping maybe Carrie could talk some sense into Martha. I wished I could play a tape for her to let her hear her Goddaughter's cries. But I knew. They stick behind their family, right or wrong. I couldn't trust them. They all stopped speaking to me the day I was removed from my home. They erased me from their lives, a hurtful feeling that they would endure themselves as Jennifer erased them from her life. She did the same thing that they did, yet they wondered why. Jennifer knew they would try to get her back in Martha's life, defending Martha's actions, not caring or even believing the horrible things that were done to her. I stood behind my daughter. What was happening was not ok. They were right about me brainwashing Jennifer. I instilled in her mind that what these adults were doing to her was wrong, a crime. Anyone who defended it, they were vapor. I guarded Jennifer against anyone who thought about speaking on Martha's behalf. To me, they were as nuts as she was. Jennifer knew on her own who to trust and who not to. It was a game we knew well. Martha had a lot of people convinced that she was the poor victim. I did not blame these people for they couldn't fathom nor even believe, as it was just as hard for me to believe that my child and I were Martha's prisoners. They didn't see her that way. In Martha's new world, she is charming, sweet, intelligent, and a businesswoman. In my world, she has bloodshot eyes, horns sticking out of her head, a long hot fork that she can stick me with as she wishes. I was getting notions again. Did her new husband know this side of Martha? Was he in on it, or maybe he does not know. If that were the case, then Martha would be lying to him as well as her family and friends. And I am a fool. Would he stand by her side if he found out what she did to her own daughter? Jennifer often told me that in most of Martha's voicemail messages, Martha was phony, speaking as if someone was standing there that she had to impress, a voice of no concern, a tone unrecognizable to her 15-year-old child, a sophisticated storybook mother, as if nothing were wrong between them. Other messages, no one to impress, A recognizable tone, reprimanding. Jennifer and I were the only people in the world that saw these two people.

March 18, 2007, it was a Sunday evening, and Jennifer and I were at one of the local car dealers. It was closed, but I found that it was a great way to shop for cars. You don't have a salesman following you, asking you a hundred questions. Jennifer was months away from getting her driver's license, so I thought I would take her to look at cars to see what she liked. There were about 12 Dealerships within several blocks. We looked around for about a half-hour, Jennifer pointing out what she liked. She liked the Chevy Equinox and the Nissan Murano. We were out for about an hour and at the third dealer. I was bent down looking through a window of a car when Jennifer interrupted me and said, "Dad, hurry up, turn around. Guess who's in that white car that's pulling in the dealer behind us?"

I looked up and what do you know? It was Rod and his family in a white unmarked police car.

"Did they see us, Jennifer?"

"Yeah Dad, they looked right at us."

"Come on Jenn, let's get out of here."

We went across the street where my car was parked, jumped in and headed home. All the way home, Jennifer was saying,

"I told you so, I told you so."

I didn't know what to think. Was that a different car or the same one? Why would Rod lie? Probably just a coincidence.

March 23, 2007, counselor #3 session 19 (Jennifer alone)

Jerry: Hey Jennifer, how are you?

Jennifer: Good.

Jerry: Just me and you today, as you may recall.

Jennifer: Yeah

Jerry: So, anyway, what's been going on in the life of Jennifer?

Jennifer: Nothing really

Jerry: No? Ok. Well, what would you like to talk about today? Ah, you know this is your time.

Jennifer: Nothing.

Jerry: Nothing?

Jennifer: No.

Jerry: Ok. Well, we got to talk about something ha, ha, ha, otherwise we're going to have a long 45 minutes.

Jennifer: Nothing really.

Jerry: Ok, anything happened between you and your Mom that you want to talk about?

Jennifer: No.

Jerry: No, Ok um, do you want me to pick something to talk about?

Jennifer: I guess,

Jerry: Ha, ha, ha, ha, that's a risky, that's a risky thing. Boy.... . You know honestly I was trying to think of something to talk about with you today if you didn't have anything you wanted to talk about.... . and um...you know I thought uh maybe we could talk about forgiveness but then you know there is no way I could push forgiveness if nobody isn't ready to forgive so I thought well that probably doesn't make sense to talk about um...so I was really hoping you would have something for us to talk about Jennifer.

Jennifer: No

Jerry: No? Um.... well let's think last time you were here, you and your Mom were here together, and you talked about uh when you went over to pick up some stuff at her house. And um... one of the things we talked about the fact that uh she turned like a wedding picture for you to see... and you didn't appreciate seeing you know her and Todd in the wedding picture, you thought it was like, I don't know you didn't say rubbing your nose in it but, you know that was the sense I got. . Uh do you want to talk about that anymore?

Jennifer: No, not really.

Jerry: Ok.... I know your grandpa is sick because your Mom had mentioned to me, um do you remember I spent a little time alone after uh you guys left. Uh your grandpa is sick, how is he doing?

Jennifer: I...don't know.

Jerry: You don't know? He was in the hospital, as she told me.

Jennifer: Yeah.

Jerry: Were you close to grandpa?

Jennifer: Not really.

Jerry: Not really? Were you close to Grandma?

Jennifer: No, not really.

Jerry: No? Ok, who were you close to in your, you know, extended family?

Jennifer: I don't know, no one really, I guess. I'm close with my one cousin now that's on my Dad's side.

Jerry: Un huh, hmm, ok. .... Jennifer what, what do you think happened in your family? Why do you think things went so bad?

Jennifer: Like I said before, because my Mom went...crazy!

Jerry: Your Mom went off the deep end.

Jennifer: Yeah,

Jerry: Um hm, ok. . . And um...when you say she went off the deep end, when did you feel she started going off uh as you put it up when your Mom went crazy, when do you think she started going crazy?

Jennifer: Um, ... like at the beginning, everything like as soon as she asked my Dad for a divorce.

Jerry: Um hm, um hm, ok now I'm not really good with chronologies, so give me like month and year so again if you would.

Jennifer: I want to say July..... 2005

Jerry: July of 2005, ok, so roughly uh a year and a half ago, right.

Jennifer: Yeah

Jerry: Yeah, ok, and that's when you started noticing uh you know, changes in your Mom.

Jennifer: Um hm.

Jerry: Ok, and uh what changes seemed to make it seem like she was going crazy?

Jennifer: Uh well like I said before, arguing and just everything. Basically everything we talked about before really.

Jerry: Um hm. Alright, and uh .... When that happened, um what explanation did you give yourself about what was going on?

Jennifer: What do you mean?

Jerry: Well, you saw a change in your Mom

Jennifer: Yeah

Jerry: A big change apparently, and um...you thought uh my gosh my Mom is acting really crazy out of character here. What was your explanation for why she changed in that way?

Jennifer: Um probably Todd.

Jerry: Ok, now you didn't know at the time she was involved with Todd, did you?

Jennifer: Uh yeah, I did. I found out the day that she told me about the divorce.

Jerry: Ok, so she told you the same day.

Jennifer: Yeah, I believe it was later that night,

Jerry: Yeah ok, and uh what did your Mom tell you about Todd, about her relationship?

Jennifer: That's when she started asking me about um, that... That's when she just started asking, telling me oh if you see a picture of him and stuff then um you know you'll see what I mean or if you talk to him or meet him you'll see what I mean and things like that and that's basically where yeah, where that went.

Jerry: So that was literally the same day that you found out

Jennifer: I think so; it was a while ago, so I don't

Jerry: Your memory might be foggy, but it was pretty close together.

Jennifer: Sure, yeah.

Jerry: Ok, and um...did she tell your Dad the same day that she told you that she wanted a divorce?

Jennifer: I....... think so, I'm not sure, I think so though

Jerry: Yeah, um hmm

Jennifer: I think it was like earlier that day. But I'm not positive.

Jerry: Um hm, hmm. Ok, ok. And you didn't have any incline that things were going bad

Jennifer: No

Jerry: between Mom and Dad, so it kind of like took you as a surprise

Jennifer: Yeah

Jerry: Yeah,....... Did you feel like uh, I think from what you said in the past, I think I know the answer to this but you really feel like she tried to push Todd on you

Jennifer: Yeah

Jerry: In a certain sense, yeah, yeah, boy. What advice would you give uh in a similar situation if they wanted to preserve a relationship post-divorce?

Jennifer: Um, I don't know. I guess that I would say like let the kid make up their own decision and like just stay the same person you are, you know even though things are going to be different but remain the same way toward the kid and not, don't push them into anything or try to take them away from anything or anything, just like let them make their own choices and decisions and let them feel how they want to and stuff.

Jerry: Um hm ok, do you feel like your Mom disrespected your decisions, not your decisions uh your feelings?

Jennifer: Yeah

Jerry: Yeah, ok, and what feelings do you feel uh that your Mom disrespected?

Jennifer: Well, because I didn't want to meet him or anything, and like she just kept trying, so I don't know what you would call that. As a feeling but yeah. I don't know.

Jerry: Um hm. Uh she didn't respect your readiness anyway. For one thing, and uh, but did she actually, was she actually pushing for you to meet Todd?

Jennifer: Um, well

Jerry: Or was she trying to sell you that he's a nice guy and

Jennifer: Well both because um like, like I said before um when she said oh when you meet him and see you'll understand what I mean or something like that and then the other time where she was like oh we'll get a house a pool and on and on and all this stuff, and then we'll go on vacation, we'll have all the same things like that. That's basically meeting him because if you are going to be staying with him, you know, it's no different.

Jerry: Um hm, hm. Well, it was too much too fast, too soon, that's for sure. You know.... hm.... . You really felt like uh, she really didn't understand probably what it was like for you to get the news. . . About the divorce I mean.

Jennifer: Say that again

Jerry: I said you really didn't feel like she understood what it was like for a kid to hear that news. Her parents were getting a divorce.

Jennifer: Yeah, like cause, I guess she hasn't been through it so she wouldn't know cause she would always say oh I know things are hard and things like that but, she wouldn't understand because she was never in that situation as a kid. So.

Jerry: Um hm, um hm, yeah true. It's true. Nobody can understand something like somebody who's uh been through it. . You know I've worked with families for a long time uh you know before I had kids I would work with parents and uh, you know you really don't understand uh like some of what they're talking about until you have a family of your own, you have your own kids, and you go through it. There is no substitute for the experience that's true. Yeah, yeah, when your Mom first told you that she was uh going to get a divorce from your Dad, what was your initial reaction?

Jennifer: Um, I was shocked, I guess.

Jerry: Yeah, did belief,

Jennifer: Yeah, because I didn't see anything wrong.

Jerry: Un hm. Hm. Kind of like how could it happen to us was your initial reaction.

Jennifer: Yeah and because everything seemed normal like they always been so, I don't know, nothing seemed different.

Jerry: Um hmm. Um hmm. Ok, and then what did you feel as the shock wore off?

Jennifer: Um, I don't know; all I remember is just being shocked for a while, like I ended up talking to my friends and stuff. I called one of my friends; I was going to go on a trip with her, just to kind of get away for a couple of days. And like even she was shocked. All my friends that found out they couldn't believe it because they, I always had friends over and stuff like that and they always thought things were fine too>

Jerry: Um hmm

Jennifer: I was just shocked for a while.

Jerry: Um hmm. So you were shocked that your friends were shocked too sounds like

Jennifer: Yeah

Jerry: You know uh, you always had friends over, they didn't see anything that indicated that it was a troubled household, I guess. Hmm……. I think one of the things that happened is that uh you know your Mom was like using the nuclear family kind of model for a blended family situation. Um, do you know what that means?

Jennifer: No,

Jerry: Um, A blended family is like after there is a divorce a lot of times after people divorce, each person has kids from a first marriage and they are trying to blend a bunch of people together to create a new family. That's a blended family. A nuclear family is what you had, you know the Mom the Dad and you know the kids, that's a nuclear family and a blended family is what people try to create afterward. And um a lot of times what happens is …. Uh the parents are trying to create like a nuclear family, let me put it, in trying to create a blended family they use a nuclear family model. And uh they have kind of like these mitts of instant love that they operate according to. So like um it's kind of like they put these expectations on people that are really unrealistic because there isn't instant love in a blended situation. Am I making sense to ya?

Jennifer: No

Jerry: Alright. Let me try again. Let me just bring it down to your situation. Like your Mom put an expectation of instant love on you that you were instantly supposed to have, if not love at least warmth and positive regard for Todd. Right,

Jennifer: Yeah ok,

Jerry: And um, that's realistic for a bunch of reasons. One uh, you were still reeling from the shock of the divorce. Number two, hush the loss of your nuclear family, in a way, it's like a huge loss. I mean uh enormous, you know, and when people are grieving, they can't reattach to somebody else. Uh number three, um it's a complicated situation for kids because they're trying to work out a relationship with both parents and like the expectation that you would instantly bond with Todd uh it kind of made your situation as a kid with a divorced family more complicated because you're trying to work out a relationship with both parents. And um like this myth of instant love it puts enormous pressure on people.... and creates uh a lot of uh, a lot of anger, uh sometimes. Did I get it that time? Did that make sense?

Jennifer: I think so, so basically

Jerry: Tell me what you got

Jennifer: Basically, my Mom was trying to put pressure on me to like Todd and vice versa so

Jerry: That instant love part.

Jennifer: Um you said a blended family. I wasn't ready, (softly) the nuclear family was broken up

Jerry: Yeah, yeah, and yeah. I worked with this lady. Her name was Ester Walt, and she wrote a book called the remarried family. She was a Doctor at the University of Chicago. Um she died of cancer a while back but uh, anyway, I learned a lot from her. Uh, I was fortunate enough to work with her for many years, and I learned a lot about remarried families from her. That was one of the things I have learned is that uh people place these uh expectations of instant love on kids. Sometimes they place it on stepparents too, you know, in this case, we're talking about you. And uh that expectation uh because in a way, it um ...it's just far beyond where kids are ready to go emotionally. Uh it creates inter-distention between a kid and a parent, and it makes it seem to the kid like a parent is from outer space. Uh kind of like so out of touch, I mean. With where the kid is at. And um you know the parent gets so intent on creating this blended family that they put this unrealistic expectation on the kid and that creates a lot of pain.... . If your Mom would have gone slower with that and been more respectful of uh like your feelings in your face would that have made a big difference in how you coped with it??

Jennifer: I don't know because she didn't so....

Jerry: Right, yeah, but it would have been better if she were more in touch...with your readiness, no drought..... What else do you feel she disrespected as far as your decisions, as far as your feelings?

Jennifer: I don't know, I guess that was it.

Jerry: Um hmm

Jennifer: That's basically everything right there.

Jerry: Um hmm, hmm. Ok so one of the biggest things is, uh you know that she really tried to push uh a relationship with Todd uh you know too fast.

Jennifer: Yeah, that and other things.

Jerry: Yeah, other things we've talked about too. Ok, after she told you in July of 2005 that she was going to pursue a divorce um what other signs made you feel like she went crazy?

Jennifer: Um well, she was acting differently like I said before, and we were getting into more arguments; she was just totally different. Really!

Jerry: Um hmm, um hmm. Yeah, you said she was more argumentative

Jennifer: Yeah

Jerry: Uh, At That Point, ok. And uh what do you make, what do you make of that?

Jennifer: What do you mean?

Jerry: Why do you think uh she got more argumentative uh at that time?

Jennifer: I have no clue

Jerry: No clue?

Jennifer: No, She just did.

Jerry: Evidently, um, scared maybe?

Jennifer: No, I wouldn't say scared

Jerry: Of losing you, I mean

Jennifer: No, because I was staying with her, so it didn't make any sense. My Dad wasn't even there. She's I don't know, she just changed, but I wouldn't say she was scared.

Jerry: Um hmm, hmm. Ok, maybe, later on, she got afraid of losing you. But uh not at that point.

Jennifer: No, because she was already pushing me away. So. .

Jerry: Hm ok, alright. Um .... what else um you know, could have happened uh that would have been more respectful to you besides the Todd thing?

Jennifer: I have no idea because, like I said, she didn't do anything to you know so.

Jerry: Yeah, you had a complicated, you had a real complicated situation. Your divorce was more complicated than most. The divorce in your family at least what I think uh you know I think it was complicated by virtue of the fact that you didn't see it coming, it was more complicated by the fact that um your Mom was leaving your Dad for another, I think that kind of adds to the other spouse's pain. Uh that's an extra complication. Uh you know it was certainly complicated by the fact that your Mom made you know kind of pushed you to make like you know, a real rapid transition. It was complicated by the fact that your Dad went through an intense period of depression afterward. Your situation was more complicated than you know what most kids have to go through. Not that it's ever easy, don't get me wrong, but I think your situation was more complicated than most. You agree with me on that wouldn't you?

Jennifer: Yeah

Jerry: Yeah, Did you feel in essence, you got like, the things your Mom did drag you into the conflict between her and your Dad?

Jennifer: Wait, what?

Jerry: Do you feel like the things your Mom did drag you into the middle of her problems with her and your Dad?

Jennifer: Um like, are you saying like what she did to me? Got me into the middle of what was going on?

Jerry: Yeah,

Jennifer: Um, well yeah because, Yeah um, because like I don't know everything like it had to do like certain things we would argue about it would have to do with my Dad and stuff so it kind of like put me in that place too. Like if my Dad needed something, she wouldn't give it to him and things like that but she wouldn't talk to him to give it to him. It was things like that. I don't know if that's what you are saying.

Jerry: Yeah. So let's see if we are on the same page. So would you like to have to carry messages back and forth?

Jennifer: Um,

Jerry: Your Dad would need something and she wouldn't talk to him. She would say Jennifer tell your Dad Yada yada yada.

Jennifer: Um, kind of, yeah I would say yeah. Because I don't know it was things like that so, there has been so much and it's been so long so I don't remember every little thing.

Yeah, she placed me there plenty of times.

Jerry: Kids usually say they want to be left out of it.

Jennifer: What?

Jerry: Kids usually say they want to be left out of it, you know.

Jennifer: Yeah

Jerry: They don't want to be forced to pick. They don't want to be um, carrying messages back and forth you know they don't want any of that. ... What worries did you have like your family was going through this whole thing?

Jennifer: I don't know

Jerry: Did you have a lot of anxiety?

Jennifer: Meaning like?

Jerry: Well like you know what anxiety is? Apprehension because you don't know what is going to happen, that kind of thing. Discomfort

Jennifer: Uh, no.

Jerry: I mean things were falling apart, your life as you knew it was falling apart right

Jennifer: Yeah

Jerry: And you didn't know kind of like the future was going to look like

Jennifer: Yeah, yeah.

Jerry: So you had to have that apprehension, anxiety however you want to say it. Otherwise, you would be out of touch. Everybody would at a time like that. (Short silence) When did the divorce actually start? I mean um, did your Dad leave the house right away? After your Mom told you in July?

Jennifer: No,

Jerry: No,

Jennifer: They were staying there but then my Mom had my Dad kicked out or removed from the house however you want to put it. So,

Jerry: Um hmm. How long was that? Between finding out?

Jennifer: I have no idea.

Jerry: Well that must have been traumatic, you know. And um, when that happened, were you there when that happened?

Jennifer: Um, no I was um, well first I was at my Dad and Mom's friend's house, and I was like spending time with like them because they have like, they have two kids and I grew up with them and so I was staying with them cause they're like around my age and they're kind of like family, family friends. And so I was staying by them for a couple of days and um she took, the people where we were at they took me to, because my Mom was out of town for a couple of days for work. That's what she said and so I went to stay with my Dad for a day or that night and the next morning. I was with my Dad and the next morning I guess my Mom was back in town and she was at work and she called me and asked me if I wanted to have lunch with her but um, I wanted to stay with my Dad and I don't know it was kind of weird why all of a sudden she was asking and I was like I haven't seen Dad, and she's like well I would really like you to come have lunch with me, I just got back and I don't know if she was like I got to talk to you or something. I don't know. And then finally my Dad was just like, ok I'll drive you over there. So he drove me over and I went up to my Mom's work and then she was like, ok well we're going to go to lunch or something, we'll go to lunch and then. Yeah I guess, and then she said we were going to stop by one of my friend's houses or something. So we left and we went to lunch and I was going to call my Dad. I told him that I would call him later. So then, I got to um my friend's house and then my Dad was calling me and then I went to pick up my phone and my Mom took my phone away. She wouldn't let me answer it. And she was like well we have to talk. And I was like well why can't you let me call Dad first and I told him that I would tell him you know, or I told him that I would call him. And she's like no you can't call him. And I was like why not and I got really mad. So then we were at my friend's house. We went um in one of the rooms and she was talking to me and she told me that I couldn't see my Dad, that I couldn't be anywhere near him, I couldn't have any contact with him or anything like that. And like I didn't know why. She was just like you can't because I'm scared or something over something stupid. And she's like, Oh well he said that he was going to hurt me or hurt you or something and I knew that wasn't true, I was just with him you know for a whole day and I spent the night there. And so like I thought that was so ridiculous. And like me and my Dad, it was weird because we had a feeling that something was up. All of a sudden, she was just calling and wanting me to come over right now. And...I don't know it was weird and so my Mom I guess later on that night she went to the house and she had the locks changed. And so I guess my Dad had to go and the police went to the house because my Dad, as soon as he got home like 2 minutes later the police got to the house and they told him that he had so much time to pack his stuff and get out. And like he didn't know what was going on and that's why I thought, I knew she was lying there, and that it wasn't true because I was just with him. And I spent the night with him and everything and we were fine you know. And so I couldn't talk to him or anything. So

Jerry: Um hmm. So you felt that whole thing was kind of devious?

Jennifer: Yeah like there was no point. Me and my Dad and like, (starting to cry) And like I came home and there was a letter from my Dad cause I guess in the time that he had, he wrote me a note, but I was like there was no need you know, she just made things worse.

And, cause there was nothing wrong. She was staying with him. When I went on vacation with my friend they stayed there, they were there for, I'm pretty sure my Dad was still living at the house for a couple of weeks and then she had a business trip and I guess that's what she said. Downtown or something. She went out of town and I was already by like our friend's house before she went and then I came like the next day. I stayed with my Dad for the rest of the day and then I spent the night and that's when my Mom called me the next day. So that didn't make absolutely no sense.

Jerry: Um hm, um hm. Hm. So when your Mom was on this business trip, you were with your Dad when she was on this trip.

Jennifer: No. I was at a friend's before she left, like I went the day before and spent the night there and she went, I went with my Dad.

Jerry: You were with your Dad when she was out of town.

Jennifer: Before she left town, they had both taken me to a friend's house. And then they went home and I spent the night there and then the next day, she left. Then I think I spent the night there again and then she was still gone and then that day I went to my house where my Dad was at and then I spent the rest of the day with him and then I spent the night and then the next day. But she wasn't, I didn't, like she wasn't far from home though, she was like 2 hours away from downtown Chicago or something and for

Jerry: So part of the time you were with friends and part of the time you were at home with your Dad.

Jennifer: Yeah

Jerry: I see, I see. And your Mom knew you were going to split the time between your home and your

Jennifer: No, I was supposed to stay there but like, I was supposed to stay at the friend's house but um my aunt or well I consider her kind of like an aunt I guess but um, she was like oh, do you want to spend time with your Dad and I was like yeah. She's like 'cause if you want to spend time with your Dad so I went over there and cause I was like calling him on the phone too and, we told him I was going to come and he was like ok so I went there so...

Jerry: Ok, so you kind of felt like this whole thing was kind of devious in a way?

Jennifer: Yeah, it was unnecessary, like there was no point to it, kind of like, there was no reason that I shouldn't be able to talk, see or contact my Dad in any way through email. So (sniffling)

Jerry: Well that's huge, that's huge. You know, cause we talked about before uh if somebody's like preventing access to a parent, you know during a divorce uh that's a huge problem. And um if somebody is pushed to have a relationship with a new person, that's a huge problem too. You know but the uh you know kind of being blocked from seeing your Dad, that's a biggie. Uh maybe when you and your Mom come in you know maybe that's an aspect that you know we could talk about to get your feelings out.

Jennifer: I've already talked about it with her. It doesn't change with all the last counselors.

Jerry: It might not, it might not, um that's kind of what counseling looks like. Um, I'll help you to talk about it with her. Um ok, well we're just about out of time um did you have a good time? Um........ Feel like it will be a break for you from school?

Jennifer: Yeah

Jerry: And I know you will not be sad that you will have a week before you have to come back here ha, ha, ha. I know that, uh, but I accept it so I guess I will see you in two weeks which will be Friday the 6th of April but uh

Jennifer: Yeah, the 6th

Jerry: I will be seeing your Mom tomorrow, by the way, she wasn't able to make it last week uh so we set it up for tomorrow.

Jennifer: I thought she was out of town.

Jerry: She was out of town last week, I think she came back today, which I think is uh why she made it on a Saturday.

Jennifer: Oh, because yesterday she told me she was going out of town today in the afternoon and she wasn't going to be home for a week, cause I was calling her and I needed to get something from the house. Yesterday I called her.

Jerry: Well, if that's the case, I must have misunderstood what she said but uh. So I guess I'll find out tomorrow morning.

Jennifer: Yeah, cause I called her yesterday and I asked her cause I needed to get something, I wanted to see if I could come this weekend and get something from the house. She's like well, if you want to come, you could come now if you want. I was like can't I come tomorrow or another day, she goes, well I'm leaving tomorrow afternoon going out of town and I'll be gone for the weekend, and I was like oh, ok. She was like actually, I'll be gone for the whole week. So

Jerry: You know what, she, your Mom had left me a message about scheduling stuff and it was a long message. I might have misunderstood what she said so this may be my screw-up.

Jennifer: Ok

Jerry: This wouldn't be the first time I screwed up. So we will see tomorrow. Alright well enjoy your trip. Ok

Jennifer: Yeah

After this session, Jennifer came out of the room with Jerry right behind her. As soon as I saw him, I stood up and said, Um, I was wondering if you had a couple of minutes, I have a couple of questions for you. Yeah, Jerry replied, and I followed him back into his office, shut the door behind me as Jennifer waited outside the room. . Jerry sat down in a chair on the opposite side of a couch in which I sat down. At first, I was nervous because I had a running recorder in my pocket. But like Jennifer said, after a few minutes, you forget it is there.

Me: I'm just curious, I mean, what do you think about Jennifer?

Jerry: I think she is a neat kid. And I think she's doing very, very well as far as I could see. Uh you know she's doing well uh academically. She's involved in uh quite a few things uh you know she was telling me about uh the orchestra trip she is going on

Me: Boston

Jerry: Yeah, I wouldn't mind going to Boston myself.

Me: Yeah, Um see I'm curious as, I mean how long are you guys going to keep her here?

Jerry: Well basically, Tom, what's keeping Jennifer here is uh the court order.

Me: Ok let me ask you about the court order. What do you know of the court order?

Jerry: The court order that I have, the copy that I've seen, is that uh...the therapy is supposed to go on for a minimum of one year.

Me: Right.

Jerry: And the next

Me: Or, or, if the parents, which they got me on that one. Her mother will keep her in here for years if she can, the rest of her life. But um, I mean basically what is your job? I'm curious.

Jerry: The way I look at my job is that I'm trying to heal the relationship between Jennifer and her Mom and uh you know that's kind of the way I see my Job...and um you know I think uh you know it's an, it's an enormous task. That's how I see my job.

Me: I mean um, to me I'll tell you what...Martha is going to lose her forever by keeping her in counseling. That's only hurting her and the courts suggested that they have no idea, no idea. The courts don't even know on February first that Martha threw Jennifer out of her home. They don't know about all of the events that I'm sure Jennifer has spoken about. She has told it a hundred times. I mean you as a person, I mean you have children. What do you think it does to a kid that has to relive a year and a half ago over and over and over again? And you see Martha. I know her, she isn't admitting anything. In order for somebody to say they are sorry, somebody to accept the apology, the person has got to admit it, and she admits nothing, she did nothing wrong. And that's going to kill her in her lifetime, in her relationship with her daughter. I mean, I always tell Jennifer,

Yeah, I don't like Martha very much because Martha got me thrown out of the house. Yeah, I had a suicidal thing, hey I was with the woman for 20 years. She broke my heart but I never threatened anybody else, but to get me out of the house so she could continue dating. She went to the courts and said, Oh he's going to kill me and he's going to kill my daughter, and that is untrue. You know the 14th amendment states a man can't be evicted from his home and deprived of life, liberty and property without due process of the law. And they ignored that Law. Ok well we'll see what she says but, but let me tell you what a liar Martha is. And you know there are two sides to every story. Martha stated on Thursday the seventh that she announced the divorce to me. And she stated that very evening that I told her I was going to kill her boyfriend. Ok, and yet in her affidavit to the courts she was scared to death. And that's why the restraining order came. Yet Martha came back home Friday. She cried and we spent the weekend together, I'm sorry this happened Tom. So she contradicted herself and the courts didn't see that. She's a good liar and it's going to cost her, her child. And I think what everybody is doing, the courts suggested that they wanted her in counseling because she didn't talk to her mother. In other words they want to know why. Jennifer has amazing stories of abuse and they are the same every time. I wasn't living there, but I've witnessed what she did in front of us and I'm telling you, you are going to damage this kid for life...because I know you are making money, did you know I'm paying for half of this? Did you know that?

Jerry: Uh no I didn't

Me: No, no, I got half the bill, I paid half the bill for the first one and the second one. That's a shame because outside of this, they say Jennifer is not normal.

Jerry: Well Tom, that I could help you with you know actually the insurance company is paying for this. I just paid Martha $800.00 for the last counselor.

Jerry: yeah but it can't be from me it's through the insurance company

Me: No, no, but when this is all done, after two or three years of counseling, I'm going to pay half of the bill.

Jerry: Well, Etna pays me

Me: Right, right, all the co charges, the co-pays, she inflates that whatever, that's my business. I'm telling you right now the courts want to know why she isn't talking to her mother. Not ok, here is your job to get these two together. She's been through heck and back.

Jerry: Um hm.

Me: And you don't see her stories and...and that's sad because you are just going to damage this kid.

Jerry: Yeah

Me: She is an A student; they said she is not normal. I've talked to other counselors at school and other people and attorneys. They usually said kids that have problems in divorce are failing at school. You see, she is fine up until the day she walks in here. She's happy, she is laughing. And as long as Martha can ride this court paper, in three years that kid is never ever going to speak to her again. That's what kind of damage it's causing. I don't control that. I tell her if you want to talk to your mother you go right ahead. But I'm telling you right now that is my daughter, nobody knows her better than me.

Jerry: Um hm

Me: and you are killing her. Martha is pushing her every week coming in here laughing in her face, Martha laughs in her face. It's a joke to her. And if you don't see that, all you are going to do is destroy a child.

(Short silence)

Jerry: Well, the way I look at it is Tom, um you know I know that Jennifer doesn't want to be here. And I know the only reason that Jennifer is here is that the court has ordered her to be here.

Me: Right, because of crooked attorney's that's why.

Jerry: Well she pretty much told me uh if it weren't for the court she wouldn't be here now

Me: Who said that?

Jerry: Jennifer

Me: Right, right, exactly.

Jerry: Yeah so, the way I look at it, you know I'm a family therapist and you can call it idealistic, but my goal is always to try and help kids to come out of a divorce a good relationship with both parents. Now I can't force uh healing

Me: Ok let me ask you this, what do you think about what this child told you her mother did to her?

Jerry: Uh I think that uh Jennifer has a real hard time of it and I've said that to Jennifer, and I think that um that Martha did things uh that uh you know made the divorce, divorce is always hard on a kid. But I think that Martha did things that made it even worse. Now I said that to Jennifer.

Me: But she doesn't admit them, does she?

Jerry: Uh she does, she admits some mistakes. Yeah Yeah, Martha does

Me: Did she tell what she did, Martha is nuts. All she does is grind and grind. Outside of here, she has got you fooled, she's got the courts fooled. She comes in here like this, she has all of you fooled because outside of here she is wicked. You see what she did with that picture. She knew that would hurt that kid. Jennifer is devastated by this whole thing so now we go to the house. What does she do, she puts a picture out there, knowing it will hurt her. I mean that's negligence, that's malicious.

Jerry: I would say that, I believe we are talking about turning the picture

Me: Right, putting it out there so Jennifer can see it

Jerry: I think, I think that was wrong.

Me: Yeah you know what it is, it never ends. It's never going to end.

Jerry: And I think you know, you can ask Jennifer I've said this uh that I think there were other mistakes Martha made too you know the problem between the two of them um its complicated. Martha did things, she made mistakes along the way, she made poor choices along the way

Me: Yeah it started out as mistakes but when you keep punching somebody and punching them and punching them, and punching them, and punching them. It's no longer a mistake. I told you she's got you fooled, she has everybody fooled. She comes in here, I've known her for 22 years. She can be the sweetest person in the world but outside of here she's evil. She laughed in her face when she took the truck and left us stranded. Jennifer was crying, she laughed in her face. It's funny. But she comes here, oh, I'm sorry, now I'm sorry and then she is going to do something tomorrow. You are never going to stop her. She wants to beat this into thsis kid, forget what happened to you and come be my daughter on the weekend she don't even want her full time. Come see me. You know whatever, when her significant other sees his kids she doesn't have that. That's her fault.

Jerry: Well here is how I look at it Tom um you know my job is to try and have them, to have

Me: And you haven't seen Jennifer has been through how many sessions 40 in a year, in a year?

Jerry: Not even 6 months, I don't know how many with the other guys

Me: but I mean to me as a human being.... this little girl walks in your office and you are killing her and you're just going to keep on doing it aren't you, for money.

Jerry: Well I do it because I have a belief as a family therapist that uh kids should come out of it

Me: Right, if the two parents are normal. Do you know what abuse is? And do you know the definition of brainwashing? Do you know that?

Jerry: Yeah

Me: What is it?

Jerry: Uh a person becomes emerged with another that they have no ability to think on their own.

Me: Um it's a coercive way to give a person new beliefs and new ways of thinking of things, replacing their true facts with beliefs of their own.

Jerry: Um hm, um hm.

Me: And basically Jennifer says that's what she is getting like you are trying to brainwash her into forgetting what happened to her without dealing with it. That's what counselor number two did too. No it didn't happen to you, this is what happened to you, that's brainwashing.

Jerry: Yeah I think if you ask Jennifer about her session today we were actually talking about stuff that hurt her I didn't try and like

Me: Yeah but she tells me, I'm the only adult she trusts because of what she went through.

Jerry: Yeah, but if you ask, if you were to ask her about her session today I don't think she would tell you that I tried to convince her of something that didn't happen.

Me: No but she tells me, she tells me that, that she'll explain what happened to her in her life and her mother never speaks, and you explain why she did it as if you were there.

Jerry: Sometimes, you know what sometimes, sometimes that does happen

Me: But yet, but yet, she says you don't explain. Do you know what that kid went through when you are thrown in the street at 14 years old, when you are thrown in the street in the dark? That's neglect, that abandonment, that's abuse. And everybody wants to say that didn't happen to her. When I found her freezing, you are, I'm telling you...everybody is damaging this kid. So you are going to hold her because the court says so you are going to hold my kid a prisoner for a year.

Jerry: Well here is what I'm doing Tom, I'm trying to be respectful of the fact that uh you know Jennifer doesn't want to be here I mean as you could see. Basically, we are having about two sessions a month with her and her mother. Because I have been seeing each of them individually. I'm trying to be respectful of the stress for Jennifer, that's one of the ways in trying

Me: Right, but don't you think making a kid relive a nightmare over and over and over. I could see if she is coming in here, if she is messed up on the street. I'm sure you deal with all kinds of kids like that, their grades aren't doing, and they are kids with problems. And see, this child is an A student. She just got awards today that came home for the student of the month. Where is your justification that this kid isn't well? You see, you know what, I'm not an idiot. The thing is what Martha wants and what she is paying for is she wants a relationship with Jennifer. That's what she's paying for and your job is to get it, because a real compassionate person would say well wait a second let me throw a red flag up there, your mother did what to you, and you question the mother and you see well hay, I can't fix something if this person is going to keep denying it, see but we know who you work for. I've been through this, I've been through this.

Jerry: Well you know I do help, you know I do help Jennifer talk with her mother about uh

Me: She has told her a thousand times.

Jerry: As something happens. You know I do

Me: And Martha says she didn't do it, she admits the small things. Martha never threw her out, Martha didn't chase her around the house, Martha didn't take, I know Jennifer, that's my kid she told me what she did, deleted pictures, she, she emotionally abused that kid. And she doesn't admit all that stuff. And that kills that kid. You want to say you are sorry. A long time ago, I tried to help Martha. Once I realized she was nuts, because you see what she did with the picture? Next week is going to be something else, and next month is something else laughing in her face. The day before court, she called Jennifer and told her, your Dad better sign those papers and if he doesn't you are going to be put away. Is that normal to you? Is it normal to threaten a child like that?

Jerry: No, no,

Me: What do you think about that?

Jerry: Uh, I think kids should be left out of marital politics.

Me: Right.

Jerry: I mean absolutely

Me: But you don't care about that, your job is to get Martha what she wants right,

Jerry: My job is to try and help Jennifer and you know

Me: Ok, alright you just said Jennifer, you want to help Jennifer, what does Jennifer want?

Jerry: You know it's my belief

Me: I'm asking you a question

Jerry: Jennifer doesn't want to be here

Me: Right, No she doesn't want a relationship with her mother and do you know why. Because the law and all of these adults won't let her heal. You know I can show you a letter from the only counselor I ever trusted, which was the first one......because see Martha wasn't involved. This woman got to know Jennifer on her own.

Jerry: Um-hm

Me: Then she got to know Martha and she realized what's going on and she said the kid needs to heal on her own time frame.

Jerry: Um- hm um hm

Me: See, you got two people wanting something out of this

Jerry: Um hm

Me: Your Job is to get Martha what she wants. Jennifer doesn't want to be here, she cries, it's killing her and you don't care about her. You care about Martha because she's where the money is coming from. I'm not an idiot and you are destroying my kid. That's all I'm telling you. That's a shame, that's a shame as a family man, I'm, and I'm a smart human being. I see a problem with two people, you know what, Martha, and nobody can help you, only god can help you. Only God can help you.

Jerry: Ok

Me: But you know what you are going to do, you are going to hold, she knows it kills Jennifer. She knows it kills her to be here and instead, you know what if this was me. Jennifer and I had problems in the beginning because they were trying to brainwash her against me. You know what, I didn't drag her through counseling. I let her, Ok, I let her heal and we worked things out. And that's why I have the relationship I have with her. But, she is destroying that kid. And she's never, she is going to take her into counseling every Friday until she is 18. You know what? Martha is never going to see her kid from 18 until she dies because you are holding her a prisoner. It's punishment. What doesn't she want to do, this is what I'm going to do to her. I mean and you should see that, you're in here with her, you know it's killing her. You know she cries and doesn't want to be here. And she won't accept Martha being her mother because of what she did and she keeps grilling. Every time you know, the last counselor every month, it was something new that Martha did.

Jerry: Um hm.

Me: So to Jennifer ok, you know in the beginning she had that, that chance. You know what, Mom, stop what you are doing. No, Martha does it again and again and again and again. I mean you control your own destiny. I mean I don't need a counselor or the law to make my daughter like me. If I can't do it on my own, I'm not going to do what she hates. That's what you do for the love of your child.... . And see Martha expects you, you go in there and get my daughter for me. And it isn't going to happen. I mean she's not 2; she's 15; she's very intelligent and

Jerry: I know that, I know that,

Me: So you are going to keep her in here for a year, Martha is never going to let her go. You are going to destroy that kid. All you are doing is

Adding to it. .

Jerry: Well what I can do Tom, is I could try and make it as least stressful for Jennifer as possible.

Me: It's not about that

Jerry: Well

Me:It's not about that, it's about Martha making Jennifer come to see her.

Jerry: Well the way that I Look at it, you know, just philosophically, I've been doing family therapy for a lot of years. I do believe that kids are supposed to come out of divorce um

Me: Yea um I've seen a lot of divorces, my parents were divorced

Jerry: Yeah

Me: and they didn't get along and this and that, and they broke up. You see nobody went off the deep end and started accusing of murder and throwing their kid in the street. That's going above and beyond

Jerry: Um hm

Me: that's vicious, that's negligent, she threw her kid out three times, she gave her kid away, and she didn't give me custody,

Jerry: Tom, we're going to have to wrap it up

Me: yeah, I'm just telling you

(Jerry gets up and starts walking me to the door)

March 29, 2007, Jennifer was going to Boston with her orchestra class for 5 days to compete with other schools for a chance to play with the Boston Symphony Orchestra

March 31, 2007, Jennifer while on her trip in Boston, Martha made her usual once-a-day call to Jennifer. This time she actually had something else to say.

"Hi, Jennifer!"

"What do you want, Mom?"

"You know you are missing out on some good things."

"Oh Yeah, what is that?"

"Well, you have a step-brother and step-sister."

Jennifer angrily replied, "What, oh no you didn't. First of all, I do not have a step-brother and step-sister and second, why would you say something like that and I don't even have you in my life."

Jennifer hung up.

What is wrong with Martha? Has she lost her mind? What was she like around those kids? Did she act like a loving mother? Oh I'm sure if those kids were around her, she acted like the perfect step-mom. What did these kids think of her as I am sure she pretended to be kind, trying to gain their trust as she threw her own child away like a piece of garbage. Nothing has changed with Martha as she was still trying to force life on her daughter that she wanted no part of. A strange comment that Martha thought would suddenly change her daughter's mind as she thought what was wonderful to her, would lure her daughter back into not into her life but theirs. As for Jennifer, it was just another nail Martha drove into her own coffin.

April 3, 2007. Jennifer had a school concert. Martha called Jennifer about an hour before the concert. As usual, Jennifer did not answer, and Martha would leave a voicemail.

"Hi Jennifer, this is Mom. You are probably getting ready for your concert tonight. Um I just want to let you know I'm not going to make it tonight so I hope you have a good time. If you want, give me a call later. Bye."

For Jennifer, this was good news. She hated Martha showing up at anything. She was no fool to Martha's split personality. Martha would usually show up either minutes before the concert started or minutes after. Always noticeable to the kids on stage as Martha's entrance would show fear as she looked around the room for me, assuring that she can sit on the opposite side where she will be safer. Overly dressed, Martha knew her entrance was noticeable. To Jennifer, it was just an act.

April 13, 2007 Counselor #3 session 20, Martha and Jennifer

Jennifer and I walk up the stairs into the waiting room. As we walked in, the counselors door was opened, and I noticed Martha sitting in Jerry's office, Jennifer walks in and shuts the door.

Jerry: We were just talking about your grandfather. Your Mom was giving me a medical update. Do you want to fill Jennifer in maybe, or do you already know, I don't know.

Martha: Do you want to know?

Jennifer: No, I don't, doesn't matter.

Martha: Ok.

Jerry: Ok. Um......but anyway just to finish my thought on, my neighbor was saying he actually lost all taste uh after his heart problems, which they attributed to the medications he was on. So uh if your Dad got a taste for the wrong things ha ha ha. .

Martha: Umm, he got a taste for everything.

Jerry: Maybe it's not so bad in some ways, I guess.

Martha: ha, ha.

Jerry: Anyway, welcome Jennifer. Uh you were out of town on a little trip or something last week, I guess huh?

Jennifer: Nods

Jerry: Ok, good time, I trust, alright can I ask where you went or is that .... a secret?

Jennifer: Silent.

Jerry: It is I guess but you had a good time. Alright, well it has been a while since I've seen you. I saw your Mom alone last week uh but uh gosh what's it been three weeks since I've seen you? I could look but I think it's about that. What would you guys like to talk about today?

Jennifer: I have something. Um well you know how last time I was saying how she never stops, like, when we were talking about the picture and stuff when we went to the house. Last time we had a session.

Jerry: Yes.

Jennifer: And um well now she is trying to say or to get me to feel bad or like to want me to come with her and stuff saying that I'm missing out because I have a stepbrother and stepsister. So that's just proving my point that even more that she just keeps pushing it and it's just she has her life, I have mine. Just let it be.

Jerry: Ok, ok and what did you take that to mean that your Mom mentioned you have a stepbrother and a step-sister, what did you think that to mean?

Jennifer: Well I don't so, that's how I take it to mean (sarcastic) and she's like your missing out, you could be seeing them and stuff and it's like , is that supposed to get to me in some way saying that I have a brother and sister in which I don't. No.

Jerry: Um-hm, well...um...what do you want Mom to understand about her mentioning that you had a stepbrother and stepsister?

Jennifer: Just don't.

Jerry: Not to do it. Ok and maybe you could say a little bit about uh you know why that's important to you.

Jennifer: Because I don't have a stepbrother and step sister.

Jerry: Ok.

Jennifer: and she's just trying to push something like, just to bring something up, yeah I don't know:

Jerry: Yeah, stepbrother and stepsister is kind of a legal creation. You know it's uh, when we talk about brother and sister normally we talk about somebody who is blood-related, so you don't have a blood relationship with them, that's true and um even psychologically uh I mean people have psychological bonds to brothers and stepsisters but uh if it is somebody you have never met and I believe you have never met them right.

Then of course you wouldn't feel much of any bond to them. That's understandable. Um you compared it to the picture thing, which we talked about in here the last time you went over to your Mom's house. How is this similar to the picture...

Jennifer: Well I'm just saying she never stops, there is always something that happens and she is like oh, like when she says she doesn't do anything well that just proves that she keeps going, she keeps dragging things on and adding more things to like, to what she does to me but yet she says she doesn't do anything, Well that's just proving it, she says she won't do anything anymore or she never did. That's why she pulled out that picture and then now this, so what I said was true, it doesn't stop.

Jerry: Ok so pushing you to accept

Jennifer: Well I mean just for anything, she just doesn't stop.

Jerry: Ok so pushing you to accept, that's kind of like another straw on the camel's back so to speak.

Jennifer: Yeah.

Jerry: Ok, ok. Do you want to ask any questions to help understand what Jennifer is saying, Martha?

Martha: I only mentioned the stepbrother and stepsister because you said that um you were glad that I was upset and sad because I have no children, no child in my life and that's when I brought that up

Jennifer: No, you said that before, you told me that I was missing out on my life and it could be better if I saw you and that I'm missing out because I have a stepbrother and stepsister.

Martha: I said you could have a relationship and a good time with me and your Dad.

Jennifer: No, I have enough of a relationship with my Dad, not you!

(Silence)

Jerry: Um why did you bring up the stepsister and stepbrother, I don't understand

Martha: Well, we were talking about it and she said that I was sad or I was upset and or I don't remember the word but that I didn't have a child or anything and she was happy that I was miserable or keep crying a river or something like that, I said well that's not true, there are children in my life and you have a stepbrother and stepsister.

Jerry: Ok so were you hurt by what Jennifer said?

Martha: No I'm kind of use to it,

Jerry: Were you hurt by what Mom said?

Jennifer: Ha ha ha no she tells me my life is miserable, I don't really care what she says. If she thinks I'm going to listen to her. I'm not, I'm not stupid, if she was telling me how my life is miserable and basically how it could be better and stuff when I'm the one happy, I don't need to be here. Apparently, my life is the one that's not miserable. Hers is, if I have to come here and deal with her every week. She is the one that's having the problems, not me so yeah I said, I was like yeah well my life isn't miserable you know...

Martha: You are not here because your life isn't miserable ha, ha, ha.

Jerry: Ha, ha, actually

Jennifer: No, no,

Jerry: Ha, ha, ha. I think all three of us have a problem ha, ha, ha, I would like to feel successful, I don't feel successful. You know to be here and you're here because you are trying to repair your relationship with your Dad so we all have a problem I guess. Um but to get back to the um .... Issue you were raising. To you this was kind of like turning the picture for you to see. It was kind of the same

Jennifer: Wait, say that again.

Jerry: Um when your Mom said you know about the stepbrother and stepsister, to you, it was similar to turning the wedding picture for you to see.

Jennifer: No, no, I'm just saying that's adding on, she always does something more.

Jerry: Well in that um, that's legitimate in the sense that um .... . when kids go through a divorce they feel like they didn't have much sense of control over their life and they feel like um when the family is splitting up um, it's a huge loss and they have no control over what's happening.... and it may be that um when you turned the picture for Jennifer to see or mentioned you know the stepbrother and stepsister, it kind of like pushing her to accept something that although in reality, she's not kind of like ready to accept and recognize.

Martha: Um-hm.

Jerry: Um, I don't know if I ever told you guys this but I do over the years I've done a lot of family therapy and I used to work with a lady who wrote a book The remarried family. Her name was Sandra Dalton and uh, Sandra is now dead. Uh but one of the things that she said kids a lot of times have problems with is that bond retaining to the remarried family are like pushed prematurely or too hard and um I think maybe the best way for you to uh think about what Jennifer is saying Martha, it's just something she is still not ready to accept.

Jennifer: And not going to be.

Jerry: Maybe you never will, who knows.

Jennifer: I know I never Will.

Jerry: Ok

Jennifer: She just doesn't get that yet.

Jerry: But um like recognizing your marriage or recognizing relationships with the kids, Todd's kids that's just not where she could go right now. And the more you push it, um probably the more it drives her away. Is that fair in saying?

Jennifer: Yeah.

Jerry: Ok, um

Martha: Well how did the orchestra competition go?

Jerry: I was just going to say one more thing.

Martha: Oh.

Jerry: Then we could get off of this unless you guys want to continue. Um the other thing I was going to say was um, although you're having, you have some bond now with Todd's kids, that doesn't replace the spot in your heart that Jennifer has right.

Martha: Um-hm.

Jerry: Ok, and that spot is always going to be kind of like uh, on reserve for her.

Martha: Yep. Always

Jerry: So just because

Jennifer: (sarcastic) Yeah!

Jerry: You have a relationship with Todd's kids doesn't mean that, that excludes her if she chooses to have a relationship with you, right.

Martha: Yeah

Jerry: Ok, and ...even though you choose to have a relationship with Todd's kids...um in reality, do you have an expectation that Jennifer have a relationship with them?

Martha: No.

Jerry: Ok

Jennifer: But yet she brings it up, and another thing didn't we say that you wouldn't tell her like before um like what to say and think and stuff because basically

Jerry: Did I just do it?

Jennifer: Yeah.

Martha: Ha, ha, I'm not telling you

Jennifer: Ok, here, I could do this too, I could talk to someone and on my behalf and say , oh well don't you think that you're thinking or you think that you know she is wrong because she did this and bla bla bla, and they could go yep, yep, you are basically saying it and they, come on

Martha: I tell you all the time

Jennifer: Yeah ok, ok.

Martha: I am always here for you.

Jennifer: Whatever.

Martha: Maybe you don't listen to the messages when I leave you messages but

Jerry: Let me just ask you, I didn't uh tell your Mom what to say when you were telling her uh you didn't like it when she brought it up about the stepkids

Jennifer: No, but

Jerry: But I just did now

Jennifer: Yeah.

Jerry: Um, I saw that as a little different because I saw that as helping your Mom to talk about her own experience of things. I didn't like try and redefining

Jennifer: No but basically, No I'm not saying that but I'm saying basically if you're trying to get her to talk about it then she should be able to say it herself, not you say it and ask her ok well, you know you still have a place in your heart for Jennifer, she goes yeah and stuff like that. That's not having her say it herself, she didn't say it herself. That's what I'm saying, you have to say something for her and then her have to come up with an answer for herself.

Jerry: Yeah, honestly um, I knew your Mom felt that way because like I told you I met with her last week and she had brought that up.

Jennifer: Ok then she could say that.

Jerry: She could have yeah and I think it would have been better if she did. I knew it was in there and that's why I didn't cut that off because I wanted her to say what she said to me last week.

Martha: Nobody ever could replace you Jennifer.

Jennifer: So you are trying to say it now that doesn't, I don't, once again I don't care because I don't believe you. For the five hundredth time.

Jerry: It may not work now but that's why I was saying, that's why I asked a question

Jennifer: Ok that's why I brought it up

Jerry: I'm glad you did, I'm glad you did. I tell you where I'm at with things um..... It may be that you and your Mom are always going to have uh different experiences of events around the divorce, and it may be that uhhhh because each of you literally had different experiences that will have different narratives about the divorce. I'm not going to try to get those narratives to match up anymore. So uh I think maybe what you'll find is that like um, if you talk about your experience of things uh I'm not going to try and correct your perception of things because you thought like I've done that right. Ok so I'm going to try, I'm going to try not to do that now, you got to know that um I may try and help you guys have a therapeutic conversation so like if your Mom says something to me that I think would be helpful for her to say to you, I may like do something to get it out, that still might happen. That's what I did a little while ago. Um and this is nobody's thought but my own. Um……my guess is like sometimes you're like so careful that you might, that may be why you didn't say it on your own

Martha: Um-hm

Jerry: But anyway I don't want to be a laborite but truly she did say that last week. Um you were going to ask another question and I kind of like elongated things.

Martha: I'm just wondering how the orchestra concert went if you ended up winning?

Jennifer: That's my business.

Martha: I'll just have to make a phone call

Jennifer: I know you are just going to do it anyway so why even ask.

Martha: I rather talk to you about it and get information from you

Jennifer: Well I don't talk to you about anything else so why even try.

Martha: Because you are my daughter and I care.

Jennifer: Uh yeah, keep telling yourself that.

(Silent)

Jerry: Do you have other things you want to know about?

Martha: Um-hm

Jerry: Ok well

Martha: Uh did you ever go back to the orthodontist, the dentist and the eye doctor?

Jennifer: Taken care of, taken care of, and taken care of. , once again uh my business.

Martha: You know Jennifer you are my daughter and I care about you and

Jennifer: No, no, you do not have anything over any of that so no,

Martha: I pay for insurance and I pay bills on a monthly basis so you could have braces.

Jennifer: Uh, Dad pays some of them too. So don't even. Because that's why the last time I went to the Ortho I couldn't go because the bill wasn't paid so Dad had to pay him.

I couldn't make another appointment, hmm so you could hmm all you want.

Martha: I should have brought a copy of it with me.

Jennifer: Yeah. .

(Silence)

Martha: I think I have it with me.

Jennifer: I don't really care, I know what the lady told me.

Martha: I know what I paid.

Jennifer: Ok.................. .

Jerry: The last time the two of you were together, um there was a song you had asked your Mom to look up. It was by the Dixie Chicks as I recall. Um, did you look it up?

Martha: Um-hm.

Jerry: Ok um, I have not looked it up and so I have not seen the lyrics. Can I see them?

(Martha hands Jerry the paper)

Jerry: Not ready to make nice. Should I read it out loud?

Jennifer: I don't care, I already know the lyrics, and I could tell you exactly what I mean by it. I know some of the lines you guys they're going to take and say oh well it's a good thing but

Jerry: I'm not going to say, I haven't even read it yet.

Jennifer: I know but I know

Martha: Not ready means you are not ready yet.

Jennifer: No

Jerry: Ok let me read it.

Jennifer: No you obviously didn't pay attention. Not ready is not ready, Does it say not ready yet? No. ....

(Jerry reads silently)

Forgive, sounds good

Forget, I'm not sure I could

They say time heals everything

But I'm still waiting

I'm through with doubt

There's nothing left for me to figure out

I've paid a price, and I'll keep paying

I'm not ready to make nice

I'm not ready to back down

I'm still mad as hell, and I don't have time

To go 'round and 'round and 'round

It's too late to make it right

I probably wouldn't if I could

'Cause I'm mad as hell

Can't bring myself to do what it is

You think I should

I know you said

Why can't you just get over it?

It turned my whole world around

And I kinda like it

I made my bed, and I sleep like a baby

With no regrets, and I don't mind saying

It's a sad, sad story

When a mother will teach her daughter

That she ought to hate a perfect stranger

And how in the world

Can the words that I said

Send somebody so over the edge

That they'd write me a letter

Saying that I better

Shut up and sing

Or my life will be over?

I'm not ready to make nice

I'm not ready to back down

I'm still mad as hell, and I don't have time

To go 'round and 'round and 'round

It's too late to make it right

I probably wouldn't if I could

'Cause I'm mad as hell

Can't bring myself to do what it is

You think I should

I'm not ready to make nice

I'm not ready to back down

I'm still mad as hell, and I don't have time

To go 'round and 'round and 'round

It's too late to make it right

I probably wouldn't if I could

'Cause I'm mad as hell

Can't bring myself to do what it is

You think I should, what it is you think I should

Forgive, sounds good

Forget, I'm not sure I could

They say time heals everything

But I'm still waiting

Jerry: Ok you asked your Mom to get it and read it. How did you want to use it?

Jennifer: Ok can I see it, just so I could look at it? Alright ha, ha, ha, ok. Um well I know you got, well she probably thought since forgive sounds good like I want to forgive her and stuff but the whole base of the song what the song is meaning um like something happened between her and her Mom and um, that even though how many people say that you should forgive and stuff but she says she is not going to cause she can't forget it and all that but that's why it says forget I'm not sure I could and how its saying how time heals everything which is commonly said you could easily say. Um but I'm still waiting saying that it hasn't healed it's been you know so long to the point where she's just had it. And then I'm through with doubt there is nothing left for me to figure out, I know what happened there's nothing left for me to figure out, I know what I want I don't want to you know be, have any part to do with her. And then especially here is the big part, the one we were just talking about earlier. I've paid the price and I will keep paying because I like, so much has happened and she keeps going on like I was saying earlier with the picture and saying about the stepbrother and stuff meaning I'll keep paying, and then the chorus where it's I'm not ready to make nice. Um, it's too late to make it right, because it happened, there is nothing you could do about it. It's way too late. Um and then I wouldn't make it right even, like it says I probably wouldn't if I could. So even if I could make it right I wouldn't because there is too much that has gone on. Um and then it says can't bring myself to do what it is you think I should. Whatever she thinks, counselors think and stuff. Can't do it because like before too much has happened. And then it says I know you said can't you just get over it. She said that before you need to get over it. You said that before and um it says it turned my whole world around and I kind of like it, It did turn my whole world around you know I don't have two parents and all that but I like it. I'm with my Dad, I'm happy, you know I have even a closer relationship than I did with my Dad before. And then it says um let see.... well I made my bed and sleep like a baby like I got on with my life and it's fine. Um with no regrets and I don't mind saying. I have no regrets with what I did, you know. Um it's a sad sad story when a mother will teach her daughter that she ought to hate a perfect stranger. That's perfect because it is sad when your Mom can teach you how much hate people have in them and you know how you can easily dislike someone before you get to know them.

Jerry: Who is the person?

Jennifer: Well it could be like for anyone, a mother will teach a daughter to hate a perfect stranger. Like basically, I can't trust anyone because if I thought I trusted her a long time ago and it ended up, I couldn't, how do you trust a perfect stranger and how do you like, like a perfect stranger if you, you know, like that. Basically, you taught how to hate someone you don't even know yet. Um uh let's see... and how in the world can the words that I said send somebody so over the edge that they would write me a letter saying that I better shut up and sing or my life will be over. That's basically saying how can um , well. like how can everything just come down to where I don't get a decision and that I get something from a judge saying that I have to go to counseling or like I get consequences basically saying write me a letter saying I better shut up or sing or my life will be over, that if I don't go to counseling me and my Dad get in trouble and stuff like that which I don't have no choice, that's basically what that's saying and then it's the chorus all over. And um pretty much, yeah. Here ya go. (Jennifer hands Martha the paper)

Jerry: Um Can you summarize as best you can what Jennifer was trying to tell you from the lyrics from the song?

Martha: Well Jennifer, we did have a relationship, and we could have a relationship

Jennifer: He said summarize what I said, not give your own opinion, there is a difference.

Martha: Summarize what you said, what you have been saying that you don't want a relationship with me no matter what and you can't trust anybody.

Jennifer: Yeah

Martha: But that's not true

Jennifer: How do you know, you're not me?

Martha: Well I'm summarizing.

Jennifer: Saying that's not true, that's giving your own opinion.

Martha: You're right, I did. .

Jennifer: Yeah I know.

Martha: People change Jennifer, and sometimes change you don't like it and sometimes it's for the better for someone and not for someone else.

Jennifer: Ha ha ha, ok, ok, ha, ha, ha, you're downing yourself on that one. If people change ok, maybe it's not good for someone else ok, well right back at ya. People change and maybe it's not good for someone else. I've changed, I don't want to talk to you, don't want to have anything to do with you so basically, it's not better for you so there you go.

Martha: You say you don't have a choice but you do,

Jennifer: No, I don't, am I sitting here? I could walk out of this room and nothing will happen?

Martha: No

Jennifer: Ok then, is that a choice?

Martha: Your choice is

Jennifer: Wait No, no, no, no, is that a choice? That's what I thought. That's what I said. Ok, continue.

Martha: You do have a choice because you chose to be with your Dad, and I let you.

Jennifer: Ok no.

Martha: I could have continued to fight it in court, but I let it go because I wanted you to be happy.

Jennifer: Yeah ok, whatever.

Martha: And as far as a choice, you made the choice not to want to see me anymore.

Jennifer: Yeah and that's not my problem that you can't handle that. It's yours and you did it to yourself.

Martha: Well how do we change things moving forward?

Jennifer: You leave me alone, that's how.

Martha: I'm not

Jennifer: Oh no, no, no, but people change, and it happens for the better of some and not for others, didn't you just say that?

Martha: But what do we have to do to make things better?

Jennifer: Nothing, leave me alone. That's what you have to do.

Martha: Well I can't do that and I won't do that.

Jennifer: You got your life, I have mine, that's it. You can't do that, then it's too bad for you because I've moved on. Even though how much you say in that conversation, how my life is miserable, I moved on and I'm fine.

Martha: I didn't say your life is miserable.

Jennifer: Yes, you did.

After these sessions, Jennifer would often vent, sometimes crying in anger at her harsh imprisonment. I could only listen as my stomach acids boiled from her stories. I was completely helpless. I was a prisoner too. After this session, I decided to stop taping the sessions. I was exhausted. There was nothing that I could do to stop Martha and the court-ordered counseling. There were many times I wanted to show Martha the book hoping to back her off the insane manipulated counseling sessions. I told Jennifer my intentions as I knew I would get her opinion. Jennifer said, Dad you're not going to scare her. Besides, she will be more shocked when she finds out there is a book about her in stores. Let her buy one. My daughter didn't need my help anymore in counseling. Her answers were better than any answer I could ever give her. Although she has cried in many sessions and felt beat up, she gave many beatings in return, leaving two college-educated adults without words from some of her intelligent answers, stopping the sessions dead in their tracks, sending Jennifer on her way so that they can regroup after being outwitted by a child. I was guilty of preparing Jennifer for these sessions, telling her don't let them put words in your mouth, don't let the counselor tell you his versions of events, don't let them talk about court, don't give them information on where we go, who we're with. The things that have nothing to do with the court-ordered counseling because mother and daughter do not get along.

April 14 2007, I called the realtor to find out what was happening: No answer.

April 15, 2007, I called Jerry,

"Hey Jerry, this is Tom."

"Hi Tom, how are you?"

"I'm fine; I have a couple of questions for you."

"Sure Tom, what can I do for you?"

"Well Jerry, do you remember back on March 24th you had a counseling session with Martha alone, one day after you saw Jennifer?

"Yes, I remember."

"Well what if I told you that I can prove Martha was out of town on that day, that I actually drove over there to see that not only was Martha's Truck not there, but there were no lights on in your office."

"I'm not sure what exact day you are talking about Tom"

"Jerry, maybe I could call the insurance company and see what days you charged them for her visits. So if you charged them for days she was out of town, that would be fraud"

“I don’t know what you are talking about; I will have to check my records Tom."

"Speaking of records, Jennifer would like a copy of her records as well. She has a legal right to her records. If you do not give her the records, I will have an attorney get the records for her. Ok Jerry?"

"Ok Tom, I'll look into it."

I hung up.

Monday, April 16, 2007, Jennifer had a Badminton game. Martha showed up and they argued.

Tue, April 17, Martha called Jennifer and told her that they will discuss this with Larry.

April 20, 2007 Counselor # 3 session 21

April 27, 2007 Counselor and Martha.

May 2, 2007 Jennifer and I went out to dinner. While eating, I asked Jennifer, What you really want from the house?"

Her reply was, "I don’t know Dad, and it’s been a long time since I’ve been there. Nothing I could think of."

"Well this is how I feel Jennifer; I don’t want anything at all if we have to go there with police hovering over us."

"Whatever Dad, that’s up to you."

I knew Jennifer could care less. I wasn’t sure if she understood how I felt, but I believe she did. I did know my friends and family would think that I was crazy. These things were worth money, valuable, and necessities. I guess you would have to be me to understand. These were things Martha and I shared, Memories. For all the torture she has put me through, nothing was worth more than letting Martha have every last thing from our past, knowing that I, too, left every memory behind. Taking no part of her with me. It was the principal, I wanted Martha all alone to box and bury our life together. I also did not want to give Martha the satisfaction of standing over Jennifer and me observing our pain as we gather what she has allowed us to have in the presence of her police protection as well as the audience. I refused to let her write that chapter in her story. However, later Jennifer called Martha to tell her that she wanted pictures.

May 4, 2007 Counselor says Martha will not be attending. Session 22

May 13, 2007, Jennifer was at home alone on the computer when Martha instant messaged her. Jennifer explained her slang in writing. U = you, 2 = to, ne = any, w/ = with, c = see, ur = your or you are, b = be, urself = yourself, cuz = because.

mfrawley2428 :(Martha) How are you?

Auto response from FUNGI1031 :(Jennifer) I am away from my computer right now.

FUNGI1031: well, now that u r talkin 2 me horrible

mfrawley2428: I love you & want you to know that I am here for you.

FUNGI1031: I think I just threw up in my mouth

FUNGI1031: I dont need u so get over it

FUNGI1031: u have a problem w/ letting go of things

FUNGI1031: I and Dad let go so now it's your turn

mfrawley2428: You're my daughter & I'll never let go. l

FUNGI1031: no im not so get over urself . . . . . you're more pathetic than i thought

FUNGI1031: why is your thing still mfrawley? Don't u know how 2 move on . . . . . u dont deserve that name ne way!

FUNGI1031: especially cuz its my last name. . . . U shouldnt have ne thing 2 b a part of it

FUNGI1031: . . . . ???? THAT'S WAT I THOUGHT

mfrawley2428: i love u 2

Auto response from FUNGI1031: People always LIE

FUNGI1031: if u considered that love that i would like 2 know wat goes through ur head w/ tod . . . . . wow that must b a sad relationship mfrawley2628: i didn't get around to changing it

FUNGI1031: yeah c my away message. . . . fits u well cuz if u dont love someone and ESPECIALLY wen u remarry. . . . . u usually go w/ the knew guys name. . . . . i cant believe u tell a story that Dad is holding on

FUNGI1031: its u

mfrawley2428: i divorced your Dad, not you. i will never let go of u.

FUNGI1031: apparently not cuz ur still carrin his name around. . . . . . . man now i feel bad 4 Dad cuz that has 2 b sickining 2 kno that u still have MINE AND MY DADS name on ur aim becuz it already is makin me want 2 puke!!! And get a grip i already let go of u a LONG time ago . . . . . so ur NEVER GOING 2 GET NE WHERE BY SAYIN THAT SO SAVE UR BREATH 4 UR OTHER KIDS

mfrawley2428: Jennifer i pray that 1 day you can relieve ur self from all the pain and anger

FUNGI1031: there is no pain and anger. . . . Just wen u come around so if u left me ALONE (poof all gone) but u have a hard time doing that ms. godly person over here

mfrawley2428: i'm not the 1 that walks around wearing a cross around my neck

FUNGI1031: OK. ur just jealous cuzz i LOVE MY DADDY and NOT you. . . . . . .

mfrawley2428: not jealous, just sorry that you can't see or realize how much i love u

mfrawley2428: no 1 can show u love if u don't let them in

FUNGI1031: keep feelin sorry for urself then ur good at that ne way

mfrawley2428: i don't feel sorry 4 myself - only u

FUNGI1031: oo i already kno wat love is,. . . . . i get enough from my Dad. . . . . ur the one who doesnt kno wat love is. . . . . . Love isnt the same as hate . . . . ooo wait sorry i forgot it is 2 Martha scumm

FUNGI1031: i don’t feel sorry for myself

FUNGI1031: there is nothin 4 me 2 feel sory for myself for

FUNGI1031: im the normal one who still has a life

mfrawley2628: u have 2 parents that love u

FUNGI1031: nope i have 1 that loves me more than 2 would love ne child. . . . . DADDY

FUNGI1031: . . . . once again that's wat i thought

mfrawley2428: if that's what u believe, no one can change that. i do love u more than u will ever know.

FUNGI1031: and i hate u more that u will ever kno

FUNGI1031: so keep tellin urself that. . . . . ur talkin 2 a wall right now get used 2 it cuz i did. . . . . ur not gettin that ne where near a place where i will listen 2 wat u say. . . . So now i am done b/c that was just a waste of my time and i am going 2 go finish livin the rest of my 15th year in my life that u will never c from now until forever

May 14, 2007, Jennifer and I moved into a motel in Countryside. With May 22nd around the corner, I feared that with Martha living somewhere else, she would attack my living conditions. An easy win in court, the immediate removal of a child. With restraining orders still lying over my head, Martha could take Jennifer somewhere and not have to tell me. I figured at least the motel had two beds with maid service. If they attacked me, at least I could say we're just staying a few weeks because we were buying a house. People do it all the time. Like everything else I've lived through, I've always felt safer on the move. I hated Martha knowing where we were living. It was a different feeling Martha not knowing. It was much more peaceful for Jennifer and me. A time to drop our guard, a feeling of safety and freedom.. Just to be safe, I paid my rent for May on the apartment. We would move things to a storage unit I bought a month earlier at night. My building manager worked nights. I told no one except for Ray. I said nothing to my landlord as I would not ask for my security deposit. Although this was wrong, I had to be smart, no matter what the cost. For the safety of my little girl and me, money was no object. The cost for my peace and security was over $300.00 a week. As other people considered this a waste of money, I couldn't buy enough of it. How much is your sanity worth? For me, priceless.

The motel was less than five blocks from where I worked. Jennifer would walk to Jenny's house to catch the bus with her. She lived just around the corner. I told Jennifer not to tell any of her friends where we were staying except for Jenny. I didn't have to explain; Jennifer knew by now. Jenny would come to hang out and even stay overnight sometimes. Jenny's parents knew we were staying there, it seemed they knew of our circumstances and understood. I'm not sure how much Jenny told her parents but we never told her not to tell. Jennifer and I trusted this family. All we had in the motel room was a cooler, our clothes, a Laptop computer, and a printer. I needed these things for Jennifer to do her homework. We were eating out often and we were getting sick of it. There was a dollar store right through the parking lot of the motel. We would go there and buy bread, peanut butter and jelly, Drinks, paper plates, milk, paper bowls and silverware. The dollar store had food as we would buy cereal and other snacks. We had a nice little table by the sliding glass doors where we would eat our meals. We didn't have a table and chairs in our apartment. Jenn would make me laugh, while eating at the table for the first time, she said, "Wow this is nice Dad." We would make the best of things. We treated it like a vacation. Any place that Martha didn't know we were there, was a vacation to us. We had cable as well, what more could we ask for.

Jenn was living her life going to the park and hanging out with Jenny as well as other friends. She just lived in a motel. Jennifer never showed any shame. She believed in me and knew that one day we will have our own place again. We enjoyed our time in the motel, when she was there, we would listen to our iPods, watch movies, play cards, wrestle, what else you do when you're doing time as we would call it. Jennifer and I never changed, we were the same people, just without the finer things we once had. When I was alone, I would lay on the bed writing my story for hours, sometimes days in a row. Although we were comfortable there, we were very cautious. I knew the Manager and he knew my story. Jennifer would stop in the office in the morning for juice and donuts before going to school. He was always looking out for her. He let us stay in the back of the motel off the busy street to avoid anyone seeing us. He also assured me if anyone asked if I was staying there, he would tell them no. For now we felt safe but we knew it would be short-lived.

May 21, 2007, 9:30 am while at work, I called Ann the realtor.

"Hello Tom," she said.

"Hi Ann," I was just wondering why no one has called to inform me where the closing is going to be as well as the time?"

"The attorney didn't call you Tom?"

"No he did not, I asked you to have him call me over a week ago."

"I'm sorry Tom Ann said, why don't I call them now and have them call you back, so that they can let you know what is going to take place. I'm so sorry about the furniture Tom, I think Jennifer's furniture is by Martha's Mom's house or in storage."

"Well Ann I'm used to it."

"Tom let me call them so that you can get the information you need."

At about 10:30 am, I checked my phone. There was a voicemail. I went into the bathroom.

"Hi Tom, this is Joanne from the attorney's office. I have the information you need for the closing. Call me back at this number." I immediately called. Joanne answered, "Hi Tom, do you have an email address or fax number?"

"I have an email address I replied!"

" Can you give it to me please," she asked. I gave her my address.

"Ok Tom, I'll send you the information right away."

"Thanks, I said, bye!"

My cell phone was capable of sending and receiving emails. After about an hour, I checked my phone for any emails. There was none. I decided to give it another hour and I would check it when I was at lunch. I had lunch from 12 to 12:30. During lunch, I checked my mail once again. Still no mail. I figured maybe she was busy, and it was her lunchtime as well. At 1:30 pm, I called Joanne. She answered, "Hi Dalton's law office."

"Hey Joanne, I didn't get any email from you."

"You didn't, Tom?"

"No, I didn't."

"Well, I sent them to the address you gave me, Tom. Give it to me again. I gave it to her again, and she replied, "Yes this is the address I sent them to. Let me send them again, Tom."

"Ok I said, I'll check my mail again later."I hung up. I didn't want to keep running to the bathroom so I decided I would wait until my shift was finished. I got off work at 4:30 that evening, went straight home, sat down and turned my home PC on. Once again, still no email from Joanne. I was getting frustrated, I was tired of being second hand to anyone that had anything to do with the process of my divorce. Angry and annoyed, I called Ann back. She answered, "Hi Tom. Wow I thought, I didn't tell her who I was. I guess with her big payday just around the corner, she didn't want to miss my calls. They were important now.

"Did you talk to the attorney Tom?"

"No, I talked to his secretary Joanne and she said she was going to email this morning at 10:30. I talked to her again at 1:30 and she claimed that she sent them. After I told her I didn't receive them, she promised to send them again."

"Let me call them back and see what happened, I'll call you back Tom."

"Ok," I said and hung up.

Sarah called back within a few minutes, "Tom Joanne said she sent you two emails; maybe they were spammed."

"No, Sarah," I said, ``they will not be spammed unless I receive them first and manually choose to spam them."

"Well I don't know what to tell you Tom."Well Ann, you know what I think, I think it is rude considering you told them two weeks ago to call me and now just 24 hours before the closing, and I am still trying to get information. I have no idea where or when the closing will be held. I am so used to the people around Martha being rude to me."

"Maybe you should call Joanne again Tom, she should be able to tell you the address and Time."

"Yes, but it would sure be nice to have the same privileges as Martha, have the paperwork of what is going to take place beforehand. I guess I'll call her again," I replied.

"You know what, Tom, I can at least give you the address. It will be at 1666 west Horror Grove at 11:30 am."

May 22, 2007, closed on the house.

May 29, 2007, I picked up Jennifer at 4:45 after working a nine-hour shift. While going back to the motel, I asked Jennifer, "Did your Mom call today?

She replied, "No, but Jerry did and he said there is no more counseling."

"Really," I said as my heart dropped. What did he say, Jennifer?"

"Hi Jennifer, this is Jerry."

"Yeah," Jennifer replied.

"Well, I told you I would call you after I have seen your Mom and I just wanted to let you know there will be no more counseling, I'm resigning."

Jennifer said, "Ok."

"I feel there is nothing I could do because you don't want to come to counseling with your Mom or by yourself, I feel we are not getting anywhere. So I'm sending you, your Mom, and your

Dad a letter with recommendations. I recommend you going back to the counselor you and your Dad first went to. I'm recommending that you go without your Mom at the frequency they could take you. If that counselor cannot take you, I know a family therapist that you can see by yourself. Your Mom will not have to go. I'm not sure if your Mom will fight to keep you with me for the court order of a minimum of one year. I discussed it with your Mom already, and I'm going to send you a letter."

"Ok," Jennifer said.

"Ok good luck Jennifer, bye."

Jennifer hung up.

Although my daughter and I were extremely happy as freedom was staring us right in the face, I was stumped. Why now, why all of a sudden? Was Jerry's words true? Did he really feel that way or was Martha behind the whole thing? Why would he recommend that only the child seek alternative counseling? Why not the mother? Did he actually feel that Jennifer had all the problems and Martha was perfectly normal? What an amazing diagnosis from a man with over thirty years of experience in psychotherapy. That evening Martha left a single voicemail,

"Hi Jennifer, it's just me. I wanted to see how you are doing. I love you and miss you. Give me a call, bye."

Jennifer did not call.

May 30, 2007, Martha left this voicemail for Jennifer.

"Hi Jennifer, its Mom. I know Jerry called you yesterday. I'm just wondering what you think about what he said, so give me a call if you want, bye."

May 31, 2007, I had Jennifer call Martha. My daughter and I knew Martha's games well. She doesn't do anything unless it benefits her and her alone. We were curious as to Martha's motive. Jenn made the call.

"Mom, so what's going on with counseling?"

"You don't have to see Jerry anymore Jennifer, he feels that he can't help you but he is going to recommend that you see another counselor. That's if you want to."

"Are you going to take that paper to court, Mom?"

"No Jennifer, it's up to you if you want to go. Jennifer I love you and. .

Jennifer interrupted, "No, no, no, no, don't go there Mom. So nothing is going to happen to Dad and me?"

"No Jennifer," Martha replied.

Jennifer hung up.

I got upset that Jennifer hung up. "Jennifer, what's wrong with you? Your mother just set you free, you do not want to get her angry. If you get her mad, she will punish you. All she has to do is take that letter to the court and you are right back in counseling. Be smart, Jennifer."

Jennifer stared at me for a second, saying nothing as she held her cell phone up in the air and hit a button. She recorded the whole conversation of her mother stating she would not have to attend counseling anymore. I was silent for a moment and then said, "Jennifer you are a smart little girl."

I want you to call your mother back and see if she will talk to me. Jennifer called Martha, she agreed and Jennifer gave me the phone.

"Martha," I said,

"Yeah," she replied.

"What games are you playing now?"

"I'm not playing any games, Tom."

"Well why all of a sudden is counseling over?"

"The counselor felt he couldn't help Jennifer anymore. He also said you and Jennifer think he is siding with me.

Well guess what Martha, he admitted to my face alone in his office that he was brainwashing Jennifer."

"He didn't say that to me, Tom."

"He's not going to say that to you, Martha."

"Brainwashing Tom?"

"He didn't say brainwashing, I did Martha. I told him that Jennifer tells you what happened to her and he gives her new ways to look at things, defending what you have done to her. Just like the second counselor."

"Tom, counselors give people new ways to look at things to help them."

"Yeah Martha, new ways that are not the truth. You pay these counselors just like you are the one who decides that they will get the job so basically they work for you. You let these people hurt our daughter."

"What are you talking about, Tom?"

"You know what I'm talking about Martha. Do you know counselor number two had Jennifer pretend that she was in court testifying against you as he played the judge. What the hell is that Martha?"

"Counselors ask questions, Tom."

"About court Martha, that's interrogation. My counselor, who has over 40 years of experience, said that is insane questioning for a child. She also thought having a child in counseling 3 times a week is excessive. Funny Martha, the exact times of Jennifer's softball games. She cried, "Daddy they took my softball away. What a punishment."

"Tom, the counselor, felt that Jennifer needed more counseling."

"That's B.S. Martha, all you do is lie."

"You know Tom, you are the one who hired Rachel Davis for Jennifer."

"I'm not stupid Martha, she was clearly on your side. According to their code of ethics, Rachel was supposed to have the same loyalty to Jennifer as any other client. She has seen Jennifer only once; she hardly returned Jennifer's phone calls. But yet, Rachel talked to you all the time, including emails. She didn't email me. When she was in court, she sat by you and ignored me. Whatever Martha, I'm not going to sit here and argue with you about all this."

(Martha starting to cry) you know Tom, I just want to know where my daughter is when you go out of town."

"What for, Martha? You haven't been in her life for a year and a half. Funny every time I let you know that I will be out of town, someone breaks into my apartment."

(While crying) "With my daughter living there, why didn't you call the police and get fingerprints."

"They are the police Martha, just like my landlord described Rod to a tee with his white police car. Rod told me about when that happened and he said he got rid of his white car before that happened. Yeah Martha, he told me that too, but the day after he told me, I saw him in a white car. Nobody tells the truth, you are all liars. This is the life I live, the life you gave me. My daughter and I live in fear. People were following Jennifer and me just like the men standing around Jennifer's baseball games. You should know me Martha, I grew up on the street."

"Tom, I took your truck by myself. Rod didn't have anything to do with it."

"You know what Martha, I didn't call you to argue about all of this."

"Tom, what can I do? I don't want to hurt Jennifer anymore, I send her money and she gives it back."

"Giving your daughter a card on her birthday or holidays with twenty dollars or whatever doesn't justify you being a good mother. It's too late, I can't help you. I know you like a book, you do what other people think you should do. You never listened to me when I said back off of our daughter before you lose her forever. You didn't listen, you didn't care as you punished her over and over again. That's on you. But anyway I have nothing more to say, we are just wondering what you will do next. "Got to go, have a nice life."

"You too," Martha said.

I hung up.

Martha needed to listen to herself talk as she boldly stated that she didn't want to hurt Jennifer anymore. I could only take that like she knew what she was doing was hurting her child. An admittance to guilt. This was not the first time she said that—a contradiction as to Jerry alone making the decision to end counseling. Basically giving me the incline that she was in charge. The expectation of me to believe anything that comes out of her mouth as she is sympathetic to someone wanting to rob her daughter after she admits to robbing the truck that carried what little possessions that she allowed her child to have. Though I'm sure of Martha's innocence that she was unaware, the truck contained her child's sole possessions, only upon finding out she would hold them for ransom. As she stands behind that, I am solely responsible for the hiring of Rachel Davis, ignoring the fact that the courts appointed her, the same courts that granted Martha's every request. A remarkable conversation, similarities of Jennifer's counseling as Martha explains her events of what happened to me. New ways of thinking of things, other than my beliefs. Was she trying to brainwash me, It sure seemed that way.

A few days later Martha called Jennifer. I could hear Jennifer talking a room away.

The conversation:

No mom divorce is not just a normal thing everyone goes through. You had an affair, you cheated on your husband that makes you a whore. And you expect me to go live with you and the man you cheated on my father with. Never going to happen.

Jennifer, your dad and I didn't get along.

Mom stop, you and Dad were kissing, hugging and laughing in the swimming pool a week before you wanted the divorce. Keep telling lies, you believe you own lies. Whatever makes you look good?

I have a question Mom, did you promise to that man the same you did with my father. I promise, for richer and poorer till death do you part? What can't answer Mom, that's what I thought?

I grabbed my keys and left. I always thought Jennifer should be a lawyer, she leaves everyone speechless.

May 29, 2007, we received this letter by email from Martha.

Ms. Jennifer Frawley

**03 East Avenue

Hodgkin's, IL 6*****

Dear Jennifer,

As I indicated in our phone conversation earlier today, I have decided, after much consideration and considerable consultation with colleagues, to resign as your therapist. This letter will explain my reasons and set forth some recommendations that I believe will be more helpful than continuing our work.

I recognize from your frequent statements that you do not desire either family or individual psychotherapy with me. Consequently, we have never been able to establish a working alliance or a therapeutic alliance. For that reason, it serves no purpose for you to continue counseling with me.

You have been through many stressful family disruptions in the past two years. These disruptions have included the loss of a positive relationship with your mother, the dissolution of your intact family, and the near loss of your father.

Although there has been significant family disruption, I believe that there is too much hurt, anger, and suspicion in your family system to allow for effective family sessions. In fact, requiring further family therapy likely would increase your stress level significantly.

I believe that individual counseling could be beneficial to you, but I believe that my prior role interferes with working individually with you. I believe that counseling must recognize that you have a choice. Not only do you have a choice about your interactions with your mother, but you also have a choice about your therapist and your counseling.

With these factors in mind, I make the following recommendations:

1.) Family therapy should be suspended indefinitely. It should resume only when you are ready. If in the future you should desire a return to family therapy, I suggest that you contact The Family Institute at Northern University (8**) 773-0**0. The Family Institute has a satellite location, so location should not be a hardship.

2.) I recommend that you return to your first therapist for individual counseling therapy with likely be more productive because both you and your father trust and favor that therapist. You can work out the frequency of the sessions with her.

3.) Should your first therapist be unavailable to work with you, I would suggest that you contact The Family Institute at the number given above. The family institute also provides individual counseling.

I know that our work over these past eight months has been stressful for you. I hope that these recommendations facilitate constructive changes in your counseling. I have communicated these recommendations to your mother, and I am mailing a copy of this letter to your father. I wish you well in the future, and I hope that peace returns to your life.

Sincerely,

Jerry

Could this be true? Was it finally over? My heart would drop as I looked into Jennifer's eyes. Relief and worry at the same time. I didn't have to say anything as Jennifer would do all the talking. Was Martha setting Jennifer free for the sake of her child's sanity, or was counseling taking time away from her new life as she now resided over an hour away. Thoughts hurting my head as Martha was fading out of the Mother-daughter court-ordered counseling. Was my request for the records that would scare Jerry into resigning? Did he feel what he was doing was wrong? Did greed finally catch up with these evil souls? I may never know. After reading the letter carefully, I knew one thing: it clearly left the door open for Martha to request a 4th counselor. I asked for the records because I believed Martha and Jerry were committing fraud charging Martha's insurance for visits while she was out of the state. Could this have been the reason? I could never be sure. I was, however, sure that this letter is no different than the sessions. Statements like the loss of a positive relationship with her mother. Jennifer's hurt and anger. A poor mother, an angry child. Suspicion, why would anybody be suspicious. Jennifer never mentioned she had a problem with her father's near loss, which is absolutely nothing about the hell inflicted by Martha; nothing at all is wrong with her mother. Was he blind, or was he pretending to be. There were notions in my head again. Why I was not included in Jerry's decision to resign? Jerry didn't even have the decency to call me, never about anything. I found it kind of odd when rescheduling; he would call a child, not the parent. Oh I take that back, he would call the non-custodial parent to convey the message. I still felt Jerry's letter was another slap in my face. My stomach continued to bleed. The most amazing thing about this resignation was Jerry and Martha, over the months, stressed that they were following a court order. If that were true, then why weren't the courts notified? Based on my experience, not following a court order was contempt! However, this was something Jennifer and I were used to. The only people that had to follow the rules were us. Martha was definitely exempt!

Although free of counselors, my daughter and I would be forever scarred. We lived in a different world as opposed to anybody we knew. We lived in constant fear. While walking down the street, we would often turn around to see if we were being followed. If someone was staring at us, it would make us nervous. My hand would shake every time I would open the mailbox, fearing the famous manila envelope from Mr.Burnburg or the Cook County Court System. I feared ever getting married again, especially in Cook County, Illinois. I now fear anyone in power. This would extend to my 15-year-old daughter, who continues to live in constant fear, as she walks to friends' houses; she frequently looks over her shoulder to see if she is being followed. She pointed out every time a Cook County Sheriff car would drive down our street, look Dad, there is the sheriff. Do you think they are looking for us, saying things like Dad that man on the corner keeps staring at us? She has nightmares of the day the police will come to her home and take her Daddy away and bring her to the evil mother who tortured her.

A sad day in America as she is taught in school about the bill of rights, the constitution, freedom of speech, innocent until proven guilty, that we live in the free world of democracy, only to learn in the real world the very people designed to protect her, are the people she fears most. All for money, a life sentence of living in fear. What a sad way for a child to go through life as her abusers take their families on tropical vacations with the money they received for emotionally abusing a child. I guess you would have to have a conscience to feel anything. Was Jennifer the first, or were there dozens before her? Maybe, even hundreds. How many more? How many will it take to make a grown human being see that they are hurting children? Will they ever see it at all? I know one thing, these two counselors Jerry and John, felt my presence. For now, they think that they have gotten away with the torturing of my daughter—a huge mistake on their part. I am an angry man, an angry father who was dedicating his life to seek justice against these licensed child predators. From this point, I vowed that I will never stop searching for the people who have power over them, people that are not corrupt and have a conscience. I know there are good people out there, I just have to find them. Even if Martha is brought down with them. Although I know I'm going to feel bad, if I let her get away with it, I will have to let them. That's not going to happen, especially that she ran the show, hurting her own daughter. There is nothing she could say to me, no tears that she could cry to make me dry her big brown eyes. She laughed in our faces as we cried for almost two years, and I'm sure she is not done yet. Jennifer and I continued on our pursuit for freedom and happiness.

June 6, 2007, I bought a mobile home.

Just the feelings in my body as well as the notions in my head, it was an indescribable feeling, a huge boulder off my back as I could now stand a little taller.

I was hoping that this was the moment where the people who were pushing me around for Martha would see a guy just trying to make a life for himself and his daughter. I was hoping they would see that I was defenseless, that they would have some compassion, especially that I didn't do anything to them, that they could feel something for picking on someone they didn't even know, just for a favor for a woman who hates him. I was even hoping that even Martha could somehow gain some kind of feelings, that maybe she would give up her torture and help us that she would see all the hell she put us through did not stop us from our will to survive. I guess the last part was just wishful thinking.

Some of my friends were concerned that Martha would use this as another way to disgrace me. He lives in a trailer park. He is trailer trash, a comment most people use due to the fact that they have bigger, more expensive things; they think that gives them the right to consider themselves better as well as more important than people that have less than them. Amazing as in their college-educated worlds, they are taught "Fortunate, Less Fortunate," then they take that out into life, and it becomes "You're Trash, I'm Treasure."

I would be lying if I said I was not one of those people.

I didn't care what people thought anymore. It is easy to stand on the side and tell people what they should do and what you think they should do, when the reality is what they can do, what they need to do. Expectations, as they would call it, you are expected to live a certain way, you are expected to have expensive things, expected to dress in certain fashions, expected to be intellectual in order to be accepted in the world of the middle or upper class. In my new world, I'm expected to survive. I lived on the street, in my vehicle, in other people's homes; to me I was in heaven. I have seen something different than the class I've once belonged to as I was now living in a class that those people only talk about. They are clueless as they judge. Through all of the hell I have been through I've gained great knowledge. I would learn to see things that most people cannot or refuse to see, even better, I lived it. As upper society looks down on people based on the way they live and the price of their possessions, they are judged on the outside, judged by their shells. I guess I was fortunate to see inside all of the shells. In the trailer park world, I've seen things differently than I once thought or have been told. I didn't see what the rest of the world's description of such a life, I saw an old couple that was retired that enjoyed this affordable way of living after decades of marriage and love. They would sit outside in the summer along with elderly friends that live close enough to walk to each other's houses, and talk about old times over some beer and wine. No, they don't have a big house, or a condo with elevators and balconies, yet they are happy. I have seen a divorced mother of two small children working a nine-to-five job, alone with no support from the father, an affordable way of life, to give her children a better life than her own. I watched as her children ran all through the park playing and riding their bikes. They knew only one world, childhood. I've seen a young married couple with three children as they both work jobs, their house is newly sided, a yellowish color with white shutters and doors, beautiful landscaping that drapes all along the entire front of their home that sits sideways, a home 44 feet in length. I watch as they sit on their porch at night, along with glowing lights surrounding their awning and landscape. The kids are laughing and playing running around the porch as Mom and Dad sit in chairs talking about their day over a cold beverage. I watch as these people go to work, come home, have dinner, watch TV, go grocery shopping, have family birthdays, as well as celebrate the holidays. I've seen many nice, even new, vehicles. The same make and models that were parked in driveways of the seemingly better grade of humans. So as society sees this lesser class world as trash, they fail to see that this less fortunate world lives the exact same way as they do. The only difference is the price of their possessions. Wait a minute, there is one difference. In this world, these souls don't dwell on what the expectations or what the seemingly upper class thinks. They spend their time living life. I have found myself caught in this crossroads of judgment several times. Meeting new people, when asked where you live, I've sometimes found myself stalling before I answered. For a moment, I felt my answer was going to embarrass me. I was almost ashamed to say it, but after what I've been through, I said it like I was proud. I didn't care what people thought anymore. I don't have to lie to impress anyone. I've learned a lot from Jennifer's friends. That there are many people in the upper class that do not judge by what you have but who you are. Her friends thought our home was cool, that Jennifer was lucky to have her very own bathroom. It is only fair to say in all walks of life, there is good as well as bad.

As society often lives their lives by standards and expectations, they base their status of importance on money-making, ignorant to what life is really about. Putting money at the top of their list for happiness, their life passes them by, only in the end to find that the most precious things in life cannot be bought.

My brother Paul is all too aware of that true reality. At the young age of 28, he made his fortune at the Chicago board of trade. Smart and successful, he expanded his success by teaching others as they joined his growing business. A wealthy man got married and decided to settle down and raise a family. Paul's first son was born with a rare fatal disease with no known cure or treatment. Paul would now shift his successful energy to saving his son. His success meant nothing other than a source to seek treatment as well as a cure. A harsh reality that money cannot buy Paul's son's life. Don't get me wrong, it takes money for treatment and to find a cure but more than that it takes people who have it, to be compassionate and use it for helping people. Not using it to hurt people or judge them. As Paul uses most, if not all of his fortune, to find a cure, not only for his son but all of the children who have this fatal disease, I say this, he is now less fortunate than you and I, what class is that. As we live our lives divided into classes, we all fail to see that there is only one class that matters, the class of life.

May 2, 2008

Jennifer and I arrived home from Michigan where we spent the weekend helping Roy, Dianna, gram and Pa put all the boats and other crafts in the water for the summer. After emptying the car of luggage and other things Jennifer went out to check the mail. She came back inside and sifted through the mail. I sat on the couch exhausted from the 2 ½ hour drive. Just then Jennifer said oh boy a card from Mom. She opened the card and said she has a typed letter Dad. I didn't say anything as Jennifer continued to read the letter silently. She was somewhat teary eyed when she looked at me and said, "What a crock of shit." She then read the letter aloud.

The letter:

Jennifer,

For the past 9 months I've been sending you $500 a month for living expenses. I've trusted your word that you were attending college. This is the last check I'm sending. I've been sending you this money on blind faith. From this point forward no more.

I wish you would go away to college, spread your wings and experience life. Don't let your Dad hold you back from growing and living life to the fullest. I have the means to help you. The payoffs for attending college and achieving your degree are something you will never regret. The benefits will help provide you for a better future.

One thing you don't know is that every time I would put money away to save for you to go to college your Dad would say stop, we live for the day, and Jennifer is going to get a full scholarship, so you don't need to save money. I argued no, you have to save and if she gets a scholarship that's a bonus, then she'll have spending money. I always said I want Jennifer to have the opportunity to go to college after high school the way it should be done, not by working a full time job and going to school at night. I missed out on the college experience because my father didn't want to pay for me to go. I started saving for you so you could go.

I am here to help support you. I want to be a part of your life, but you won't let me. You are my daughter and I love you dearly, at some point this has to change. I'm here for you and always have been. You have always been the center of my life, number one in my heart, my single most important priority in my life and I never replaced you. Someday I hope you understand this.

People go through divorces everyday and things don't go to this extreme. Sometimes life just happens and changes are made. I know the way things were handled weren't the best, but there are no instructions. I didn't turn you away, I fought to keep you, but it only pushed you away. It is your father who keeps us apart. If it wasn't for the things your Dad has said and done I truly believe you would be a part of my life. It's a pity for your Dad, he's smothering you the same way he smothered me. The only reason I stayed with him as long as I did was because of you. Hopefully one day you will realize that I never stopped loving you. My love for you will never end.

It's up to you, what you choose to do. You are the one in control. It's up to you to call me. It was your choice to live with your Dad. I tried to stop you, but couldn't.

My heart is broken because I am not a part of your life. You hold the key to us having any kind of relationship, but you won't let me in. The choice is yours and always has been. We've missed the last 4 years of life together. I miss not seeing and talking to you. I miss taking you on trips to places you've never been before.

There will always be a place for you in my heart, in my life and in my home. I love you more than anything in the world and miss you more than you can ever imagine.

I love you, Mom

I was so upset with what Jennifer just read to me, I got up, picked up the car keys from the table and headed to the door.

Jennifer said, "Where are you going Dad?"

"Just out Jenn."

"Where Dad?"

"I don't know Jenn, just out."

I closed the door behind me, got in my car and started driving. I went to the restaurant where Jennifer works. I sat at the bar drinking beer after beer talking to no-one. I am just thinking about Martha's letter. It was really bothering me, especially the comment about me smothering Martha. That was untrue. The accusations of smothering Jennifer as well. It was the same ole thing Martha bashing me to Jennifer. She was never going to let up on her crazy stories. After a few beers I received a text from Jennifer.

"Where are you Dad?"

I replied, "I'm at the restaurant, do you want me to pick you up to come here?"

"No Dad, I figured you were there and I'm walking and I'm just about there."

A few minutes later Jennifer tapped me on the shoulder. I turned around and Jennifer handed me her phone and said, "Read this."

She walked away to go say hello to some of her co-workers. I looked down at Jennifer's phone to see what she was talking about. It was an email she sent to her mother.

Jennifer's email:

Subject: YOU'RE NOTHING

Here we go with all of your bullshit lies. The $500 dollars you have been sending me you said were for living expenses. . . . NEVER did you say anything about it being for college because you said you cut me off from college money before second semester. By the way look at my e-mail address I'm sending you this from! It's called a college email address. . Wouldn't have one if i wasn't attending. . . . Just in case you're too dumb to figure that one out.

You're a real cold blooded BITCH. I didn't want to go away to college because there is no point in spending thousands of dollars to just take gen eds and that was my decision NOT my fathers so quit blaming him. It has absolutely nothing to do with him. And I am living life to the fullest . . . . . something i WOULDN'T be able to do at a major university! I dont give a shit about your money or you having the "means" to help me so screw you. I'm not an idiot and know that attending college will get me where i want to be in life so I'm not regretting anything but OBVIOUSLY you are considering your message. . . feeling sorry for yourself?? HA!

And that's a crock a shit about saving money for college. I'm not working a full time job but do have 2 and go to school because I can! You bring up saving money for me to go because your father wouldn't let you. . . . Yet it's funny how you're doing the exact same thing he did . . . . . you're "cutting" me off of that "money" that you supposedly saved. But that's fine, I don't need your money.

Plus, another lie. . . . "My single most important priority" haha wow. . . . You've got to be joking. . . . . . if that was true you wouldn't have kicked me out, you wouldn't have put me through counseling and the abuse there when i didn't want to go, you wouldn't have had my transportation of my Dad's truck and left ME stranded, you wouldn't have taken my house and dog from me, you wouldn't have taken all the furniture for me and my Dad to start over, you wouldn't have kept my belongings and memories from me, and you sure as hell wouldn't have tried to make me go see a doctor to get checked to see if my own father raped/molested me. . . . . i could go on and on but you're not worth my time. But all these things were done for YOU, what you thought was your benefit because you're selfish and only thought about yourself. . . . You thought things like that would only affect my father but considering i was living with him it affected me too but your too damn stupid to realize that . . . . . so open your eyes!! People do go through divorce everyday. . . ok i dont care but YOU caused it to go to this extreme because shit you did started to bite you in the ass and you just kept going to try to get your way but you keep losing the fight. . . . So give it up already. It doesn't matter anymore what you do to me or my Dad anymore, it wouldn't be anything new or anything we couldn't handle. We've rolled with your punches and keep going strong. . . . You're shit only makes our relationship stronger because it just shows me more and more the manipulative, crazy bitch you have become. So those your line about life sometimes changing . . . . . hope you're handling it well because your life changed and you screwed up . . . . . mine was obviously for the better. . . . THANK GOD!

You're two paragraphs contradict each other. . . . One says it's my Dads fault for keeping us apart yet the other says it was my decision. So which one is it?!?! Do you even re-read the shit you write because it just makes you look like an even bigger idiot. Reality check . . . it's the things you said and have done that caused me not to have anything to do with you . . . . . not anything involving my Dad. But you always have to have someone to blame because you don't want to handle the guilt. . . . . Karma is a bitch and it must be hitting you hard. So apparently its pity for you not my Dad . . . . . too bad i don't have any for you and never will. He's not smothering me. . . . You were the one who did. He lets me make my own choices like an adult and always has . . . where you on the other hand haven't. So I thankfully made the right choice in judgment and I will NEVER regret my decision. So you best find some tape for your broken heart but just remember, it will always be flawed. . . . . . And you're the only one to blame.

Now stay the hell out of our lives!!! Don't send me any more pitty cards, i don't care about the money or anything. This is your last connection because you are crazy and I dont need your stupid threats about cutting me off when you already did a long time ago. . . . It didn't matter then and it's not going to now. You don't mean shit to me and never will . . . all you are is just another stranger walking down the street that i don't have to see. So FUCK YOU . . . have a nice life. . . . . Mine is already great and I don't need you to screw it up any more. Your connection is now being disconnected! THANK GOD!

Jennifer served 17 months of her 2-year weekly sentence of psychotherapy for the crime of not surrendering her soul to an abusive mother. Having already served over 40 sessions with three different counselors Jennifer refused to give up as she rather do time than surrender her mind. Emotionally wounded from many battles, she remains a force to be reckoned with, vowing to last until the very end, sending a message that there are some souls so powerful that even money is not a large enough weapon to defeat them. Jennifer's fight was not just for herself as she often told me she feels sorry for the younger, weaker children that were also caught in this web of torture. Hoping that her screams will be heard everywhere across the U. S. rattling the king-size beds of politicians everywhere, awakening them from their pleasant dreams, pulling them into a child's nightmare, leaves me wondering, will these dream wizards wake the children or will they ignore the screaming young souls who cry for their help and go back to sleep.

Jennifer is a sophomore in college and maintains an A average as an honor roll student. She continues her passion for playing the violin and is a content, happy young woman.

As for Martha, the new Mrs. Todd Scum, is currently living in Northern Illinois. Martha stated in her first restraining order that I was a product of a broken home abused by my stepfather. A true statement as true as Jennifer is now a product of a broken home abused by her blood mother. Martha continues to hold her own child hostage, backed by the power of the Cook County Court System.

For Todd Scum, Martha fell in love with me, the man, and you, the wallet. A woman once told me I'd rather be eating a hamburger in a dive with someone I loved than eating steak in Paris with someone I didn't.

I did feel sorry for Martha's family, I knew deep down inside they all loved Jennifer and missed her. But they, too, have no one to blame but themselves. Jennifer's Papa died, never getting the chance to say goodbye.

You all may have gotten away with a crime against a child, but you couldn't take her soul. She was smarter than all of you. Shame on you, pick on someone your own size, or should I say of equal power.

However,

For the two women Judges who sentenced my daughter to years of psychotherapy, Judge number one, how could you do that to a child you have never met. I presented evidence from the very first counselor stating that the child was perfectly fine as well as a journal from my child stating what was happening to her with John Dawson. You were god! I begged you to listen. You ignored it. You refused to look at the evidence.

Judge number two, you wouldn't even let me explain. You were going to lock me up in a cage for protecting a little girl—shame on you. You took away all of my possessions and forced me to pay large amounts of money based on erroneous documents.

Rachel Davis, You were hired to protect my child. Even though it was once you met her, you heard her cries, she told you what was going on, yet you sent her to her abuse—shame on you.

Mr. Burnburg. Your big house is built with people's pain and each brick is made out of a child's tortured soul.

Mr. John Dawson, your torture chamber is no longer a secret. Everyone knows what you have done to an innocent little girl.

As for Martha, there is no sentence that a court can hand you that is far more punishment than the sentence your only child will hand you on the day she turns 18. A life sentence without your child. A married man walked into your life with the promise of travel and riches. For that, you torture your only child. You are evil. You sold your soul to the devil, you can never buy it back. You have created a story of lies, hatred and punishment to hide the truth of your affair. This is your story, I just wrote it.

Me, I make no excuses; I see the truth for what it is. As far as my marriage, I must have done something wrong to lose the person I loved my whole life. Maybe I didn't tell Martha I loved her enough, maybe I didn't make enough money, or ever travel with her when she often asked. Obviously, she wasn't satisfied with me. The one thing I don't understand is what I've done so wrong that any one person could hate me so much. I do not hate Martha; I hate what she has done. I hate what she has become. The Martha I knew for years was not capable of this hatred. I truly believe she was the one who was brainwashed. Martha always needed people to assure her she was doing the right thing. With the courts, her boyfriend and her family in her corner, she was unstoppable. However, I will never forgive her, nor is there any excuse for the pain and suffering she caused our daughter and me.

I was abused as a child and now as an adult. Forced by the courts to take my child to over a year and a half to her abuse and punishment, knowing what was going to happen is mental cruelty as well as torture on me. Enough to make even the toughest fathers cry. Beaten as a child, I was punched in the face, kicked in the stomach, thrown down a flight of stairs, beaten with boards and bats, black eyes, and bruises. As the courts and Martha considered this, and this alone, abuse, they were very wrong. The bruises go away. You remember the hate, the mental cruelty, and the humiliation. The beating is over in minutes. The punishment and mental cruelty last a lifetime. Martha, along with the courts, threw her child and me on the streets, took our belongings, our home, our money, our cars, as well as our freedom. The one thing they could not take was a father and daughter's love. No one is that powerful. As Parents, we try to protect our children from abuse, never preparing for when a parent becomes abusive. Nevertheless, I have overcome every obstacle the Courts and Martha has thrown at me. Evicted from my home, stripped of my rights as the 14th Amendment of the Constitution ensures that no State shall "deprive any person of life, liberty, or property, without due process of law. " Family Court routinely deprives citizens of their children and assets without due process. Men are evicted from their homes without a hearing. Family Law enables the court to violate citizen's rights under color of law by using the subjective "best interests of the children " as the overriding principle. I encourage everyone who has been through what I have to tell your story. Only then will the judges' Attorneys' Counselors' and Police follow the real law as they will never know if the people as well as children that they serve their injustice will tell. Don't keep it a secret. I believe that all divorce court appearances should be recorded. No one should have the power to access these files except the people whose lives are inside them. All counseling sessions should be recorded and accessible at any time to any party involved. I find it ironic that counselors hide behind the privacy act. When you go into a store to shop, you are not alone in that aisle. There are cameras following you everywhere. Watching you put items into your cart. Watching to see if you steal. Counselors are thieves too. They steal freedom, happiness, and young minds. How much is that worth as opposed to a can of corn?

We do not want people to feel sorry for us but be proud. It doesn't matter what's written on paper, It's what's in your soul. Although tortured souls, we are good souls, powerful souls. For over two years, I have fought for my daughter with only a $90 suit and my will. I have won.

People work hard their whole life buying homes, saving to send their children to college, and have a comfortable retirement until death do they part. In the midst of a divorce comes the loss of friends, family, and a spouse. If that is not enough, the Illinois Cook County Court System takes over. It has revolving glass doors that never stop spinning as they suck in its victims by the hundreds. People enter these famous glass doors to fight for their equal share of everything they have put into their marriage for years, including their children, only to exit with a fragment of their lives as the courts, attorneys, and counselors, prospers from the already broken souls who enter. Our current court system of today is in need of major reform. The hallways should be lined with photos of their victims who suffered the lost money, property, children, and in some cases, their freedom. I feel before a Judge sentences children to years of counseling, they should at least meet their victims. It is terribly wrong for a single human being, having the sole power to control the destiny of thousands. I wrote my story in the hopes of sending a message to whoever has the power to change the current system that preys on people's life savings as well as the innocent young minds of their children.

I dedicate my book to Jennifer, the most courageous soul I know.

I wake up every morning

The sun is not so bright

The secrets that I keep

Makes it always seem like night

Evil is all around me

Everywhere I stare

Every waking Moment

More than I could bear

Punished for loving my daughter

Sentenced to life in hell

By a force so powerful

There is no one to tell

Hated by a woman

I once called my wife

Lies to everyone

As she destroys my life

She threw away her child

Into the gates of hell

A mother gone wild

An innocent little girl

Two evil men

Ordered by the law

To take this child's soul

For a mother who wants it all

In a closed room

A man and mother there

Torturing a little girl

Her father is unaware

Taking the child's thoughts

Replacing them with lies

A helpless little girl

Sits in the corner and cries

Her father in the next room

Hears his daughter's cries

There's nothing he could do

For if he does

Jail is his demise

There is nowhere to run

There is nowhere to hide

No one gives a care

What we have bottled up inside

Licensed by the law

They run their living hell

Overlooking one thing

That child was going to tell

A story of a crime

A kidnapping of a mind

A counselor and mother's goal

To brainwash a child

To torture her innocent soul

Written by Tom Finley

Made in United States
North Haven, CT
05 November 2026

21769186R10257